DAILY DOSE
of
KNOWLEDGE™

WEST
SIDE
PUBLISHING

Consultants:

Ellen Cutler has a B.A. and M.A. in art history. She is currently a lecturer in art history at the Maryland Institute College of Art. She has been a freelance writer since May 2000.

Andrew Dell'Antonio is head of musicology and ethnomusicology at the School of Music at the University of Texas at Austin. He has won a number of awards for teaching and scholarship, and his research focus is on changing models of musical listening from the 16th century to the present day.

Dr. Anthony Edmonds is George and Frances Ball Distinguished Professor of History at Ball State University and the author or coauthor of seven books. He was a contributor for *The Sixties Chronicle, The Fifties Chronicle,* and *American West Chronicle.*

Joanne H. Edmonds, Ph.D., is a professor of literature at Ball State University, where she is also an honors college dean.

Robert Wolff, Ph.D., has published more than 50 research articles and 24 articles/books for the general public. He specializes in spiders, earthworms, bacteria, and human health.

Contributing Writers: Tina Adler; Patricia Barnes-Svarney; Sandy Becker; Victor Cassidy; Ellen Cutler; Andrew Dell'Antonio; Susan Doll, Ph.D.; Anthony Edmonds, Ph.D.; Joanne H. Edmonds, Ph.D.; Jane Friedman; Martin F. Graham; Jerry Guo; Peter Gwynne; James H. Hallas; Jessica Harwood; Kathryn Holcomb; Phillip Jones, Ph.D.; William Martin; Nancy McCaslin; David A. Murray, Ph.D.; Julie J. Rehmeyer; Russell Roberts; Richard A. Sauers, Ph.D.; David Stark, Ph.D.; Pamela D. Toler, Ph.D.; Cassandra Willyard

Facts verified by Betsy Rossen Elliot, Donna Halper, and Regina Montgomery.

Introduction: Awaken Your Inner Intellectual ■ 7

Sunday ■ Music

Monday ■ Science & Nature

Tuesday ■ Visual Art

Wednesday ■ History

Thursday ▪ Literature

Friday ▤ Biography

Saturday ▤ Miscellaneous

Index ▤ 374

Awaken Your Inner Intellectual

ONE OF THE BEST ways to keep our minds sharp, particularly as we age, is to try to learn something new every day. This doesn't necessarily require continued schooling or laborious topical research. Rather, it is achievable simply by taking a few minutes each day to read something of substance.

That is the inherent beauty of this collection. With 365 informative passages—one for each day of the year—you'll enjoy learning something new each day. The unique power of this approach as an instrument for broadening knowledge is what provides the inspiration for *Daily Dose of Knowledge*™.

Daily Dose of Knowledge™ presents daily offerings of topical information drawn from seven different themes, each corresponding to a particular day of the week. The topics are not in order of importance or chronology, so there's no need to work through this book in an orderly progression from cover to cover. Rather, you can choose any topic that interests you as a starting point, using the days of the week as a guide. The daily themes are as follows:

Sunday—Music

Discover the gifted individuals, timeless compositions, musical genres, technical innovations, and societal influences that have shaped music over the past millennia.

Monday—Science & Nature

A fascinating exploration of the wonders of the human and natural world ranging from human genome sequencing to the geography of earthquakes and volcanoes.

Tuesday—Visual Art

A broad examination of virtually every visual art form developed from prehistoric times to today along with the visionaries behind their creation.

Wednesday—History

From the founding of Hinduism in 1500 B.C. to 9/11, an extensive survey of the events that have shaped our world through recorded time.

Thursday—Literature

Scriptures and classics, sagas and comic books—a far-reaching look at the most influential and inspiring literary works and genres spanning human history.

Friday—Biographies

Life stories of those who have influenced human history and civilization—many of whom you will know. If you don't know the others, you definitely should.

Saturday—Miscellaneous

A wide-ranging look at pretty much everything and anything not explored Sunday through Friday.

Each passage is concise—one page in length. By reading a passage every day, you'll explore all seven themes each week and learn about 52 unique topics relating to each theme over the course of a year. In addition, select articles feature additional tidbits of information, called "Postscript," that add depth and insight into the person or event featured.

The result is a profound expansion of one's overall intellectual capacity.

So delve into *Daily Dose of Knowledge*™ and build your cranial depository of knowledge. Don't try to ingest the entire volume at once. Just take a few minutes—whether at bedtime, while riding the commuter train to work, or while soaking in the bathtub—and read one mind-stimulating passage every day.

Learn something new. Feed your brain. Enrich your mind. And enjoy cultivating the intellectual stirring deep inside of you.

Johann Sebastian Bach

WHILE JOHANN SEBASTIAN BACH'S (1685–1750) music has been praised for its genius in the popular press, Bach would have been perplexed and probably appalled at the notion that he had "superhuman" creative capacities. Bach was born into a family of musicians and fathered several performers/composers himself, two of whom (Carl Philipp Emanuel and Johann Christian) gained significantly more renown in their own lifetimes than their father ever received (or even sought).

A consummate craftsman, Bach was conscious of his place in a legacy of hard work and dedication to a carefully practiced skill—in his case, playing the keyboard for Lutheran worship. As a young man, he worked systematically to copy and model both his keyboard technique and his improvisational skills on the great workaday Lutheran keyboardists of an earlier generation: Buxtehude, Pachelbel, and others whose work is relatively unknown today. In his prime, Bach became the most renowned keyboard player in central Germany. He specialized in organ technique and served as a testing consultant to the great organ-builders of the time.

Bach had many students, and the most successful became upstanding and dedicated organists for some of the top churches of the area. Unlike some of his contemporaries, such as Handel or Telemann, Bach published very little music during his lifetime. All of his publications were for keyboard, designed as teaching tools for the professional Lutheran organist.

Several decades after Bach's death, his vocal works were "rediscovered" by Mendelssohn, and his complete opus was cataloged and printed as one of the first historical compendia of a bygone composer's "master works." But those who admired Bach in his own lifetime praised him for his dedication to his instrument and to the teaching of his craft (both in performance and in improvisation, in which his skill—honed through decades of constant practice—was legendary).

The vast majority of Bach's works that are so highly valued today—the *Brandenburg Concertos,* the cantatas, the partitas for violin—were essentially forgotten between his death and the "Bach Revival" of the mid-1800s. But, partly through the agency of his two famous sons, Bach's keyboard works remained a key teaching tool for expert musicians, serving as a resource for such luminaries as Mozart and Beethoven.

Cloning

CLONING IS NOTHING NEW, if by "cloning" we mean "producing geneti-cally identical copies." Plants have been cloned for centuries by the low-tech method of taking cuttings. Frogs were cloned 60 years ago by a process known as *nuclear transplantation:* The nucleus from a tadpole's intestinal cell was removed and injected into a frog egg that had its own nucleus removed. The egg developed into a frog that was the clone of the donor tadpole.

Of course, it's a little more complicated with mammals. Frog eggs are large and laid by the thousand, and the embryos develop in ordinary pond water. Mammalian eggs are few and fragile, and embryos have to be returned to a surrogate uterus to develop.

Dolly the sheep, cloned in Scotland in 1996, is probably the most famous cloned mammal. She was created by removing the nucleus from a mammary cell of one ewe and putting it into the egg (from which the nucleus had been removed) of another ewe. Dolly is the genetic clone of the mammary cell nuclear donor.

Dolly

For cloning to be successful, the donor nucleus, whether it comes from a mammary cell, a skin cell, or some other adult body cell, must be "reprogrammed" by the receiving egg so it acts like the nucleus of a newly fertilized egg and starts dividing and differentiating to form an embryo. In Dolly's case, the embryo was implanted in the uterus of a surrogate mother.

Right now, mammalian cloning is very inefficient. It took the Scottish researchers 277 tries to get Dolly. So, those who have qualms about the implications of cloning humans need not fear an army of identical clones any time soon.

Although there are widespread ethical concerns about human reproduc-tive cloning (culminating in a live birth), "therapeutic cloning" may be more widely accepted. In this procedure, rather than implanting the cloned embryo in a gestational surrogate, embryonic stem cells are derived from it. These stem cells would be a perfect match for the nuclear donor, so any therapeutically useful cells or tissue made from them could be transplanted into the donor with no fear of immunological rejection.

Paleolithic Painting: Chauvet Cave

THE WORLD'S OLDEST WORKS OF ART—more than 400 red ochre and black wall paintings of lions, panthers, bears, owls, rhinoceroses, hyenas, buffalo, and more—were completely unknown until 1994, when three cave explorers found them in Chauvet Cave (named for one of the explorers), near Vallon-Pont-d'Arc in the Ardèche region of southern France. The cave contains animal images etched into its walls, along with hand and palm prints made by the artists. There is also a single wall drawing of a woman's hips and legs with the head and torso of a bison, often called the Sorceror.

In 1995, when archaeologists began to explore the Chauvet Cave to document its contents, they found a string of three chambers totaling 1,700 feet in length, a connecting gallery, and three vestibules. Carbon arc dating put the age of the artworks at more than 30,000 years (though these dates have since been challenged). The cave floor is littered with animal remains, including 55 bear skulls, along with ibex and wolf skulls.

The Chauvet Cave proves that humans drew and created works of art far earlier than anyone dreamed they could. Cave paintings exist in many places, but those at Chauvet are the oldest known—and unique for their employment of shading and perspective in images of overlapping mammoths. Art historians had always believed that these techniques were invented thousands of years later.

One animal, possibly a bison, is composed entirely of red dots. Until the discovery at Chauvet, the creation of this painting technique, known as *pointillism,* was credited to Georges Seurat, a 19th-century French artist. Archaeologists were also astonished that the Chauvet Cave painters chose to depict predators instead of the usual animals of the hunt—horses, cattle, and reindeer—that are painted in other Stone Age caves.

The half woman-half bison sorcerer image suggests that the Chauvet caves may have been used for religious ceremonies. Variations in the ages of the cave's contents have led some archaeologists to posit that people visited the cave as late as 25,000 to 27,000 B.C.

Unfortunately, the entrance to Chauvet Cave is now gated, and it seems unlikely that the public will be allowed to visit any time soon.

The Black Death

Over a period of five years, from 1347 to 1352, a horrific epidemic ravaged Europe, killing millions, devastating cities, causing widespread panic, and shaking social institutions to their foundations. This natural holocaust—today recognized as bubonic plague—was fearfully referred to as "the Black Death."

Highly contagious, the disease caused fever and painful swelling of the lymph glands, known as *buboes*. Spots appeared on the skin, red at first and then turning black.

Death came swiftly. Italian writer Boccaccio observed that the victims often "ate lunch with their friends and dinner with their ancestors in paradise." Anyone who began spitting blood and saliva was as good as dead.

The pestilence arrived in Italy in October 1347 aboard several Genovese merchant ships returning to Messina from the Black Sea. Many of the crewmen were already dead or dying of the mysterious disease, which quickly spread to the countryside.

The cause remains a mystery, but modern study indicates that the original outbreak occurred in China in the early 1330s. The plague primarily afflicts rats, but it can be transmitted to humans by fleas—in this case by the oriental rat fleas from black rats.

The pestilence quickly spread throughout Europe. Those who attempted to tend the sick quickly fell victim to the plague themselves. Any contact with the afflicted or their clothing was a virtual death sentence. "They sickened by the thousands daily, and died unattended and without help," wrote Englishman Samuel Pepys. "Many died in the open street, others dying in their houses, made it known by the stench of their rotting bodies."

Over the next five years, an estimated 25 million people—one-third the population of Europe—succumbed. England alone lost an estimated 70 percent of its population, falling from seven million at mid-century to two million by 1400. Smaller outbreaks continued to claim victims for another 300 years.

In addition to corpses, the pestilence left a multitude of social ramifications in its wake. The great number of dead created labor shortages long after the disease had passed. The ensuing tension between feudal lords and serfs resulted in peasant revolts in England, France, and elsewhere.

The Canterbury Tales

WRITTEN BY GEOFFREY CHAUCER in Middle English and dating from the 14th century, *The Canterbury Tales* are the most well-known medieval literary work written in English. This collection of both serious and funny stories is framed by a pilgrimage from the South London borough of Southwark to the city of Canterbury, where the pilgrims plan to visit the shrine of St. Thomas Becket, martyred in the 12th century in the Canterbury Cathedral. Having gathered at the Tabard Inn, the pilgrims agree to a plan proposed by their host, Harry Bailly, which calls for each pilgrim to tell two tales en route to Canterbury and another two on the return journey. In fact, only 24 tales are told by the group of 29 pilgrims, with Chaucer himself telling 2 of the 24.

Even better known than the tales themselves are the colorful and often humorous descriptions of the pilgrims as they are introduced in The Prologue of the *Tales*. The Oxford Cleric, for instance, has become an archetype for the bookish academic totally focused on learning; the Squire, so lovesick that "he slept as little as a Nightingale" typifies youthful passion; the Wife of Bath, who has outlived five husbands, embodies female energy and exuberance.

Taken together, the tales give a cross section of medieval English society; only the uppermost and lowest levels (the aristocracy and the peasant class) are missing. As is appropriate for a work from this period, there are a number of characters connected to the church, yet their behavior is generally hypocritical. Of the clerical characters, only the Parson is truly admirable: "Christ and his Twelve Apostles and their lore/He taught, but followed it himself before."

The tales told are linked by prologues and epilogues in which the pilgrims comment on their stories and respond to those of others. Each tale is appropriate to its teller. For instance, the Knight tells a tale of courtly love, while the cook—a vulgar and pugnacious character—tells a bawdy tale of deception and adultery that parodies courtly love. The Pardoner, who famously begins by boasting about his own covetousness, tells a tale of covetousness, showing how that sin leads to other kinds of sinful behavior.

Altogether, the *Tales* present an engaging pageant of medieval life that has influenced subsequent generations' perceptions of the Middle Ages. According to English dramatist John Dryden, Chaucer "has taken into the compass of his *Canterbury Tales* the various manners and humors... of the whole English nation in his age."

Confucius (c. 551–479 B.C.)

CONFUCIUS IS BELIEVED to have been born in 551 B.C. in the state of Lu in present-day Shandong province. His birth name was Kong Qui. His disciples called him *Kongfuzi* or *K'ung-fu-tzu,* meaning "Great Master Kong"; transliterated into Latin his name became Confucius.

Born during a time of much turmoil, Confucius developed a philosophy of righteous behavior based on a belief in man's innate morality. To him, the ideal person would strive to behave morally, would show respect for both superiors and inferiors, and would serve as an inspiration to those aiming to live fulfilling lives.

Rather than formulate a rigid set of rules, Confucius encouraged individuals to think for themselves and to make proper ethical choices. Such people, he said, would take "as much trouble to discover what was right as lesser men take to discover what will pay." He believed these ethics should guide everything from the relationship between father and son to that between emperor and subject. The ideal government, he said, was simply a reflection of the ideal family.

Confucius held a minor government job in Lu, eventually rising to the post of justice minister. However, after years of service, he grew disenchanted with the politics of his prince, which were much at odds with his own ethical standards. Around age 50, Confucius resigned from his government job and embarked on a 12-year journey around China, espousing his view of the ethical life.

As far as is known, Confucius never wrote down any of his teachings. He might have been forgotten entirely had it not been for his followers, who recorded his sayings—or at least the gist of them—in a collection of books known as the *Analects.* Confucianism, which is based on Confucius's teachings, was not popular during his life. However, in time his philosophies became central to Chinese life, affecting everything from education and government to interpersonal relationships.

Though sometimes followed as a religion, Confucianism lacks reference to an afterlife and other spiritual concerns generally considered integral to religious thought. Nevertheless, at least one of the master's maxims bears a striking resemblance to Jesus' "Golden Rule." Asked by a follower for "any one word that could guide a person throughout life," Confucius is said to have replied, "How about shu: never impose on others what you would not choose for yourself."

Kabuki Theater

KABUKI IS A TRADITIONAL form of Japanese theater combining *ka* (song), *bu* (dance), and *ki* (skill) in highly stylized performances. Dating back to the 1600s, Kabuki is geared toward the general public, unlike the more intellectual and subtle Noh theater of the Japanese nobility.

Ironically, though created by a shrine maiden named Okuni in 17th-century Kyoto, Kabuki roles—including those representing women—eventually came to be played entirely by men. The men specializing in these female roles are referred to as *onnagata*.

It was not always so. Originally, Kabuki theater featured large casts of women performing dance routines. Since many of these women were also prostitutes, the Tokugawa Shogunate entirely banned women from the casts in 1629. Young boys dressed as women took over these roles, but that did not help the situation much, and this practice was also eventually banned. Only after mature men assumed all dramatic roles was the moral dilemma resolved.

While troubling to modern sensibilities, the ban on women is credited with raising Kabuki to a higher level. Now drama and skill took precedence over dance, transforming Kabuki into a true dramatic art involving music, dance, and mime, along with lavish costumes, elaborate staging, and heavy facial makeup instead of masks. Highly stylized choreography and greatly exaggerated gestures are standard. Kabuki may also feature interplay between the actors and spectators. Actors pause to address the audience, and the audience responds.

Themes include commentary on contemporary events and depictions of historical material, such as the famed story of the 47 Ronin. A typical program will present a play on a domestic theme, followed by one or two dance plays featuring ghosts or other fantastical beings, concluding with a large dance finale. Performances often revolve around what the Japanese refer to as *kanzen-choaku*, which translates to "reward the virtuous and punish the wicked."

Today, both the Kabuki Theater and the National Theater in Tokyo present regular performances, and there are several performing Kabuki troupes that continue to preserve the historical tradition.

Georges Bizet's *Carmen*

POLITICAL CHANGES in late 19th-century Europe caused many musicians to forge their approach into a specifically "national" style (such as Mussorgsky in Russia, Verdi in Italy, and Gottschalk in the United States). The flip side of the "nationalism" coin was a renewed interest in the "exotic other." In the late 19th century, composers increasingly created musical works that explored Asian, African, or even American topics—not in an "anthropologically correct" way, but rather as a reflection of European fantasies of remote lands and their mysterious, sensuous inhabitants.

French composer Georges Bizet (1838–1875) played up the exoticism of the title character in his opera *Carmen* (1875), a Spanish gypsy who seduces a young corporal named Don José into mutiny, toys with him, and finally rejects him, whereupon he kills her in a jealous rage. Although Bizet incorporates some Spanish and Gypsy music into the dramatic score, *Carmen* is ultimately a French opéra-comique.

Carmen is one of many late 19th-century female operatic protagonists whose seductive musical allure and ability to disrupt the male-dominated status quo seem to actually *require* their murder in order for the story to come to a nonthreatening close. In many other operas, the leading (and fatally doomed) female character projects a mixture of sensuality and purity—most Verdi and Puccini heroines fit this bill. But Bizet splits those two characteristics between the entirely sensuous Carmen and the virginal Micaëla, Don José's fiancée, who unsuccessfully tries to dissuade him from following Carmen to their mutual doom.

Although initially denounced for its "immorality," Bizet's *Carmen* has become one of the most popular operas in current repertory. Carmen's opening song, the "Habanera" ("Love is a rebellious bird/that nobody can tame") is a favorite excerpt for mezzo-soprano singers and one of the most memorable operatic melodies. The other famous song in the opera, featuring Carmen's new flame (and Don José's rival), the toreador Escamillo ("Toreador, Love Awaits You"), was the most immediately successful number and is still one of the most widely recognized operatic excerpts. Ironically, Bizet himself thought that the song was "trash," written for the lowest common denominator of his audience.

The popularity of the opera has led to a number of film versions and some remarkable adaptations. *Carmen Jones*, reset in an African American context by Oscar Hammerstein II, was a successful stage show as well as a 1954 film, using an adaptation of Bizet's musical score.

Antibiotic Resistance

D OCTORS AT THE Centers for Disease Control recently reported a
study showing that in 2005, 19,000 people in the United States died
from MRSA—methicillin-resistant *staphylococcus aureus. S. aureus* are
fairly common bacteria and are generally not dangerous, but they can
cause serious health problems in people who are weakened by old age
or illness. And the bacteria are resistant to even the newest, last-ditch
antibiotics, so a mild infection in a healthy person can sometimes get out
of hand and become fatal.

S. aureus are not the only microbes becoming resistant to antibiotics.
Humans are in an "arms race" with the bacteria that make their living
by making people sick. We devise new and different antibiotics, and the
bacteria evolve resistance. How do they do this?

Disease-causing microbes thwart antibiotics by interfering with their
mechanism of action. For example, penicillin kills bacteria by attaching
to their outer cell walls, then damaging the walls, causing the bacteria
to die. (Human cells do not have "walls"—only an outer membrane—so
penicillin doesn't harm our cells.) Resistant microbes, however, either
alter their cell walls so penicillin can't stick to them, or they produce
enzymes that dismantle the antibiotic itself.

Alternatively, the antibiotics erythromycin and tetracycline attack bacterial ribosomes, the structures within a cell that enable it to make proteins.
Resistant bacteria have slightly altered ribosomes, so drugs can't bind to
them.

How can bacteria develop antibiotic resistance so fast? For one thing,
they reproduce (by cell division) every hour or so, which means they can
evolve very rapidly. And, of course, any bacteria with antibiotic resistance
would be the ones to survive two weeks of penicillin. More important,
many of the genes for antibiotic resistance are carried not on the main
bacterial chromosome, but on separate small rings of DNA called
plasmids. These plasmids can be shared between bacteria—even between
bacteria of different species. This means that any resistant bacteria, even
harmless ones, can potentially share their resistance with the next *strepto-
coccus* that tries to give you a sore throat.

How did we get into this alarming jam? By using antibiotics. Antibiotics
are everywhere today, so bacteria get plenty of practice in evolving and
sharing mechanisms of resistance. Of course, antibiotics can save lives
in certain situations. But other times they're taken when not helpful or
necessary, such as if someone has a viral infection.

Li Tang and
Chinese Landscape Painting

L I TANG, WHO FLOURISHED between about 1080 and 1130, was a pivotal artist in the shift of Chinese landscape painting from the Northern Song style (960–1127) to the Southern Song style (1127–1279), specifically the shift from a panoramic to a partial view accompanied by greater freedom in execution and choice of subject matter. Born in Ho-yang in China's Honan province, Li Tang spent most of his life in K'ai-Feng, the provincial capital, where he was an important member of the Painting Academy and a friend of Emperor Hui Tsung.

At this time, he painted panoramic Song Dynasty–style landscapes, but he also worked in fine line to produce lively rustic scenes featuring people, birds, and water buffalo. In 1122, the Mongols invaded northern China and took the emperor prisoner. Li Tang soon relocated to Hang-chou in the south, where he became the influential founding master of its new painting academy.

Wind in the Pines Amid Myriad Ravines (1124) is an ink and slight color painting on silk executed by Li Tang in Hang-chou and now preserved at the National Palace Museum in Taipei, Taiwan. A tremendous rock formation dominates the center of this painting, with trees, rocks, and possibly water below. According to Laurence Sickman and Alexander Soper in *The Art and Architecture of China* (1956), *Wind in the Pines* observes all the traditions of its time, but has "a new quality of intimacy and lyricism."

What makes this design more striking than paintings by earlier Chinese landscape masters are "the stronger contrasts in light and shade, the white clouds and the finger-like needle peaks." After citing other Li Tang landscapes from this period, Sickman and Soper write that "several of these works are done, not with the densely packed, 'small axe-stroke' ts'un [technique for depicting wrinkles on a mountain, hill, or rock], but in relatively broad washes, a 'large axe-stroke' ts'un, and soft, flowing brush-strokes in the drawing of the trees." Paintings of this kind established Li Tang as the precursor of a style that peaked in the 12th century with two Academy painters, Ma Yuan and Hsia Kuei.

The Holocaust

O N THE NIGHT of November 7, 1938, a German diplomat was shot in Paris by a Jewish youth. He died two days later. This event set off two days of anti-Jewish violence throughout the Reich that would become known as *Kristallnacht* (Night of Broken Glass). Civilians joined Nazi storm troopers in ransacking more than 7,500 businesses and damaging more than 1,000 synagogues. Some 30,000 Jewish men were arrested and sent to concentration camps. The persecution of German Jews that Adolf Hitler had initiated when he assumed power in 1933 finally set in motion the first stage of what was to become known as the "final solution to the Jewish question."

Emigration of German Jews was seen as the initial "solution," but as the number of Jews in German hands grew following the invasion of adjacent countries, the Nazis sought another solution. Reinhard Heydrich, the head of the Security Service, the intelligence arm of the SS, convened a meeting with key German leaders to determine the next course of action. "Another possible solution to the [Jewish] question," meeting notes stated, "has now taken the place of emigration, i.e., evacuation to the east." It was silently understood by all participants that "evacuation to the east" meant extermination.

By the end of the war, more than 15,000 concentration and death camps had been established in the German-occupied territories, primarily in Eastern Europe. By the end of World War II, the total number of Jews killed by their Nazi captors surpassed six million.

"Kill without mercy," Hitler instructed his subordinates following the invasion of Poland. "All men, women and children of Polish descent or language. Only in this way can we obtain the living space we [the Aryan race] need." In addition to Jews, thousands of political prisoners, Jehovah's Witnesses, homosexuals, Gypsies, physically and mentally disabled people, and civilians of conquered territories were either killed immediately or sent to camps for extermination or to be worked to death.

Following the war, many of the German architects of the final solution avoided punishment by killing themselves or escaping from the Allied occupation. One notable figure, Adolf Eichmann, who oversaw the railroads that transported prisoners, escaped to Argentina, only to be captured by Jewish agents in 1960 and taken to Israel. Found guilty of war crimes, Eichmann was hanged almost two years later. Hitler himself is believed to have committed suicide by gunshot and cyanide poisoning in a German bunker on April 30, 1945.

Voltaire's *Candide*

T HE SHORT NOVEL *Candide, ou l'Optimisme* (1759) is today the best-known work of the Enlightenment writer, journalist, playwright, and critic François-Marie Arouet (1694–1778), whose pen name was Voltaire. He was inspired to write the book after the Seven Years' War and the 1755 Lisbon earthquake, and he invokes the theme of evil throughout. In the allegorical *Candide,* written in a light and breezy style, the main character's enthusiastic optimism wanes after he goes through a series of horrific and comic misadventures. The book has a matter-of-fact tone that wittily parodies other romantic adventure plotlines and skewers various senti-mental, philosophical, and religious ideas.

The main character is the naive young man Can-dide, an illegitimate child of "the most unaffected simplicity" whose face is the "index of his mind." He falls in love with his cousin Cunégonde, daughter of the Baron of Thunder-ten-Tronckh. Dr. Pangloss, tutor of both Cunégonde and Candide, is an optimist who mindlessly repeats, through the most horrific adventures, that "everything is for the best in the best of all possible worlds."

Candide joins the army after he is forced to leave the castle because he's caught kissing Cunégonde. He is flogged, almost burned as a heretic, and witnesses the devastating 1755 Lisbon earthquake. After killing an Inquisitor and a Jew who had been "sharing" Cunégonde, Candide flees to South America. Becoming separated from Cunégonde, Candide and his tricky servant Cacambo wander into El Dorado, a utopian community where they acquire great riches. But on their return to Europe, Candide is cheated out of them all. After learning that Cunégonde is captive in Constantinople, Candide travels there, meeting Cunégonde's brother and Dr. Pangloss again on the way and hearing of their own misadventures.

After many improbable events, Candide, Cunégonde (old and ugly by now), Dr. Pangloss, Cacambo, and two other companions of their journeys settle on a small farm, where Candide finally renounces Dr. Pangloss's optimism, concluding: It is best "to cultivate one's own garden."

Candide freely satirizes kings, the army, war, the nobility, the Catholic Church, and Protestantism, but its main satirical target is the optimism of Gottfried Leibinz. In his book *Theodicy,* Liebinz famously wrote that we live in the "best of all possible worlds" that God could have created.

The Buddha (c. 563–483 B.C.)

SIDDHARTHA GAUTAMA, known as the Buddha, was a colorful figure whose meditations and philosophies became the foundations of Buddhism. However, few facts are known about his actual life. He was born the son of a tribal chieftain in the foothills of the Himalayas in the late sixth century B.C. When he was 29, he rejected the Hindu concepts of dharma and karma, became a wandering ascetic, and spent the rest of his life teaching his new doctrine in the kingdoms of northern India. When he died, at the age of 80, his followers were only one small band among the many heterodox sects that appeared in northern India in the seventh to fifth centuries B.C. His *bhikkus* (disciples) and teachings were largely unknown until the Mauryan emperor Asoka converted to Buddhism nearly 200 years after Siddhartha's death.

The Buddha of legend has a more elaborate story. When Prince Siddhartha was born, a seer proclaimed that the prince would become either a great king or a holy man. Upon hearing this, Siddhartha's father hoped his son would become a great king and sought to protect him from the miseries of life.

Despite his father's efforts, Siddhartha saw an aged man, then a man covered with sores and shivering from fever, and, finally, a corpse being carried to the cremation grounds. Aware for the first time of age, illness, and death, the prince was troubled. A fourth sign brought Siddhartha hope: a religious beggar with a look of joy.

Unable to forget these things, the prince abandoned his family and kingdom the night his first son was born. Searching for liberation from sorrow, he became first a wandering ascetic, then a forest hermit, owning nothing but the robe he wore. One day while sitting beneath a pipal tree, Siddhartha vowed that he would not move until he had solved the riddle of suffering. Although tempted repeatedly by Mara (a demon who is said to have sent beautiful women to seduce Siddhartha to distract him from reaching spiritual enlightenment), Siddhartha sank deeper into meditation. On the forty-ninth day, he understood that sorrow comes from desire, and that man can overcome sorrow by ridding himself of desire. At this moment, Siddhartha became the Buddha, or the "awakened one."

For 40 years, the Buddha taught, and the number of his disciples increased. When he was 80, he traveled north to the hills of his youth, preparing his followers for his death. His last words were "All things decay. Strive diligently."

Cannibalism

ACCUSATIONS OF CANNIBALISM, substantiated or not, were used as an excuse for colonial exploitation. Today, the assertion that a prehistoric or "primitive" culture may have practiced either ritual or nutritional cannibalism arouses immediate suspicion as many early reports of cannibalism have been challenged and proven false.

Accounts of cannibalism in more recent times usually come from firsthand accounts, which are not verifiable and can easily be dismissed as hearsay. However, anthropologists have several ways of looking into the past and determining whether a given pile of prehistoric human bones and artifacts show evidence of cannibalism. For instance, cut marks on ancient bones are studied to see if they are similar to marks typically found on butchered animal bones. Ancient cooking vessels are also studied. Anthropologists will analyze scrapings from the inside of pots for evidence of human muscle proteins, as this would indicate that human flesh had been cooked within. In addition, some long bones exhibit a characteristic called *pot polish* where the ends of the bones appear smooth. It is believed that this trait was caused by the bones rubbing against the sides of a pot during cooking.

The chronicler Bernal Diáz accompanied Cortés in 1519 as he marched into Mexico to subdue the Aztecs. He left an eyewitness account of human sacrifice and cannibalism among the Aztecs. Recently, anthropologists studying at several sites in Mexico found bones that show evidence of cannibalism. Still, there is disagreement about whether the practice arose for nutritional reasons or as part of a religious ritual. The Mexican highlands had no big game or domesticated animals, so it seems possible that cannibalism arose from a shortage of animal protein.

The Fore tribe in New Guinea is also reported to have practiced ritual cannibalism, nibbling on the cooked brains of the recently deceased. This claim has been challenged, yet it remains supported by an interesting fact. A disease called *Kuru* was once prevalent among the Fore and is now dying out with the decline of cannibalism. Kuru is a prion disease, like the infamous Mad Cow Disease, and such diseases are only transmitted through contact with, or consumption of, infected flesh.

Long ago, the Anasazi people lived in New Mexico. They disappeared some 1,000 years ago. It is now believed that they practiced cannibalism as well. An Anasazi site dating from A.D. 1150 yielded dried human excrement containing human muscle proteins. This appears to be good evidence that the fellow who deposited it there had digested human flesh.

The Caccini Family

IN THE LATE RENAISSANCE, Giulio Caccini (1551–1618) was a pioneer in the "invention" of opera as well as one of the more renowned leaders in a new and highly influential tradition of solo song. Indeed, Giulio claimed to have invented both a new, radically expressive singing style and a notational practice—coupling a singing line with a shorthand bass/chordal notation, called *basso continuo* or "figured bass"—that became the musical linchpin for decades to come.

Since a number of Giulio's contemporaries similarly laid claim to inventing the basso continuo—and since Giulio was renowned even in his own day for his tendency toward self-promotion—his boasts should be taken with a grain of salt. Still, his approach became the springboard for a significant reconfiguration of the Italian song tradition.

An established teacher, Giulio Caccini aimed to pass his singing craft on to the rest of his family. His "musical household" was a widely praised institution. Giulio's first wife, Lucia Gagnolanti, was a singer who died when her children were still young. His eldest daughter, Francesca (born in 1587; died after 1640), known as "la Cecchina" ("the songbird"), was probably the most prolific of a small handful of successful female performer-composers in the early 1600s.

Francesca is the first woman known to have composed operas. In 1628, her opera *La Liberazione di Ruggiero Dall'isola d'Alcina*—commissioned by the archduchess of the Medici court, for whom Francesca worked—was performed in Warsaw, Poland, marking the first time an Italian opera was performed outside of Italy. In addition, Francesca was a singer and played the harp, lute, keyboard, and guitar. She also wrote poetry and song lyrics.

Francesca's career was significantly limited because of her gender; women who performed in public were considered little more than prostitutes. However, she was supported by the female regents who subtly governed Florence in the name of the underage duke.

Francesca disappeared from public view after she married a nobleman and gave birth to a son. While her father sought the limelight to the very end, Francesca may well have realized that as a woman she could have a more stable life if she avoided public music-making of any sort.

Settimia Caccini (1591–c. 1638) was Giulio Caccini's youngest daughter. She was a successful composer and singer. Guilio's son, Pompeo Caccini, was also a singer.

Galileo Galilei

A LONG WITH NICOLAUS COPERNICUS and Isaac Newton, Galileo Galilei (1564–1642) was a giant of early modern science. His father, a musician and wool trader, wanted his first-born to become a doctor. When Galileo announced his intention to become a monk, his father quickly enrolled him at the University of Pisa to study medicine. There, the young man became fascinated by mathematics and—bored with medicine—ultimately dropped out of the university. He learned enough mathematics to offer private lessons, and in 1586 he published his first book, a study of Greek mathematician Archimedes. In 1592, he was named a chair in mathematics at the University of Padua where he spent the next 18 years. In 1609, he began building a series of telescopes that enabled him to make several discoveries—particularly that four moons orbited Jupiter—which helped overturn Aristotle's and Ptolemy's theory that Earth was the center for the circular motion of all heavenly bodies.

This confirmation of the work of Copernicus (who had believed that Earth rotated on its axis daily and circled the sun once per year) profoundly disturbed officials of the Catholic Church, who continued to revere the view that Earth was the center of the universe. In 1616, Cardinal Bellarmine, Archbishop of Capua, issued an injunction forbidding Catholics from holding or defending Copernican doctrine. Galileo, however, continued his research, hoping that his study of tides would further support the notion that Earth itself was not stationary but moved in its own orbit.

In 1632, he published his major work in defense of the Copernican system, *Dialogue Concerning the Two Chief Systems of the World Systems—Ptolemaic and Copernican*. The Catholic Inquisition banned the work and ordered Galileo to come to Rome to appear before the Inquisitors. Found guilty of violating the 1616 injunction and forced to recant his Copernican "heresy," he was sentenced to life in prison, which was later commuted to a lifetime of house arrest. Even under these circumstances, he managed to write another major work, *Discourses on Two New Sciences* (1638), which laid the groundwork for the science of mechanics.

When Galileo died in 1642, he was not buried in consecrated ground for fear that the Church would object. His books were not removed from the Catholic Index of banned books until 1835. In 1992, Pope John Paul II finally admitted that "errors had been made by the theological advisors in the case of Galileo."

The Elgin Marble Controversy

THE PARTHENON STILL inspires awe 2,500 years after its completion. But for the last 200 years, its sculptures have been embroiled in controversy. In the early 19th century, many were removed and exported to England, where they have remained ever since. The fate of these sculptures—known as the "Elgin Marbles," after the man responsible for their removal—has been hotly debated between those calling for their return to Greece and those who argue that they should stay in Britain.

Considered by many to be the world's most perfect building, the Parthenon (built between 447 and 432 B.C.) was conceived as the centerpiece of Pericles's ambitious building program. Its interior housed a 42-foot-high gold-and-ivory statue of Athena (since lost) by the sculptor Phidias (c. 490-c. 430 B.C.).

Phidias—who later went on to create one of the Seven Wonders of the Ancient World, a colossal statue of Zeus at Olympia—determined the design for the sculptural program of the Parthenon but left much of the actual carving to others. The sculptural decoration consisted of 92 metope reliefs depicting mythological battles, pediment figures representing the birth of Athena, and a 500-foot-long frieze devoted to the Panathenaic procession.

The Parthenon's subsequent history was tied to that of Athens. After the city came under Ottoman control in 1458, the building was made into a mosque. Later used to store gunpowder for the Ottomans, the Parthenon exploded in 1687, blowing off the roof and destroying many of the remaining sculptures. Throughout the 18th century, the Parthenon sculptures were literally up for grabs, with foreign travelers breaking off pieces to take home with them.

Such was the state in which Lord Elgin found the Parthenon in 1800. A permit from the Sultan enabled Elgin—British ambassador to Constantinople from 1799 to 1803—to remove 17 pediment figures, 15 metopes, and 56 frieze slabs. Elgin sold the sculptures to the British government in 1816, and they have been housed in the British Museum ever since.

The debate over the Elgin Marbles has new relevance today amid the recent opening of the New Acropolis Museum. The museum will display the Parthenon sculptures remaining in Athens in a stunning space in which one writer found it "impossible to stand . . . without craving the marbles' return."

Mao Tse-tung

THE SON OF A PROSPEROUS FARMER, Mao Tse-tung (1893–1976) preferred books to farm work, graduating from a teachers' school in 1918. As a student, he discovered the philosophies of Marx and Lenin and came to see socialism as the solution to China's many problems.

In 1921, Mao served as Hunan's delegate to the meeting founding the Chinese Communist Party. He and fellow Communists worked with Sun Yat-sen and the Kuomintang (Nationalist Party) until Sun Yat-sen's death in 1925. The Kuomintang was taken over by Chiang Kai-shek, who quickly pushed the Communists out.

In 1927, Mao helped create a Soviet-style government in Jiangxi Province, organizing an army and redistributing land. By 1930, this rogue government had established authority over several million peasants. Chiang's Kuomintang set out to erase this threat. In 1934, in danger of being overwhelmed, Mao and his comrades began a 6,000-mile fighting retreat known as the Long March. Of the 80,000 who started, only about 8,000 survived, with Mao emerging as the uncontested Chinese Communist leader.

Over the next ten years, holding out in remote Yan'an, Mao formulated "Maoism"—essentially adapting the philosophies of Marx and Lenin to fit China's agrarian peasantry. Communist propaganda billed Mao as a compassionate revolutionary, but those who deviated from his party line were treated harshly.

Japan's invasion of China in 1937 interrupted the warfare between Mao and Chiang. The Nationalists and the Communists made a show of allying to fight the invaders, but they spent much of their efforts positioning themselves for the showdown they knew would follow.

After WWII, civil war again erupted in China, but now the Communists were stronger. By 1949, Mao had expelled Chiang and the Nationalists from the mainland and established the People's Republic of China.

Mao's reputation diminished following his death in 1976. There was criticism of his failures and his ubiquitous "cult of personality." Despite his mixed legacy, "Chairman Mao" transformed his nation. Under Mao's direction, China became a major player on the world stage, a stature that has continued to grow in the new century.

Albert Camus

ALBERT CAMUS (1913–1960) was one of the most prominent mid-20th-century French writers and intellectuals, winning the Nobel Prize in Literature in 1957 and becoming the youngest author since Rudyard Kipling to be so honored.

Born in French Algeria to a Spanish mother, Camus lost his father during World War I, which left the family destitute. Nevertheless, the precocious Camus managed to attend the University of Algiers. When he contracted tuberculosis at age 17, he was forced to prolong his university studies, but he eventually earned the equivalent of a master's degree.

Responding to the political crises of the 1930s, Camus wrote for various journals. He also belonged to L'Équipe (the team), an Algerian political theater group. Camus joined the Communist Party in 1935 out of sympathy for the Spanish Republican government during Spain's civil war but was expelled two years later for also joining the Algerian People's Party. During World War II, Camus became famous in France as a correspondent with the underground resistance publication *Combat*. He became friends with writer and philosopher Jean-Paul Sartre, whose work influenced him.

Camus's 1942 essay *The Myth of Sisyphus* introduced the idea of "the absurd," using the familiar story of Sisyphus and his pointless, never-ending task of rolling a stone up a hill. Even as he struggles against the "indifferent universe," Sisyphus doesn't despair. In fact, he has a personal "rebellion," another theme of Camus's works.

In the novel *L'Étranger* (usually translated into English as *The Stranger*), also published in 1942, Camus's central character, Meursault, reflects on his life while awaiting execution after he kills a man seemingly at random. Meursault refuses the consolations of religion and conventional habit but dies at peace because he accepts "the indifference of the universe" and his own responsibility for his actions.

That "absurdism," as it came to be called, differed from nihilism and was cemented even further by Camus's novel *The Plague* (1947), in which the character Dr. Rieux serves the plague-embattled citizens of Oran, in French Algeria, with the words, "We refuse to despair of mankind. Without having the unreasonable ambition to save men, we still want to serve them."

Strongly moral in his writing and his life, Camus continued to be a political pacifist. He died in a car accident in 1960.

Helen Keller (1880–1968)

CERTAINLY THE MOST revered example of an American who overcame physical disabilities, Helen Keller was born in Tuscumbia, Alabama, to a prominent family. At 19 months old, she contracted a "brain fever" that left her blind, deaf, and mute. Keller's uncle urged her parents to institutionalize her at age six when she became subject to violent tantrums. However, on the recommendation of famed inventor Alexander Graham Bell, her parents hired a young graduate from the Perkins School for the Blind to teach Helen to communicate. Anne Sullivan patiently worked with her until finally, in 1887, Keller understood and said the word *water*—an iconic moment in the history of the disabled, immortalized in the award-winning play and film, *The Miracle Worker*.

From that point on, Keller became a voracious reader and writer. She graduated from Radcliffe College and spent much of the rest of her life working to improve conditions for the disabled. Indeed, she became an almost iconic symbol of courage, dedication, and faith—a shining example of what true grit could accomplish. Her memoir *The Story of My Life* (1903) has been translated into 50 languages. Keller was also instrumental in establishing an endowment in her name for the American Foundation of the Blind. Famed American writer Mark Twain paid her the ultimate compliment when he remarked, "The two most interesting characters of the 19th century are Napoleon and Helen Keller."

There was another side to Keller's life that is less well-known to the public: She was a political and social radical for much of her life. She joined the Socialist Party but found it too moderate for her taste; she left it for the far more radical Industrial Workers of the World. She spoke out for birth control, civil rights for black Americans, and women's suffrage. A committed pacifist, she opposed U.S. entry into World War I, and when the war was over, she condemned the deportation of immigrants for political reasons. She was even investigated by the FBI in the 1950s due to her radical ideology.

In a curious way, her social and political views were in sync with her ideas about the disabled. She very much believed in doing all she could to stamp out injustice and discrimination—against any person or group. This is perhaps the ultimate legacy of a woman who was more complex than her conventional image would suggest.

Cher Ami

PIGEONS HAVE CARRIED MESSAGES for almost as long as humans have needed to send them. In 776 B.C., the names of the winners at the first Olympic Games were "air-mailed" to the cities of ancient Greece via pigeon. In 1851, before telegraph wires had encircled the globe, an entrepreneur named Julius Reuters used pigeons to send breaking news across Europe. Pigeons also provided essential strategic support in times of war. One of the most famous of these military birds was a carrier pigeon named Cher Ami, or "Dear Friend" in English.

In the final months of World War I, American troops pushed through the Argonne Forest toward the Meuse River, suffering horrific losses. On October 2, 1918, soldiers from the 77th Infantry Division under the command of Major Charles W. Whittlesey, who would become known as the "Lost Battalion," found themselves isolated in a ravine, pinned down by German guns. Unprepared for a siege, they soon ran out of food, water, and ammunition. Their situation worsened as shells from their allies, so-called "friendly fire," suddenly began exploding around them.

Cher Ami was now the only one who could relay their location and dire circumstances to the Allied leadership. Whittlesey penned a note on a scrap of paper: "We are along the road parallel 276.4. Our own artillery is dropping a barrage on us. For heaven's sake, stop it." On October 4, he sent for the pigeon keeper, Omer Richards.

With the note attached, Richards released Cher Ami, and the bird spiraled up into the sky as a German sharpshooter took aim. Cher Ami would survive this attack, and apparently a few others, ultimately making his way to the American headquarters. When he arrived, the capsule containing the message hung from the remains of his shattered leg. Still, his mission was successful, and on October 8, forces arrived to rescue 194 men—all that remained of the original 554 soldiers of the Lost Battalion.

Sadly, Cher Ami died from his wounds on June 13, 1919. He was awarded the *croix de guerre* medal by the French government for having delivered several important messages and for his courage. In 1931, he was also named to the Racing Pigeon Hall of Fame. The Organized Bodies of American Racing Pigeon Fanciers also recognized Cher Ami's service in World War I, and he was awarded a gold medal. Cher Ami's remains can now be found at the National Museum of American History in Washington, D.C.

Musical Worship in 17th- and 18th-Century North America

WHILE THE MAIN GROUPS of colonists on the Eastern seaboard of North America in the 1600s and early 1700s shared a national allegiance to England, they reflected at least two significantly different religious paths: The "Pilgrims" and "Puritans" in New England came out of a Calvinist Protestant tradition, while those in the Virginia colonies were primarily Anglican.

In musical terms, the New England groups were dedicated to simple congregational singing of psalms, without the use of instruments or complicated harmonies, in church (in keeping with their Calvinist roots). The Virginians, on the other hand, inherited the somewhat more complex tradition of the English anthem, and their churches tended to have dedicated choirs, though their resources were significantly less elaborate than those available in mother England.

Because only a small percentage of the population could read music, New Englanders came to rely on a method called "lining out" for their musical worship in a church service: The leader would sing one line of a psalm (either from a book or by memory), and the rest of the congregation would repeat that line. The process would continue for the duration of the scriptural text. Over time, this led to members of the congregation taking what some church leaders considered "inappropriate liberties" with the melody in repeating the psalm line and thus to a "unison repeat" that was anything but unison.

Those who objected to the "disorder" resulting from lining out (as well as the increased duration of psalm singing that it caused) created a push in the late 1600s for increased musical literacy, so that all worshippers could sing simultaneously from a music book without relying on the lining-out process. This approach (established through "singing schools") caught on remarkably well and led to increasing demand for new arrangements of sacred songs—arrangements that some church leaders deplored as too elaborate and "distracting" to focus on the text, but that became the linchpin of a more progressive approach to congregational singing throughout the English colonies. This eventually opened up a space for the first self-proclaimed (and self-taught) American composer, William Billings (1746–1800), whose music fused sacred tradition with an emergent nationalist fervor.

Chaos Theory

CHAOS THEORY is the branch of mathematics that attempts to account for the fact that many systems are not successfully described by the linear equations used in traditional math and physics. The "chaos" in Chaos Theory doesn't mean messy or disorganized; it just means non-linear and, hence, virtually impossible to predict.

A common example is the weather, where tiny changes in atmospheric conditions in the Pacific Ocean can produce enormous changes in a weather system by the time it reaches New England. Another common example is a pool table, where tiny variations in the air currents, bumps on the tabletop, and the force of a given shot make it impossible to predict where the ball will end up after ten ricochets off the table rim.

Such systems are called nonlinear. The equations that describe them contain a lot of exponents, and the graphs that map them contain curving lines instead of straight ones (hence the description nonlinear). This means that tiny changes in the initial conditions can lead to enormous variations in the final result, and seemingly simple systems can produce complex behavior. A simple mathematical demonstration of this is the fact that $2^{10} = 1064$, while $2.1^{10} = 3503$. A small increase in the number taken to the tenth power yields a product more than three times greater.

An early pioneer of Chaos Theory was meteorologist Edward Lorenz. In 1961, using an early version of a computer to run his weather simulations, he found that very small changes in the initial assumptions produced big differences in the weather predicted at the end of the run. His discovery was actually an accident: He repeated a computer simulation by entering values from a printout, rounded to three decimal places. The original simulation had used values carried to six decimal places. To his surprise, the second simulation gave a completely different outcome. It turned out that simply rounding the numbers to more or fewer decimal places made a big difference in the end result. In 1972, he gave a paper at a meeting of the American Association for the Advancement of Science, entitled "Predictability: Does the Flap of a Butterfly's Wings in Brazil set off a Tornado in Texas?," thus coining the term "the butterfly effect," commonly associated with Chaos Theory.

Many important systems are now thought to be nonlinear. For example, the evolution of life on Earth may be such a system. A tiny change in, say, the percentage of oxygen in the atmosphere a billion years ago might have resulted in an unrecognizably different collection of living creatures today.

The Book of Kells

T HE BOOK OF KELLS is considered the most remarkable of some 50 surviving manuscripts produced by Irish monks in the early Middle Ages. Its contents feature the four Gospels of the New Testament—each a Latin account of the life of Christ—with lavish illustrations and decorative passages. The text was handwritten by scribes around the late eighth

century in a monastery probably located on the small, remote Isle of Iona located off the west coast of Scotland. Images of Christ, the Virgin, and the Evangelists accompany the text, surrounded by distinctive abstract forms. It is believed that as many as four artists worked on the manuscript.

The principal decorative motifs consist of interlaced, swirling lines, sometimes called Celtic knots, which bend and curve, suggesting organic forms such as plant stems or snakes. There are also discs and circular shapes, as well as bold geometric outlines that are used to form both enlarged letters and abstract shapes. One of the best-known pages is found at the beginning of the Gospel of St. Matthew. Known as the *Chi Rho Iota* page because of the prominence of the three Greek letters (XPI) that stand for "Christ," it features an extravagant display of opulently colored lines and patterns as well as scattered images. Visible within the letters and interlaces are the head of a man (possibly Christ or a monk), several angels, and cats and mice fighting. Colors in the manuscript were derived from both local and imported materials, some of which were very costly. Gold was simulated by orpiment, a yellow compound derived from arsenic.

Tradition associates the Book of Kells with the legendary St. Columba (or St. Columcille), a sixth-century saint. Whether Columba worked on parts of the book himself or whether it was produced to commemorate him, the manuscript is said to have left Iona some time after its completion, possibly in the wake of a Viking invasion. It was in the monastery at Kells, Ireland, by 1006, when it was reported to have been stolen. The book was found buried "under a sod" with its gold and jewel-encrusted cover removed.

Since 1661, the Book of Kells has been located at Trinity College in Dublin.

The Atlantic Slave Trade

THE ATLANTIC SLAVE TRADE was a critical part of the British economy in the 18th century. Ships sailed from Britain to the west coast of Africa with trade goods such as firearms, gunpowder, alcohol, cotton textiles, beads, knives, and mirrors. These goods were traded for slaves. The slaves were then shipped across the Atlantic under conditions so barbaric that slave traders expected to lose as many as 30 percent of their captives on each trip. The survivors were sold to plantation owners in the West Indies and the American South. Slave-produced cotton, tobacco, and sugarcane were then shipped back to Britain.

Every step of the triangular trade brought enormous profits to Britain. Liverpool was the largest slave-trading port in the world. British manufacturers produced cheap goods, especially for the African market. By the last quarter of the 18th century, one-third of Manchester's textile production was shipped to Africa. British ships transported 50,000 slaves a year. The sugar economy was so dependent on slavery that West Indian plantation owner John Pinney declared it was "as impossible for a man to make sugar without the assistance of negroes as to make bricks without straw."

Despite the economic importance of the slave trade, increasing numbers of Britons questioned its morality. In 1783, the Society of Friends (Quakers) established a committee to publish "such information as may tend to the abolition of the slave trade." The movement took more formal shape in 1787 with the creation of the Society for the Abolition of the Slave Trade, financed by both Quaker and Evangelical businessmen, one of whom, William Wilberforce, became the movement's spokesperson in Parliament.

In 1807, Parliament enacted a law abolishing the slave trade in the British colonies and making it illegal to carry slaves in British ships. The practical impact of the legislation was limited. If anything, the scale of the trade increased. Brazil replaced Britain as the most important slave-trading nation. Other European companies continued to trade in slaves, often with money from British investors. British slave traders continued to sail under foreign ship registrations. The efforts of the British navy to enforce the ban simply resulted in higher prices.

But for Wilberforce and his colleagues, the 1807 legislation was the first step in a campaign to abolish slavery altogether. Wilberforce was on his deathbed when the Abolition of Slavery Act was finally passed in 1833. British slave owners received compensation for up to 40 percent of the estimated market value of their slaves; the slaves received nothing except their freedom.

Virgil's *Aeneid*

*T*HE *AENEID*, written by Latin poet Publius Vergilius Maro (70–19 B.C.), known as Virgil in English, is considered one of the great epic poems in the Western tradition. It has been almost as influential on art and poetry as Homer's epics. But whereas Homer's were composed in performance out of an oral tradition and only written down hundreds of years later, Virgil's epic is self-consciously literate, composed and written by a single author. *The Aeneid* is written in dactylic hexameter, the same meter used in Homer's *Iliad.*

While the Trojan Aeneas was a minor character in the *Iliad,* Virgil expands his story into Roman national mythology to both imitate and rival Homer's epics. *The Aeneid* shows events from the perspective of Aeneas's own time, after Rome had defeated Carthage and absorbed Greek culture.

In the poem, Aeneas, a descendant of Venus, flees Troy with his son Ascanius, carrying his father, Anchises, on his back. With a fleet of Trojan ships, Aeneas seeks to fulfill the gods' command to build a city in Italy. Two attempts are defeated by bad omens and plague. The Trojans are cursed by Harpies, creatures with women's heads and birds' bodies, which were portrayed in Homer's *Odyssey.* But they also encounter friendly inhabitants.

After he loses his father and a storm blows him and his companions to Carthage (modern-day Tunisia), Aeneas encounters the Carthaginian princess Dido, who explains how she founded Carthage after fleeing Phoenicia (in modern Lebanon) to escape family intrigue. Dido falls in love with Aeneas, and they live together until the gods remind Aeneas of his duty to found a city. As he leaves, the heartbroken Dido commits suicide with Aeneas's castoff sword on a funeral pyre of possessions he left behind.

A storm blows the Trojans to Sicily. When they arrive in Italy, Aeneas is allowed to visit the underworld to see his dead father. While there, Aeneas sees a pageant of events in a glorious Roman future. Aided by Tiberinus, god of the river Tiber (which flows through Rome), Aeneas receives a friendly reception from King Latinus. But Latinus's queen, Amata, stirs up local tribes against him. Led by Turnus, whom the queen wants to marry her daughter Lavinia, the tribes begin a war against Aeneas's Trojans. When Aeneas travels to get support from neighboring tribes, he meets his patroness, Venus, whose husband, Vulcan, has forged him divine armor. In a final battle against Turnus and his forces, Aeneas is wounded but finally kills Turnus.

Benjamin Spock (1903–1998)

A RGUABLY THE MOST trusted and popular author of child-rearing manuals in history, Benjamin Spock was born in New Haven, Connecticut, the son of a successful attorney and a stay-at-home mother. As the eldest of six, he gained considerable early experience in caring for children. Spock lived up to his parents' high expectations when he gradu-

ated from Yale University and later received his MD at Columbia University in 1929, finishing first in his class.

From the outset of his career as a pediatric specialist, Spock was convinced that he could best serve his patients by understanding their psychological needs as well as their physical ones. He studied psychology for six years, becoming one of the few pediatricians with this type of training. His background led him to disagree with the methods of infant care that were popular at the time. As propounded by John Watson, parents were advised to follow a strict regimen of eating, sleeping, and bowel movements. Watson also warned parents against showing excessive affection for their young children. Spock advocated a much more flexible approach.

Inspired by his new ideas, Spock published *The Common Sense Book of Baby and Child Care* in 1946. He was stunned to see it become an immediate best seller. His views that parents should not commit to a rigid schedule in caring for infants and especially should not be afraid to show affection helped revolutionize child care in America and beyond. During his lifetime, the book went through seven editions, was translated into 40 languages, and sold more than 50 million copies,

In the 1960s, Spock became a high-profile opponent of the Vietnam War. He was convicted of conspiracy to abet draft evasion during the war (a conviction overturned on appeal) and ran for president on the People's Party ticket in 1972. He participated in antinuclear weapons demonstrations in the 1980s and '90s. Indeed, his political activism—and that of many young people in this period—led some political and religious conservatives to blame what they saw as his excessively permissive views of child rearing as the root cause of anarchic, youthful rebelliousness. Spock, on the other hand, emphasized his flexibility. He even believed that an ultimate goal of parenting was "to civilize" children.

The Koran

FOR MUSLIMS, the Koran is the literal word of God, written on a tablet preserved in heaven and revealed to the Prophet Muhammad by the archangel Gabriel.

The title "Koran" means "The Recitation" in Arabic and describes the manner of the book's transmission. According to Muslim tradition, around A.D. 610, Muhammad retreated to a cave in the hills outside of Mecca to engage in solitary prayer. Gabriel came to him in his sleep. Three times the angel commanded, "Recite!" Three times, Muham-

mad asked, "What should I recite?" Gabriel replied, "Recite in the name of your Lord who created, created man from clots of blood. Recite! Your Lord is the Most Bountiful One, who by the pen taught man what he did not know."

As a result of this vision, Muhammad took on his role as the messenger of God: sent to confirm and correct the scriptures previously given to the Jews and Christians. He described his task as bringing people back to the religion revealed to Abraham, which he called Islam, meaning "submission."

Noted for the beauty of its Arabic, the Koran is composed of 114 chapters, called *suras,* revealed to Muhammad over a period of 22 years. Traditionally, these have been arranged in order of length, rather than chronologically or according to content.

It is uncertain whether the entire Koran was written down during Muhammad's lifetime. Members of the Companions of the Prophet memorized portions as they were transmitted orally and received. An authorized version was established under Uthman, the third caliph, who ruled from 644–656. This remains the authoritative text of the Koran for Muslims, though the absence of vowels and diacritical markings in the Kufic script (in which the revelations were originally written) means that variant readings are recognized as having equal authority.

Because the Arabic of the Koran is believed to be the revealed language of God, all Muslims learn to recite the scripture in Arabic—no matter what language they speak or read—and chanting the Koran is an art form. Memorizing the entire Koran is seen as an act of devotion, bringing honor to those who do it.

Beethoven's *Eroica* Symphony

LUDWIG VAN BEETHOVEN (1770–1827) arrived in Vienna in his early twenties, having been encouraged by one of his patrons that he would "receive the spirit of Mozart [who had recently died] from Haydn's hands." It would have taken a rather substantial ego to withstand such an intimidating charge—those two were, after all, arguably the most famous Viennese musicians of the day. Beethoven, however, was clearly up to the task, and he consciously chose to program works by both Mozart and Haydn alongside the premiere of his own First Symphony in a well-advertised concert on April 2, 1800.

Around this time Beethoven became increasingly self-conscious about his role as a musical pioneer. He was also growing more aware of his own hearing loss. The notion of heroic struggle became an important artistic trigger, and this can be seen most clearly in his Third Symphony, the so-called *Eroica* (Italian for "heroic"), which Beethoven began composing in 1803.

At the time Beethoven began working on this symphony, General Napoleon Bonaparte was leading the French armies to heroic deeds. The title page of Beethoven's draft bears the name *Bonaparte,* and the opening movement of the work has often been described (almost since its 1804 premiere) as a "heroic narrative" involving a musical idea that is presented, "disrupted," and then transformed into a powerful statement.

The second movement of the work provides a somber marchlike tune, similar to funeral marches written in the French Revolutionary style by such composers as François Joseph Gossec. This alternates with a contrasting musical idea based on a fanfare, bringing together two powerful military-music tropes. After a somber scherzo, the last movement is a complex assemblage of variations on a melody that Beethoven had created for his ballet *Creatures of Prometheus.*

The original title of the symphony was changed: Rather than *Bonaparte,* it is now known as the *Eroica,* a title that was directly provided by Beethoven, who further stated that it was "composed to celebrate the memory of a great man," without indicating a name. Indeed, Beethoven is said to have canceled the dedication in anger upon hearing of Bonaparte's decision to be crowned emperor (thus relinquishing the equality of status that so many European intellectuals found fascinating about the French revolutionary spirit). However, the truth is more subtle, since there is evidence of Beethoven's admiration for Napoleon more than a decade later.

Influenza

I F ONLY WE COULD get a flu shot that lasts a lifetime, just as children nowadays get immunized against measles, chickenpox, mumps, and a number of other formerly troublesome viral diseases.

Some years are bad flu years, with many people falling ill and many victims suffering serious illness. Other years the virus is not as bad. The problem is, each strain is always a little different, so a vaccine that protects against all of them hasn't been developed.

Influenza, or "the flu," is caused by a virus consisting of genetic material (RNA) packaged in a shell made of proteins and waxy fats. Two proteins, hemagglutinin and neuramidinase (H and N to the scientists who study them) protrude through the shell, like spikes. These proteins help the virus attach to and enter the cells it infects. They are also what our bodies recognize as invaders and what we produce antibodies against.

The reason we can keep getting the flu year after year is that these two proteins keep changing, so our bodies' immune systems can't recognize them—and a new flu vaccine must be developed every year. The measles virus, in contrast, is stable over time, so one attack of measles (or a shot of measles vaccine) confers lifetime immunity. Why are some viruses stable and others not? Scientists believe the reason is that the flu virus can infect birds and pigs as well as humans, while measles and most other common human viruses infect only us. While the virus is growing in one or the other of its animal hosts, it has the opportunity to exchange genes with different viral strains and may pick up a new H or N gene to try out on us next flu season.

In 1918, just as World War I was ending (and before there were any flu vaccines available), more than 20 million people died in a worldwide flu pandemic. The flu killed more people than the war had. More Americans died in four months of the 1918 flu epidemic than have died of AIDS in the past 20 years. Hoping to discover what made the 1918 flu strain so virulent, scientists have been extracting viral fragments from victims' lungs, which have been preserved in hospitals all these years, and also from victims frozen in the permafrost in Alaska and Spitsbergen, Norway. So far, they have managed to reconstruct the 1918 virus and have devised a vaccine that seems to protect mice. Perhaps by the time another extremely virulent flu strain comes along, we will be ready with a vaccine that protects humans. Even now, tens (perhaps even hundreds) of thousands of people around the world die from influenza each year.

Trompe L'Oeil Realism

T WO PAINTERS IN late-fifth to early-fourth century B.C. Greece, Zeuxis and Parrhasios, staged a competition to see who could produce the more realistic painting. Zeuxis's effort was a painting of grapes so luscious that it caused birds to come peck at them. When Zeuxis tried to lift the curtain from Parrhasios's painting—only to realize that the curtain was itself the painting—he conceded defeat, reputedly explaining, "I have deceived the birds, but Parrhasios has deceived Zeuxis."

This famous story, recorded later by the Roman writer Pliny, epitomizes the central aspect of trompe l'oeil: the ability to fool the viewer. A French term meaning "to fool the eye," trompe l'oeil is the most intense form of realism—the genre that best reflects the notion that the function of art is illusionism.

Illusionistic painting was absent from much of the Middle Ages: The Italian painter Giotto (c. 1266–1337), credited with its revival, is the subject of another legendary anecdote about trompe l'oeil: Giotto is said to have painted flies so persuasively that artist Cimabue tried to shoo them away.

While works that might be called "proto-trompe l'oeil" were produced in early Renaissance Italy, it was in 17th-century Holland where artists, spurred by developments in the field of optics, created works so realistic they could actually confuse the viewer. Artists like Cornelius Gijsbrechts (c. 1630–1675) portrayed such subjects as letter racks whose persuasively rendered textures appealed to the viewer's sense of touch.

Staircase Group

Dutch artists also depicted objects hanging on a wall that seemed to emerge from the canvas and enter the viewer's space. An example of this is *Violin Suspended from a Peg* (after 1674), attributed to Jan van der Vaart (1647–1721).

About 100 years later, American artist Charles Willson Peale (1741–1827) included an actual step in front of his painting *Staircase Group* (1795), which depicts his sons peeking out from behind a doorway. Installed within the doorframe of Peale's studio, the painting is said to have fooled George Washington, who allegedly tipped his hat to the two young men as he walked by.

The Battle of the Somme

ONE OF THE LARGEST battles of World War I, the British offensive at the Somme River was intended to break the stalemate of trench warfare and relieve German pressure on French forces at Verdun in 1916. British General Douglas Haig gathered 13 British and 11 French divisions for an attack along a 25-mile front. He even brought in cavalry to exploit the expected breakthrough. French General Ferdinand Foch and British General Henry Rawlinson both questioned the wisdom of the operation, but all objections were brushed aside.

The battle opened with a seven-day artillery barrage. More than 1.7 million shells were fired on the German positions. On July 1, Haig's infantry went over the top, not realizing how ineffective their artillery had been. The troops were massacred. German forces had waited out the bombardment in deep underground dugouts, then they emerged to mow down the British infantry. British forces suffered almost 60,000 casualties on the first day alone, including nearly 20,000 dead, making it the bloodiest day in the history of the British army. German casualties seemed almost negligible—about 8,000.

Undeterred, Haig continued the attack for the next four months. The battle deteriorated into a stalemate with only minor gains. The operation finally sputtered to a close in mid-November with the Allies having advanced only five miles since July 1.

The cost was catastrophic. Postwar statistics indicated that 419,654 British and 204,253 French were killed, wounded, or captured, and another 146,431 were listed as missing. Whole units were wiped out, including the so-called "Pals" battalions made up of men from the same town—even the same family—who had enlisted to serve together. German losses at the Somme are in dispute but were probably somewhere between 465,000 and 650,000.

Less than two years later, in August 1918, Haig again attacked at the Somme. By then, the German army was not what it had once been, but plenty of hard fighting remained. The Germans were pushed back over a wide front to the vaunted Hindenburg Line, which was then breached in late September.

But it was the appalling casualties of the first battle that would remain forever associated with the Somme and came to symbolize the horror and futility of war. As German officer Friedrich Stenbecher wrote, "Somme. The whole history of the world cannot contain a more ghastly word."

Arthur Conan Doyle

"**Y**OU DON'T KNOW Sherlock Holmes yet . . . Holmes is a little too scientific for my tastes; it approaches to cold-bloodedness . . . He appears to have a passion for definite and exact knowledge."

This passage from *A Study in Scarlet* (1887) marked the first-ever mention of Sherlock Holmes in print. Holmes quickly became a bigger international phenomenon than his creator, Edinburgh doctor Arthur Conan Doyle (1859–1930), could have imagined. Fresh from the University of Edinburgh, Doyle produced this first Holmes story while awaiting patients in a slow Portsmouth practice. *Beeton* magazine grudgingly published the story in its 1887 Christmas Annual, while complaining about "cheap fiction." But readers soon clamored for more. In 1890, Doyle sold *The Sign of Four* to *Lippincott's Magazine. Strand Magazine* encouraged Doyle to write a series of Holmes stories, and thus a series of timeless icons were born: the brooding, pipe-smoking, violin-playing (not to mention cocaine-injecting) Holmes; his foil, the sensible Doctor Watson; kindly housekeeper Mrs. Hudson; and well-meaning but bumbling Inspector Lestrade. *The Adventures of Sherlock Holmes* followed in 1891–1892, and *The Memoirs of Sherlock Holmes* from 1892–1893.

Despite Holmes's overwhelming popularity, Doyle was bored with him by 1891: "I . . . feel [toward Holmes] as I do towards pâté de foie gras, of which I once ate too much." In 1893, he penned *The Final Problem,* in which Holmes plunges to his death alongside his arch-nemesis, Professor Moriarty. Though readers mourned and *Strand Magazine* lost 20,000 subscriptions, Doyle refused to bring Holmes back, saying: "He takes my mind from better things."

However, the years diminished Doyle's steadfastness. His wife, Louise, contracted tuberculosis, and Doyle tended her faithfully until her death in 1906. He filled idle hours writing *The Hound of the Baskervilles*, which was released to eager readers in 1902, followed by *The Return of Sherlock Holmes* in 1904–1905. In 1907, Doyle married Jean Leckie. All seemed well—until the Great War, when Doyle lost his son, his brother, two nephews, and two brothers-in-law. Sinking into depression, he became (like many Britons after the Great War) an avid disciple of Spiritualism, debating such debunkers as Harry Houdini. The steadily darker and more gruesome Holmes stories that followed, including *The Valley of Fear, His Last Bow,* and *The Case-Book of Sherlock Holmes,* had by this time become tools to raise money for Doyle's crusade.

Agrippina the Younger (A.D. 15–59)

AGRIPPINA THE YOUNGER was the great-granddaughter of the Julian emperor, Caesar Augustus. Her first husband, Gnaeus Domitius Ahenobarbus, was also Agrippina's second cousin. Their union resulted in the birth of the infamous future emperor Nero.

Although married, Agrippina was believed to have had an incestuous relationship with her brother Caligula, emperor of Rome. She also threw herself at the still-married Galba, a prominent aristocrat and politician, but was thwarted by Galba's mother-in-law, who is said to have given her a public reprimand and a literal slap in the face.

In 39, Agrippina and her sister Livilla plotted to murder Caligula and make Lepidus the emperor of Rome. However, their attempt failed—the sisters were exiled and Lepidus was executed. Caligula, his wife, and daughters were murdered in 41, and Claudius (Agrippina's paternal uncle) became emperor.

As ordered by Claudius, Agrippina and her sister returned from exile, though Agrippina was now a widow—her first husband had died during the 40–41 winter. Passienus Crispus became her second husband. Although happily married, Crispus was forced by Emperor Claudius to divorce his wife in order to marry Agrippina.

It is likely that Agrippina's ambitions for Nero led to the untimely death of her second husband around 47—some believe that she poisoned Crispus to gain his estate. According to Suetonius, Agrippina then exploited her familial relationship to seduce Claudius. Marriage between uncle and niece had, up to that point, been regarded as incest. Claudius, however, forced a change in the laws to arrange the union.

As empress, Agrippina arranged for Claudius to adopt her son, Lucius, whose name was changed to Nero following the adoption. When Claudius died suddenly in October 54, many believed Agrippina had arranged his death by poisoning him with mushrooms. She had noticed Claudius favoring his son Britannicus for emperor over her son Nero, which provided motive for his untimely death.

Nero was only 16 when he became emperor. Agrippina tried to take power herself, as regent, with little success. When she interfered with Nero's affair with the wife of a senator, he showed himself to be her true son and planned her murder. When Agrippina survived the deliberate sinking of her boat on the Bay of Naples, Nero ordered her execution. Agrippina was killed at her country home in 59, at age 44.

Music for the Home: The Piano

T HROUGH THE LATE 1700s, pianos—like all musical instruments— were constructed by hand in specialized craftsmen's workshops: Even the most productive European manufacturers only built a couple dozen pianos a year. However, innovations in construction technique (first larger workforces, later mass-production approaches and steam technology) increased European production of pianos by a factor of 100 between the late 1700s and the mid-1800s. The English firm of Broadwood produced more than 2,000 pianos yearly. Both the quantity and economies of scale made pianos increasingly available to the rising middle classes—having a piano in the house became a necessity for those aspiring to social distinction.

While both men and women learned to play piano as part of their cultural upbringing, the instrument became increasingly associated with women in the 1800s. Some highly respected professional female pianists emerged. Especially prominent was Clara Wieck (1819–1896), who later married Robert Schumann and became a crucial performer and advocate for his music. More often, women were highly proficient amateurs, and sometimes pupils of the most famous male pianists of the day (Chopin and Liszt, among others, gained considerable income and fame by working with wealthy female students). Women's keyboard skills were considered to be most appropriate, however, as auxiliary to their domestic duties. Music could serve to charm and attract a spouse and to entertain family and friends in the home (perhaps also to accompany devotional singing), but public performance was considered distasteful and contrary to a well-bred woman's goal of being unobtrusive.

Facilitated by the invention of lithography at end of the 1700s, which allowed for greater production and lower costs of sheet music, arrangements of popular orchestral and operatic excerpts for piano were marketed to the increasing middle-class public by a growing number of publishers. Sometimes these included "piano four hands," involving two performers playing side-by-side on a single instrument—often a socially sanctioned opportunity for courtship. This expansion in "home consumption" of various musical genres allowed both the development of a new repertory designed specifically for amateur entertainment and the codification of a "lasting" repertory of great musical works for the edification of the rising bourgeoisie. While these categories ("entertainment/edification") were initially fluid, the distinction between the two eventually became an important feature of late 19th-century musical sensibility.

"Behind the Wall": Music in 17th-Century Convents

"*THE CLOISTERING OF WOMEN may be necessary, so that the young girls do not remain in the paternal house at the risk of losing their honor, not only to outsiders, but also to the household servants, and what is worse, even to their own brothers or perhaps also to their own fathers!*"

Thus wrote a gentleman living in Bologna, Italy, at the beginning of the 1600s. He was referring particularly to girls whose mothers had died, leaving them without maternal protection. During that period, in cities such as Bologna and Milan, as many as 60 percent of girls from the upper-middle classes were enrolled (or perhaps unloaded) in convents—with or without their consent.

Yet, this was not necessarily as bleak a fate as it might appear to 21st-century sensibilities. For some time, convents were great centers of musical excellence. Thus, a musically inclined girl might be sent to a convent specifically to continue her musical career, which would otherwise end with marriage since public performance was considered unseemly for a woman. She would frequently receive musical training at home in preparation for taking the veil and might also be offered a dowry reduction from a convent eager to add her talents and experience to their ranks. Even within the convents a good deal of musical training took place: instrumental as well as vocal—despite the fact that musical instruments were often officially banned from cloisters.

Catholic religious leaders were divided on the advisability of encouraging (even allowing) nuns' musical devotion—some chastised and penalized the nuns under their authority for the "frivolousness" of their musical activity, comparing the allure of their voices to that of witches or sirens. Others, however, maintained that the nuns' "invisible voices" (the nuns' music carried over the walled divider between the public spaces and the nuns' inner church) could provide the faithful who were attending events in the convents' public churches a foretaste of the ineffable music of paradise.

These dedicated and talented women have recently had their musical practices beautifully re-created by several ensembles. Noteworthy recordings include works by Lucrezia Vizzana from the 1620s (*Musica Secreta*, on Linn Records) and by Chiara Cozzolani from later in the century (*Cappella Artemisia*, on Tactus Records).

Barbara McClintock (1902–1992)

GENETICIST BARBARA MCCLINTOCK completed revolutionary work in the 1940s and '50s that led to her discovery of genetic transposition, or "jumping genes." However, her discoveries initially met with skepticism from her colleagues, and it took decades for technical advances in molecular biology to prove that her work was valid. In 1983, she was recognized for her astounding work, receiving the Nobel Prize in Physiology or Medicine for her achievements.

McClintock's groundbreaking work began while she was a graduate student at Cornell University where she was part of a group studying maize genetics. At that time, little was known about DNA, and most genetic studies focused on chromosomes and genes. The scientists at Cornell knew several of the genes that determined kernel color. They also determined how kernel colors are predictably inherited.

Thomas H. Morgan had experimented with fruit flies and found that chromosomes carry the genetic material and that the genes are arranged in a linear fashion along the chromosomes, like beads on a string. (He received the Nobel Prize in 1933 for this work.) Scientists had also learned that the chromosomes came in pairs, one from each parent, usually attached near the center to make an "X." The paired chromosomes could recombine, trading genes from one of the pair to the other, but it was believed that the genes generally stayed on the same chromosome and in the same linear order.

McClintock made her most valuable discovery while doing research at Cold Spring Harbor on Long Island. She carried out her experiments by growing corn in a garden plot behind her lab. Fertilization was controlled by covering the flowers to protect them from random pollination, and they were dusted with pollen from a known source. McClintock found the maize exhibited an unexpected pattern of colored and multicolored kernels that couldn't be explained by traditional genetic theories. She believed that the genes controlling kernel pigment had transposed, or "jumped," to another location in some cells.

Her results were largely ignored for years, as they contradicted the genetic theories of the time. Fifty years later, we understand that there are indeed *transposons,* genetic elements that can pop out of the chromosome and reinsert somewhere else, which activate or prevent the expression of genes. These transposable elements have been found not only in corn and other plants, but also in fruit flies, bacteria, and yeast.

The Unicorn Tapestries

THE ORIGIN OF the Unicorn Tapestries remains a mystery, but the seven hangings were most likely created between 1495 and 1505. From at least the late 17th century to the early 20th century they belonged to the de La Rochefoucauld family in France. Looted from the family's chateau during the French Revolution, the tapestries were bought back from some farmers who were using them to cover vegetables in a barn. John D. Rockefeller, Jr., saw them at an exhibition in 1922. He purchased them and then presented them to New York's Metropolitan Museum of Art in 1937.

The Unicorn in Captivity

Formally known as *The Hunt of the Unicorn,* the hangings were woven from threads of wool and silk, dyed with vegetable colors, and twined with silver and gold. It took a team to create these tapestries. First, someone had to imagine the story. This person clearly knew the pagan myths as well as the Christian symbolism associated with the unicorn. This might have been the buyer or possibly a scholar-advisor. Nearly all the plants, flowers, and animals carry symbolic meanings associated with the life of Christ and also with the idea of marriage. Then designers produced full-scale models for the weavers to follow. Finally, skilled weavers translated the images into gorgeous tapestries.

There are seven episodes in the series. In *The Start of the Hunt,* well-dressed hunters gather with their dogs and servants in a moment of great excitement. They discover their prey when *The Unicorn Dips His Horn into the Stream to Rid It of Poison.* The stream is represented as an elaborate fountain, and various animals gather around the unicorn and wait for the chance to drink. As the hunters attack with spears, *The Unicorn Leaps the Stream.* Then *The Unicorn Defends Himself,* kicking out and impaling a dog on its sharp horn. Finally, the hunters resort to subterfuge, and *The Unicorn Is Tamed by the Maiden.* Only in the company of a chaste young girl can the creature feel at peace. The hunt is ultimately successful, and *The Unicorn Is Killed and Brought to the Castle.* At last we have *The Unicorn in Captivity.* Restored to life, with droplets of blood marking its wounds, the legendary beast lies in an enclosure in the shade of a pomegranate tree within a field of wildflowers.

The British Conquest of India

THE BRITISH ORIGINALLY went to India not as conquerors but as traders. The British East India Company was just one of several European companies that received licenses from the Mughal emperors and their subsidiaries to establish trading posts in India. As long as the Mughal empire remained strong, the employees of the East India Company simply focused on buying spices and textiles at the best price.

When Mughal Emperor Aurangzeb died in 1707, the empire began to fall apart. Six emperors sat on the Peacock Throne in Delhi between 1707 and 1719. Former Mughal feudatories became independent kingdoms that paid only formal allegiance to the Mughal emperor.

The growing power vacuum in India offered new opportunities for other European trading companies and their armies. Joseph François Dupleix, the governor of the French trading company, was the first to recognize the profits to be gained from involvement in the succession struggles that developed in the new Indian states. The British were quick to follow his example. The trading companies, which previously operated as clients of Indian rulers, soon became king-makers.

In 1756, the British became involved in the internal politics of Bengal when 20-year-old Siraj-ud-Dawlah succeeded his grandfather as the Nawab (provincial governor) of Bengal. Powerful interests in Bengal were willing to pay the East India Company for help in dethroning the young Nawab in favor of his uncle, Mir Jafar. The final treaty between Mir Jafar and the East India Company included substantial payments not only to the East India Company, but also to the army, the Company's council in Bengal, and individual council members.

On June 23, 1757, Robert Clive, a former bookkeeper turned military officer, led 800 European and 2,000 Indian soldiers against Siraj-ud-Dawlah's forces at the Battle of Plassey. Although he was seriously outnumbered, Clive was confident of victory: Siraj-ud-Dawlah's most important general was Mir Jafar, who had promised not to take the field. At the end of the day, Mir Jafar was the Nawab of Bengal, but Clive was the state's real ruler.

Mir Jafar's treachery cost him—and his successors—far more than money. Unable to meet their financial commitments to the East India Company, successive rulers of Bengal ceded additional trading privileges, territory, and finally political control to the British. Officially a vassal of the Mughal emperor, the East India Company became the major political power in India, ruling territory from Sri Lanka to the border of Afghanistan.

Robertson Davies's Deptford Trilogy

T HE DEPTFORD TRILOGY consists of the three most famous novels by Canadian writer Robertson Davies: *Fifth Business* (1970), *The Manticore* (1972), and *World of Wonders* (1975). The plots of all three novels hinge on two connected events.

In 1908 Deptford, Ontario, a ten-year-old boy, Percy Boyd "Boy" Staunton, throws a snowball at his friend and rival Dunstable Ramsay. The snowball misses Ramsay and instead hits a pregnant woman, Mary Dempster, wife of the town's Baptist minister. As a result, Mary gives premature birth to a baby, Paul, who has birth defects. Fifty years later, Boy Staunton's body is found at the bottom of a lake with a stone in his mouth, just as he is about to assume an important office. A chain of guilt between these two incidents connects all the major characters.

Considered the best of the series by some, *Fifth Business* is narrated by Dunstan Ramsay (who has changed his name) as a letter to the president of a college from which he is retiring as headmaster. Ramsay's letter recounts his lifelong fascination and rivalry with his childhood "friend and enemy" Boy Staunton, who became a rich and successful businessman.

Ramsay believes that he is responsible for the care of Mary Dempster, who slid into mental illness after Paul's birth and difficult early months. While serving in World War I, Ramsay sees a vision of her as a Madonna during a battle in which he loses a leg. Never marrying, he spends years studying with a Catholic order devoted to researching lives of sainthood candidates. Becoming convinced that Mary Dempster is a saint, he supports her for the rest of her life.

While writing the trilogy, Davies underwent Jungian analysis, which plays a central role in the series. *The Manticore* focuses on the Jungian analysis of David Staunton, Boy's son, a lawyer who tries to understand his relationship to his wealthy father through his analysis.

The third novel, *World of Wonders,* is narrated by Paul Dempster, who has grown up to become a famous magician under the stage name Magnus Eisengrim. He tells his story between breaks of a film in which he plays Jean Eugene Robert-Houdin, the first modern magician.

POSTSCRIPT

■ *Fifth Business* was 40th on the American Modern Library's list of the 100 best novels of the 20th century.

Alfred Hitchcock (1899–1980)

BORN ON AUGUST 13, 1899, in a working-class section of London, Alfred Hitchcock was the son of a greengrocer. His entrance into the film industry occurred in 1919 when he landed a job as an intertitle-card designer for the London branch of Famous Players-Lasky, a part of Paramount Pictures. He worked his way up to assistant director by the mid-1920s. Hitchcock's training in a Hollywood-based studio influenced his keen craftsmanship and his attitude toward popular film. After the studio changed hands, Hitchcock was sent to Germany in 1925 to direct his first two features, *The Pleasure Garden* (1925) and *The Mountain Eagle* (1926). There, he was inspired by the Expressionist directors, whose visually driven films were marked by deep shadows, oblique angles, a heightened emphasis on set and costume design, and subjective camera techniques.

In 1927, Hitchcock returned to England to direct his first mystery thriller, *The Lodger* (1927), which became a breakthrough film, garnering attention from both the press and the public. His reputation grew with another thriller titled *Blackmail* (1929), which became England's first sync-sound film. He continued to hone his craft in England, directing such early favorites as *The 39 Steps* (1935) and *Sabotage* (1936). In 1939, he signed a contract with David O. Selznick and moved to Hollywood, where he enjoyed his greatest success. Hitchcock became a household name in the 1950s when he hosted a television series that bore his name, *Alfred Hitchcock Presents,* though he rarely directed the series' episodes. The 1950s became his most creative decade, producing such classics as *Rear Window* (1954), *Vertigo* (1958), and *North by Northwest* (1959) before culminating with his masterpiece, *Psycho* (1960).

The artistry of Hitchcock's films was largely overlooked by intellectuals and critics during his lifetime. Working in the underrated thriller genre, Hitchcock's absolute command of filmmaking techniques made his films so entertaining that the entertainment value masked the artistry as well as his dark themes and cynical vision of humanity. Beneath the suspense and black humor lurks the master's view of a modern world where the innocent are falsely accused of hideous acts, appearances are deceiving, everyone is guilty of something, and evil can be anywhere.

The Cabinet of Curiosities

WHILE THE AVERAGE PERSON today would not go shopping for a stuffed bird, the horn of a unicorn, a perpetual motion machine, a mummy's hand, or paintings by Raphael and Caravaggio, these were once hot items for Europe's elite. For Renaissance-era princes, such items were essential to create a display (sometimes an entire room) of their odd collections. Such a display was called a cabinet of curiosities.

Even at that time, the impulse to collect art alongside curious objects was nothing new. In fact, the residences of the Roman Emperor Augustus (63 B.C.–A.D. 14) housed statues, paintings, and wonders such as "the huge remains of monstrous beasts which had been discovered on the Island of Capri." Later, during the Middle Ages, the treasuries of monarchs and religious institutions amassed artworks, manmade marvels, and natural treasures, including seashells and ostrich eggs.

In keeping with their predecessors, prominent 16th- and 17th-century Europeans assembled collections juxtaposing artwork, manmade and natural rarities, and scientific instruments, often in a seemingly haphazard manner. The keepers of these curiosities prized the marvelous over the commonplace, and their collections sometimes reached epic proportions. However, there was a hidden motivation for the immense popularity of the cabinet of curiosities. The thousands of cabinets that sprang up reflected the era's preoccupation with human ability and the urge to understand all aspects of the physical world. Collectors hoped to capture both the wonder of human achievement and the complexity of nature.

The cabinet of curiosities also took on an important political connotation, especially in Germany. By the late 16th century, nearly every court contained a cabinet of curiosities that would be shown to important visitors. For these rulers, the cabinet of curiosities was a visual demonstration of their intellectual and political power, legitimizing claims to authority and serving as an effective diplomatic tool.

One of the most spectacular cabinets belonged to Holy Roman Emperor Rudolf II, who ruled from 1576 to 1612. Housed in the Hradschin Palace in Prague, Rudolf's collection included paintings by Albrecht Dürer and Pieter Brueghel, astrological and astronomical devices, and natural wonders, including a botanical and zoological garden complete with live animals. While it was regularly used for formal diplomatic purposes, the collection also served an educational function by providing examples for artists to study and emulate in their own works.

Hildegard of Bingen

COMPOSER HILDEGARD OF BINGEN (1098–1179) is one of the earliest individuals in European musical history about whom we have biographical information. She authored a collection of poetic and musical works that arguably surpasses the output of any of her male contemporaries.

Hildegard was born of a noble family in what is now the Rhineland-Palatinate region of Germany. She took vows at age 14 at what later became a Benedictine convent and eventually founded two female religious communities (the first near Bingen, hence her name) and served as their de facto leader. She was the first woman to take this sort of initiative. Though she is often described as an abbess, there is controversy about whether that term should apply, since she was never officially conferred the title by the church, though Holy Roman Emperor Friedrich Barbarossa—a close relative—did address her as "abbess" after she founded the second convent.

Political and religious authorities of the time (including a number of popes) consulted Hildegard and held her in high regard, largely because her religious visions were thought to be extraordinarily powerful. She also undertook extended preaching missions over the course of a decade, which was truly exceptional for a woman of the time, and she wrote texts on botanical and medicinal matters as well as extended commentaries on scripture.

All of Hildegard's songs are sacred, connecting to her religious visions. She lived in a time when the European tradition of sacred plainchant (now known as "Gregorian chant") was being expanded from a nominally God-given set of prayers (tradition held that Pope Gregory had been visited by the Holy Spirit in the form of a dove, who had sung the prayer melodies in his ear) to a broader set of spiritual songs reflecting human interaction with the divine. Accordingly, Hildegard's melodies are more expansive and elaborate than Gregorian chant, revealing patterns of musical organization that reflect a remarkable creativity.

Hildegard's music has been recorded by a number of ensembles that specialize in medieval repertory and has also served as the inspiration for more creative reworkings, including *Monk and the Abbess: Music of Hildegard von Bingen and Meredith Monk* (1996) and *Lux Vivens*, featuring Jocelyn Montgomery and David Lynch (1998).

Mining Precious Metals

Precious metals, including gold, silver, and platinum, are valued for their scarcity as well as for their unique properties, such as luster, nonreactivity, and malleability. Because of their desirable qualities, these precious metals have been mined for thousands of years. Today, they are most commonly used in jewelry, as coinage, in works of art, or purely for investment purposes.

Since gold does not tarnish or form alloys readily, it was one of the first metals to be discovered and recognized. It has been used as decoration and currency for more than 8,000 years, when the Egyptians discovered it in exposed veins with quartz. Today, however, gold is usually mined as an ore, a combination of many minerals that include small amounts of gold. Because gold is so valuable, mining companies can process ore with as little as 0.015 ounce of gold per ton of rock and still make a profit.

Gold ore is extracted from underground mines and open-pit mines. The gold is leached from the ore with a dilute cyanide solution and passed through activated carbon, which selectively absorbs the gold. It is often refined through electrolysis, which separates impurities by passing an electric charge through the gold ore.

Like gold, silver is often found in conjunction with other metals. Today, most of the world's silver is produced as a byproduct when refining other metals, including gold, copper, and lead. But since modern methods for separating silver from other metals were not available to ancient civilizations, silver was probably first mined in its natural condition. There is evidence that native silver was mined in ancient Greece and used as currency.

Although gold and silver have always been deemed valuable, platinum, an exceedingly rare metal, was not always seen as precious. Platinum was first discovered in the 16th century in Colombia, which was then part of the Spanish Empire. The Spanish saw this metal as a nuisance since it was associated with gold, and it made the gold difficult to recover. The name of this metal is derived from the Spanish word for silver, *plata*, because of its close resemblance to silver.

Native platinum is a mixture of six metals: platinum, palladium, rhodium, ruthenium, iridium, and osmium. Like the other metals, platinum ore is recovered from both open-pit and underground mines. After the ore is blasted out of the ground, it is crushed and mixed with water, then pumped through air to form a "froth flotation." Platinum group metals adhere to the bubbles and are selectively removed and then further refined.

Michelangelo

MANY OF MICHELANGELO'S (1475–1564) works are iconic master-pieces familiar even to people with little interest in the history of art. However, two works in particular secured his fame in sculpture and painting: the marble sculpture *David* (1501–1504) and the frescoes on the ceiling of the Sistine Chapel (1508–1512).

The figure of *David* was originally commissioned for placement atop a buttress of the Florence cathedral. The marble for the project posed a daunting challenge: It was too flat to easily accommodate a figure of the prescribed height; moreover, the block had already been cut into by another sculptor. But even with these constraints, the figure of idealized manhood that Michelangelo created was so extraordinary that it was relocated to the heart of the city.

David

In 1506, Michelangelo was summoned to Rome by Pope Julius II to discuss the Sistine Chapel. Considering himself a sculptor, not a painter, Michelangelo originally declined the commission to paint the Chapel's ceiling, but he later accepted. By the time the work was completed in 1512, the vault was filled with more than 300 images depicting the narrative of Genesis, from the creation of the world to the life of Noah. Interspersed throughout the Old Testament images, naked youths called *ignudi* lounge on the painted architecture and hold various decorative and symbolic elements.

Michelangelo's work was both admired and despised. Soon after it was erected, *David* was stoned, probably by opponents of the political regime that commissioned it. During an uprising in 1527, the left arm and hand were shattered, although the pieces were preserved until repairs could be made. In the 19th century, *David* was moved into the Galleria dell'Accademia to protect it from further weathering, and in 1991 a deranged Italian painter smashed the toes on one foot with a hammer.

While the images of the Sistine Chapel ceiling were much admired—and Michelangelo was brought back in 1535 to add a Last Judgment to the altar wall—the ignudi were a source of dismay. In 1565, one of Michelangelo's students, Daniele da Volterra, was hired to cover the figures' nakedness with veils and loincloths, for which he earned the nickname *il Braghettone*, or "the maker of breeches." Other additions in the interest of modesty were made in the late 16th century and over the next 200 years.

Oliver L. Brown et al. v. *the Board of Education of Topeka (KS) et al.*

THIS LANDMARK SUPREME COURT decision from 1954 is one of the most important turning points in American judicial history. In a 9–0 vote, the Court threw out the legal ground for racial segregation in public schools and provided the legal basis for the civil rights revolution of the 1950s and 1960s.

The Court overturned an earlier ruling, *Plessy* v. *Ferguson* (1896), which maintained that states could legalize racial segregation so long as "equal" facilities were provided for the segregated group—the so-called "separate but equal" doctrine. After *Plessy*, a number of Southern and border states promptly established racial segregation targeting African Americans, ranging from separate public schools and public transportation to the use of separate Bibles for black witnesses to swear on in South Carolina. In 1954, the Court ruled that "the doctrine of 'separate but equal' has no place. Separate educational facilities are inherently unequal."

The decision was the culmination of two decades of work by the National Association for the Advancement of Colored People (NAACP) to over-turn school segregation. Led by lawyers Charles Houston and Thurgood Marshall, the NAACP saw the piecemeal erosion of separate but equal when, in 1938 and 1950, the Court ruled that law schools at the universities of Missouri and Texas had to desegregate because facilities could not be equal. The *Brown* decision went further, as it relied on the testimony of social scientists such as Kenneth Clark, who showed that segregation created a self-image of inferiority in black children, impeding their ability to learn. The decision caused celebrations among blacks and cries of doom among many whites.

In 1955, the Court dealt with the implementation phase of the *Brown* decision. Realizing that school segregation and white racism were deeply ingrained, especially in many white Southerners, Chief Justice Earl War-ren convinced the Court to call for implementation "with all deliberate speed." To many Southern leaders, this opened the door for a series of tactical delays ranging from state legislatures interposing their authority between the Court ruling and the people of their states, to the closing of school districts, to physical violence and intimidation. Although this slowed integration considerably for a number of years, Court decisions—sometimes backed by federal troops, as in Arkansas in 1957 and Mississippi in 1962 and later by the Civil Rights Act of 1964—ultimately achieved legal school desegregation.

Jack Kerouac's *On the Road*

JACK KEROUAC SUFFERED through six years of rejections before his most famous novel, *On the Road,* was finally published by Viking Press in September 1957. This thinly veiled autobiography recounts his travels across the United States and Mexico in the late 1940s. He typed the first draft in only three weeks in April 1951 on a 120-foot-long roll of thin drawing paper as a single paragraph in an experimental, stream-of-consciousness style with a lyrical cadence. He used the real names of his friends, particularly his travel companion, Neal Cassady, in this draft; in later revisions, he changed Neal's name to Dean Moriarty and his own to Sal Paradise.

On the morning of the publication of *On the Road*, Kerouac bought a copy of the *New York Times* to read its review of his book. "Just as, more than any other novel of the Twenties, *The Sun Also Rises* came to be regarded as the testament of the 'Lost Generation,'" reviewer Gilbert Millstein wrote, "so it seems certain that *On the Road* will come to be known as that of the 'Beat Generation.'" Not all reviews were as positive, but Millstein's prediction about the social impact of the book was right on target.

In his novel, Kerouac describes a free, unstructured way of life that opposed the conformity and materialism of postwar America. His characters question societal expectations, listen to jazz music, have a number of sexual relationships, and experiment with drugs. As a result of *On the Road*, Kerouac was seen as the voice of his generation and the father of the Beat and Hippie movements.

Kerouac was unprepared for this fame, however, since it took him away from what he enjoyed most in life: writing spontaneous prose and poetry. Extremely introverted, he increasingly isolated himself from others and died in 1969 from the effects of years of drug and alcohol abuse.

POSTSCRIPT

■ Although *On the Road* was an account of Kerouac's travels, he did not learn to drive until he was 34. Neal Cassady, himself an important figure in the Beat Generation, was the driver and navigator.

■ The 120-foot-long first draft scroll still exists. It was purchased in 2001 by Jim Irsay, the owner of the Indianapolis Colts, for $2.34 million and has been circulating to universities and public libraries across the United States since 2004.

■ While it is often assumed that *On the Road* was the result of a spontaneous outburst of creativity, Kerouac had been planning the book for a number of years and often referred to the journals he kept during his travels with Cassady.

Henry Ford (1863–1947)

PERHAPS THE MOST influential businessman of the 20th century, Henry Ford spent much of his youth helping his father on the family farm in Dearborn, Michigan—a task that he despised. In his spare time, he tinkered with farm machinery, trying to improve it. Ford fled rural life in 1879, moving to Detroit, where he worked as a mechanic. He joined the Edison Illuminating Company in 1891, and his mechanical skills soon led to his appointment as chief engineer.

The promotion gave Ford time to devote to side projects, and in 1896 he completed his own "gas buggy," the Quadricycle.

Having found a passion for building automobiles, Ford helped found the Ford Motor Company in 1903. By 1908, he decided to focus on creating a cheap and easy-to-build car that would revolutionize the American economy and the lives of most of its citizens. He combined a fundamental insight—that "everybody wants to be someplace he ain't"—with his dazzling ability to understand the logic of machines and built the Model T Ford. By 1916, its price had dropped to $300, and the revolutionary assembly-line technique pioneered by Ford enabled the company to produce a finished product in less than two hours. By 1926, Ford Motors was selling half the automobiles purchased in the United States.

Without a doubt, this man's monumental accomplishments sparked American economic growth in the early 20th century and provided millions of Americans with a geographic mobility unknown before Ford. But his life revealed interesting and sometimes disturbing paradoxes. Ford was a revolutionary innovator, but he resisted making any changes to the Model T even as his competition developed new models. He was a pacifist who opposed World War I, yet he welcomed praise from German dictator Adolf Hitler. Although partly responsible for massive urban growth, he hated cities, seeing them as dens of iniquity. Perhaps most damning, he was virulently anti-Semitic, and he used his own newspaper, *The Dearborn Independent,* to spread venomous charges against what Ford saw as a Jewish conspiracy to dominate the world. Finally, some would argue that mass-production of automobiles has led to a morass of pollution and urban gridlock—ironic for a man who had hopes the car would enable people to escape the cities that he so hated.

J.R.R. Tolkien's *The Lord of the Rings*

JOHN RONALD REUEL TOLKIEN'S (1892–1973) *The Lord of the Rings* may be the best-selling and best-loved work of literature of the 20th century, having an estimated 150 million readers worldwide. The story of the hobbit Frodo Baggins's quest is even credited with creating the genre of fantasy literature. Over the years, Tolkien's work has inspired films, video games, Web sites, merchandise lines, and countless imitators.

A talented linguist, Tolkien invented several languages. In 1917, he began creating the mythology and history of the fictional setting of *The Lord of the Rings,* which he called Middle Earth, to give his languages a context. He would spend the rest of his life developing Middle Earth, while both raising a family and working as a professor at Oxford University. As an expert on northern European languages, literature, and mythology, Tolkien incorporated elements of Germanic and Finnish mythology, Anglo-Saxon literature, the Bible, and Greek tragedy into his work. He never intended to publish much of this material; however, following his death, his son Christopher worked to see that it was released.

Tolkien's first successful nonacademic publication was *The Hobbit* (1937). He first wrote the lighthearted tale of Bilbo Baggins for his children, but he published it at the urging of his friend C. S. Lewis, who would later write the popular *Chronicles of Narnia* fantasy series. In *The Hobbit,* a group of dwarves and a wizard named Gandalf recruit Bilbo Baggins to help recover treasure from a dragon. Originally, *The Hobbit* was not intended to connect to the elaborate mythology of Middle Earth, but when Tolkien's publisher asked him to write a sequel to his unexpectedly popular book, Tolkien drew on his constructed mythology. This sequel would become *The Lord of the Rings*. While Tolkien intended for his new work to be a single book, his publisher separated it into the now-familiar three volumes to cut printing costs.

Thanks to the recent movie adaptations of *The Fellowship of the Ring, The Two Towers,* and *The Return of the King,* a new generation has discovered Tolkien's work. Released between 2001 and 2003, the film trilogy was groundbreaking. Together, the three movies were nominated for a total of 488 film awards and won 264 of them, including 17 Oscars.

POSTSCRIPT

▇ *The Hobbit* developed from a single sentence Tolkien wrote on a student's blank exam: "In a hole there lived a hobbit."

From Oral to Written: Chant and Neumes

NOT ALL WORLD CULTURES have developed the notion that sound can be conveyed through markings on paper (music notation). A system of music notation to accompany poetic verse was developed in classical Greek culture, but that methodology was forgotten in Europe through the age of the Roman Empire and the early Middle Ages.

When Charlemagne—emperor of the Franks—agreed in the year 800 to make Roman Christianity the official religion of his empire (which covered much of modern-day France and Germany in central and southern Europe), the pope sent emissaries to teach the Frankish people how to pray.

At the time, Christian prayer involved the use of specific melodic formulas (*plainchant*). Initially the emissaries taught orally, by rote: The student repeated the melody and prayer back to the teacher until the teacher was satisfied with the accuracy of the student's reproduction. Then they moved on to the next prayer. This was a very time-consuming process and was only as good as the student's memory; since there were hundreds of prayers to learn, it was easy for the student to become confused.

Eventually, some enterprising teacher or student decided to create a visual shorthand above the prayer text so that the student could remember the "shape" of the melody after the teacher had left. This kind of graphic notation, called *neumes,* gradually became more precise and complex over several generations until musicians began to use it not only to jog their memory but to create new melodies and transmit them easily to other places.

Thus notation became a central aspect of the European musical tradition, and the ease and widespread literacy in notation allowed musical styles to spread and intermingle, creating a rich web of musical traditions by the late Middle Ages.

POSTSCRIPT

■ The syllables used for singing musical scales in the Western tradition (think of the "Do-Re-Mi" song from *The Sound of Music*) are derived from the opening syllables of successive stanzas of a hymn to Saint John the Baptist. Medieval teachers realized that the syllables were sung on progressively higher notes, so they used them in a row to create singing primers for their students.

Migration

EACH SPRING, hundreds of millions of monarch butterflies leave their alpine sanctuaries in Mexico and California and head north on paper-thin wings in search of fragrant milkweed fields. In the fall, their offspring—or their offspring's offspring—return, instinctively navigating thousands of miles to their ancestral refuge.

Monarchs aren't the only organisms to carry out such extraordinary feats. Sea turtles, whales, geese, and many other animals make predictable, often seasonal, journeys to breed, find new sources of food, or bask in a warmer climate. These animals rely on an inner biological calendar and environmental clues, such as changes in day length, to tell them when it's time to move. Internal or external signals can trigger profound biological changes: For example, hormones prompt some animals to gorge themselves in preparation for the long trek.

Preparing for the journey, however, is only half the battle. Once migratory animals have taken to the air, land, or sea, they must figure out where they're going.

For some species, the process is relatively simple. They let the wind or water currents carry them along. But others follow a more complex process. Monarchs carry a map in their genes. Snow geese, on the other hand, must learn by following their parents all the way from Canada to New Mexico.

Many other species navigate the same way humans do—using landmarks and celestial clues to keep them on track. Like ancient mariners, birds and other animals can use the position of the stars to find true north. Pacific salmon, which spend their adult lives feeding in the open ocean, return to the freshwater streams where they were born to breed. Scientists believe that salmon rely on chemical clues in the water, which they can then taste or smell, to locate their birth streams.

But salmon and other animals may also harbor a sixth sense. Researchers now believe that many animals—including birds, turtles, whales, and rainbow trout—have the ability to navigate using information about the intensity and inclination, or angle, of the earth's magnetic field.

Byzantine Icons

IN THE BYZANTINE EMPIRE, an *icon* was an image of Christ, the Virgin Mary, or a saint intended as an object of devotion. Byzantine icons essentially functioned as "stand-ins" for the holy figures they portrayed. In the words of a sixth-century writer describing his response to an icon of St. Michael: "The viewer trembles as if in his actual presence."

The Byzantine icon is today seen as one of the most enigmatic art forms. The powers associated with these objects are difficult for many people in this day and age to grasp. The images themselves—which gaze out at the viewer with mysterious remoteness—appear strangely aloof.

Perhaps most intriguing is their "timelessness." Byzantine icons remained remarkably consistent over the course of 1,000 years. Icon makers—who remained anonymous until the 13th century—adhered to conventions that prescribed how themes were to be depicted. Conventions for every type of image were established by a prototype. Legend has it that the prototype for the Virgin of Hodigitria—in which Mary holds the Christ child on her left side, and "points the way toward Salvation" with her right hand—was painted by St. Luke, whose model was the Virgin herself.

Legends surrounded other icons as well. Among the most intriguing are those concerning acheiropoietos icons. Such icons, produced by divine inspiration (*acheiropoietos* means "icon not made by human hands"), were thought to have miraculous powers of healing and protection.

The Kamouliana icon is an image of Christ imprinted on a piece of linen, found in the mid-sixth century; the imprint, in turn, made an imprint on the dress of the woman who found it. Both images were considered acheiropoietai. The icon was housed in a special shrine in Constantinople and taken into battle, while the copy was carried in processions and helped raise funds for a church and village destroyed in a raid.

Eventually, the veneration accorded to objects such as the Kamouliana icon was deemed dangerously close to idolatry. This ultimately led to Iconoclasm (726–843), which involved not only the banning of icons but also their physical removal or defacement. At St. Sophia in Constantinople, mosaic icons of Christ were scraped off, while the faces of other figures were smeared or replaced with crosses. The tesserae with their names were picked out one by one.

In 843, Empress Irene ended Iconoclasm—an event still celebrated on the first Sunday of Lent as the Triumph of Orthodoxy. Ever since, the icon has been central to Orthodox Christianity.

Murder of the Romanovs

BORN MAY 18, 1868, near St. Petersburg, Russia, Nikolai Aleksandrovich Romanov succeeded his father, Tsar Alexander III, in 1894. He married Princess Alexandra of Hesse-Darmstadt that same year, and they eventually had four daughters and a son.

Mild-mannered Nikolai possessed mediocre political skills and could not cope with the rising tide for constitutional reform in Russia. Lacking political flexibility, he stubbornly clung to the autocratic tradition of the 300-year-old Romanov dynasty.

Russia's entry into World War I on the side of the Allies doomed the Romanovs. Military catastrophes, economic hardship, and growing unrest on the home front resulted in the Russian Revolution and Tsar Nikolai's abdication. By November 1917, the Bolsheviks, led by Vladimir Lenin, had gained control of the government.

Lenin intended to put the tsar on trial for "crimes against the people." He ordered the imperial family held under house arrest in Ekaterinburg.

In the end, Lenin decided not to risk a public trial. On the night of July 16, 1918, as anti-Bolshevik White Russian forces drew near, the tsar; his wife, Alexandra; daughters Olga, Tatiana, Maria, and Anastasia; son Alexei; the family doctor; and three servants were led into the cellar of the house and shot, stabbed, and clubbed to death.

Fearing possible martyrdom of the Romanovs, the corpses were buried in a secret unmarked grave. Rumors that daughter Anastasia had miraculously survived circulated for years, but all claimants proved to be pretenders. Not until 1991 was the mass grave located and excavated. The remains now rest in St. Peter and St. Paul Cathedral in St. Petersburg.

The murder of the imperial family was a carefully calculated act, carried out by order of Lenin and the Soviet government chief, Yakov Sverdlov. The removal of the Romanovs not only deprived the anticommunist White Russians of a powerful rallying point; it marked a clear and dramatic departure from the old system and opened a one-way door to the new.

"The execution of the Tsar's family was needed not only in order to frighten, horrify and instill a sense of hopelessness in the enemy but also to shake up our own ranks, to show that there was no turning back, that ahead lay either total victory or total doom," wrote Bolshevik leader Leon Trotsky.

Ironically, the Russians were soon to find that, with Lenin in power, they had only traded one despot for another.

The Waste Land

THIS LONG POEM (434 lines), written by T. S. Eliot (1888–1965) and published in 1922, is a key Modernist text and probably the most important poem written in English between the World Wars. As the title implies, the poem speaks to the disillusionment and loss of purpose associated with the years after World War I.

For early readers of the poem, the central metaphor of the "waste land" was emblematic of their own feelings that the world had changed irrevocably. Readers since this period have continued to connect with the poem, which speaks to contemporary concerns about alienation from the past, destruction of the environment, and loss of faith in formerly respected institutions and creeds.

The poem is highly allusive, full of quotations and half-quotations from a variety of languages and literatures; it contains snatches of dialogue, song, poetry, and even nursery rhymes. The meaning of specific lines may be obscure for first-time readers of the poem. Quotations are often fragmentary, and transitions seem arbitrary. However, the five sections of the poem take readers on a "journey."

The poem's five sections are entitled "The Burial of the Dead," "A Game of Chess," "The Fire Sermon," "Death by Water," and "What the Thunder Said." Throughout, imagery associated with the legend of the Holy Grail and with ceremonies of fertility and rebirth suggest rituals and beliefs from the past along with tentative suggestions that some of these may still prove sustaining: "These fragments I have shored against my ruins." In his Notes, Eliot refers readers to Jessie L. Weston's *From Ritual to Romance* and to James George Frazer's *The Golden Bough*, two works that influenced his writing.

The poem begins with the famous line "April is the cruelest month" and continues with words and images that despairingly deny the positive sense of renewal traditionally associated with spring. The last words of the poem are three repetitions of *Shantih,* a word associated with the *Upanishads* (sacred Hindu texts) and meaning, according to Eliot's notes, "The Peace which passeth understanding."

Ho Chi Minh (1890–1969)

ONE OF THE MOST controversial and enigmatic world leaders of the 20th century, Ho Chi Minh was born Nguyen Sinh Cung in Nghe An Province in what would become modern-day Vietnam. (After assuming a number of aliases, he changed his name in 1940 to Ho Chi Minh, which means "Bringer of Light"). His father, a scholar and itinerant teacher, opposed the French occupation of his country and their ill treatment of local peasants. He instilled in his son a sense of hatred for French colonization and the rigid class system.

As a young man, Ho traveled to the United States, Africa, England, and finally France, where he became active among Vietnamese nationalists. In France, he petitioned U.S. President Woodrow Wilson to make Vietnam's independence from France part of the peace treaty ending World War I; Wilson refused.

Rebuffed by Wilson, Ho joined the French Communist Party, as he thought it was the best chance for Vietnam to become independent and be rid of a dominating French upper class. Between 1919 and 1945, he was trained in Moscow, created the Indo-Chinese Communist Party, and allied with the United States in fighting against Japan during World War II. He was without question the most powerful and revered nationalist leader in Vietnam in 1945, when his party, the Viet Minh, declared independence from France and named Ho the president of the Democratic Republic of Vietnam. After a bloody, eight-year struggle to maintain control, France capitulated, and Ho's forces controlled the northern half of the country. But half of the country wasn't enough; Ho was determined to unify Vietnam under Communist control.

Because of Ho's commitment to Communism, the United States was determined to prevent South Vietnam from falling to the North. Opposing what it interpreted as aggression from the North, the United States became involved in a conflict that lasted from 1954 to 1975 and caused bitter divisiveness in America.

Ho Chi Minh did not live to see the ultimate victory of his cause in 1975 when South Vietnam surrendered to North Vietnam, but he remained a powerful presence. To many Vietnamese and progressive groups throughout the world, he was a hero—a dedicated, firm, but gentle nationalist who inspired the liberation and reunification of Vietnam. To other Vietnamese and many Americans, Ho was a brutal Communist dictator who oppressed his people, caused the needless deaths of millions, and presented a threat to the security of the United States.

Stonehenge and the Early Inhabitants of Britain

STONEHENGE IS A CIRCULAR setting of large stone blocks located about eight miles north of Salisbury, in Wiltshire, England.

Nobody really knows who built Stonehenge or why. However, archaeological evidence provides a clear indication of when Stonehenge was built, and everyone agrees that it is a remarkable feat of engineering and construction. The builders dug the ground with deer antlers, shoveled the earth with shoulder blades of cattle, and moved huge, heavy stones considerable distances by roller, sledge, and raft.

The stone circle is aligned upon the sunrise at the summer solstice, suggesting a communal knowledge of astronomy. Most scholars believe that the stone circle and associated structures were used for religious rites.

Archaeologists divide the construction of Stonehenge into three phases:

Stonehenge I (c. 3100 B.C.): A circular earth bank and ditch roughly 330 feet in diameter were constructed. Just inside the earth bank is a circle of 56 holes, called *Aubrey Holes,* that held wooden posts.

Stonehenge II (c. 2150 B.C.): The posts in the Aubrey Holes were removed, and the holes were partially filled with soil or cremation deposits. Timber structures were erected in the center of the circle, also at the northeastern entrance. Pillars of igneous rock called *bluestones* were brought to the site from mines in present-day Wales (possibly by land and water routes) and erected in its center, forming two concentric circles.

Stonehenge III (c. 2000 B.C.): Silicified sandstone boulders from the Salisbury Plain (*sarsens*) measuring up to 30 feet long and weighing 50 tons were mined, dragged to the site, skillfully dressed, and placed in different settings. About 80 sarsens were erected in a 108-foot-diameter circle of 30 uprights capped by a ring of stone lintels. This enclosed a horseshoe formation of five large stone uprights capped by lintels (*trilithons*). Later, 20 bluestones from Stonehenge II were arranged in an oval setting, which was succeeded by a bluestone horseshoe that remains to this day.

Early Opera

THE WORD OPERA in Italian means "work," a very nonspecific term that does not designate sung drama in any way. Indeed, the term used to describe the results of early experiments with musical theater was *dramma per musica*—drama through, or for, music. Certainly, sung drama quickly became one of the favorite forms of multimedia entertainment in Europe and eventually North America (only displaced by the movies in the early 20th century), so the genre of "opera" has great fascination for audiences and scholars alike.

Historians have long struggled to determine when the first opera was created and performed and have been stymied by the fact that there is no obvious "first work" that was acknowledged as entirely different from traditions that had preceded dramma per musica. In other words, many of the components that coalesced into the tradition of opera had been around long enough that the creation of the genre was not a single-occasion event.

Two separate places and traditions can be singled out as significant. The first are the experiments at the court of Florence around 1600, which reflect the sponsoring Medici family's goal of recasting themselves as the heirs to the classical tradition of ancient Greece and Rome. The earliest surviving example of this Florentine court opera tradition was created by Giulio Caccini and Jacopo Peri for the celebrations surrounding the marriage of a Medici princess to King Henry IV of France. However, the opera was performed only a couple of times within the period of a week, had very limited public appeal (one patron famously described the simple musical recitation as listening to chanted mass for several hours), and was never produced again until modern revivals.

The other tradition, which began in Venice around 1630, was self-consciously designed to appeal to a broad public—admission was charged, and all who could afford the ticket were welcome to attend (while the Florentine court tradition was by invitation only). Theaters competed both for audiences and for superstar singers, who were paid large amounts for their "drawing power."

However, most of the music for the earliest examples of this tradition was not preserved. When new, it was closely guarded by the troupes of singers and musicians who relied on it for their livelihood. And a previous season's musical work was quickly outdated to a public that craved novelty, so it wasn't deemed worth preserving (except to pilfer and rearrange for a new production).

Antioxidants

COULD CHOCOLATE and red wine actually be good for you? Maybe. Both contain antioxidants, which are natural chemicals that inhibit oxidation of certain molecules. The jury is still out, however, as to whether these antioxidants can really help you live a longer and healthier life.

Antioxidants are believed to protect our cells from highly reactive ions called *free radicals.* Free radicals form naturally when our cells break down food, and they can also be produced by tobacco smoke and radiation. Free radicals can damage our cells, and they are implicated in cancer, heart disease, and the aging process. Antioxidants, however, can neutralize these free radicals.

One class of antioxidants, called *polyphenols,* is found in grape skins. So in addition to wine, antioxidants are also plentiful in grapes and grape juice. When making red wine, grape skins are not removed, so red wine contains much higher levels of antioxidants than white wine. In the laboratory, the antioxidants derived from grapes are shown to inhibit cancer cells in a culture dish. And another study showed that drinking a glass of red wine daily reduced the risk of prostate cancer. However, these studies are still considered preliminary.

Chocolate also contains the polyphenol class of antioxidants. Dark chocolate contains a high percentage of cocoa solids, so it has twice as many antioxidants as milk chocolate. Also, milk interferes with the absorption of antioxidants. As a result, eating milk chocolate or drinking milk with dark chocolate will prevent antioxidants from being absorbed.

Antioxidants are also found in a variety of other foods, including fruits, vegetables, nuts, grains, and meats. Vitamin A, Vitamin C, and Vitamin E already have familiar health benefits, but they also have antioxidant properties. Another potent antioxidant is beta-carotene, which is found in carrots and other orange fruits and vegetables. Tea, coffee, soy, and oregano are other known sources of antioxidants.

Taking supplements containing antioxidants is not recommended. Large clinical trials have not proven any benefit from taking antioxidant supplements, and some suggest they can even be harmful. The best course of action is to eat a healthy, well-rounded diet that includes a variety of fruits and vegetables. Red wine and chocolate probably shouldn't be included primarily for their antioxidant properties—better to rely on the fruits, grains, nuts, and vegetables for those.

Cast-Iron Architecture:
The Eiffel Tower

OTHER TOWERS ARE much taller—not to mention more modern (most of the building isn't heated in winter or cooled in summer). Still, the Eiffel Tower—a relic of the 19th century—is the beloved symbol of a great city and the world's most famous cast-iron structure.

The 7,000-ton Eiffel Tower stands on a 1,400-square-foot base in the center of Paris, France. The structure of exposed cast-iron latticework is made of 18,000 pieces of metal, joined by 2.5 million rivets, and covered with 60 tons of paint.

The 984-foot, four-sided tower stands on four legs, which angle inward and upward toward the tower's first level (189 feet up). Beneath each pair of legs is a spacious semicircular opening. Above the first level, the sides of the structure angle inward again, leaving a trapezoid-shaped opening as they lead to the second level (379 feet, 8 inches up). A long, slim tapering structure leads upward to the observation deck (905 feet, 11 inches high), which is topped by a television antenna that brings the tower's total height to 1,052 feet, 4 inches.

More than three million people visit the Eiffel Tower each year. Riding the elevator or climbing the steps, visitors can stop at the first level to buy souvenirs and eat in a popular restaurant. More steps lead to the second level, which has animated displays and a swanky dining spot. After taking 1,665 steps (or the elevator), visitors reach the observation deck with panoramic views of Paris.

Gustave Eiffel, an engineer who specialized in metal construction, designed the tower, winning a competition that had more than 100 entrants. The tower was intended to be a temporary symbol for the World's Fair of 1889, and many French intellectuals hated it. Guy de Maupassant, who is known for his short stories, signed a manifesto against "this vertiginously ridiculous tower," and the poet Verlaine rerouted a journey near Paris to avoid seeing it. Nature lovers declared that the tower would harm birds. However, the Eiffel Tower was not pulled down after the World's Fair ended because most Parisians had grown fond of it.

The Spanish Inquisition

FOLLOWING CENTURIES of control by the Moors (Muslims from North Africa), a coalition of Europe's Catholic kings drove them from most of the Iberian Peninsula in the 13th century. Although their armies had been defeated, many Moors remained in Spain. (They held the stronghold of Granada until 1492, when they were driven out of the province by the Spanish army.)

A large Jewish community also existed in Spain, making it the only country in Western Europe with a multicultural population of Catholics, Jews, and Muslims. These groups lived in relative harmony until the end of the 14th century, when persecution of non-Catholics began. Hundreds of Jews were killed in a series of persecutions in the larger cities of Spain. To save their lives, many Jews and Muslims converted to Catholicism.

Many Spaniards distrusted these *conversos* (new Christians), believing that these recent converts were still practicing their old religions. Consequently in 1478, King Ferdinand II and Queen Isabella pressured Pope Sixtus IV to give them the authority to institute an inquisition in Spain to purge the country of heretics.

Tomás de Torquemada, named the inquisitor-general in 1483, created tribunals in most major Spanish cities to find and try heretics, primarily among *conversos* communities. After the tribunals were established in a city, an *Edict of Grace* would be issued calling for citizens to confess to their heresy. The tribunal would then encourage citizens to denounce the heretics who did not turn themselves in. The accused would be defended by a member of the tribunal. Torture was often used to solicit a confession, and once a person was convicted, sentences ranged from fasting or prayer to execution for those refusing to repent. More than 13,000 *conversos* were tried and hundreds executed in the first decade of the inquisition. Those unreconciled Jews were banished from Spain in 1492 to remove any ties they might have with *conversos*.

Protestants and Moriscos (Muslim converts to Catholicism) became the subjects of the Inquisition in the 16th century, and the practice was even carried to the New World before finally being abolished in 1834. In more than 300 years of religious persecution, as many as 5,000 "heretics" may have been executed.

POSTSCRIPT

■ The "lighter" side of the Inquisition was portrayed in sketches by the British comedy group Monty Python and in Mel Brooks's movie *History of the World, Part I*.

Emily Dickinson

Although only a few of her poems were published during her lifetime, Emily Dickinson (1830–1886) is today considered a major poet, whose body of work (1,789 poems) has been the subject of serious scholarly attention. Even so, many of her poems are unknown to the general reader, and most people think of her as a whimsical nature-loving recluse, an image fostered by poems such as number 324: "Some keep the Sabbath going to Church—/I keep it, staying at Home—/With a Bobolink for a Chorister—/And an Orchard, for a Dome."

Dickinson's poetry, however, contains a vast range of intriguing voices and situations. At times, the "I" of the poem imagines herself dead or dying; at other times, the persona is recently bereaved. The poems can be passionate, as in number 249: "Wild Nights—Wild Nights!/Were I with thee/Wild Nights should be/Our luxury!" At other times, the voice is singularly cool: "The Soul selects her own Society—/Then—shuts the Door—." The Dickinson persona may be a married woman who misses her unmarried state (732) or an unconventional woman who comments ironically on the respectability of gentlewomen who are horrified by "freckled Human Nature." In 754, one of Dickinson's most enigmatic poems, the persona describes herself as a loaded gun who serves and guards an unnamed "master."

In style, Dickinson's poems take the meter of ballads or hymns, yet the poet experiments with these traditional forms, employing eccentric vocabulary, frequent use of dashes, and seemingly random capitalization, as well as violent imagery. These devices, together with the author's courageous examination of the human condition, create a highly individualistic body of work; a Dickinson poem is almost instantly recognizable.

Little is known for certain about Dickinson's emotional life, despite widespread rumors of an unhappy love affair. Although she became increasingly reclusive, she was a loyal and attentive friend to those in her circle. In her late 20s, she began assembling her poems into packets—sheets of folded stationery threaded together. Having accepted what she called her "Barefoot-Rank"—that is, knowing that she would not be understood during her lifetime—she left her poems for posterity.

POSTSCRIPT

■ An anthology entitled *Visiting Emily* is a collection of poems inspired by Dickinson's life. One of the poems in this book is entitled "Taking Off Emily Dickinson's Clothes" and was written by Billy Collins, U.S. Poet Laureate from 2001 to 2003.

Edward Kennedy "Duke" Ellington (1899–1974)

ALONG WITH LOUIS ARMSTRONG and Charlie Parker, Duke Ellington was arguably one of the most important giants of 20th-century jazz. His multitude of talents—as a player, a composer, an arranger, and a leader of both large bands and smaller groups—made him a crucial figure.

Ellington was born in Washington, D.C., into a middle-class family. His father was a butler in the White House and later designed blueprints. Young Ellington took piano lessons but at first seemed uninterested in music. As a teenager, however, he became fascinated with ragtime piano music and played a few gigs at his high school (during one, a friend started calling him "Duke"). His interest was further piqued when, during a vacation trip, he fell under the spell of "hot" pianist Harvey Brooks, who changed Ellington's life. Duke recalls, "After hearing him, I had a real yearning to play."

Duke dropped out of school, married, had a son, and moved to New York in 1923 where his band, the Washingtonians, grew in popularity. He played a number of major clubs, including the famed Cotton Club, a landmark venue during the Harlem Renaissance of the 1920s. Ellington reached national fame when his band was broadcast live across the United States via radio on "From the Cotton Club."

In 1924, he made his first recordings, including his own composition, "Choo Choo." Three years later, he signed with agent and publisher Irving Mills, whose shrewd knowledge of the music business led to record contracts with major labels such as Columbia and Victor, as well as a European tour and more concert dates in the United States. By the 1930s, Ellington was probably the most popular jazz musician in America.

Ellington's career reached its peak in the 1940s when he composed several longer jazz suites, most famously "Black, Brown, and Beige," a somber riff on black struggles in America, which premiered in Carnegie Hall in 1943. Even after the decline of the popularity of big bands in the 1950s and 1960s, when smaller combos became the dominant jazz format, Ellington's influence remained powerful, as artists such as Dave Brubeck and Miles Davis wrote and recorded tributes to "the Duke." His numerous awards include a Grammy Lifetime Achievement Award, the Presidential Medal of Freedom, and the French Legion of Honor.

The First World's Fair

ORGANIZED UNDER the direction of Queen Victoria's husband, Prince Albert, the Great Exhibition of the Works of Industry of All Nations was held in London in 1851. It was the first of the international exhibitions of industry and technology that would become known as World's Fairs.

Crystal Palace

The exhibition was housed in the so-called "Crystal Palace," which got its name from a commentary on the hall in the satirical magazine *Punch.* Built in less than nine months, the hall itself was a monument to British innovation and technology. Essentially a giant greenhouse, its framework of cast-iron columns and girders was built with prefabricated parts from Birmingham. Nearly 300,000 panes of glass made up its walls and roof.

The grand affair was intended as a celebration of Great Britain's position as the "workshop of the world." Contributions were requested from all over the world, but more than half of the 14,000 exhibits came from Britain and its colonies. Displays included machinery, crafts, and fine arts. Other wonders included the Koh-i-noor Diamond, on loan from Queen Victoria herself, and a 24-ton block of coal, which stood outside of the entrance. The arched Centre Transept, which housed the world's largest organ, was used as both a circus tent and a concert hall. In the park surrounding the exhibition hall, there were copies of statues from around the world, a replica of a lead mine, and the first exhibition of life-size dinosaur models.

Between May 1 and October 15 of 1851, the exhibition drew more than six million visitors. Prince Albert emphasized its educational and practical value, writing, "The products of all quarters of the globe are placed at our disposal and we have only to choose that which are best and cheapest for our purposes." However, most visitors agreed with *Punch* that the exhibition was "Britannia's great party."

World's fairs showcasing industrial and technological advances remained quite popular following London's 1851 exhibition until the 1933–1934 Century of Progress in Chicago. Beginning with the 1939 World's Fair in New York, the focus of such international exhibitions shifted from industry to celebrating national culture and identity.

Lutheran and Calvinist Reforms to Musical Worship

FROM THE BEGINNING of the Christian Church, worship was sung, drawing on the traditions of Jewish practice with which early Christians were familiar. As Christian clerics of the Middle Ages sought to create increasingly intense prayers, the songs they developed became more and more elaborate, a tradition that was regularly chastised as too extravagant by more conservative elements of the Church. It is thus no surprise that the use of music and singing was a key consideration for the 16th-century reformers who sought to bring Christianity back to its original pure form.

Theological reformers Martin Luther (1483–1546) and Jean Calvin (1509–1564) had strong opinions and gave specific directions to their followers concerning the use of music. Their approaches had both strong similarities and important differences. Both men insisted that the reformed Christian faithful should worship through collective song, using the vernacular (the language of the common people—for example French or German—as opposed to Latin, the official language for worship in the Church of Rome until 1963), and clear, comprehensible modern translations of scriptural texts.

Calvin sought to go "back to basics" by deriving worship songs almost exclusively from the Psalms, which he saw as providing the core "sung worship" repertory from the Bible. Calvin forbade his followers from using instruments or singing harmony in church, since that would distract the worshippers with "ear candy."

Luther, on the other hand, was very fond of complex music (he was a fan of one of the most prominent composers of the time, Josquin Desprez) and encouraged its use, as well as the incorporation of instruments into worship services. Luther was especially interested in providing simple songs (*chorales*) to his followers that paraphrased biblical texts or messages in several straightforward and memorable stanzas. Collective singing of these chorales formed the backbone of the Lutheran worship service. Musicians would then elaborate on the chorale melodies through both keyboard improvisation and more complex vocal and instrumental compositions.

This difference accounted for the significantly different musical developments in Calvinist and Lutheran traditions over the centuries. While Calvinists did not seek to foster elaborate worship music, Lutheran composers created sacred works of great complexity that are still used to this day for both worship and enjoyment.

Finding a Cure for Cancer

SINCE CANCER IS ONE of the most common and deadly diseases on the planet, millions of dollars have been directed toward research into finding a cure. But, despite the time, thought, and money put into this effort, late-stage cancer is still incurable. And even if cancer is caught early, the most viable treatment options are limited to surgery, chemo-therapy, and radiation therapy, all of which have serious drawbacks. Surgery will work only if the cancer has not already started to spread. Radiation therapy can kill tumor cells, but it also kills the surrounding healthy cells. Chemotherapy kills all rapidly dividing cells, including both cancerous cells and healthy stem cells, causing diarrhea and hair loss.

Why is cancer so difficult to cure? Cancer is a breakdown in the function of cells, which makes it impossible for the immune system to detect the resulting tumor cells. Devastating diseases that have been nearly eradi-cated in the past, such as small pox or polio, are caused by viruses that can be recognized and destroyed by the immune system. But a tumor cell is not a virus, nor is it a bacterium that can be killed with an antibi-otic. Tumors are made of the body's own defective cells. While medical arsenals are full of tools ready to fight invading organisms, we have yet to develop a drug to selectively kill our own malfunctioning cells.

There are promising discoveries being made, however, in understanding the genetic causes of cancer. If we understand how cancer forms on the genetic level, there is a greater possibility of developing new treatments. Recent studies show that cancer is caused by mutations in genes that control how a cell grows and divides. When cell division controls break down, the cells divide continuously and create a mass of cells known as a tumor.

One possible way to fix malfunctioning genes is through gene therapy. If a gene that controls cell division is reintroduced into tumor cells, it will inhibit the division and spread of the tumor. The challenge is delivering the gene into all the tumor cells and also making sure the surrounding healthy cells are not affected. Also, each tumor is caused by a different type of mutation, so therapies must be developed for each specific combi-nation of mutations.

Despite the challenges, genetic research in cancer has paid off in devel-oping some successful new treatments. For example, cancers due to the HER2 gene in breast tumors can be destroyed by an antibody specific to this gene.

Francisco Goya

FRANCISCO JOSÉ DE GOYA WAS raised in Saragossa in northern Spain. He began his art studies while in his teens, and in 1774 moved to Madrid to design tapestries. By 1789 he was employed by King Charles IV, producing portraits and mural designs.

Goya's private vision often seems in conflict with his obligations as a court painter. In the *Family of Charles IV* (1801), the royals mill about in an ornate chamber. Their portly figures and homely faces are depicted with appalling candor. In fact, a 19th-century French critic described them as "the corner baker and his wife after they won the lottery."

A terrible illness in 1792 left Goya physically fragile and deaf, and he turned to smaller-scale works. During the next 15 years, he would produce some of his finest portraits, including the *Duchess of Alba* (1797).

The struggle between secular rationalism and the worldview of traditional Catholicism infuses the etchings Goya published as the *Caprichos,* or *Caprices* (1799). A famous image shows a man asleep at his desk, while bats, owls, and a large cat circle him. The caption reads: *El sueño de la razón produce monstruous* ("The sleep of reason produces monsters"). The meaning is unclear. Does the absence of reason create monsters, or is reason itself an amoral condition that brings such things about?

In 1808, the armies of Emperor Napoleon invaded Spain. The next six years were marked by horrific actions by both the French armies and the Spanish resistance. The inhumanity of war is the theme of a suite of prints called *Los desastres de la guerra (Disasters of War)* that present unspeakable acts with the immediacy of an eyewitness account.

Ferdinand VII returned to the throne in 1814, but his regime was as harsh as the French occupation had been. Goya's work became even more moving and culminated with the so-called "Black Paintings," depictions of murderous gods, witchcraft, and pathetic creatures. One of his most famous and powerful works, *The Third of May: The Execution of the Defenders of Madrid* (pictured) was also painted at this time.

In 1824, Goya went into exile, settling in Bordeaux, France, where he died in 1828.

The Salem Witch Trials

SAMUEL PARRIS WAS born in London and arrived in New England in the 1660s. His father, a cloth merchant, maintained a sugar plantation in Barbados and, upon his death, Parris went to the island to claim his inheritance. When he returned to the colonies, he brought with him a slave by the name of Tituba to serve the Parris household and care for his daughter, Elizabeth.

Parris continued to work as a merchant and began preaching. Eventually, he became Salem Village's minister. Parris, harsh and stern, had qualities characteristic of Puritan leaders. Members of Puritan households had no entertainment and little joy in their lives. The Parris household was no exception. Elizabeth and her cousin, Abigail, turned to Tituba for entertainment and were fascinated when Tituba told them about voodoo and other island practices.

A few months after learning about voodoo, Elizabeth and Abigail became feverish, convulsed, twitched, and had unexplained seizures and fits. Doctors who examined them decided their symptoms were caused by witchcraft. Ann Putnam, a friend of the girls, developed the same type of symptoms. As more of their friends became afflicted, a hunt ensued for the witches who had caused the girls' problems. The girls identified Sarah Good, Sarah Osborne, and Tituba as the witches who caused their afflictions.

Sarah Good and her family were beggars and were despised by the people living in Salem Village. Sarah Osborne, a neighbor of the Parris family, had been on unfriendly terms with them over a legal dispute concerning the ownership of her property.

At trial, Good said she had been falsely accused, but she was found guilty and sentenced to die by hanging. Osborne maintained her innocence throughout the trial but died in a Boston jail before a verdict was rendered. Tituba admitted she was a witch and was placed in prison, where she named other witches.

The witch hunt then began in earnest. More than 100 people were arrested and imprisoned, and trials were held throughout the Salem area. Many individuals were found guilty, and several were hanged.

In 1706, Putnam apologized to her church for having accused people of being witches, acknowledged that those she had accused were innocent, and said that Satan had deceived her in making her believe the way she had.

The King James Bible

THE WORKS OF SHAKESPEARE and the King James Bible (sometimes called the "Authorized Version" by the British) are the two most important influences on English literature in the past 400 years.

In 1603, King James VI of Scotland, a moderate Puritan (Calvinist or Presbyterian), became James I of England. On a tour of England to claim the throne, James was handed a petition allegedly signed by 1,000 Puritan ministers (no copy survives), complaining that the Anglican Church established by Henry VIII was still too "popish" (Catholic). In response, James convened the Hampton Court conference in 1604, where Puritan leader Dr. John Rainolds asked "that there might be a new translation of the Bible, because those which were allowed in the reign of King Henry the Eighth and Edward the Sixth were corrupt and not answerable to the truth of the original." Although the result was supposed to supersede other Bibles in official services of the Church of England, James never actually "authorized" the translation.

However, James, a theologian himself, directed the translating committee's work through 15 instructions that steered a middle course between radical Puritanism and established Anglicanism. He instructed the translators to follow the Bishops' Bible (the translation then used in churches) as closely as possible; to avoid unfamiliar translations of words, such as the radical Puritan "congregation" instead of "church" or "washing" instead of "baptism"; and to use marginal notes minimally, only to explain Latin or Greek words or to relate one Bible verse to another.

Forty-seven unpaid scholars, including Anglican bishops, Puritan clergy and lay scholars, and linguists, worked on the translation. They divided into two committees at Oxford, two at Cambridge, and two at Westminster. Each committee translated certain parts of the Bible, and in 1609 a review committee met to harmonize the parts. The original "Authorized" Bible was published by Robert Barker in 1611. Minor revisions continued to be made in later versions.

Notwithstanding minor revisions in 1629 and again in 1638, the King James Bible was the most widely accepted English Protestant Bible for 250 years. In 1881, a group of 50 scholars substantially revised its language. Since then, many other translations have competed with the King James, but none has had as wide an influence.

Frank Lloyd Wright (1867–1959)

FRANK LLOYD WRIGHT, the son of a poor minister, was born in Wisconsin shortly after the end of the American Civil War. As a young man, he apprenticed for a local builder and took classes at the University of Wisconsin. In 1887, he moved to Chicago and got a job as a tracer for an architectural firm. The following year he found a better-paying drafting position with Louis Sullivan and Dankmar Adler. Sullivan in particular influenced Wright's attitudes toward architecture.

The quiet neighborhoods and beauty of Oak Park drew Wright to the community to build his personal residence. After moving to Oak Park, Wright also opened his own firm. He developed a new style of residential architecture, the Prairie style. Breaking from traditional styles of architecture, Wright used low sloping rooflines, horizontal lines, banks of windows, and cantilevered projections to convey warmth and to project the image of a home that would fit in with the surroundings of a prairie landscape.

Though married, in 1911 Wright returned to Wisconsin to build a new home for himself and his mistress. He named his home Taliesin, a Welsh word meaning "shining brow," because he positioned the home on the projecting edge of a steep hill. This home reflected the elements of the Wisconsin environment. Wright used Wisconsin limestone for the home's chimneys and sand from the local rivers to mix into the stucco walls.

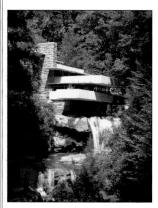

Organic architectural concepts are also visible in Wright's famous Fallingwater, a private residence in Pennsylvania. Set in natural surroundings, Fallingwater is constructed of natural limestone and is positioned over a stream and waterfall.

Fallingwater

Wright is also well-known for commercial building designs and for the functional furniture he designed for the interiors of many of his Prairie-style homes. He built more than 400 homes, and most of them have survived.

Wright's final project was designing the Guggenheim Museum in New York. However, he didn't live to see it completed. Wright died on April 9, 1959, after complications from intestinal surgery.

The Geography of Earthquakes and Volcanoes

EARTHQUAKES ARE SUDDEN disturbances inside Earth that generate seismic waves in the crust. They happen all the time; most of them are so small that sensitive instruments are needed to detect them. When major earthquakes occur, they do considerable damage to the land—affecting agriculture and public works—and to cities, resulting in destruction of buildings, roads, and bridges. Some earthquakes cause tidal waves or tsunamis, which spread destruction over a wide area. They can cause catastrophic loss of life and property, sometimes even changing the course of history.

Earthquakes take place when rock on Earth's crust fractures due to the buildup of strain during geological processes. Strain is created by heat escaping from the core of Earth or movement of Earth's tectonic plates. Though most earthquakes occur beneath the sea, those that attract public attention are generally near continental coasts or island chains. The Pacific Ocean rim is an especially active area.

Volcanoes are places where molten rock has erupted to Earth's surface. They can be the familiar conical structures—funnel-shape depressions filled with molten rock—or long fissures in Earth's surface. When volcanoes erupt, they do tremendous damage in the short term: destroying property and creating tidal waves. The fumes and dust they release into the atmosphere can also affect the climate for long periods of time.

Sixty-two percent of volcanoes occur along the Pacific Rim. Roughly 45 percent exist in the island chains of the east Pacific Ocean, and 17 percent occur in mountain chains. Large areas of the earth have no active volcanoes but may have those that are extinct.

Around 1200 B.C., the ancient Mediterranean cities of Troy, Mycenae, and Knossos disappeared without apparent cause. Some archaeologists have suggested that numerous earthquakes in succession (an earthquake storm) may have caused their destruction. The Harappan people lived in the Indus River valley in present-day India for roughly 2,000 years but disappeared around 1900 B.C., an event that some scholars attribute to catastrophic earthquakes.

In the late ninth century, the Mayans of Central America suddenly abandoned Quirigua and Benque Viejo, important cities. Some archaeologists attribute this to earthquake activity. Others doubt these speculations, calling them the "Godzilla Attacks Babylon" theory. The question remains open.

English Madrigals and Ayres

MOST PEOPLE WHO have sung in a choral ensemble—and indeed, most parents who have attended a middle- or high-school vocal recital—have encountered English vocal works of the late 1500s called *madrigals*. Elizabethan courtiers absorbed Italian fashions of all sorts, and they quickly picked up on the Italian upper-class custom of amateurs singing simple secular part-songs for recreation.

The Musician with the Lute *by Caravaggio*

Both English and Italian madrigals featured flowery poetic texts that often hid mildly spicy double-entendres (enough for a gentleman to glance meaningfully at his lady-love while singing, making her blush appropriately), and were designed to easily be sung by amateurs (usually three to six people at a time) for an evening's enjoyment. This was not music intended for a listening audience—singers and listeners were one and the same, allowing for genteel and refined interaction. Madrigals crossed the blurry line between artistic and popular music; they were meant to be performed and enjoyed by just about anyone.

Many English madrigals just had new English text added to music by Italian composers. Some of the musicians who "translated" the Italian madrigal into an English phenomenon also contributed to the ayre tradition, a uniquely English approach to expressive song. Foremost among the celebrated composers who worked in this tradition was John Dowland (1563–1626). Dowland was a lutenist, and all of his ayres feature that instrument prominently, sometimes paired with a single voice, other times as an optional resource along with four equal voice-parts. His motto was *"Semper Dowland semper dolens"*—always Dowland, always sorrowful—and his melancholy music reflected this. Another uniquely English trait of Dowland's music is the format of his sheet music, which allows four musicians to sit or stand around a table and each read from their parts.

Dowland's ayres have inspired many elaborations and performances. Most recently, former Police bassist Sting has recorded a number of Dowland songs to the accompaniment of a modified lute. More experimental but also deeply expressive approaches can be heard by the Dowland Project, and a beautiful "historically informed" take was recently offered by the English ensemble Virelai.

Restoration Ecology

HUMANS HAVE TRIED to repair their surrounding landscapes and ecosystems for thousands of years. Yet the science of restoration ecology has emerged as a field of study only within the last 20 years. Extensive damage from industrialization as well as poor regulation of air, water, and soil pollutants have led to a sharp demand for technologies to help repair the harm caused by human intervention. In particular, ecological restoration aims to reintroduce native animals and plants, control soil erosion, eradicate weeds and invasive species, and revegetate the habitat.

Many conservationists consider restoration ecology the practical side of ecology. One crucial aspect of this field is studying soil composition. The dirt under our feet is host to thousands of microorganisms and other creatures, such as earthworms, that ultimately determine the health and diversity of above-ground vegetation and animals. Another important aspect is analyzing the dynamics of the ecological community: Are jack-rabbits overrunning the prairie land? Should more wolves be introduced? Will the wolves inadvertently kill off other native, and possibly endangered, animals? These are all questions restoration ecologists face when cleaning up a negligent factory's mess or repairing the damage caused by the poor planning of a well-meaning farming community.

Of course, nothing's a cure-all. Some critics argue that restoration ecology is a reactive, rather than a proactive, effort and too much money is spent fixing a damaged ecosystem when better planning and tighter regulations could have prevented the situation in the first place. Other critics warn that the field is still in its infancy, and that humans, as of yet, cannot replicate true natural environments. The lesson here is that perhaps we should strive to protect the environment and call in the restoration ecologists when they are inevitably needed.

POSTSCRIPT

- The U.S. government is currently spending billions of dollars trying to keep the Florida Everglades from drying up. It is perhaps the largest and most expensive restoration project ever attempted.
- Many research institutions offer graduate programs in restoration ecology. The University of Wisconsin's lab spans 1,200 acres.
- In the last five years, hunters have killed 140,000 goats in the Galapagos Islands in the largest eradication campaign in the world. Natural vegetation is already growing back.

Chartres Cathedral

DOMINATING THE SKYLINE of the town of Chartres located southwest of Paris, the Chartres Cathedral is one of France's finest surviving examples of early Gothic architecture.

The dimensions of the present interior make Chartres one of the most spacious churches in France, measuring more than 45 feet across the nave (central passage) and 120 feet from floor to ceiling. It uses pointed (rather than round) arches, a hallmark of the Gothic style, introduced north of Paris in 1145. Chartres and other Gothic churches like it constitute engineering marvels, involving limestone blocks precisely fit together without concrete. The soaring height of these churches was made possible by strategically designed skeletal ribs supporting thin shells of stone. Outward thrust was balanced by flying buttresses located on the exterior, featuring bridgelike struts that surrounded the outer walls.

The west facade of Chartres reveals its long building history, stretching across four centuries. There is a stark difference between the two towers, one plainer and simpler, reflecting the earlier Romanesque period, and the other taller and pierced with extensive carving and embellishments, representing the late, flamboyant Gothic aesthetic. The latter was not completed until 1513, following the earlier tower's collapse. A rose window of stained glass occupies the facade's center, constituting only a portion of the 220,000 square feet of colored glass in the cathedral.

Sculpture on the "Royal Portal" of the west entrance includes distinctive statues of kings and queens attached to jamb columns on either side of the portals (doorways). Although elongated and stylized, they are noted for their kind faces and welcoming presence, a contrast from the intimidating images found on earlier church sculpture. Similarly, the calm, gentle Christ figure above the portal reinforces the theme of salvation, which awaits those who enter the church, as they step from the outside world into a light-filled, soaring paradise on Earth.

The Royal Portal also includes much secular content, such as the labors of the months, personifications of the liberal arts, and zodiac signs. These reveal the role of the Gothic church as a community center in which concerts, plays, and lectures all took place, alongside traditional Christian worship.

The Trinity Test

AT 5:30 A.M. ON JULY 16, 1945, in an isolated section of the Alamagordo Bombing Range near Los Alamos, New Mexico, the first nuclear weapon was successfully tested. This test was the culmination of a series of scientific breakthroughs in the early 20th century.

Most important were the first splitting of an atom in 1932 by two British scientists and the first successful experiment, in 1938, in which a uranium atom was split (called *nuclear fission*) by two German physicists. This last event led to fears that the Nazis might be working on a nuclear weapon as World War II loomed, which helped convince U.S. President Franklin Roosevelt to authorize an American nuclear weapons development initiative.

Code-named the Manhattan Project, this massive enterprise enlisted thousands of scientists and engineers to work on various components of the project. Army General Leslie Groves, who was the director of the overall project, instituted a code of absolute secrecy. Different aspects of the project were developed at different locations, with workers unaware of what was going on at sites other than their own. For example, scientists at the University of Chicago conducted the first controlled nuclear reaction, while those at Oak Ridge, Tennessee, separated nuclear fuel from natural uranium. Meanwhile, the Hanford, Washington, facility produced plutonium.

Once the different fuel and hardware had been developed, University of Chicago physicist Robert Oppenheimer directed the actual creation of the weapon. Charges that Oppenheimer might have had connections to the Communist Party were brushed aside in part because his scientific brilliance and administrative and diplomatic skills were vital to the project. At Los Alamos, Oppenheimer oversaw a race against time that contained all the elements of a first-rate suspense novel, as he and his colleagues worked around the clock to produce the bomb before the Germans or Japanese did.

The race was won when the test succeeded. The explosion unleashed a force equivalent to 21 kilotons of TNT, which created a fireball that fused desert sand into a green glasslike solid and left a bomb crater almost 2,400 feet across.

From the use of atomic bombs on Japan to end World War II, to the nuclear standoff between the United States and the Soviet Union during the Cold War, to our current fears of nuclear terrorism, the legacy of the Trinity Test is a powerful one.

"Beowulf"

WRITTEN DOWN ANONYMOUSLY, this long poem (more than 3,000 lines) in Old English uses pagan and biblical references to glorify the heroism of Beowulf, who as a young warrior defeats the monster Grendel and his loathsome mother, and who in old age, as a king, must again defeat a ravening monster—this time a dragon. The period of the poem's creation is uncertain; it may have occurred as early as the seventh century, or it may date from the time of the only surviving manuscript, around A.D. 1000.

The world of the poem is a harsh one in which humanity is ruled by fate or destiny: "Fate goes ever as fate must." This world also prizes courage, however: "Often, for undaunted courage/fate spares the man it has not already marked."

Although called an epic, the poem does not, as J.R.R. Tolkien pointed out, consist of the kind of narrative traditionally associated with the epic genre. The story is organized around three great battles, with a lapse of 50 years between the first two (with Grendel and his mother) and the final one with the dragon, in which Beowulf receives fatal wounds, though the dragon is defeated.

Grendel and his mother are described as descendents of Cain. In addition to biblical references, the poem also contains numerous allusions to Germanic myth and legend. The dragon, Beowulf's final antagonist, will perhaps remind contemporary readers of ways in which Tolkien, known for his analysis of the poem, has created in his novels his own version of gold-hoarding dragons.

A revered and much-studied text, "Beowulf" is a work that Western literature almost lost. It survives in only one manuscript, and that one was almost destroyed by fire in the early 18th century. Thanks to the Electronic Beowulf Project, digital images of the manuscript are now available; the original is housed in the British Library in London.

The poem has been widely translated into modern English and many other languages as well. A popular contemporary translation by Nobel prizewinner Seamus Heaney was published in 1999. Also popular is a short novel entitled *Grendel,* published by American novelist John Gardner in 1971. This work, which retells the story from Grendel's point of view, is widely taught in schools and universities along with "Beowulf."

A 2007 film version of the poem stars Ray Winstone as Beowulf. The cast includes Anthony Hopkins, John Malkovich, and Angelina Jolie.

Frederick Douglass (1818–1895)

FREDERICK AUGUSTUS WASHINGTON BAILEY was born a slave in 1818 in a town on the eastern shore of Maryland. His mother was an African American, and his father was probably white. In 1838, Douglass escaped slavery by posing as a free black sailor. Once in New York, he adopted the last name Douglass to foil slave hunters who wanted to

capture him and return him to slavery. He also married Anna Murray, a free black woman he had met in Baltimore.

Having escaped slavery, Douglass devoted his life to advocating civil rights for all people. In 1841, Douglass spoke at an abolitionist meeting in Nantucket, Massachusetts. His moving speech brought him to the attention of the great William Lloyd Garrison, a leading abolitionist. Garrison asked Douglass to become a spokesman for the antislavery movement, and soon the talented orator was speaking all over the North and Midwest.

In 1845, Douglass published his memoir, *Narrative of the Life of Frederick Douglass, an American Slave*. He departed for a lecture tour of Ireland and England shortly after the book came out and returned to America in early 1847.

Douglass moved to Rochester, New York, and started a weekly abolition newspaper called *The North Star*, which he published until 1860. He became involved in women's rights and in 1848 was a speaker at the first Women's Rights Convention in Seneca Falls, New York.

Douglass became friends with abolitionist Gerrit Smith and also met John Brown. After Brown's failed raid on Harpers Ferry in 1859, Douglass went to England briefly to avoid accusations that he helped Brown plan the raid. In 1863, two of Douglass's sons joined the Union army. Lewis served with the famous 54th Massachusetts, and Charles was in a cavalry regiment. Douglass was known to have criticized President Abraham Lincoln for not moving faster to end slavery, but by 1865 he had become a wholehearted Lincoln supporter.

After the war, Douglass moved to Washington and married a white woman (for which he was widely criticized) after his first wife passed away. He also held two positions in the District of Columbia government and was minister to Haiti from 1889 to 1891. Douglass died suddenly on February 20, 1895, of a heart attack.

Early Recording Technology

THOMAS EDISON MADE the first recording of human speech ("Mary had a little lamb") on December 6, 1877. Six weeks later, he patented his phonograph. It used cylinders wrapped in tinfoil: A diaphragm activated a stylus, which pressed indentations into the tinfoil as the cylinder rotated. Sound waves were recorded as variations in the depth of the helical groove.

Edison was far from alone in the field—others had tried to record sound before him. Later, in the 1880s, there was an explosion of recording technology. Augustus Stroh in England recorded the words "mama" and "papa" on brass disks. In 1885, the U.S. inventors Chichester A. Bell and Charles Sumner Tainter developed a device like Edison's, using a wax cylinder instead of tinfoil to deliver a much better sound. The German-born Emile Berliner created a machine that recorded sound as a wavy line, making a spiral on a flat disk. The initial recording became a master from which large numbers of thermoplastic records were pressed and could then be played back.

Early recording and playback devices were acoustical. They collected and applied sound without amplification to actuate the diaphragm of the record-cutting device. Only the loudest sounds recorded well, and there was little subtlety to performances. Shortly before World War I, the U.S. scientist Lee de Forest invented the Audion vacuum tube amplifier, which greatly amplified sound power without sacrificing quality. During the 1920s, electrical sound recording and reproduction rapidly supplanted mechanical technology. This dramatically improved the ease and range of recording as it delivered a better playing quality.

Commercial exploitation of sound recording followed advances in technology. In 1894, Emile Berliner manufactured and sold 1,000 electric- or hand-powered record players and 25,000 records—seven-inch hard, rubber disks. In 1896, Eldridge Johnson introduced the first low-cost record player with a motor. Berliner and Johnson merged their firms in 1901 to create the Victor Talking Machine Co. with its trademarked dog listening to "His Master's Voice." By 1903, record firms had begun to market recordings of celebrity opera stars like Enrico Caruso. In 1906, the Victor Company introduced the first cabinet phonograph, the Victrola.

As recording technology continued to improve, music recording transformed society. Record companies recorded classical music, jazz, folk songs, and gospel. Popular songs on romantic themes sold in huge numbers, helping to create today's entertainment industry.

Music at the French Court Under Louis XIV

KING LOUIS XIV OF FRANCE (who reigned from 1643 to 1715) was probably the most powerful monarch of that country in the early modern era. His grandfather, Henry IV, had converted from Huguenot Calvinism to Catholicism and signed the Edict of Nantes in 1598, ending a half century of bloody religious civil wars. The French elites were eager to build on the stability that Henry and his son Louis XIII promised, but when Louis died prematurely, leaving a young child—also named Louis—as heir, there was great concern that chaos could once again descend on the French state. The younger Louis, however, was well supervised and proved to have a tremendous skill for exerting order and control; his reign was the longest and most stable of any monarch of a major European nation. In the process, Louis XIV created a centralized state that was the envy of rulers for generations to come.

Also much envied—and used as a template by many of his contemporaries—was Louis's use of music as a symbol of power and grace in both secular and sacred contexts. Early during his rule, Louis fostered and danced in the choreographed court ballets that had fascinated both his father and grandfather. Later, he championed the shift from the lute to the keyboard as the "favored" instrument for French nobility.

Louis surrounded himself with the best and brightest musicians in his kingdom and beyond, and especially encouraged his protégé (and dance teacher) Jean-Baptiste Lully in the development of a uniquely French tradition of musical theater that was as influential as it was spectacular. Louis also took advantage of his status as king-by-grace-of-God in fostering an elaborate tradition of sacred music at court that later was also very influential in England (leading to the establishment of the choral-orchestral *anthem*) when Charles II, his cousin, was reinstated as king of England after the end of the Commonwealth.

Some composers who wrote music for Louis's court were Lully (dance and musical theater), Denis Gaultier (lute music), Louis and François Couperin (harpsichord), and Michel Delalande (sacred vocal music).

POSTSCRIPT

■ At the age of 14, Louis danced in a court ballet. He appeared at the close of the ballet as "the sun" and was so pleased with the image of himself as the source of light and the center of the system around which all objects must revolve that he styled himself "the Sun King" for the remainder of his reign.

Deforestation

IF FORESTS ARE MANAGED wisely, lumber can be a renewable resource in a thriving natural area. However, only about 13 percent of the world's forests are currently being managed, and only 2 percent are protected by reserves. As a result, deforestation is occurring at an alarming rate. About 30 to 50 percent of the world's forests have already been destroyed. Worse still, on average an area the size of 20 football fields is cleared away each minute. Consequently, trees are being cut down much faster than they can regenerate.

The causes of deforestation include logging, construction, and agriculture. Tropical rain forests are especially in danger because of the common practice of "slash and burn" methods to clear new land for agriculture. Since the soil in rain forests is nutrient-poor, with most of the nutrients tied up in the living systems, crops can only be grown on the newly cleared land for a few years. Then the land is abandoned, and more land is cleared.

Healthy forests are important to our quality of life for many reasons. Most important is their role as natural regulators of carbon dioxide in the atmosphere. Carbon dioxide is the most common greenhouse gas contributing to global climate change. While humans are releasing more and more carbon dioxide into the air, we are also destroying the forests that have the capacity to capture this carbon dioxide from the atmosphere. Therefore, deforestation is also a major contributor to global climate change.

As forests disappear, so, too, will the animals that depend on this ecosystem for survival. Forest habitats must be preserved to prevent the extinction of wildlife species. With this in mind, many preservation projects are currently under way. For example, old-growth forests in the northwest United States are protected from logging in an effort to save the northern spotted owl from extinction. Preservation of the rain forest is of particular concern since the rain forest is home to about half of all species on Earth, even though rain forests only cover about 7 percent of Earth's dry land.

POSTSCRIPT

▓ Each year, an area of forest equivalent to the state of Indiana is cleared.

▓ The African island country of Madagascar only has 5 percent of its rain forest remaining. The rest has been cleared primarily by slash and burn methods for farming.

Photographers of the Civil War

THE AMERICAN PHOTOGRAPHER Mathew Brady (1823–1896) learned to make daguerreotype pictures in 1841, less than two years after this early photographic process was demonstrated in Paris. He opened a gallery in New York City and quickly gained prominence.

While in London to show his pictures at the Great Exhibition of 1851, Brady met a Scottish photographer, Alexander Gardner (1821–1882), and persuaded him to join his business venture. With an additional gallery in Washington, D.C., and a grand new space in New York, Brady was the leading maker of photographic portraits in the United States. His sitters included celebrities and statesmen, from the circus impresario P. T. Barnum to Presidents Millard Fillmore and Abraham Lincoln.

Ulysses S. Grant, as photographed by Brady

In 1861, following the outbreak of the Civil War, Brady sent photographers to document military life, equipping them at his own expense. Printing technology in the 1860s did not allow the use of photographs in newspapers, but crowds filled Brady's galleries to see images of encampments, officers, and blasted battlefields strewn with the dead.

Brady anticipated that he would make a fortune from sales to private individuals and especially the U.S. government. In fact, the enterprise led to financial ruin, as survivors and their family members did their best to forget the horrors of the war. Although Brady continued to make photographs for the rest of his life, he never regained the economic heights he had enjoyed as a portraitist. Moreover, he and Gardner quarreled over the fact that all images were presented under Brady's name rather than the name of the individual photographer. Gardner soon broke with Brady.

In 1866, Gardner published a two-volume work, *Gardner's Photographic Sketch Book of the Civil War.* Photographers received credit for their images, and evocative captions and dramatic accounts of the circumstances accompanied each picture. The *Sketch Book* was never a financial success.

After the war, Gardner produced an early example of a "photo essay." He made portraits of the defendants accused of assassinating President Lincoln, then documented preparations for their executions. His final photograph shows the coffins and freshly dug graves.

The Birth of Christ

CHRISTIAN TRADITION HOLDS that Joseph led a donkey carrying a very pregnant Mary into Bethlehem on December 25 to register for a Roman census. Unable to find a room, they spent the night in a stable, where Jesus Christ was born. Heralded by angels, shepherds came from their fields to pay homage to the Savior. While the mother and baby were still in the stable, three kings arrived carrying gold, frankincense, and myrrh as gifts.

Not all of this story is supported by the authors of the four Gospels. Matthew's Gospel simply states that Jesus was born in Bethlehem in Judea during the time that Herod was king. (Biblical scholars place Christ's birth somewhere between 6 B.C., since Herod died in about 4 B.C., and A.D. 4, which was the approximate date of a Roman census.) Matthew adds that three kings from the East followed a star to the house where Jesus was staying. Neither Mark nor John relay the story of Christ's birth. The Gospel of Luke gives the fullest description of the event. He references a census, Bethlehem, a stable, and the shepherds.

The day and month of Christ's birth are not given in the Gospels, but Christians traditionally celebrate it on December 25. That date has been disputed by biblical scholars. December in Palestine is extremely cold and, contrary to Bible passages, shepherds would not be in the fields with their flocks in the winter. They would house their animals in October and remain inside until early March. It is also impractical that Jews would be required to travel any long distances at that time of year.

The Romans celebrated a winter festival, Saturnalia, between December 17–24. December 25 observed *solis invicti nati,* to honor the birthday of the unconquered sun. This was the celebration of the winter solstice when daylight began to grow noticeably longer. It was a period of celebration, filled with gambling, drinking, and the giving of presents.

Christians did not celebrate the birth of Christ early in the history of the Church. Unable to banish the celebration of solis invicti nati, the Christian Church spiritualized it by initiating the celebration of the "Feast of the Nativity of the Sun of Righteousness"—in other words, Christ's birth. Church leaders hoped that using the same date for this religious holiday would bring more nonbelievers to the faith. They also incorporated some of the Saturnalia customs, particularly the giving of gifts. Using a pagan festival as the model for the celebration of Christ's birth has continued to be controversial and has, over the centuries, alienated many Christians from celebrating this religious holiday.

Charles Dickens

AFTER WILLIAM SHAKESPEARE, Charles Dickens (1812–1870) is the most popular and influential writer in English. His stories, popular in his own lifetime, continue to define Victorian England for millions of readers and have inspired countless films, musicals, plays, cartoons, TV shows, and lines of merchandise.

Dickens's father, a Navy clerk, was imprisoned for debt in the infamous Marshalsea Prison, forcing 12-year-old Charles to work ten-hour days in a factory blacking boots and pasting labels on bottles to help support his family. These experiences helped shape Dickens's outlook, and his commentary about poverty and social conditions found its way into his later fictions, including *Oliver Twist* (1839) and *Little Dorrit* (1855–1857).

With only four years of total schooling, Charles educated himself by reading and became a magazine reporter. The instant success of his first novel, *Pickwick Papers* (1836), launched his career as a novelist.

Magazines then published novels one chapter at a time. Many of Dickens's novels reflect that structure, building suspense at each chapter's end and juggling separate characters and storylines. Mechanized printing, steamship and rail travel, increased literacy, and lower postage costs helped Dickens reach large audiences. However, weak copyright laws cost Dickens income from unauthorized editions.

Today, Dickens's best-known work is *A Christmas Carol*, which tells how four ghosts visit miser Ebenezer Scrooge on Christmas Eve. This and other Christmas stories helped revive Christmas celebrations in England, which had declined since Puritan days. Other popular novels include *A Tale of Two Cities*, *Great Expectations*, and *David Copperfield*.

A workaholic who feared falling back into poverty, Dickens wore himself out giving dramatic readings of his works that often earned more than his novels themselves. He died of stroke in 1870, leaving an unfinished *Edwin Drood* and ten children.

POSTSCRIPT

- In spring 2007, a "Dickens World" theme park opened in Kent, England. It features Scrooge's haunted house, Fagin's Den, and a Victorian schoolroom.
- In 1841, huge crowds on New York docks called out, "Is Little Nell dead?" to the ship carrying the final installment of Dickens's *The Old Curiosity Shop*, which tells how Little Nell and her grandfather flee from an evil loan shark.

Henri Bergson (1859–1941)

F RENCH PHILOSOPHER HENRI BERGSON never received the widespread public recognition that his fellow 20th-century philosophers Jean Paul Sartre and Bertrand Russell did. Nonetheless, Bergson was a major thinker who was one of the first to try to integrate the discoveries of modern biology into a system that would help comprehend the nature of human consciousness.

Born to a Polish Jewish father and an Anglo-Irish mother, Bergson's life was strangely similar to that of his more well-known French compatriot, Sartre; Bergson was born in Paris, educated at the École Normale Supérieure, and taught for a number of years in French *lycées* (secondary schools). While teaching in various positions, Bergson published works espousing his philosophical theories. Like Sartre, he also became involved in politics, serving on several French diplomatic missions and acting as president of the Committee on International Cooperation of the League of Nations. Rather than try to become exempt from the anti-Semitic laws issued by the pro-Nazi French Vichy government, he officially registered as a Jew in 1940. He died of chronic bronchitis in 1941 before suffering the consequences of this declaration of solidarity with fellow Jews.

In his major philosophical works, *Matter and Memory* (1896) and *Creative Evolution* (1907), Bergson argued that intuition is in fact more powerful and profound than intellect. He modified Darwin's theory of evolution, claiming that "the creative urge," rather than natural selection, is the driving force behind evolution. Human intellect evolved as "an instrument of survival." But he believed intuitive insights transcend intellect and reason and "allow us to find philosophic truth."

Naturally, philosophical empiricists like Russell criticized Bergson for not illustrating how intuition could function without relying on intellect. But other philosophers, including William James (who befriended Bergson), saw value in his attempts to go beyond a mechanistic view of the natural world. Indeed, Sartre himself incorporated his fellow Parisian's idea of no-being into existentialism. And novelists Marcel Proust and John Dos Passos were influenced by Bergson's concept of nonlinear time. Thus, a thinker who is off the radar screen of most literate people nonetheless has had a marked influence on modern thought.

Music and Film: The Silent Era

THE PHRASE *SILENT FILMS* implies the absence of sound, but this was certainly not the case for much of the silent era (1885–1927), when movies were accompanied by live sound in one form or another.

The most common form of live sound was music. In the nickelodeon era (roughly 1906–1914), pianists performed along with the "flickers," sometimes accompanied by a trap-drummer. Also common were mechanical musical instruments, such as player pianos or other self-playing devices. Live musicians who performed in nickelodeons seldom had time to prepare before a new program of films was introduced. Some nickelodeons changed films daily, and every morning the musician had to accompany a new film not seen before. These musicians soon learned to anticipate love scenes, comic chases, rescues, and so forth, by learning filmic conventions. They became quite adept at improvisation.

Around 1911, palatial-style theaters overtook the nickelodeon as the primary venue for motion pictures. With the advent of movie palaces and the rise of the feature-length film—which occurred around the same time—musical accompaniment became more important to the film-going experience and also more sophisticated. A 1922 survey by *Motion Picture News* revealed that 30 percent of U.S. theaters had small orchestras, 46 percent used large organs, and only 25 percent made do with pianos.

The rarest and most expensive score was one originally composed for a specific film, for example, the way Dmitri Shostakovich composed all original music for *New Babylon* in 1929. More common were semi-original scores that combined famous musical selections with original pieces, such as Joseph Carl Breil's music for *The Birth of a Nation*, which used "The Ride of the Valkyries" to great effect, but also included love songs by Breil himself. D. W. Griffith always took a personal interest in the scores for his feature films, including those for *Intolerance* (also by Breil) and *Broken Blossoms* (by Louis F. Gottschalk).

Also used were scores consisting of stock melodies for orchestras, which were sent with the films by the distributor. However, most of the time, the distributor provided a list of musical cues. The cue sheet gave the approximate time and a short description for each scene in the film. The musician in charge (the orchestra conductor or a small-town pianist) would consult a source like Erno Rapee's *Motion Picture Moods*, which indexed musical themes for stock scenes like "action" that could easily be accessed and adapted to the film. An experienced silent-film musician was familiar with these set pieces and could combine them into an exciting live score to add vitality and expression to the viewing experience.

Italian Opera in an Age of Superstars

BY THE EARLY 1700s, Italian opera had spread to most of the cities and courts of Europe. While admission was open to the public, the nobility and royalty were entitled to the best seats, usually in "boxes" that were elevated and open on two sides—forward to the stage and back to sitting rooms where one could snack, play cards, and "socialize" (sometimes with women whose specialty was high-class "socializing") during the majority of the three- to four-hour show. Since boxes were rented out by the season, it was not uncommon for a nobleman to go to most performances of a production—upwards of 10 or 20—and spend most of his time conducting various sorts of business in his box, moving to face the stage only when his favorite singer(s) had a featured song or set piece (aria).

The hierarchy of audience placement was reflected in the casting. The "first man" (*primo uomo*) and "first woman" (*prima donna*) were contractually entitled to the most (and most showy) arias, during which they would strut to center stage and receive the admiring cheers of their patrons and fans. It was common for a singer to be asked (whether by authentically enthusiastic backers or by people planted in the audience for just such a purpose) to repeat an aria—twice, three times, or even more.

While the superstar women (the term *prima donna* has of course survived into modern English) were well compensated, the leading men were even more spectacularly paid—and almost all of them sang in the same range as the women (soprano, mezzo-soprano) because they had been prevented from reaching puberty by an "unfortunate accident" that had taken place in their youth. (The practice of castration was illegal and punishable by death or excommunication in Europe, but somehow many hundreds of sweet-voiced boys had convenient "accidents" of this sort.)

While this practice seems barbaric from a modern sensibility, a profession in singing (either for the stage or for the Catholic Church, which at this point was still forbidding women from singing in church services) was the most profitable career available for many younger sons of poor families. For a skilled and fortunate (and highly trained) singer, it could be substantially profitable indeed, both for the individual and for his extended family.

Superstar *castrati* (who tended to prefer the term *musico*, "musician") continued to rule the serious musical stage into the early 1800s. Mozart wrote a number of roles and some sacred music for specific *castrati*.

Artificial Photosynthesis

PHOTOSYNTHESIS IS THE PROCESS by which plants use the energy of
light to transform carbon dioxide into carbon-containing compounds
like sugars, which plants use to fuel their metabolism. What if we could
perform photosynthesis in a lab and make useful carbon-containing compounds, like fuel for our cars, with just the energy of sunlight? Scientists
with the U.S. Department of Energy are working on precisely this idea,
which is known as *artificial photosynthesis.*

The problem with copying photosynthesis in a test tube is that the
natural chemical components of the
plant cell do not work if you remove
them from their natural environment
within the leaves. Therefore, scientists must create alternate catalysts,
molecules that encourage a chemical
reaction to take place, to replicate the
natural catalysts in the plant cell.

The first steps of photosynthesis are called the *light reactions,* in which
plants capture light energy. First chlorophyll, the pigment that makes
plants look green, absorbs light, which "excites" electrons. The energy of
these electrons is used to split water (H_2O) into a waste gas, oxygen (O_2),
and protons (H+). The protons are then used to generate ATP, a short-
term energy storage molecule.

The process of splitting water to produce oxygen is difficult to carry out
in the laboratory. To replicate this step, scientists are working on creating artificial complexes with metals such as ruthenium to replicate the
natural complexes in leaves.

The last steps of photosynthesis are sometimes called *carbon fixation*
because in these stages, the carbon atoms from carbon dioxide are fixed
together as they are converted into glucose, a six-carbon sugar. The
bonds between the carbon molecules in the glucose now store the energy
produced during the light reactions in a more stable form.

So another key part of the process of replicating photosynthesis is
actually turning the carbon dioxide (CO_2) into carbon-containing
compounds that are useful fuels. There are already catalysts that can convert carbon dioxide into carbon monoxide, which can be used as a fuel,
but these catalysts are inefficient and slow. To make artificial photosynthesis practical, a better catalyst must be developed.

Jan van Eyck's
Giovanni Arnolfini and His Wife

THE PORTRAIT OF Giovanni Arnolfini and his wife, painted by Jan van Eyck in 1434, was completed at a time during which Bruges (Belgium) ranked as a premier commercial and cultural center in Northern Europe. The prosperity of Arnolfini, an Italian merchant residing in Bruges, is reflected in his fine clothing and the furnishings of his home. Besides serving as indicators of Arnolfini's wealth, the possessions cluttering the interior are said to carry hidden meanings. The dog, for

example, signifies fidelity; the whisk broom, wifely duties; the single lit candle in the chandelier, the presence of God.

Certain symbols reinforce the spiritual message that human sin is redeemed by Christ. The oranges on the windowsill, which recall the forbidden fruit from the Garden of Eden, refer to original sin, while scenes from Christ's life and crucifixion carved into the medallions of the mirror frame are reminders of salvation.

The extreme detailing demonstrates the virtuosity of van Eyck in using oil paint, a new medium at the time. Oil paint yielded richer color, more accurate simulation surface textures, and more natural illumination than older media, such as tempera or fresco, had ever permitted. The artist's technical brilliance extends to the reflection in the convex mirror, which reveals two men entering the room.

The resemblance of these men to witnesses at a ceremony, coupled with the phrase after the artist's signature written on the wall ("Jan van Eyck was here in 1434"), indicate to some that the panel was intended as a pictorial wedding document. Other clues include the position of Giovanni's hand, raised as if taking an oath, and his shoes on the floor, a symbol of holy ground, which would be associated with the sacrament of marriage.

However, the appearance that Giovanni's wife is pregnant would seem to contradict the notion of a wedding, although she is probably gathering her full skirt at her waist, thus giving only the *illusion* of pregnancy. This, coupled with the depiction of St. Margaret, the patron saint of childbirth carved on the bedpost, suggests the *hope* of child-bearing.

Defeat of the Turks at the Gates of Vienna

HAD IT NOT BEEN for the gallant defenders of 17th-century Vienna, modern-day Europe might be an entirely different place, known more for its mosques than its cathedrals.

In 1682, parts of Hungary fell under the domination of the Ottoman Empire, raising fears among European Christian leaders. Encouraged by this success, Grand Vizir Kara Mustafa, commander of the Ottoman army, turned his eyes to the Hapsburg capital of Vienna and its Catholic population.

By June, Mustafa had marched into Austria, prompting Holy Roman Emperor Leopold I and his court to flee. The Turks reached Vienna on July 14 and laid siege to the city.

Defense of Vienna fell to 16,000 Christian troops, including civilians with no military training. Mustafa's army numbered some 200,000.

Despite the glaring discrepancy in manpower, the Turks lacked sufficient heavy artillery to breach the city's walls. Whenever Mustafa's men achieved a breakthrough, the defenders threw up barricades and held the attackers at bay.

As the siege continued, the city's food and ammunition supplies began running low. But help was on the way. Fearful of the Ottoman threat to Christian Europe, Pope Innocentius XI appealed to European Catholic rulers to help the embattled Hapsburgs. In accordance with a mutual defense treaty signed with Leopold the preceding March, Polish King Jan Sobieski set out with 30,000 men to aid the beleaguered city.

Joining up with the Austrians and Germans in mid-September, Sobieski attacked the Ottoman army outside the city. Caught by surprise and with Polish heavy cavalry charging toward Mustafa's headquarters, the Turks broke and fled. The Ottomans limped back to Belgrade, where the Grand Vizir was strangled and beheaded as punishment for his unsuccessful venture.

Having turned back the Ottoman threat, Sobieski received acclaim as the savior not only of Vienna but of all Europe. His victory ensured that Christianity would remain the primary religion of Europe. Pope Innocentius XI attached so much importance to this event and his own supplementary role in it that his monument in St. Peter's Cathedral bears a relief rendering of Sobieski's victory.

Virginia Woolf

A MAJOR MODERNIST WRITER, Virginia Woolf (1882–1941) rejected the traditional realist novel in favor of an impressionist style. In many of her novels, the action is primarily internal—events are seen not from the outside but from within a character's stream of consciousness.

For example, in *Mrs. Dalloway* (1925), protagonist Clarissa Dalloway prepares for and then hosts a party for friends and colleagues of her husband Richard, a member of Parliament. Her thoughts during the day and evening that the novel takes place include memories of her childhood and adolescence, thoughts about the recently ended war (World War I), speculations about death, and trivial worries about the party.

Other important Modernist works include *To the Lighthouse* (1927), *The Waves* (1931), and *Between the Acts* (1941). Woolf was an exponent of modern fiction in her essays as well. In "Mr. Bennett and Mrs. Brown" (1924) she attacks the realism of novelist Arnold Bennett, calling for a more experimental and internal approach to characterization.

Woolf has also been hailed as an iconic feminist writer. In most of her work, gender roles are explicitly or implicitly examined; in *Orlando* (1928), for instance, the hero encompasses both genders. In her justly famous essay "A Room of One's Own" (1929), Woolf insists on the fundamental need for the resources and independence necessary for women to realize their creative potential.

Woolf grew up in a literary family. Her father, Leslie Stephen (1832–1904), was a highly regarded man of letters, and both Woolf and her sister, Vanessa, though not sent to University as were their brothers, developed their literary and artistic interests in a household where books were read and ideas discussed. After the deaths of their parents, the young women, together with their brothers, became the center of the Bloomsbury Group, who gathered to discuss the arts. Group members included essayist and biographer Lytton Strachey; art critic Clive Bell, who married Vanessa, herself an artist; and former civil servant Leonard Woolf, who married Virginia in 1912.

As Virginia's husband, Leonard conscientiously attempted to provide the kind of atmosphere that would enable his wife to write. Plagued by recurrent bouts of mental illness, Woolf nevertheless left an impressive body of work—essays, literary criticism, and novels, as well as letters, diaries, and short stories. She committed suicide by drowning herself in 1941.

Linus Pauling (1901–1994)

LINUS PAULING IS REMEMBERED both as an influential chemist and a humanitarian. He holds the honor of being the only person to ever win two unshared Nobel prizes: the 1954 Nobel Prize in Chemistry and the 1962 Nobel Peace Prize.

Pauling was born in Portland, Oregon, in 1901. He lost his father at age nine, and his widowed mother struggled to raise her three children. At age 11, Pauling, a voracious reader, became avidly interested in insects and started collecting butterflies and beetles. By age 13, he had found his life-long love: chemistry.

Pauling worked his way through school, earning a bachelor's degree in chemical engineering from Oregon State College in 1922 and a Ph.D. in chemistry from the California Institute of Technology in 1925. His innovation was in applying the principles of physics to chemistry, specifically the application of quantum mechanics to chemical problems. He published prolifically in a variety of fields, using X-ray diffraction to examine the structure of molecules and studying the properties of hemoglobin in hereditary anemia. Pauling won the 1954 Nobel Prize in Chemistry for his research into the nature of the chemical bond.

Already renowned for his expertise in chemistry, Pauling took up the cause of informing the public about the dangers inherent in producing and testing nuclear weapons. When the first nuclear bombs were produced in the 1940s, most Americans did not realize that there were possible long-term effects from exposure to radiation. Pauling was aware of the hazards, and he was committed to ending the open-air testing of nuclear weapons. In the late 1950s, he started a petition warning the public about the dangers involved in testing nuclear weapons. The petition, signed by 11,000 scientists worldwide, encouraged politicians to recognize the need for a treaty limiting bomb testing. For this work, Pauling was awarded the 1962 Nobel Peace Prize.

One bump in the road of Pauling's career came from the fallout of his passionate belief in the healing qualities of large doses of vitamin C. In 1970, he published a book entitled *Vitamin C and the Common Cold*, followed by a book about vitamin C and cancer a year later. Scientific research did not back up his claims, which cost him both reputation and money. However, he went on to promote good nutrition and published a book in 1986 called *How to Live Longer and Feel Better*.

The Origins of Native Americans

AMERICANS OF EUROPEAN descent generally think of Native Americans as the "original" inhabitants of the Americas, but of course they are also immigrants, albeit of much greater antiquity.

Where they emigrated from, and when, has been a topic of vigorous debate among anthropologists, geneticists, and linguists. Most agree that the majority of Native American populations—here when the Europeans arrived—came across the Bering Strait from Eurasia toward the end of the last Ice Age (about 12,000 years ago). Sea levels were lower, and Siberia and Alaska were connected by a land bridge. This theory is supported by genetic similarities between Asian populations and Native American populations. It is also supported by the discovery of stone tools in Clovis, New Mexico, which are estimated to be about 11,500 years old.

However, the Bering Strait theory rests partly on failing to find archeological evidence of older Native American inhabitants. Thus, every discovery of potential older relics presents a challenge. For example, human remains and tools found in southern Chile are now believed to be at least 13,500 years old. These tools are different from the ones at Clovis, suggesting a different origin for the population. It is believed that these people must have come by sea along the Pacific coast from Southeast Asia or even the South Pacific. There are also remains in Brazil and the southeastern United States that may date back as far as 50,000 years ago.

In addition to genetic relationships and archeological evidence, there is also information from Native American languages. Some linguists categorize the many indigenous languages into three groups—Eskimo-Aleut in the far north, Na-Dene in most of Canada and also the American Southwest, and "Amerind" to encompass all the rest. Such a grouping supports a theory of three successive waves of immigration. Other linguists have suggested that the extreme diversity of New World languages could not possibly have arisen in only 12,000 years and propose earlier and more numerous migrations from Asia and also Europe and the South Pacific.

In short, the linguistic, DNA, and archeological evidence do not always agree in assigning dates, relationships, and origins.

One thing on which nearly everyone agrees is that the present Native American population is only a tiny remnant of a much larger population, most of which died out after the Europeans arrived. Most were victims of new diseases brought by the Europeans, as well as warfare and social disruption.

G. F. Handel and the English Oratorio

GEORG FRIDERIC HANDEL (1685–1759) created a successful career in England in the early 1700s by defining himself as a specialist in Italian music, particularly opera. English upper-class audiences were swept up in the fashion for things Italian, and Handel—who had spent a decade perfecting his training in Italian musical circles—exploited that fashion very effectively. But when Italian opera fell out of favor in the 1730s, Handel risked losing his livelihood; instead, he effectively reinvented himself, pioneering a new kind of musical work: the English oratorio.

Handel's English oratorios draw on several musical traditions that Handel cannily understood to be appealing to his wealthy patrons. They all have sacred topics, most of them Old Testament stories. Like opera, they are narrative and dramatic, but they are not designed to be fully staged: Singers playing the individual parts just stand on a stage without scenery or physical action. In the tradition of Italian opera, solo sections alternate with elaborate and grand choruses derived primarily from the self-consciously nationalistic English Anthem, along with some elements from Handel's early training as a Lutheran organist.

While there is controversy about whether Handel's early oratorios were as "popular" as was later claimed—Handel probably initially relied on the same small elite audience as he had during his days as an opera composer—certainly their success grew gradually through the middle decades of the 1700s. English audiences were happy to forget that Handel had been the figurehead for the Italian theatrical tradition that was now dismissed as decadent and were very receptive to the generalized message of morally upstanding biblical stories told through grand and intense musical gestures.

Handel's oratorios were the first musical works in history to be kept in regular performing repertory for more than a generation after their composer's death. Indeed, some (for example, *Messiah*) are performed consistently even to the present day.

Handel's *Messiah* is probably the best known of his oratorios, though it is atypical in a couple of ways. First, it draws from the New rather than the Old Testament. Second, it is not clearly narrative, consisting of a series of fairly disconnected images making up three large sections ("The Birth," "The Passion," "The Aftermath"). Many contemporary performances only present the first part of the oratorio, which tells the Christmas story, though they generally also include the final chorus of the second part, the famous "Hallelujah Chorus." The third part, with texts primarily from Corinthians, is seldom performed as a whole.

Game Theory

IMAGINE THAT YOU and a friend have just been arrested. The police have enough evidence to convict each of you for assault with intent to rob. But they really want to charge you with armed robbery. To make that tougher charge stick, they need one of you to testify against the other.

The police lead you to separate rooms for interrogation and offer you a deal. If you testify against your friend, you'll get off scot-free as long as she doesn't testify against you. Your poor friend, however, will go to jail for five years for armed robbery. If she testifies against you, too, you'll both go to jail, but the term will be lessened for your cooperation to just three years each.

You could certainly refuse to testify against your friend. But, in that case, if she betrays you, you'll be in the slammer for five years yourself. If she stays loyal and also refuses to testify, you'll each get just one year of prison time for the lesser charge of assault with intent to rob.

So what do you do?

If what you care about most is minimizing your own prison time, you'll rat out your friend. If she betrays you, too, you'll get three years for squealing instead of five. Even if your friend stands firm, squealing will set you free, while keeping mum will leave you rotting in jail for a year.

Of course, your friend is facing the same decision, so the selfishly rational thing for her to do is to testify as well. But that leads to an ironic result. If you both squeal, you'll each end up in jail for three years. You'd both be better off if you stayed loyal and only had to serve a year in prison. Yet your personal self-interest drives you away from this better outcome.

This is the classical conundrum of the "Prisoner's Dilemma." It is the canonical paradox of an entire branch of mathematics, called *game theory*. Game theory is the science of mathematically deducing the best strategy when actions affect one another.

Game theory has now shed light on a huge range of disciplines, from economics to evolutionary biology to political science to neuroscience to quantum physics.

POSTSCRIPT

▨ John Nash won the 1994 Nobel Prize for his foundational work in game theory during the 1950s. The category for his prize was economics. The book and movie *A Beautiful Mind* depict Nash's struggle with schizophrenia.

Sandro Botticelli

HIS PATRONS INCLUDED several Medicis and one pope, and today crowds flock to see his paintings at the Uffizi. Yet Sandro Botticelli's talents weren't always so highly valued. The creator of *The Birth of Venus* (c. 1485) fell out of fashion in the early 16th century, his dreamy heroines and decorative style appearing out-of-date alongside Michelangelo's robust nudes and Leonardo da Vinci's *chiaroscuro*. For the next few hundred years, Botticelli's reputation languished in obscurity.

The Birth of Venus

During the first decade of his career, Botticelli primarily made portraits and religious works. His *Adoration of the Magi* (c. 1475)—a painting that features a self-portrait of Botticelli— made the artist famous. Around the time he painted this work, Botticelli began his long-standing association with the Medici dynasty, which was then at the peak of its power.

Botticelli is best known for *Primavera* and *The Birth of Venus*. The paintings' mythological subject matter reflects two related Renaissance concerns: the reawakened interest in classical literature and sculpture and the pursuit of the ideal human form.

Primavera (c. 1482) also embodies the principles of Neo-Platonism, a philosophy fashionable among the Medici circle that was based on the teachings of Plato and sought to merge classical and Christian ideals. *Primavera* was painted for a minor Medici, Lorenzo di Pierfrancesco, probably on the occasion of his marriage. The painting seems to illustrate the renunciation of lust, through the figures of Zephyr, Cupid, and the Three Graces.

The goddess of love is at the center of *Primavera* and is also the focus of *The Birth of Venus*, which actually depicts not Venus's birth but her arrival on the island of Cythera. Her pose, the *Venus pudica* ("modest Venus"), comes from famous ancient sculptures like the Venus de Milo.

Most of Botticelli's works were unseen for several centuries, locked away in Tuscan houses or churches—one of the reasons Botticelli was obscure for so long. This changed in the early 19th century, when these and other paintings could finally be seen by the public. The revival of Botticelli's reputation began shortly thereafter in England, where the artist attracted the interest of the Pre-Raphaelites and became the focus of a literary cult.

Abraham Lincoln

IMAGES OF ABRAHAM LINCOLN (1809–1865) are everywhere in
America. He's on both the penny and the five dollar bill. He's one of
the majestic heads on Mount Rushmore. His statue graces the Lincoln
Memorial on the mall in our nation's capital. A state capital is named for
him along with counties in 19 states.

Born in a Kentucky log cabin on February 12, 1809, Lincoln was
an average man who grew up on a small farm and was basically self-
educated. He worked as a store clerk, postmaster, surveyor, and volunteer
militiaman. He was also a lawyer of some repute in central Illinois, and
this catapulted him into a political career as a Whig party member of the
Illinois legislature from 1834 to 1841, then as a representative in Congress
for the 1847 to 1849 term.

As the North and South began to split over the slavery issue, Lincoln
was thrust into the national spotlight when, as a Republican candidate
for U.S. senator, he participated in a series of debates with Democratic
incumbent Stephen A. Douglas in 1858. Although he lost that election,
Lincoln's stand against the spread of slavery helped him earn the Republican candidacy for president in 1860.

With only 40 percent of the national vote, Lincoln defeated a divided
Democratic Party and was inaugurated as president on March 4, 1861.
A month later, the Civil War began when South Carolina troops fired on
Fort Sumter. Throughout the bloody four-year conflict, Lincoln never
wavered in his goal of reuniting the nation. By 1863, he had made the
abolition of slavery a war issue, culminating in the Thirteenth Amend-
ment to the Constitution, which outlawed slavery.

Two years later, Lincoln became the first president to be assassinated. On
the evening of April 14, 1865, John Wilkes Booth, a Southern-born actor,
shot the president in Washington's Ford's Theatre. Lincoln died the next
morning.

Lincoln's legacy includes not only his politics but also his homespun
humor and his powerful speeches, such as the Gettysburg Address and
his Second Inaugural Address. He is widely considered to be one of the
country's greatest presidents.

POSTSCRIPT

▦ Lincoln was the first president to wear a beard, thanks to an 11-year-old girl who
wrote him a letter and suggested he would look better with one.

The Divine Comedy

WRITTEN IN TUSCAN dialect by the Florentine poet Dante Alighieri
(1265–1321) between 1308 and 1321, this Christian epic, also
called a spiritual autobiography, places the poet himself as a character in
a journey through the Inferno, Purgatory, and eventually Paradise. There
are 33 cantos in each of the three sections of the poem, in addition to the
first canto, which serves as a prologue to the entire work.

Dante Alighieri

In the first canto, Dante the Pilgrim begins by telling
readers that "Midway on our life's journey, I found
myself/In dark woods, the right road lost." Here, he
meets the poet Virgil, whom Dante reveres as the greatest
of poets. Virgil explains that he will guide Dante the Pilgrim on a journey that will teach him the spiritual truths
he has lost sight of. Virgil will guide Dante through the
Inferno and Purgatory; his guide through Paradise will
be Beatrice, the heavenly representation of a woman
whom Dante the poet once loved.

God's love manifested by his gift of free will is a central
theme throughout the epic, which is crowded with characters from the
mythic and historical past as well as with Dante's contemporaries. Dante
the Pilgrim, mentored by Virgil, must learn to respond correctly to the
sinners he encounters on his journey. The sinners, possessing free will,
have chosen to sin and have hence chosen their punishments, which,
graphically described in the poem, are appropriate for their sins.

Dante's relationship with Virgil increases in complexity as the epic
progresses, with Virgil becoming an affectionate father figure who takes
pride in what his pupil has learned. Near the end of Purgatory, when he
takes his leave, Virgil reminds Dante that "your will is free, erect, and
whole—to act/against that will would be to err: therefore/I crown and
miter you over yourself." Dante is now fit for his journey through Paradise, where Beatrice shows him a world of transcendent beauty and light,
and where he apprehends the unity of all creation.

The poem is composed in *tersa rima*, in which lines of 11 syllables rhyme
aba bcb cdc, and so on. The three parts of the rhyme scheme echo the three
major parts of the poem, with these divisions emphasizing the Christian
Trinity. In addition, Dante's journey, which begins on Good Friday, takes
place during the three days in spring associated with Easter. On all levels,
the structure of the poem supports the grandeur of its themes.

Jenny Lind (1820–1887)

S WEDISH-BORN SOPRANO Jenny Lind, lovingly referred to as the "Swedish Nightingale," was praised in Europe long before her debut in America. In 1850, she toured cities across the United States, garnering praise for her voice and philanthropic work.

Lind was born in Stockholm and began singing at a young age. Her beautiful voice and virtuous character gained her great respect and popularity throughout Europe as she performed in major capitals. When Lind toured in Denmark, writer Hans Christian Andersen fell in love with her. Lind did not share the feelings; however, the two remained friends. It is thought that Lind inspired "The Snow Queen" and "The Emperor's Nightingale," two of Andersen's fairy tales.

P. T. Barnum, an American showman and entrepreneur, first heard of Lind's growing popularity during a European trip. Though he had never heard her sing, he knew she would be a huge success on a concert tour in America. He also expected he could benefit financially from her operatic skills and lovely personality.

Barnum approached Lind and offered to promote a concert tour in America. After some negotiations, she agreed. Barnum immediately began a publicity campaign to introduce Lind to America. He wrote press releases and distributed pamphlets with photos of the young star. Barnum created such interest for the singing sensation that more than 40,000 people were waiting to see her as her ship arrived in New York harbor.

Lind spent seven months touring the United States. Barnum's marketing had proven a smashing success, and crowds were delighted to see the new celebrity. In addition to promoting Lind, Barnum arranged for her to endorse products ranging from clothing and personal items to furniture.

Enthusiastic crowds met her everywhere. Lind performed popular songs as well as operatic selections. She closed her concerts with the tear-rending "Home Sweet Home." Barnum's promotion of the singer proved a sound investment—he made a fortune through her tour.

While Lind was in America she married a German musician she had known for several years. They returned to Europe and lived in England for the rest of her life.

The Parthenon

THE MOST FAMOUS surviving building from Greek antiquity, the Parthenon was built in Athens on top of a hill called the Acropolis. It replaced an earlier temple destroyed by the Persians and honored Athena, the patron goddess of Athens who was called *parthenos* (virgin). Work on the building by the architects Iktinos and Kallikrates ran 447–438 B.C., although Pheidias and his team continued to work on sculptures until 432 B.C.

In classical Greek architecture, the Parthenon is a good example of the Doric "order" (style of temple building) with Ionic elements. The columns' base was used as a unit of measurement to calculate proportions of the whole structure. The architects incorporated subtle effects by slightly bending and arcing lines of pillars and walls to create symmetry and harmony.

Panels of sculptures under the roofline, called *metopes,* display events from Athena's life as well as from Greek history. The west metopes show an invasion of Athens by Amazons, which some scholars see as a reference to the 480 B.C. Persian invasion. An interior frieze shows the Panathenaic procession, the main religious festival in honor of Athena. This was revolutionary because no previous frieze in any Greek temple had portrayed mortals rather than gods or heroes.

The Parthenon's construction provoked debate and criticism inside and outside of Athens. Athens had formed the Delian League—an alliance with other Greek city-states—against the Persians. But Athens treated the joint defense funds contributed by everyone as though they were a tribute to Athens, to be spent as Athenian leaders chose, including building the Parthenon.

When the Turks captured the area in 1456, they turned the Parthenon into a mosque, though without any structural changes other than a minaret. The main damage we see today occurred in 1687, when the Turks used it as a powder magazine. Attacking Venetians hit it with a cannonball, blowing off the roof. Further damage occurred in 1806, when the British seventh Earl of Elgin, Thomas Bruce, gained permission from the Ottoman government to remove the famed "Elgin Marbles." The Greek government is now trying to get Britain to return the statues.

The Mozart Family

WHEN MUSIC WAS CONSIDERED a trade and an artisan profession—before the notion of "genius" composers took hold—there were a number of successful musical families in Europe. Children were trained in the family trade from an early age, and marriages were often based on the professional prospects of the husband- or bride-to-be, so as to keep the family business flourishing. At the tail end of this "family business" model was perhaps the most famous European musical family: the Mozarts.

Leopold (1719–1787) was a renowned court violinist and the author of the most respected violin method book of his day. His children, Maria Anna (known as "Nännerl," 1751–1829) and Wolfgang Amadeus (1757–1791), were outstanding musical child prodigies. It is hard to know whether the Mozart children's skills were innate or carefully fostered through systematic training by their father, who emerges from his correspondence as somewhat of a hard-nosed taskmaster.

Certainly, in an age when child prodigies were all the rage, Leopold ably marketed his children to the nobility of Europe, taking them—especially the young Wolfgang—on extended concert tours throughout the continent to display their amazing talent (and, perhaps by extension, his own remarkable teaching abilities). It was during one of these tours in 1778 that the children's mother, Anna Maria, died, and this was the beginning of the disintegration of the family group.

Nännerl, whom Leopold had called "one of the most skillful pianists in Europe" when she was in her teens, had mostly remained with her mother in their hometown of Salzburg once she reached a marriageable age in the late 1760s, as was expected of well-bred women of the time. While Wolfgang encouraged her to continue composing even after she retired from touring, none of her compositions survive, and it is unclear whether she performed in public again after her marriage to a minor nobleman in 1784. It is known that after her husband died, she taught piano lessons.

Wolfgang, while maintaining a rather tense relationship with his father after his choice to leave a reliable position as a court musician in Salzburg and freelance in Vienna, went on to become a respected professional in his brief adult life. While he did have considerable successes, he died just as the notion of musical "genius" was becoming fashionable and thus was able to benefit from that idea only posthumously.

Solar Flares

SOLAR FLARES ARE some of the most spectacular events on the sun's surface. These bursts of radiation are recorded across the entire electromagnetic spectrum, from long-wave radio waves to short-wave X-rays and gamma rays. Not to be confused with solar prominences—jets and loops of ionized gases anchored to the sun's photosphere—solar flares occur in the chromosphere and outermost corona and are often linked with sunspots, the dark, cooler, intensely magnetic fields that pockmark the sun's surface.

A flare's violent explosion occurs when energy stored in a twisted magnetic field suddenly releases. This event is often compared to the buildup and release along Earth's tectonic faults that create an earthquake. Flares can occur in minutes to tens of minutes, resulting in super-heated plasma and causing electrons, protons, and heavier ions to travel at near-light speeds into space. Their frequency usually increases as the sun reaches the solar maximum in its 11-year sunspot cycle.

After nearly four decades of continually improving solar satellite data, scientists now classify flares based on X-ray brightness in the wavelengths between 1 to 8 Angstroms: the X-class flares (major events that can create long-term radiation storms); M-class (medium-size flares that occasionally produce minor radiation storms); and C-class flares (small flares that cause few problems on Earth).

Around 60 percent of M-class and stronger solar flares are associated with coronal mass ejections (CMEs), streams of highly energetic particles that originate from groups of sunspots associated with frequent flares (called *active regions*) that can cause major geomagnetic storms. If such a storm is directed at Earth, it can interact with our planet's magnetic field, producing brilliant auroras at the south and north poles. But these fast-moving, energetic particles can also influence Earth's space weather; the larger storms can cause short-wave radio blackouts, errors in navigational systems, damage to low-orbiting satellites, and problems for unshielded astronauts in the Shuttle or International Space Station.

The largest solar flare so far observed occurred on November 4, 2003, in the active region called 486—with estimates putting it at X-28 or even up to X-45. The resulting CME hurtled into space at a speed of roughly 7.2 million kilometers per hour. Although it did no damage—it was not directed toward Earth—the flare was probably not the largest in Earth's history: Scientists recently discovered evidence of an even larger "super-flare" that occurred nearly 150 years ago.

Dutch Still Lifes

DURING THE GOLDEN AGE of Dutch painting in the 17th century, Protestant authorities suppressed the use of traditional biblical subjects or saints' lives in art, considering them unsuitable for churches. Denied the opportunity to paint traditional religious themes, Dutch artists introduced moralizing messages into their realistic depictions of everyday life in Holland, including arrangements of food, flowers, tableware, and other possessions found in middle-class households. Commonly referred to as *vanitas* (from "vanity"), such still life paintings featured objects that referred to the fleeting nature of time, the fragility of perishable objects, and the inevitability of death.

An Allegory of the Vanities of Human Life *by Harmen Steenwyck*

The concept of human mortality was often driven home by the *momento mori* ("reminder of death")—an image of human remains, usually skulls and bones. These grim motifs established the foundation for *vanitas* painting when first introduced in the 16th century on the reverse side of panels showing donors, saints, or holy figures. Examples of this type, produced by painters such as the Flemish master Rogier van der Weyden, precede the Reformation. Even earlier, representations of St. Jerome typically featured the withered hermit with a skull, to evoke humility.

By the mid-17th century, *vanitas* imagery flourished in the hands of Dutch painters such as David Bailly and his pupil Harmen Steenwyck. Their still lifes included emblems of transience such as soap bubbles, pipes, half-empty glasses, skulls, candles or lamps, clocks, and butterflies. Contemporaries Pieter Claesz and Willem Claesz Heda used tables bedecked with meals, some half-eaten or interrupted, as allusions to mortality and transience.

Other *vanitas* specialists featured trophies of war (armor and weapons) to signal the futility of earthly glory. A final subgenre, *pronk* ("fancy") still lifes, presented opulent displays of exquisite luxury goods and delectable foods to both tantalize viewers and serve as reminders that the pleasures of life are ultimately fleeting and illusory.

The Glorious Revolution

JAMES II BECAME king of England in 1685 upon the death of his brother, Charles II. In the 1670s, James had converted to Catholicism, but when he became king he promised to support the political and religious status quo. However, James appointed Catholics to governmental positions, and political battles between the Catholics and Protestants in Parliament began.

James dismissed Parliament in 1685 and punished judges and officials who resisted. He even threw some Anglican bishops into the Tower of London. In 1687, James ordered Anglican clergy to read a declaration from the pulpit aimed at complete equality of religions. His increasingly alienated subjects feared that England would become Catholic.

In 1688, James's second wife, a Catholic, gave birth to a son, who became heir to the throne. Various plots emerged to overthrow James. One idea devised by government officials favored placing Mary, James's Protestant daughter by his first wife, on the throne. Mary was wed to a Dutch landholder and governmental official, William of Orange.

William planned an invasion of England and amassed the needed funds and troops. He issued a declaration indicating that the only purpose of the invasion was to maintain the Protestant religion in England, assure a free Parliament, and investigate the legitimacy of the new son as heir to the throne. William's forces landed and advanced toward London. James had sent his wife and infant son to France as soon as he learned of the impending invasion. After William's troops landed on English soil, James attempted to flee but was captured by fishermen in Faversham, England.

A provisional government was formed, and William was asked to restore order. James was asked to return to London to reach an agreement with his son-in-law. However, when it became clear that William had no interest in compromise, James took protection from sympathetic guards who allowed him to slip quietly from England into France to join his family.

William took over the provisional government, and Parliament offered the throne to him and Mary to share jointly. Restrictions were placed on the monarchy, and William and Mary ascended to the throne of England.

The agreement by which the throne was offered to William and Mary is called the Bill of Rights, but the rights are Parliament's not the individual's (as in the United States' Bill of Rights). This is historically important because it established the supremacy of Parliament over royal authority. Once and for all, England became a constitutional monarchy.

Homer's *Iliad* and *Odyssey*

THE *ILIAD* AND *ODYSSEY* were recognized by ancient Greeks themselves (and later the Romans) as their masterworks, and they continue to inspire writers and artists today. These epic poems were the encyclopedia of educated Greeks for hundreds of years and the foundation of much of Western literature. Both poems are written in dactylic hexameter, a method of phrasing commonly used by early Greek poets who sang in the oral tradition.

Scholars have long debated whether one author named "Homer" actually wrote both of these poems. He would not be considered an "author" per se but an oral singer. Such bards memorized and sang traditional texts, which they shaped and transmitted but didn't invent. Homer lived in about 700 B.C., and the poems were written down hundreds of years later. In modern times, the Trojan War itself was thought to be mythical until Troy was excavated in 1888, lending historical credence to the poems.

The war is sparked when Helen, wife of Menelaus, is "given" to the Trojan Paris by Aphrodite, goddess of love, as a reward for finding her the fairest among three goddesses. Menelaus and his brother, Agamemnon, gather Greek war leaders to attack Troy. The Olympian gods and goddesses take sides in the ten-year-long siege and even fight each other.

The *Iliad* focuses on one episode within the war—the "wrath of Achilles"—but ranges backward and forward over most of the war's events. Achilles, the mightiest Greek warrior, is semidivine and invulnerable everywhere except his heel. His "wrath" begins when Agamemnon seizes his treasures, most notably a beloved slave-girl. Achilles stops fighting until the Greeks realize his value, leaving the way open for Hector, the greatest Trojan warrior and Paris's brother, to slaughter the Greeks and almost burn their ships. When Hector kills Achilles' companion, Patroclus, the enraged Achilles finally fights, brutally killing Hector and desecrating his body. But the war only ends when wily Odysseus tricks the Trojans into bringing a wooden horse full of Greek warriors into Troy.

The *Odyssey* tells of Odysseus's wanderings after Troy's fall, as he struggles to get back to his kingdom, Ithaca; his wife, Penelope; and his son, Telemachus. Because the sea-god Poseidon is his enemy, Odysseus faces many setbacks and challenges. At home, Penelope must deal with a horde of suitors who want to take control of Ithaca. She puts them off with various tricks while Telemachus grows to manhood, aided by the goddess Athena. When Odysseus finally returns, he wreaks terrible vengeance and reunites with Penelope.

Rachel Carson (1907–1964)

Rachel Carson was born in 1907 on a small farm to ordinary parents. From a young age, she spent hours in the nearby ponds, forests, and fields. When she went back home, she wrote about them. After college at Chatham University in Pittsburgh, Carson received a master's degree in zoology in 1932. She eventually found her way to the

U.S. Bureau of Fisheries, writing radio copy for a weekly broadcast called "Romance Under the Waters." It turned out that Carson had a knack for writing about the natural world.

The *Atlantic Monthly* accepted her essay "Undersea" in 1937, at a time when the world's oceans were barely explored, let alone understood. Carson then worked her way up the Bureau of Fisheries, eventually supervising a small writing staff as chief editor of publications.

Her next break came with her first book, *The Sea Around Us*, a history of the ocean. The *New Yorker* serialized nine chapters, and the book remained on the *New York Times* best-seller list for 86 weeks. Following this success, Carson wrote *The Edge of the Sea*, published in 1953.

Carson became involved with environmental groups, such as The Nature Conservancy, and began researching the damage caused by synthetic pesticides. After four years of research and writing, *Silent Spring* was published in 1962. In this landmark book, Carson argues that pesticides greatly harm the environment and rarely limit their powers to the original pest. She introduced the concept of bioaccumulation, where a particular organism may receive only a tiny amount of pesticide, but the problem is compounded as you move up the food chain. A fish will eat lots of plankton and accumulate all of their pesticide. A bird will come along and eat the fish. And so on.

The book was widely criticized by chemical companies and lobbyists but received widespread political, scientific, and public praise. Carson was battling cancer as the book neared publication, though she managed to attend some speaking engagements and made policy recommendations to a Senate science committee. She also received a number of awards from environmental groups.

Carson died in 1964 at the age of 56.

What Is Hypnosis?

HYPNOSIS IS A TRANCELIKE state of consciousness, typically induced by a licensed hypnotherapist and used to help people improve control of their behavior, emotions, or well-being. A hypnotized person is more focused, more open to suggestion, and less critical or skeptical. A hypnotherapist may plant ideas in the patient's mind (e.g., stop smoking) but cannot induce him or her to violate their personal sense of right and wrong (e.g., commit murder).

There is considerable debate about how hypnosis works but no universally accepted explanation. Apparently, it affects the way that the brain communicates with the body through nerve impulses, hormones, and body chemicals. Some say that the hypnotic state is a form of half-sleep, but tests of blood pressure, reflexes, and physiochemistry of hypnotized subjects suggest that the state resembles wakefulness. Modern brain-imaging techniques promise to bring science closer to an explanation.

Some psychologists deny that the hypnotic state exists, stating that the patient and hypnotherapist create it according to their expectations of what the experience should be. Experiments have shown that communicating a different set of expectations to the same patient before hypnosis will lead to dramatically different results, suggesting that the hypnosis is not really an altered state of consciousness.

Hypnosis is not a cure-all, but it can help patients as part of a broader program of treatment. It is typically used to reduce fear, stress, and anxiety stemming from phobias, pain, migraine headaches, or even asthma. It can also alter negative behavior, causing patients to stop overeating or bedwetting, for example.

A patient must be open to hypnosis or the technique will not work. Commonly, the hypnotherapist makes the patient comfortable, then speaks in a gentle tone of voice about pleasant, restful things to take the patient from normal awareness to complete relaxation. From there, the patient is led to a hypnotized state. At this point, the therapist may paint vivid mental pictures of the patient in the desired condition (e.g., how healthy an overweight person will be once their diet succeeds). It is also possible to make negative suggestions so a patient, for example, associates tobacco with body odor and a repulsive appearance. Once the patient returns to a normal state of awareness, he or she feels more in control and better able to deal with their problems. Unless they enter a deep trance, patients will remember everything that was said to them under hypnosis.

Franz Josef Haydn in London

WHILE SERVING AS composer-in-residence for a noble family was a very desirable position for an 18th-century musician, it could also be precarious. This is what Austrian composer Franz Josef Haydn (1732–1809) found out when his long-time patron, Count Nicolaus Esterhazy, died in 1790. Nicolaus's son, Anton, was less dedicated to music than his father had been. While he did not dismiss Haydn out of hand, it was clear that at the not-so-tender age of 58, Haydn was facing the possibility of unemployment.

Fortunately for Haydn, Nicolaus had been generous in allowing him to publish his music and otherwise circulate it in European musical circles. (Other patrons were not so willing to share their private musicians' skills.) The reputation Haydn had gained spurred a London concert promoter, Johann Peter Salomon, to approach the composer about the possibility of a visit to England coupled with a number of lucrative commission and publishing opportunities.

Haydn left Vienna and visited London from 1790 to 1792 and again from 1794 to 1795. He was extraordinarily impressed with the musical resources and active concert tradition of that city. Haydn was also deeply impressed with the large choral works of Handel—particularly his oratorios—which were a staple of musical activity in late-18th-century London. In fact, Haydn drew directly from his London experience when he composed his powerful oratorios *The Creation* (1798)— widely considered to be his finest work—and *The Seasons* (1801). These lovingly composed oratorios, which addressed weighty religious and existential topics, contributed to the perception of Haydn as a compositional genius and allowed him to end his years basking in public glory.

Most striking for Haydn was the size and scope of English orchestras, which were significantly larger than those for which he had been accustomed to writing. They included accomplished players of a number of instruments (winds, brass, percussion) that were not commonly featured in Viennese orchestras of the day. Accordingly, the music that Haydn composed on commission for these English ensembles (the so-called "London Symphonies" numbers 93 to 98) make use of a wider and more subtle spectrum of timbre than Haydn's earlier works.

While broadening his sound palette, Haydn continued to inject his music with the humor that makes it so accessible to this day. For example, the second movement of his 94th symphony begins quietly and softly. But when the opening idea is repeated, it is interrupted by a loud and jarring chord—garnering this work its nickname: the "Surprise" symphony.

Statistics

STATISTICS IS THE SCIENCE of turning numbers into stories. Let's suppose, for example, that you want to know if women will be healthier if they take replacement hormones after menopause. You take a whole bunch of women, some of whom take hormone replacement therapy and some of whom don't. Then you watch their health over a number of years, keeping track of who gets cancer or heart disease or osteoporosis.

At the end of your study period, you've got a whole bunch of numbers, and somehow you need to turn that mess of numbers into a story that explains the effects of hormone replacement therapy. Without a knowledge of statistics, you're going to have a hard time.

But turning numbers into stories—true stories—is pretty tricky. Scientists who studied hormone replacement therapy noticed that the women who took the hormones had lower rates of heart disease. Many doctors assumed this meant that the hormones themselves protected the heart. But later analyses showed that the women who took hormones had better diets and exercised more, and thus their hearts were healthier.

This is perhaps the most common mistake made in statistics. The correlation between two things—in this case, hormone replacement therapy and lower rates of heart disease—doesn't mean that one causes the other. They may both be caused by something else entirely. Women who were more careful about their health tended to take hormone replacement therapy and to have better diets and exercise habits.

The way to avoid such mistakes is through careful statistical analysis. Because it is so easy to make false statistical arguments, Benjamin Disraeli once said, "There are three types of lies—lies, damn lies, and statistics." A bit less pessimistically, Harvard President Lawrence Lowell said that statistics, "like veal pies, are good if you know the person that made them and are sure of the ingredients." But perhaps it is American statesman Henry Clay who summed it up best: "Statistics are no substitute for judgment."

POSTSCRIPT

■ The word *statistics* is derived from the same Latin word as *statesman*. Statistics originally referred to the analysis of political data.

Brunelleschi's Dome on the Florence Cathedral

ALTHOUGH FAMOUS FOR losing a sculpture competition to Lorenzo Ghiberti in 1401, Filippo Brunelleschi went on to greater fame as the architect who designed the dominant landmark of Florence's skyline, the dome (*duomo*) of the Florence Cathedral. His commission for this project pitted him once again against his former rival Ghiberti, but this time Brunelleschi prevailed.

The nave of the cathedral had been completed in 1296, and the structure was already graced with a famed bell tower designed by the artist Giotto. The scale of the cathedral before Brunelleschi's contribution was legendary—it was said to be large enough to house the entire population of Florence. While this was an exaggeration, Brunelleschi was nonetheless charged with designing the largest dome since the one that covered the Pantheon in ancient Rome. The Florence Cathedral required a dome 150 feet in diameter, the span of the cathedral's crossing (intersection of the nave and transept).

It is believed that during a stay in Rome in 1418, Brunelleschi studied the Pantheon and other ancient monuments to help formulate his plan. He ultimately rejected the hemispheric design of solid stone used in the ancient structure, relying instead on a shell of eight sections divided by prominent ribs. Internally the dome consists of two layers, the inner of which serves as a foundation supporting the outer level. The two layers are joined by a series of arches and stone rings, but the largely hollow space between helps reduce the load and makes external buttressing unnecessary.

The dome rests on a large octagonal drum pierced with round windows (*oculi*), a common feature in ancient Roman art. At the dome's summit is an additional oculus, resembling that of the Pantheon, but with a lantern tower constructed over it. Although rightly considered a hallmark of Renaissance architecture, the dome's reliance on ribbing, pointed arches, and overall verticality places it within the orbit of Gothic art as well.

When finally completed in 1436 (construction had begun in 1420), the dome rose to a height of 375 feet. The architect Leon Battista Alberti described it as "a large structure, rising above the skies, ample to cover with its shadow all the Tuscan people." Appropriately, Brunelleschi lies buried under the dome. A Latin inscription over his tomb compares him to Daedalus, the mythological inventor of wings that carried him to the heavens.

Joan of Arc

THE HUNDRED YEARS WAR began in 1337 when English King Edward III was worried about the French claiming British land in France. He invaded France and claimed the French throne. Throughout the years, there were periodic battles, and in 1415 the British again invaded France. Fighting took place during the next 12 years, and defeat for the French seemed imminent.

Joan of Arc Kissing the Sword of Deliverance *by Dante Gabriel Rosetti*

Joan of Arc (Jeanne d'Arc), a young French peasant from Orleans, believed that God had spoken to her and that she was destined to drive the British from her homeland. Her repeated requests to the French commander were ignored until she announced the defeat of the French at a battle a few days before the commander was made aware of the defeat.

Joan was examined by doctors and clergy who were supposed to decide whether the voices she was hearing were supernatural. The religious leaders decided her claim of hearing voices was not heretical, so Joan prepared for battle as a troop commander. Before she began the campaign against the English, Joan requested that the king of England withdraw his troops from France. Enraged, the British refused.

Orleans, the last important city the English needed to capture, had been surrounded by English troops. Joan led the soldiers into battle and to a series of successes that opened the way for her to lead the soldiers to Reims, where Charles VII was crowned king (rather than his rival, Henry VI of England), settling a dispute about succession to the throne.

Joan led troops to Compiegne to defend against another English and Burgundian siege but was captured by the Burgundians as her troops retreated from battle. She was imprisoned and attempted to escape several times. King Charles VII did not intervene on her behalf, and her family did not have funds to pay ransom for her release. The British paid the Duke of Burgundy to release her to them. They decided to put her on trial as a witch because they feared her and because they were seeking revenge for her victories, including the crowning of Charles VII.

Joan was burned at the stake at the age of 19 as a result of the politically motivated and manipulated trial in Rouen. Twenty-five years after Joan's death, the pope found her innocent of the heresy charges.

The Novel in English

ANCIENT GREEK AND Elizabethan prose fictions, romances, and Spanish tales about rogues all influenced the emergence of a new type of prose fiction called the *novella* ("little new thing") in Italian. The term "novel" began to be used in English in the 18th century, when increased literacy drove the demand for new forms of written entertainment.

Novels usually presented middle-class men or women as protagonists, with plausible plots, character development, and a serious theme. Daniel Defoe's *Robinson Crusoe* (1719) and *Moll Flanders* (1722) are often considered the first English novels.

Samuel Richardson's *Clarissa* (1740–1741) was the first "epistolary" novel, presented as a series of letters. Like Miguel de Cervantes's *Don Quixote* (1605–1615), an important influence on later fiction, Henry Fielding's *Joseph Andrews* (1742) and *Tom Jones* (1749) mocked epic conventions. Horace Walpole's *The Castle of Otranto* (1764) initiated the Gothic novel, which would be developed by the Brontë sisters and Walter Scott in the early 19th century. Jane Austen's early 19th-century novels marked a breakthrough in psychological complexity, narrative voice, and examination of manners.

As mass readership developed and periodical magazines flourished, writers like Charles Dickens published novels in magazine installments, which favored multiple story lines and characters and a delayed climax. By the mid-19th century, the novel was the dominant form of written entertainment. Dickens's portraits of criminal milieus like that in *Oliver Twist* fed social reform movements. Ministers and social critics debated the novel's influence on women's morals.

As paper became cheaper, "dime novels" and "pulp fiction" (printed on wood-pulp paper) gained readers in the later 19th century. Specific genres of novels grew to include detective novels, thrillers, spy novels, Westerns, romances, and novels for children. "Serious" hardback literary novels diverged from popular paperbacks, especially after copyright laws were established in 1891. Compulsory schooling further expanded the reading public. At the century's end, H. G. Wells wrote "scientific romances" including *The Time Machine* (1895) and *The War of the Worlds* (1898), leading to the popularization of science fiction novels. In 1935, Penguin began publishing "serious" paperback fiction, with Pocket Books following four years later.

The period from 1850 to 1950 was the high point of fiction reading, which now faces increasing competition from television and the Internet.

Queen Elizabeth I (1533–1603)

ELIZABETH'S STORY BEGINS with her father, King Henry VIII. Henry was first married to Catherine of Aragon, and they had a daughter named Mary. When Catherine could not give birth to a male heir, Henry asked the pope to dissolve the marriage. When the pope refused, Henry separated from the Catholic Church, secured the divorce, and formed the Protestant Church of England. Henry then married his second wife, Anne Boleyn, who gave birth to another daughter, Elizabeth. Anne was subsequently charged with adultery and was beheaded. Henry then convinced Parliament to declare the marriage to Anne Boleyn invalid, which made Elizabeth illegitimate and restored her half-sister Mary as heir to the throne. In 1537, with the birth of their brother, Edward, Elizabeth was reduced to third in line to the throne.

Elizabeth I
by George Gower

Henry VIII died in 1547 and was succeeded by Edward. However, the new king died in 1553, leaving Mary as queen. "Bloody Mary" was determined to return England to Catholicism. She dissolved the Church of England and took extreme measures against Protestant "heretics." In return, Protestants plotted against the crown in Elizabeth's name. Although her role in these activities could never be proven, Elizabeth was confined to the Tower of London for two months soon after Mary came to power and also spent a year in custody in the palace at Woodstock.

Elizabeth gained the throne upon Mary's death in 1558. At her first Parliament, she reestablished the Church of England, an act that was opposed by both Protestant extremists and English Catholics. However, it was the Catholic opposition that proved to be the greater threat. Elizabeth's cousin Mary Queen of Scots, whose claim to the throne was supported by Catholic Europe, was the impetus for several plots against Elizabeth. After the discovery of Mary's personal involvement in the Babington assassination plot of 1586, Elizabeth reluctantly ordered her execution in 1587.

King Philip II of Spain was particularly angered by the execution. In 1588, Philip assembled an enormous fleet to invade England and overthrow the "heretic queen." However, smaller, more maneuverable British ships defeated his so-called "Invincible Armada."

Following the battle, Elizabeth would rule for another 15 years until her death in 1603. She remained unmarried throughout her reign.

Book of Job

ONE OF THE MOST challenging books of the Bible, the book of Job is also considered to be one of the greatest works of world literature. Biblical scholars believe that the story of Job originated from outside of Judaic culture and may have been revised by several writers to reflect the changing beliefs of its readers. Still, the story of Job, with its debate over why evil things happen to good people, holds an important place in the religious teachings of Judaism, Islam, and Christianity.

The story begins with an argument between God and Satan. During their discussion, God singles out Job as an archetype of a righteous servant who shuns evil. Satan argues that when provoked, even God's most loyal servant will curse him, and Satan sets out to test his theory on Job. Following a series of disasters orchestrated by Satan, Job is left without any children or possessions. Instead of cursing God, Job responds by tearing off his clothes and proclaiming, "Naked I came from my mother's womb, and naked shall I return there: the Lord gave, and the Lord has taken away; blessed be the name of the Lord" (1:21). Satan responds to this expression of piety by covering Job's body with boils.

Job and His Wife
by Georges de La Tour

At this point, Job's wife encourages him to curse the name of God. However, Job defies her instruction and responds, "Shall we receive the good at the hand of God, and not receive the bad?" (2:10). Next, Job's friends arrive to offer their advice. They believe that Job's misfortunes would not have happened without Job first committing some sin and that he should beg God for forgiveness. However, Job maintains his innocence, proclaiming that punishment without sin is unjust.

The book of Job ends with God speaking to Job. While God does not directly address Job's questions regarding his undeserved suffering, he does assert his power and authority over all of his creations. Ultimately, the question of why bad things happen to good people is left unanswered, save that it is God's will. In the end, God rewards Job for his unwavering piety, and all of Job's possessions are not only restored but also increased.

Musical Life in Spain's Colonies

GENERAL HISTORIES OF classical music tend to focus intensively on an exclusive set of European traditions, particularly those of Italy, France, and Germany, as the artistic centerpieces of Western music. This is a legitimate story to tell, given the prevalence of this music in modern-day concert halls. However, another story should be told about a musical tradition that blossomed in the Spanish colonies during the first centuries of contact between Europeans and America's native peoples. In New Spain, during the 1600s and 1700s, a type of Spanish religious song called the *villancico* gained unique New World flavor.

The villancico began as a type of secular refrain on the Iberian Peninsula during the Renaissance but was quickly adopted for religious use. While the reforms of the Catholic Church in the late 1500s reaffirmed the use of Latin for all official religious rites, a space was left open during worship for use of the vernacular, or the language of the people. In Spain, the villancico was appropriated as an informal worship song. Church musicians and poets began creating villancicos that were straightforward, jocular commentaries on religious celebrations and feasts, such as Christmas and Easter. These were designed to assist illiterate worshippers, especially new converts, in understanding the key concepts of the Catholic faith.

New World villancicos from the 17th and 18th centuries are an interesting hybrid of European musical conventions mixed with indigenous Latin and South American elements. These songs meant to involve the native peoples, whatever their background, in worship music. Many of these compositions tell stories of indigenous characters that are identified as such by their names or language. Spanish missionaries attempting to convert native peoples to Catholicism even wrote entire villancicos in native languages. For example, in Guatemala some villancicos have been found that were written in the Mayan language.

POSTSCRIPT

▪ One of the most important New World villancico poets was a Mexican nun named Sor Juana Inés de la Cruz. She is considered one of the most extraordinary Spanish-language writers of the 17th century.

▪ In recent years, a number of classical ensembles have begun making excellent recordings of this previously neglected, but musically delightful, repertory.

The Decline of Honeybees

IT HAS BEEN SAID that if honeybees become extinct, humans will become extinct also, because our food supply depends on their pollination. Fortunately this is an exaggeration, as there are many other insects—including other kinds of bees—that also pollinate our crops. It is worth noting that there were no honeybees in North America until the Europeans brought them here in the early 17th century. (There were other kinds of bees, however.) These first imported bees went wild and spread from New England and Virginia all the way to California. Regardless, the declining honeybee population is cause for serious concern.

Today, the use of commercially reared honeybees is vital to the success of up to 90 percent of American crops. (Not to mention the sale of honey.) And since 1970, beekeepers have been reporting declines in their hive populations. Wild honeybees are now almost extinct in the United States, and colonies maintained by beekeepers have also suffered dramatic losses—as many as half of the 2.5 million colonies once kept in the United States. Part of the decline is due to infestations of tracheal mites and varroa mites. In 2007, the rate of decline worsened, due to a phenomenon known as Colony Collapse Disorder (CCD).

Hives suffering from CCD have no adult bees, although dead bees are not found. The adults have disappeared, abandoning the larvae and unhatched pupae as well as all the stored food. Hive pests and other bees seem reluctant to scavenge the abandoned food and juveniles, as these attacks are delayed. As the vagueness of the name suggests, the cause of CCD is not known. Malnutrition; various pathogens, including bacteria, mites, and viruses; toxic pesticides; genetically modified crops that produce their own pesticides; stress; and even radiation from cell phones have been suspected, but so far nothing has been proven.

Recently a team of scientists did a large study analyzing the genetic material of bees from healthy colonies and also from colonies suffering from CCD. They extracted the genetic material from the bees along with whatever microbes they carried (like humans, bees carry a wide variety of nonpathogenic microbes in their bodies). When they compared them, the scientists found that most of the bees from CCD colonies (and almost none of the bees from healthy colonies) carried a virus called Israeli Acute Paralysis Virus. Perhaps this will turn out to be the causative agent, and perhaps knowing the cause will lead to a treatment.

Gericault's *The Raft of the Medusa*

*T*HE *RAFT OF THE MEDUSA* by Théodore Gericault dramatically re-creates one of the most notorious disasters in French maritime history. Completed in 1819, the large painting (193.3×282.3 in.) illustrates the conclusion of an incident that began with the sinking of a frigate, the *Medusa*, off the west coast of Africa three years earlier.

When the *Medusa* was damaged, the captain and high-ranking officers commandeered all the available lifeboats, leaving the remaining 149 passengers on a makeshift raft. At first tethered to the lifeboats that were tugging it ashore, the raft was eventually set adrift, forcing the passengers to fend for themselves on the open seas. The painting depicts the arrival of a rescue ship on the distant horizon 13 days after the accident, by which point only 15 passengers were still alive. The rest had been killed by exposure and starvation, with some survivors having resorted to cannibalism.

The story of the *Medusa* precipitated a political scandal. The tragedy was blamed on the incompetence of the captain, who had gained his appointment through political connections to the recently installed French monarchy, widely perceived as corrupt and reactionary. Inspired by accounts in the popular press, Gericault's sweeping, monumental treatment of the subject became a virtual manifesto of the burgeoning Romantic movement. With his bold rejection of the restrained compositions, idealism, and historical themes favored by the older, conservative proponents of classicism, 25-year-old Gericault suddenly found himself the leader of a new generation of artists.

To prepare his painting, Gericault constructed a replica of the raft in his studio, interviewed survivors, and sketched severed heads and limbs obtained from a Paris morgue. Bodies of his figures, painted from carefully posed friends, professional models, and survivors themselves, exhibit the idealized anatomy and artful arrangements of old masters such as Michelangelo and Rubens. However, instead of heroism or inspirational content, the viewer is confronted with a real-life horror story whose outcome is unclear. The prominent black man waving a scarf in the upper right was a survivor named Jean Charles. One of the fortunate few to be rescued, he nevertheless died several days later.

The Dreyfus Affair

O N OCTOBER 15, 1894, Captain Alfred Dreyfus, a Jewish army officer in the French War Ministry, was arrested for selling military secrets to Germany.

A military court found Dreyfus guilty in a trial notable for fabricated evidence and illegal procedures and sentenced him to life imprisonment on Devil's Island, off French Guiana. The French press, led by Édouard Drumont's virulently anti-Semitic *La Libre Parole*, applauded the verdict. Drumont, in particular, claimed that Dreyfus's actions illustrated the inherent disloyalty of French Jews.

But doubts about Dreyfus's guilt grew once the irregularities of the trial became known. When Lieutenant Colonel Georges Picquart uncovered evidence that another officer, Major C. F. Esterhazy, was a spy and that the letter that had incriminated Dreyfus was in Esterhazy's handwriting, the leftist press demanded a new trial. However, a military court acquitted Esterhazy, and Picquart was arrested. Outraged, popular novelist Émile Zola published an open letter to the president of France on January 13, 1898. Under the headline *J'Accuse*, Zola denounced the army for covering up its mistaken conviction of Dreyfus. More than 200,000 copies of the paper sold on the day the letter appeared.

The right-wing press exploded with diatribes against Zola, foreigners, and Jews. On the other side, more than 3,000 people signed a petition demanding a new trial for Dreyfus. Zola himself was brought to trial for criminal libel on February 7, 1898, in a case that kept the details of the Dreyfus affair in the international press. Zola was sentenced to one year in jail and a 3,000-franc fine, but he escaped to England.

In August of the same year, Major Hubert Joseph Henry, who had claimed to discover the letter that convicted Dreyfus, confessed he had forged documents in the case and had suppressed others in an effort to convict a man that he believed to be a traitor. Henry then committed suicide. Faced with exposure, Esterhazy fled the country. Dreyfus's appeal for a retrial was now assured.

Dreyfus was brought back from Devil's Island for a new court martial in August 1899. He was found guilty once more but was pardoned with the right to continue his efforts to establish his innocence. In 1906, a civilian court of appeals reversed the conviction. Dreyfus was formally reinstated in the army and given the Legion of Honour. Recalled to active service in World War I, he commanded an ammunition column as a lieutenant colonel.

William Shakespeare's *Hamlet*

A RGUABLY THE MOST famous play in world literature, widely translated and variously interpreted, Shakespeare's *Hamlet* was probably first performed between 1599 and 1601. The title role, with its challenges and chances for fame, has attracted actors of the highest rank, eager to enact insanity, depression, frustrated love, jealousy, and rage, while speaking poetically quotable lines. The "To be, or not to be" soliloquy, possibly the best-known speech in all of Shakespeare, occurs in Act III of *Hamlet*.

As the play opens, King Hamlet is recently dead; the king's brother, Claudius, has taken the throne and married Queen Gertrude, Prince Hamlet's mother. The king's ghost, however, has appeared nightly to the castle guards, a definite sign that "Something is rotten in the state of Denmark." By the end of Act I, Prince Hamlet has encoun- tered the ghost, who tells him that his father was poisoned by Claudius and that it is his duty as a son to "Revenge his foul and most unnatural murder."

This situation (a family member dead, a relative obligated to seek revenge) actually animates the plots of many so-called "revenge trag- edies" written for the theater at this time. Usually the call for revenge is not questioned. Shakespeare's genius is to make his protagonist a thinking, self-doubting, and introspective young man who cannot—or will not—act until he has analyzed all aspects of his situation. Grieving, erratic in behavior, and possibly insane, the melancholy prince vacillates. The effects of the original murder spread, poisoning Hamlet's relations with his mother and with Ophelia, the young woman he seems to love. Hamlet can speak freely only with his friend Horatio, who is the only other person who knows what the ghost has said.

The actor playing Hamlet must get inside the head of this most complex of characters in order to make his actions clear and credible. Outstanding interpreters of the role in the 20th century included John Gielgud, whose stage performance was called the "Hamlet of the century"; Laurence Olivier, whose 1948 film received praise and criticism for its Freudian interpretation of Hamlet's motives; Derek Jacobi, well-known for his role in the 1980 BBC television adaptation; and Kenneth Branagh, whose 1996 film version of the play has become a modern classic. Although the 1991 film adaptation starring Mel Gibson cut many key lines from the play, it has been popular with audiences.

Akira Kurosawa (1910–1998)

REGARDED AS ONE OF Japan's best-known directors, Akira Kurosawa was the first Japanese filmmaker to become popular in America. Influenced by Western literature (he adapted works by Shakespeare, Dostoevsky, and Gorky into films) and by American and European directors, he is perhaps best known for his samurai films.

Kurosawa's career in cinema began in 1936 when he answered an ad for an assistant director with P.C.L. Studios, later known as Toho Films. He learned basic filmmaking as part of Kajiro Yamamoto's team. At Toho, he also met actor Toshiro Mifune, who would star in some of the director's greatest films. Six years later, Kurosawa made his debut as director of *Sugata Sanshiro* (*Judo Saga*), released in 1943. He made ten more films during the 1940s, but it was *Rashomon* (1950) that landed him international recognition. A tale of murder and rape in ancient Japan, the film became famous for its narrative structure in which three characters offer differing points of view of the same incident, emphasizing that truth is relative, not absolute.

Like many Japanese directors from the classic era, Kurosawa focused on two types of films, *jidai-geki* (historical films) and *gendai-geki* (contemporary films). The former consisted largely of his samurai films, which attracted the largest following. With their long tracking shots, deep-focus shots, slow-motion sequences, and well-paced editing, films such as *The Seven Samurai*, *Yojimbo*, and *Sanjuro* are admired for their visual splendor. Kurosawa's contemporary dramas, which are set in modern-day Japan, are more visually subdued, focusing on complex characters and social problems. The contemporary films, including *Ikiru* and *Red Beard*, clearly show his distinctive humanism.

Though Kurosawa experienced a personal and professional low period during the early 1960s, he remained a much-admired director, winning several important awards. He won the Golden Palm at Cannes in 1980 for *Kagemusha*; he was awarded an Academy Award for career achievement in 1990; and he received the D. W. Griffith Award from the Directors Guild of America in 1992. He directed his last film, *Madadayo*, the following year.

POSTSCRIPT

■ George Lucas's original *Star Wars* trilogy was based in part on Kurosawa's *The Hidden Fortress*.

The Tour de France Bicycle Race

THE TOUR DE FRANCE was founded in 1903. It is run over a course of more than 1,800 miles (3,000 km), mostly in France, but occasionally in parts of neighboring countries. It lasts for 22 days and comprises 20 daily stages and 2 days of rest.

Riders are invited to compete as a team. Team members wear distinctive jerseys and are followed by a team car, which contains supplies. Riders

are all professionals, competing for prize and endorsement money, which today runs into the millions.

Each stage is considered an individual race. The riders may race in a group from the beginning to the end of a stage. To prevent overcrowding, a team may race the course against the clock.

The fastest rider on a stage wins that stage, and the next day wears a yellow jersey in honor of his achievement. A rider's time on each stage is added up over the course of the tour, and the individual with the lowest aggregate time is the winner. It is possible for a rider to win the overall race without winning a single stage, as Greg LeMond did in 1990.

The Tour de France alternates between running clockwise and counterclockwise around France every year. Some stages cover flat territory, while others pass through hilly country, and the most difficult—and famous—consist of punishing climbs through the Alps. Generally the rider who wins the mountain stages wins the race.

Usually, a different rider wins the Tour de France every year. Most winners have come from Europe, but U.S. resident Lance Armstrong won the Tour a record seven consecutive times between 1999 and 2005.

Almost every Tour since 1903 has been followed by charges that racers used illegal substances to dull pain or improve performance. In 1998, a rider was arrested for possession of growth hormones, testosterone, and amphetamines. Raids on hotels by tour management found that several teams were doing drugs. Riders responded by staging a sit-down strike, and though the race resumed after negotiations, it became known as the "Tour of Shame." Allegations trailed Armstrong during his long reign as race winner, but nothing was proven. Floyd Landis, the 2006 winner (also from the United States), tested positive for illegal drugs and was stripped of his title.

Louis Moreau Gottschalk

A MERICAN MUSICIANS in the art/concert tradition have always had a conflicted relationship with the European musical heritage that was long associated with "classical" music. It was well into the 20th century before American classical musicians began to shed a sense of obligation to perfect their study in Europe. Like many talented young pianists of the mid-1800s, Louis Moreau Gottschalk (1829–1869) headed to Paris at the age of 12. However, he was refused admission to the Paris conservatory because of his nationality.

The teenage Gottschalk studied privately in Paris, where he quickly gained a reputation as a remarkable keyboard virtuoso. His incorporation of Haitian Creole musical traditions into his compositions (presumably derived from Gottschalk's interaction with his white Haitian grandmother and her slave Sally) was praised as excitingly exotic.

Gottschalk toured Europe until the early 1850s on the strength of his reputation as the first performer-composer to incorporate authentic "new world" elements into his music. Returning to the United States, he proved himself very sensitive to current musical fashion, composing a number of hugely popular, emotionally intense works, which later generations often dismissed as "sentimental." He also crafted concert programs that combined arrangements of popular songs by Stephen Foster (who wrote "Oh! Susanna," "Beautiful Dreamer," and "Camptown Races") with emotional ballads and more "classical" compositions, blurring the boundaries between "high" and "low" traditions.

Through the 1850s and into the early 1860s, Gottschalk toured throughout North and Central America, with several trips (one lasting five years) to the West Indies. There he cemented his connection to Caribbean musical traditions and sought to build a compositional approach grounded in those repertories. Shortly after the outbreak of the Civil War in 1861, Gottschalk (a fervent Unionist) undertook a grueling recital tour: In the course of five years, he estimated that he gave more than 1,000 performances and traveled almost 100,000 miles by rail throughout the Union.

Forced to leave the United States by a false accusation of rape, Gottschalk spent the last four years of his life on a grand tour of South America, establishing himself as the first truly Pan-American cultural advocate. After a life of sensation and sentiment, Gottschalk's death was also sensationalized: He was said to have collapsed from malaria at a concert in Rio de Janeiro, just after he had finished playing one of his emotional works, entitled "She Is Dead."

Meta-Analysis

YOUR FRIEND SWEARS by decongestants to treat a cold, but they make you so sleepy you can't function. On the other hand, an aspirin makes your headache vanish, but no amount seems to stop your friend's head from throbbing.

It is just this kind of variation in response to medication that bedevils medical researchers, making it hard for them to figure out whether or not a drug works. What if the drug they're studying is pretty effective for most people, but the patients they enroll in their study just happen to have a poor response to it? On the other hand, the patients they enroll might have an unusually strong response, making an ineffective drug look like a winner.

One way of minimizing this problem is to study the reactions of lots of patients. The more people you study, the less likely it is that most of them will have an unusually negative or positive response. The problem is that studying lots of patients takes lots of money. As a result, researchers will often start by doing small studies, hoping that their results will still show what's going on.

If a drug works really well, a small study will probably show it to be effective. For example, although a few people don't get much pain relief from aspirin, most people do hurt less after they take it. But if a drug has a modest effect, it can be hard to tell if you only study its influence on a few people.

Often, several different researchers will do separate small studies. In this situation, scientists have come up with a trick to compensate for the narrowness of the studies. They combine the data from all the studies together and analyze it as if it all came from a single large one. This is called a *meta-analysis*.

Meta-analyses can provide more reliable information than you might get from looking at the studies separately. But they can also be misleading if not done carefully. Different studies are almost always done in slightly different ways, with varying dosages, types of patients, or formulations of a drug. And if some of the original studies were performed poorly, their results will skew the meta-analysis.

Because of this, some doctors are very skeptical of meta-analyses. And if a meta-analysis provides a really surprising result, showing, for example, that a treatment that had previously been thought to be ineffective is actually super, you should be skeptical, too.

Lorenzo Ghiberti's *Gates of Paradise*

T HE IMAGES IN RELIEF decorating the gilded bronze doors on the east side of the Baptistery of Florence (an octagonal building next to the Cathedral) represent a milestone in early Renaissance art. Completed by Lorenzo Ghiberti (1378–1455) in 1452, these sculptures are noteworthy for their effective simulation of three-dimensional space using one-point perspective, applied to compositions populated by ancient Greek- and Roman-inspired figures.

In addition to ten square panels, each showing a scene from the Old Testament, Ghiberti included 20 portrait heads and 24 full-length figures within the frames. These represented male prophets and female sibyls who foretold the coming of Christ. Michelangelo referred to Ghiberti's doors as "truly worthy to be the Gates of Paradise," giving rise to the title by which they are known today.

Gates of Paradise—*Eastern Doors (Esau & Jacob)*

Episodes depicted in the panels include the creation of Adam and Eve, Isaac sacrificing Abraham, and David and Goliath. Old Testament stories were believed at the time to foreshadow Christian themes. For example, the sacrifice of Abraham by his father prefigured the crucifixion, in which God suffered the loss of his son, Jesus Christ. Other stories, such as David slaying Goliath, held political significance. Just as David triumphed over his mightier foe, the city-state of Florence took pride in its victories over military enemies such as Milan.

Space is depicted with one-point or linear perspective, with diagonals converging toward a single vanishing point. The use of scientific perspective is seen most clearly in scenes with architecture, where lines of floor tiles and rows of classical arches align to lead the eye back to a distant vanishing point. The illusion of deep space is further enhanced by variations in relief, from sharply projecting, almost fully three-dimensional foreground figures, to extremely shallow forms in the background.

To safeguard the *Gates*, the original bronzes were moved inside the Florence Cathedral museum in 1990, and replicas were placed on the Baptistery.

The First Historians

THE FIFTH-CENTURY B.C. Greek historian Herodotus is generally considered to be the first historian in recorded history. He has been called the "Father of History" and also the "Father of Lies" because he sometimes embellished stories or included inaccurate information. Born in 484 B.C. in the Greek city of Halicarnassus on the southwest coast of Asia Minor (present-day Turkey), Herodotus eventually moved to Athens and then to southern Italy with Athenian settlers who founded the colony of Thurii, where he died in 420 B.C.

Herodotus is best known for writing *The Histories*, a lively narrative that covers the conflict between the Persian Empire and the Greek city-states that began just before he was born. His text includes the famous battles of Marathon (490 B.C.), Thermopylae and Salamis (480 B.C.), and the final Greek victory at Plataea (480 B.C.). He also related the entire history of the rise of Persia and the earlier history of the Greeks.

Herodotus did not judge the veracity of what he wrote; he simply reported what he knew or was told. When he learned of conflicting statements he included both, leaving the reader to judge which story was correct. On the whole, Herodotus was impartial, and when reporting details about other civilizations, he was generally free from racial prejudice. Even now, 2,500 years later, his narrative still makes for good reading.

Thucydides (460–c. 399 B.C.) is considered the first "scientific" historian because of the way he collected and analyzed information. Also, he left "the gods" out of his historical writings. Thucydides came from Thrace and was related to royalty there. He became a politician and admired the great Pericles as he rose in stature. In 424 B.C., during the great war between Athens and Sparta, Thucydides was elected general and sent to protect the Athenian colony of Amphipolis against the Spartans. He failed and was exiled for 20 years.

Thucydides' *History of the Peloponnesian War* covers events from the outbreak of hostilities between Athens and Corinth in 435 B.C., the entrance of Sparta into the war (432 B.C.), and the military and political events through 411 B.C. As a participant in the war, Thucydides was able to provide a fresh approach to history by giving eyewitness accounts of many events.

Unlike Herodotus, Thucydides only wrote about events that happened within his lifetime. Also, he included no social or economic passages, for Thucydides simply told the story of the military and political events of this epochal conflict that shook the Greek world.

The Lost Generation

Gertrude Stein (1874–1946) was a talented writer of experimental prose, but her place in the arts is defined primarily by her role as hostess of the most famous salon in Paris, particularly between WWI and WWII. During this time, she debated literary vision and style with Ernest Hemingway, F. Scott Fitzgerald, Sherwood Anderson, and other members of the "Lost Generation"—a term she coined to describe the disillusioned writers and artists from other countries who flocked to Paris. In addition to providing an artistic milieu in which to congregate, her salon gatherings at 27 Rue de Fleurus fostered a dialogue between European and American intellectuals.

These writers and artists came to Paris—the world's artistic capital—not to study the traditions of art or experiment with them but to seek refuge from the effects of WWI, which had destroyed the ideals of their youth. They also sought to escape an America where culture had become too narrow and provincial and where everyday life was ruled by rampant materialism.

Hemingway met Stein through a letter of introduction provided by writer Sherwood Anderson, who told Hemingway to relocate to Paris to write. Stein instantly liked the charismatic young author, who openly courted her favor. Hemingway borrowed her phrase "lost generation" for his 1922 novel *The Sun Also Rises*, thus popularizing the term.

Throughout the 1920s and 1930s, Stein experienced sometimes friendly, sometimes quarrelsome, relations with other celebrated writers who visited her salon, including Lincoln Steffens, William Carlos Williams, Paul Bowles, and Thornton Wilder. Poet Ezra Pound, another expatriate, proved too contentious for the Stein salon, but his apartment provided another gathering place for writers and artists. Sylvia Beach, a good friend of Stein's, owned and operated a popular bookstore, Shakespeare and Company, which carried the works of the expatriates. Stein, Pound, and Beach were the magnets for the Lost Generation, who were looking for meaning and guidance in their lives.

WWII provides a clear boundary for this period of expatriatism. The cultural conditions that had led intellectuals to congregate in Paris no longer existed in war-torn Europe. Stein led a quiet life in the country during the war. Afterward, she returned to 27 Rue de Fleurus to discover that her monumental art collection was still intact, but the artists and writers of her circle had scattered with the winds of war.

Walt Disney (1901–1966)

WALT DISNEY WAS born in 1901 in Chicago, Illinois. Feeling that the city was not a good environment for his family, Disney's father, Elias moved them around the Midwest, first to Marceline, Missouri, and then to Kansas City. The family would later return to Chicago, and while Disney was in high school, he also took night classes at the Academy of Fine Arts. In 1918, he attempted to join the military to fight in World War I but was turned down because he was only 16 years old. Instead, he joined the Red Cross and served as an ambulance driver.

Following the war, Disney returned to Kansas City and found employment at the Pesmen-Rubin Commercial Art Studio. There, he began experimenting with animation and met his future business partner Ub Iwerks. The two struck out on their own and started Laugh-O-Gram Films, which provided cartoons for local theaters. Later, they created a series of *Alice's Wonderland* cartoons that combined live action and animation. These were popular enough to attract a national distributor.

Unfortunately, Disney and Iwerks were making no money with their business venture. Disney moved to Hollywood in 1923 to be closer to the movie industry and his brother, Roy, and Iwerks joined him the following year. Disney developed another character and series entitled *Oswald the Rabbit* but lost the rights to Universal Pictures in 1928. Iwerks and Disney quickly devised a new character, named Mickey Mouse. His pleasing design and spunky personality made him an almost instant success, and Mickey's third cartoon, *Steamboat Willie*, was a big hit with audiences.

Disney was an innovator in the field of film animation. He wanted to create animation that consisted of more than characters engaged in physical humor. Disney also incorporated the latest film technology into his animation. *Steamboat Willie*, for example, was the first cartoon to marry animation and synchronized sound. Disney's 1932 cartoon *Flowers and Trees* was the first to use Technicolor. He was also the first to make an animated feature film with *Snow White and the Seven Dwarfs* in 1937.

Walt Disney was also a visionary businessman. He expanded his animation studio into an entertainment empire by moving into television in 1951 and opening a one-of-a-kind amusement park, called Disneyland, in 1955. When he died in 1966, he was in the midst of planning Disney World in Orlando, Florida.

Dirigibles and Airships

AIRSHIPS AND DIRIGIBLES are self-propelled, maneuverable, and lighter-than-air craft. The word *dirigible* comes from a French word meaning "capable of being steered." Any type of rigid, lighter-than-air craft can be called an airship or dirigible interchangeably. Early in their development, highly flammable hydrogen gas was used for elevating airships. Later, helium, which was more expensive but not flammable, was used.

Luftschiffbau Zeppelin, a German company, was the primary manufacturer and designer of dirigibles in the early 1900s. The German airships, called *zeppelins,* were the first to be used for commercial passenger flights. During World War I, zeppelins were also used as offensive weapons. Although visually terrifying, the airships were quite inaccurate and extremely vulnerable to attack from faster-moving aircraft and anti-aircraft weapons.

Following World War I, the Treaty of Versailles required Germany to surrender all of its zeppelins to the allied powers. However, before the treaty was signed many of the zeppelin crews destroyed their airships to avoid compliance with the terms of the treaty. Those not destroyed were handed over.

After the war, the United States constructed its first rigid airship, the USS *Shenandoah*, which made its first flight in 1923 and crossed the Atlantic the following year. The *Shenandoah* was the first airship to use helium to stay aloft. Two years after its inaugural flight, the *Shenandoah* broke into pieces during a storm and was destroyed. Germany restarted its manufacture of zeppelins when the U.S. military ordered one as part of Germany's war reparations. In 1924, the zeppelin *Los Angeles* was delivered to the United States and flew for about eight years. The British also manufactured two airships for commercial travel during this time period. Both airships eventually crashed.

Some airships manufactured after World War I were large and luxurious. One was able to seat 100 passengers, and some had dining facilities, recreational spaces, and sleeping accommodations. The U.S. navy constructed airships that were large enough to hold several airplanes.

In 1937 the *Hindenburg*, a huge German zeppelin, burst into flames as it landed in Lakehurst, New Jersey, after completing a transatlantic flight. Flammable hydrogen had been used to fuel the ship because of a military embargo on helium. In light of the *Hindenburg* disaster, and also the world's darkening political situation, the golden age of the dirigible ended.

Musical Scholarship

THE PRACTICAL AND theoretical study of organized sound dates back millennia to ancient traditions like those of China. The topic of applied and conceptual music was also a key concern of the Greek philosophers, who are often seen as the precursors of Western culture. However, the academic (or scholarly) study of music is a relative new-comer to the university system.

Following late 19th-century German scholarly models, the English term *musicology* first came into use in the early 20th century. Early proponents of musicology saw it as a "big tent" discipline that would span all aca-demic and intellectual approaches to sound. As the century progressed, university departments of music were established and classified as separate from a "conservatory" model—in which students are trained primarily to be practicing musicians rather than thinkers-about-music. Most scholars who identified themselves as musicologists focused on explaining the aesthetic and/or historical dimensions of the European "art" repertory.

As a consequence, individuals interested in other aspects of music and learning began to form separate associations: The Society for Ethnomu-sicology was established in the 1950s by researchers whose connections with anthropology led them to examine musical traditions outside the European sphere, along with folk or "traditional" music. In the late 1970s, the Society for Music Theory was founded to focus on the examination of musical works and musical-theoretical systems, which some scholars felt had been neglected in musicology's turn toward historical and stylistic inquiry. Those scholars who call themselves musicologists—a century after the term first gained currency—are indeed most closely allied with the study of cultural history. However, the American Musicological Soci-ety continues to welcome a wide variety of approaches in its membership, meetings, and professional publications.

As the American Musicological Society approaches its 75th anniversary in 2009, the scholarly study of music remains increasingly diverse—there is often productive overlap and useful collaboration in the approaches of theorists, ethnomusicologists, and historical musicologists. All three disciplines, for example, have recently begun to embrace the study of popular and mass-mediated music—establishing a challenging dialogue with colleagues in sociology, media studies, English, and other fields of study that have long approached popular music gingerly, due to their discomfort with the descriptive "mechanics" of the expressive power of sound.

Beach Erosion

IF YOU THINK moving to a new apartment or house is difficult, consider moving an entire lighthouse. A few years ago, Cape Hatteras Lighthouse in North Carolina, which stands 208 feet tall, had to be moved a quarter mile back from the beach. The reason? Beach erosion. In about 100 years, the coast had moved 1,500 feet, causing the lighthouse to be at risk of washing away.

Disappearing beaches, unstable foundations, and breakaway cliffs are not just problems in the Outer Banks of North Carolina. Coastal communities throughout the world are facing tough decisions about beach erosion. Entire cities, such as New Orleans, which lies several feet below sea level, stand to be swept away by the eroding coastlines. More bad news is on the horizon, as global warming threatens to exacerbate the already quickened erosion process.

Beach erosion has been happening since the oceans first formed. In fact, it is a necessary component of beach formation, since most of the coastal sand once came from glacier landforms that eroded away. Yet the pounding waves also gradually steal sand from a beach and either deposit it far from shore or downwind at another beach. Human involvement, whether directly to the coastline (such as by deepening inlets to allow for larger boats) or by using watercraft, has an effect on erosion as well. Geology, weather, vegetation, and many other factors also play a role.

There are several solutions, but all are problematic. One is to simply dump more sand on the beaches. However, this really just delays the inevitable. One study on the Mid-Atlantic coast suggested that the entire beach would need to be replaced every five years using this method. Other cities, like Miami Beach, have started building sea walls. This is a very contentious fix-it, as some critics claim it accelerates erosion by magnifying the intensity of the waves.

Other projects include dredging the bay or "stealing" the sand back from the ocean, but these solutions are very expensive. Regardless of the chosen method, many coastal regions are working toward long-term solutions to manage beach erosion and keep these vital resources around for generations to come.

POSTSCRIPT

▧ Dunwich, the medieval capital of England's wool trade, disappeared entirely over a few centuries thanks to the pounding surfs.

▧ When a sea wall is built perpendicular to the beach, it's called a *groin*.

Jackson Pollock

IN 1949, *LIFE* MAGAZINE asked whether Jackson Pollock was "the greatest living painter in the United States." There were those, however, who didn't think Pollock "painted" at all. His paintings were made from commercial house paint that he poured, flung, and dripped onto unstretched canvas lying on the ground or tacked to a wall. He said, "My painting does not come from the easel.... On the floor I am more at ease. I feel nearer, more a part of the painting, since I can walk around it, work from the four sides, literally be *in* the painting...."

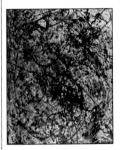

Reflection of the
Big Dipper

Paul Jackson Pollock was born in Cody, Wyoming, in 1912, but his family lived in various locations in Arizona and California. At age 18, Pollock headed east to New York City. Like many artists during the Great Depression, Pollock survived on the meager income provided to artists involved in the Works Progress Administration's Federal Art Project.

Always a heavy drinker, Pollock was treated for alcoholism in 1938. At this time he entered Jungian analysis and was encouraged to draw as a part of his therapy. Pollock soon incorporated this "automatism," or automatic drawing—random marks made at the prompting of the subconscious—into his art. Over the next few years, Pollock's paintings became increasingly abstract.

Pollock received regular, if mixed, notices from the critics and was regarded by many as a leading painter in the style soon to be known as Abstract Expressionism. In 1947, he moved with his wife, the painter Lee Krasner, to rural, peaceful East Hampton, New York. Between 1947 and 1952, Pollock created the drip paintings for which he is most famous.

At first glance, Pollock's mature paintings seem chaotic, like an explosion in a paint factory. A longer look reveals a filigree of color: Threads, drops, and swirls of paint are woven together in an all-over design, creating a sensuous texture and expressive effect. No single area of a painting commands the viewer's attention.

Early in 1956, an article in *Time* magazine gave Pollock the nickname "Jack the Dripper." Sadly, by this time Pollock was trapped in alcoholism, consumed by self-doubt, and unable to summon the imagination and strength to paint. In a tragic finale to his complicated life, Pollock died a few months later in a drunk-driving accident not far from his home.

The Crusades

IN 1071, THE BYZANTINE EMPIRE suffered a serious defeat at the hands of the Seljuk Turks, who proceeded to occupy much of Asia Minor. Emperor Alexius Comnenus sent a letter to Pope Urban II, seeking Western military aid to drive the Turks out of his territory. Instead, on November 27, 1095, the pope took the opportunity to preach a crusade against the "infidels." He declared that the Holy Land must be occupied by Christian armies and the holy places cleansed. He wanted to stop the spread of Islam and drive back the Muslims who had captured Jerusalem and other "Christian" areas.

The pope's oration stirred western Europe to action. Scores of nobles quickly signed up for an expedition to Palestine. This First Crusade was the most successful of the eight crusading expeditions that took place over the next 200 years. After traversing Byzantine territory, the Crusaders besieged and captured Jerusalem in July 1099, creating four different independent states in the process.

But the success of the Christians was short-lived. There was no overall strategic planning, and there were no coordinated plans for reinforcements or supplies from Europe. As a result, the sultan of Egypt recaptured Jerusalem in 1187. This precipitated the Third Crusade, led by King Philip Augustus of France and Richard I "the Lionhearted" of England. Richard was a superb tactician and won several battles, but in the end he failed to recapture Jerusalem.

The Fourth Crusade was diverted by Venetian greed to Constantinople, which was taken and sacked by the western Christians in 1204. King Louis IX of France was taken prisoner in the Seventh Crusade and died of disease during the Eighth. In 1291, Muslim troops captured Beirut and Acre, the last two Christian strongholds in Palestine.

The long-term results of the Crusades were much more important than the failed military aspects. Europeans discovered a taste for Middle Eastern and Asian spices, textiles, and other goods that were imported from the Muslim world, thus increasing trade and expeditions. Also, ideas and inventions from the Arab world were introduced to the West. The Crusades affected transportation, banking, and literature as well as religion and politics. Although never fought directly against the Jews, the Crusades did increase feelings of anti-Semitism in Europe.

Some cultures view the Crusades as noble and heroic feats, while others see them as acts of intolerant violence fought in the name of the church. Either way, their impact can still be felt to this day.

Mark Twain's *The Adventures of Huckleberry Finn*

*T*HE ADVENTURES OF HUCKLEBERRY FINN (1885), the most initially popular and lastingly famous of Mark Twain's novels, has been controversial from his day to ours. At first championed as a boy's adventure story, it was increasingly recognized as a major American work of fiction.

Huckleberry Finn had appeared as a character in Twain's earlier *Tom Sawyer* (1876). But while Twain narrates the former book, *The Adventures of Huckleberry Finn* is told by Huck himself. The wayward son of the town drunk, Huck builds a raft and helps a slave named Jim escape down the Mississippi River—even though Huck is convinced that doing so will send him to hell because Jim is someone else's property. Huck and Jim pass through a series of Southern towns where they encounter con men, feuds, family plots, and occasional kindness.

In a famous "Notice," Twain warned, "Persons attempting to find a motive in this narrative will be prosecuted; persons attempting to find a moral in it will be banished; persons attempting to find a plot in it will be shot." A great part of the book's initial appeal was Twain's careful use of dialects, white and black, in the characters' speech. Early reviewers either praised it as a delightful adventure tale or criticized it for being too dark and mature to be a children's book. Today's controversies revolve around Twain's liberal use of the word "nigger" (universally accepted by white readers when the book was published) and about his real views regarding slavery and African Americans, such as Huck's companion, Jim.

Supporters point out that Jim is one of the few noble characters in the book and that Twain shows the cruelty of slavery and the corruption of pre-Civil War Southern culture, with its casual violence, duels, and feuds. Critics say that Twain modeled Jim at least partly on figures from minstrel shows, a once-popular American form of live entertainment in which white performers in blackface makeup imitated and mocked African Americans in song-and-dance routines. As with other illustrated books of the period with African American characters, much modern controversy centers on the book's illustrations, some of which caricatured black characters.

Every year, *The Adventures of Huckleberry Finn* is banned from some schools or public libraries. It is regularly included in the American Library Association's list of most-banned books, yet it remains a widely read American classic and is especially popular overseas.

Stephen Jay Gould (1941–2002)

STEPHEN JAY GOULD was a scientist well known outside his professional circle. Trained as a paleontologist, Gould's primary interest lay in describing the process of evolution, and he attempted to reach as wide an audience as possible. In addition to his purely scientific research, he wrote a monthly popular science essay in *Natural History* magazine (reprinted in the collections *The Panda's Thumb* and *Ever Since Darwin*) and several best-selling books, including *The Mismeasure of Man* (a critique of psychometrics and intelligence testing) and *Wonderful Life* (about the Burgess Shale fossils found in Canada).

The Burgess Shale formation includes many wonderfully preserved fossils from about 530 million years ago, with bizarre creatures that seem to have no living descendants. Some of them have such peculiar body plans that they cannot be fitted into any existing animal classifications—for example Opabinia, with five eyes and a nose like a vacuum cleaner. Gould argued in *Wonderful Life* that chance—rather than fitness, as espoused by Darwin—must play a larger role in evolution than previously assumed. He believed that the presence of such an abundance of "trial" life forms, most of whom left no descendents, showed that some successful organisms could be wiped out by accident, leaving possibly less fit forms to take over. These ideas were controversial when *Wonderful Life* was published in 1989, and they are still a topic of debate.

As a scientist, Gould is best known for the theory of punctuated equilibrium, which he developed with Niles Eldredge. In contrast to the gradual change assumed by Darwinian evolutionary biologists, Gould and Eldredge believed that fossil records are more consistent with long periods of evolutionary "treading water" interspersed with occasional bursts of rapid change. Theirs was not a revolutionary new idea but rather a new way of focusing on evolutionary theory.

Gould was also an avid baseball fan and wrote an essay in the *New York Review of Books* reviewing Michael Seidel's book about Joe DiMaggio's 56-game hitting streak of 1941. In his review, Gould rhapsodizes about the awesome accomplishment of hitting safely in 56 consecutive games, describing the mathematical improbability of such a streak occurring by chance.

In addition to writing more than 20 books, Gould served as a professor at Harvard University in zoology, geology, biology, and the history of science. He also appeared on a number of television shows, including *The Simpsons* (as himself). Gould died from lung cancer in 2002.

Seabiscuit

BORN IN 1933, SEABISCUIT did not look like a champion. He had a plain head, short legs, a compact body, a short barrel, and a nervous demeanor. At first, Seabiscuit was used only for overnight and claiming races, the lowest ranked events in horse racing. The results of Seabiscuit's first year were so unimpressive that he was put up for sale. Tom Smith, a trainer for the racing stables of Charles S. Howard, persuaded Howard to buy the three-year-old despite his deficiencies.

Shortly thereafter, Seabiscuit rode with jockey J. Red Pollard for the first time, and horse and rider made an instant connection. Seabiscuit improved immediately and broke records at two different tracks. During the off-season, Smith worked to heal the horse physically and psychologically. Then, at the beginning of 1937, he won 11 of 15 races, which attracted the attention of the press and public. That year, he became the top money-winning thoroughbred, earning $168,580 in total. However, two events cast a shadow on his year—he lost the $100,000 Santa Anita Handicap by a nose, and the dashing War Admiral was named Horse of the Year instead of Seabiscuit.

For Seabiscuit, 1938 was a year of bad luck and bad knees. Once again, he lost the Santa Anita by a nose, and a match race with War Admiral had to be scrapped because of problems with Seabiscuit's knees. Also, Pollard was severely injured and required a substitute. Another jockey named George Woolf replaced him. Despite these setbacks, Seabiscuit bounced back in November, and the race with War Admiral was rescheduled. Wobbly-kneed, scrappy Seabiscuit managed to beat the big, regal War Admiral, finishing three lengths ahead. Millions of Americans listened to the race on the radio. Seabiscuit even snatched the Horse of the Year title away from younger contenders.

The following year, more bad luck plagued Seabiscuit as he pulled up lame after a race. Amazingly, he was able to finish the race, despite having injured a ligament in the backstretch. The season was finished for the plucky horse, and rumors circulated that his career was over. Still, Howard, Smith, and Pollard were determined for their horse to conquer the Santa Anita Handicap. In 1940, seven-year-old Seabiscuit was once again entered into the Santa Anita. He won, blowing across the finish line and setting a track record at the same time. With this win, he earned his retirement and lived on a ranch in California until his death in 1947.

Ella Fitzgerald

Ella Fitzgerald (1917–1996) is arguably the most renowned and popular female jazz singer of the 20th century. From 1936, when she made her first recording, until her death in 1996, she recorded almost 2,000 songs. Her 200 albums, which sold more than 40 million copies, earned her 13 Grammy Awards.

When Fitzgerald was very young, her parents separated. She and her mother, Temperance, like many African Americans at the time, moved north from Virginia to Yonkers, New York. As a young girl, Fitzgerald helped support her mother, stepfather, and baby sister by doing odd jobs, including running numbers for local gamblers. She also loved singing and watching the acts at Harlem's famed Apollo Theater.

In the early 1930s, Fitzgerald lost her mother to a car accident and her stepfather to a heart attack. After an incident with the police, she wound up in a reform school. She escaped but found herself without money and essentially alone.

But Fitzgerald received a major break in 1934. Her name was selected to be in a talent show at the Apollo. She wowed the crowd—who demanded an encore—and attracted the attention of noted saxophonist Benny Carter, who was in the band that night. Carter introduced her to major jazz stars of the period, most notably band leader Chick Webb, who hired her as a lead singer.

In 1938, Fitzgerald scored her first mega-hit—a jazzed-up yet puckish version of the nursery rhyme "A-Tisket, A-Tasket," which remained on the popular music charts for 17 weeks and sold more than one million copies. Her career took off. From the late 1930s to the 1980s, Fitzgerald sang with jazz greats including Ray Brown, Louis Armstrong, and Dizzy Gillespie. She also appeared on a number of television variety shows, including *The Ed Sullivan Show* and *The Tonight Show*. She spent a great deal of time touring foreign countries as a goodwill ambassador, and in 1987 she was awarded the National Medal of Arts. Fitzgerald gave her last concert in 1991.

As a singer, Fitzgerald combined near-perfect pitch with an impressive, flexible vocal range. She was perhaps most famed for her scat singing—using the voice as a musical instrument by combining nonsense words and syllables into a fast-flowing musical form.

Melting Ice Caps and Rising Sea Levels

As global temperatures rise, polar ice shelves are breaking away and melting. Melting ice caps release water into the world's oceans, and water expands in volume as it warms. As a result, the oceans have already risen 4 to 8 inches (10 to 20 centimeters) in the last century. The Intergovernmental Panel on Climate Change (IPCC) projects that the global sea level will rise another 3.5 to 35 inches (9 to 88 centimeters) by the year 2100.

Rising sea levels will have profound effects on humankind, beginning with those living on low-lying islands. For example, the Maldives in the Indian Ocean are composed of coral islands with nearly 80 percent of the land area less than 39 inches (1 meter) above sea level. Higher sea levels are expected to flood large areas of land on these islands, so many inhabitants will be forced to leave their homeland and relocate. Saltwater will contaminate freshwater supplies, causing the remaining residents to run out of drinking water. Many other island nations, including the Galapagos and Fiji, are also facing the same dismal future of constantly fighting rising seawaters that threaten to flood their territories. The Pacific island nation of Tuvalu may be the first nation lost to rising sea levels. New Zealand has been accepting environmental refugees from Tuvalu since 2003.

Mainland coastal areas will also suffer as seawater encroaches on their land. Beach erosion, flooding, and contamination of aquifers used for drinking water will become troublesome for low-lying costal areas. And in areas where sea levels are high to begin with, storm surges brought on by hurricanes could be devastating. The tragic consequences of coastal flooding due to storm surges were evident when Hurricane Katrina struck New Orleans and the Gulf Coast in 2005. The flooding could have been even worse if the sea level had been higher.

Besides the devastation to humankind, natural ecosystems will also be affected by rising sea levels. Marine ecosystems, including coral reefs, have been harmed by storm surges and warming waters. Many reefs have already undergone "coral bleaching"—when the necessary symbiotic algae leave the coral, essentially starving the coral reef. Corals will also continue to die as rising sea levels reduce the amount of light that reaches the reef. Coral reefs provide habitats for thousands of species, including fish.

It might seem like melting ice caps are a distant problem. But evidence indicates that as time passes, rising sea levels will affect our natural ecosystems and the human populations that depend on them.

Pop Art

P OP ART, A MOVEMENT with roots in the 1950s that matured and flourished in the 1960s, aimed its focus on American popular culture: advertisements, comic books, fast food, billboards, movies, and celebrities. The leaders of the movement, Andy Warhol (1928–1987) and Roy Lichtenstein (1923–1997), inflated the size of their commonplace subjects—commercial products and comic book illustrations—and presented them on monumental canvases exhibited in galleries on both coasts, incurring initial hostility from the public and critics alike. In similar fashion, Claus Oldenburg's (1929–present) "soft sculptures"—giant plastic versions of hamburgers, french fries, ice cream cones, and telephones—filled exhibition spaces from floor to ceiling.

Many have interpreted Pop Art as a reaction to Abstract Expressionism, which dominated the art scene in the 1950s but was fading by 1962, when Pop Art made its debut at the Sidney Janis Gallery in New York. Many of the artists represented, Warhol and Lichtenstein included, had worked as commercial artists. Unlike the older generation of Abstract Expressionists, Pop artists were not alienated by mass culture and material success; on the contrary, they embraced both. Their work, far from being spontaneously brushed, unique outpourings of angst, were mechanical, repetitious, and devoid of emotion. Warhol relied on silk-screening to duplicate photographs and advertising logos, and Lichtenstein used benday (stenciled) dots, a technique borrowed from commercial printing, for his comic book enlargements.

Lavender Marilyn *by Andy Warhol*

Though some perceived in Pop artists' work a critique of the materialism, crassness, and pervasive violence present in contemporary mass media, it is also possible to view the art as detached and nonjudgmental. In hindsight, Warhol's images of media stars—Marilyn, Jackie, and Elvis, for example—offer prescient commentary on the celebrity culture of today. Typically these works were derived from silk-screened publicity stills and were hand-colored to emphasize makeup, hair coloring, or other artificial means by which celebrities are glamorized and turned into disposable commodities for public consumption. The numerous images of Marilyn Monroe have a certain poignancy given that they were produced only after her suicide; they were part of Warhol's "Death and Disaster" series, which included images of car crashes, criminals, and electric chairs.

Johannes Gutenberg

I F "KNOWLEDGE IS POWER," then the Gutenberg printing press, introduced in 1440, was the instrument that empowered much of the civilized world.

Johannes Gutenberg (c. 1400–1468), a goldsmith and businessman from Mainz in southern Germany, borrowed money to pursue his experiments with printing presses and movable type in the early 1400s. His concept was not new. A form of movable wooden type had been invented as early as the 11th century by Bi Sheng in China. There are also unsubstantiated claims that Laurens Janszzon Coster (1370–1440) created a movable type printing press to print books in the Netherlands and that Gutenberg may have built upon this earlier effort.

Gutenberg taking the first proof

Gutenberg's process used replaceable individual wooden or metal letters. In fact, the genius of his invention was not so much the press itself, which was based on the screw-type wine presses of the Rhine Valley, but the separate pieces of metal type used for each character to be printed.

Prior to Gutenberg's invention, everything people read had to be laboriously copied by hand or printed from hand-carved wooden blocks. Under Gutenberg's system, individual letters were composed into words, locked into wooden forms, and inked. The paper was then pressed against the raised surface with the screw device. Once the letters were arranged into the desired text, the only time constraint was changing each piece of paper to be printed. And, unlike the old woodblock prints, these same pieces of type could be rearranged and used over and over to quickly print different texts.

In 1452, Gutenberg published his famous edition of the Bible, the first book to be published in quantity. Two hundred copies of the two-volume Bible were produced. Sold at the 1455 Frankfurt Book Fair, they cost about three times what the average clerk earned in a year. About 50 examples of the printing are known to survive today.

The Gutenberg Bible was just the beginning of what would become a flood of printed material as the technology spread. Within 45 years, approximately 2,500 European cities boasted printing presses.

Jane Austen

DURING HER LIFE, Jane Austen lived in southern England, traveled only short distances, and saw just four of her novels published. Today, she has devoted readers worldwide who call themselves "Janeites" and who meet regularly to discuss her life, her work, and the many contemporary adaptations of her writing into film and television.

Born in 1775 in the village of Steventon, Hampshire, Jane Austen was one of eight children born to Reverend George Austen and his wife. Although she received little formal education, Austen grew up in a family that enjoyed reading novels, poetry, history, and plays. When she began writing at the age of 12, her family encouraged her talent. The novels published during her lifetime—*Sense and Sensibility* (1811), *Pride and Prejudice* (1813), *Mansfield Park* (1814), and *Emma* (1815)—appeared anonymously, although her authorship became generally known, and the prince regent, later George IV, invited her to dedicate *Emma* to him. After Austen's death, her brother Henry oversaw the publication of *Northanger Abbey* and *Persuasion* in 1817.

Austen, who never married, lived with her parents and her sister Cassandra, also unmarried, until her father's death. Later, Mrs. Austen, Jane, and Cassandra settled in the village of Chawton, Hampshire, in a house provided by Jane's brother Edward. It was here that Austen enjoyed her most productive period as a writer.

When Austen fell ill (probably with Addison's disease), Cassandra and Henry took her to the cathedral city of Winchester, seeking better medical care. She died there on July 18, 1817, and is buried in Winchester Cathedral. Today, both the cathedral and the house in Chawton are places of pilgrimage for Austen readers. (There is also a Jane Austen Centre in Bath, where two of her novels are set and where Austen and her family briefly lived.)

Austen's main characters are women; her plots center on courtship and marriage, all-important concerns for women during her time. Although some contemporary critics have accused Austen of writing "chick lit," most literary scholars consider her a major writer of incalculable significance in the development of the novel. Both female and male characters are memorable—some for their wit and elegance, others as figures of fun. Characters such as Elizabeth Bennet and Mr. Darcy have been admired and idealized by countless readers; comic secondary characters such as Mr. Collins, Lady Catherine de Bourgh, and Sir Walter Elliot have become bywords for pomposity and vanity.

Jean-Paul Sartre (1905–1980)

ARGUABLY THE MOST famous philosopher of the 20th century, Jean-Paul Sartre was deeply influenced by his maternal grandfather, Karl Schweitzer, a professor of German at the Sorbonne in Paris. Sartre pursued his love of learning when he studied philosophy at the prestigious École Normale Supérieure. From 1931 to 1945, he taught at various secondary schools in France, interrupted by a year of study in Berlin in 1933 and service in the French army during World War II. Sartre was captured by the Germans in 1940 but was released in 1941 since he was thought to be unfit for military service and no threat to the Third Reich. He later became an active participant in the anti-German French Resistance. After the war, Sartre became deeply involved in left-wing politics. Ultimately, he became a critic of the Soviet Union because of what he saw as its betrayal of Marxism and of the United States because of its aggressive, dangerous foreign policy. He also maintained a life-long liaison with fellow philosopher Simone Beauvoir. Sartre died in 1980 as a result of a smoking-related illness.

Sartre is best known as a leading exponent of existentialism. Put simply, he argued that for humans, existence precedes essence; that is, we are all free to create ourselves, unencumbered by any prior conditions like original sin. In his most important philosophical work, *Being and Nothingness* (written while he was a German prisoner of war), Sartre maintained that humans create that essence by rebelling against authority, especially that of religion and traditional morality. They create their essences by "throwing [themselves] into the world, suffering there, struggling there" and continually redefining themselves. The process is never complete because humans continue to choose until death, when the process ends. Free will and human choice are thus the cornerstones of Sartre's philosophy.

In addition to his rather dense philosophical works, Sartre expressed his positions in more comprehensible literary works, especially his novel *Nausea* (1938) and play *No Exit* (1944). Although condemned by many traditionalists who found his position stark and uncomfortable since it made no room for a divine presence, Sartre nonetheless became a kind of cult figure for many young people in the 1960s who were attracted to his rebellion against authority and his focus on our power to create ourselves.

POSTSCRIPT

Sartre was awarded the Nobel Prize for Literature in 1964 but turned it down because he feared it would affect his integrity as a writer.

Jihad

SEPTEMBER 11, 2001, focused world attention on the meaning of the Arabic term *jihad*. English translations include "struggle in the path of Allah" and "holy war." Western commentators sometimes use the term "jihadi" in place of "militant," "terrorist," or "Islamist."

Today, Muslims commonly make a distinction (especially to non-Muslims) between the "greater jihad," a spiritual inner struggle for holiness of life, and the "lesser jihad," external armed conflict against non-Muslim groups for the sake of extending Allah's rule over territory. This distinction comes from a *hadith* (oral tradition) where Mohammed, returning from a battle against an Arabian tribe, told his companions he was returning from the lesser jihad to continue waging the greater jihad. However, this hadith is from a questionable tradition, and it received little attention during Islam's first few centuries.

Most references (more than 90 percent) to jihad in the Koran and in hadiths refer to armed conflict against non-Muslims. Some hadiths rank jihad as the second most meritorious deed, after belief in Allah and even before the pilgrimage to Mecca; others place it after respect for one's parents or other holy actions.

Muslim tradition divides the world into *Dar al-Islam*, "house of Islam" (the part of the globe ruled by Muslims) and the *Dar al-Harb*, "house of war" (the part of the world under non-Muslim systems). Scholar Bernard Lewis says, "The presumption [among Muslim jurists] is that the duty of *jihad* will continue, interrupted only by truces, until all the world either adopts the Muslim faith or submits to Muslim rule." Unlike the concept of "Crusade" in the Christian faith, which proved to be of limited duration and importance in Christendom, jihad was present from the beginning of Muslim belief.

Muslim legal writers recognize offensive and defensive jihad. The former could be fulfilled by supporting an army; the latter was the duty of every able-bodied Muslim. Jihad is regulated by Islamic *shari'a* (holy law). Jihadis are to avoid killing women, children, and noncombatants; to refrain from torture; to treat prisoners with respect; and to honor temporary truces and agreements made during the jihad. The purpose of jihad must be the expansion or defense of Islam, not mere booty or conquest. Only wars against infidels (non-Muslims) and apostates (former Muslims) count as jihad, not wars against rebels or bandits. Further, only captives from a jihad could be legally enslaved. At no point does jihad justify killing noncombatants.

Cole Porter

COMPOSER AND SONGWRITER Cole Porter (1891–1964) is best remembered for his clever songs, many of which debuted on Broadway but have gone on to become American classics.

Porter was born in Peru, Indiana, a small community located in the north-central part of the state. His mother came from an extremely wealthy family, who provided her with an excellent education, quality training in music and dance, and everything she needed in life. His father, not from a wealthy family, was a druggist.

Porter was very young when he learned to play the piano and violin. While he excelled at both, he devoted more time to piano because he preferred the way it sounded. Porter composed several songs and an operetta by the time he was ten. His mother quickly recognized his aptitude for music and encouraged his talent. She (with the help of her wealthy father) provided the financial backing for the publication of Porter's music.

Knowing that a good career was important to his family, Porter enrolled in an excellent boarding school that would prepare him for Yale and, eventually, law school. His years at Yale were full of music. He wrote musicals, school fight songs ("Bull Dog" and "Bingo Eg Tale" are still sung today), and many melodies for school productions. By the time he graduated from Yale, Porter had written more than 300 songs. He enrolled in Harvard Law School but soon transferred to the School of Arts and Sciences to study music.

Porter eventually left Harvard to write music in New York. In 1917, after his first production was unsuccessful, he retreated to Paris where, as a wealthy American, he could immerse himself in a social life that welcomed celebrities and international musicians. While in Paris, Porter became known for his lavish parties. In 1919, he married American socialite Linda Lee Thomas, though the marriage was primarily for social status as most people today believe Porter was gay.

Porter's return to Broadway from Paris brought him fame. His new musical *Paris* rose to acclaim, and "Let's Do It (Let's Fall in Love)" became a hit. Some of Porter's greatest songs and lyrics (including "I Get a Kick Out of You" and "All Through the Night") were written for *Anything Goes*, a musical about unusual passengers on a cruise bound for London. Though he suffered a riding accident in 1937, Porter continued to compose. *Kiss Me, Kate* became Porter's most popular musical—the production won a Tony for Best Musical, and Porter won for Best Composer and Lyricist.

Petroleum Reserves

PETROLEUM, ALSO KNOWN as crude oil, is the raw material distilled to make a variety of products, including gasoline, diesel fuels, plastics, kerosene, and asphalt. Because petroleum products are used so commonly, our petroleum reserves are being depleted rapidly. To ensure the continued production of petroleum for as long as possible, oil companies are constantly seeking new reserves.

To find new petroleum reservoirs, geologists look for a characteristic rock formation called a *petroleum trap.* First, the reservoir rock must have a high level of permeability and porosity. Forming oil can ooze upward easily through these porous rocks and collect as tiny droplets within the holes of this spongelike rock. To form a reservoir, there must also be a cap rock, an overlaying bed of impermeable rock that prevents the oil from escaping to the surface. Often the locations of these rock formations are found by drilling rock cores or by performing seismic soundings. Geologists can distinguish a difference in the sounds as they bounce off nonporous and porous rocks. Through these estimates, geologists can even estimate the amount of oil in the reservoir.

The locations of oil reservoirs have not been equally distributed around the globe. Almost two-thirds of the world's discovered oil reserves are located in the Middle East. Russia is also rich in crude oil and is responsible for 12 percent of the world's oil production. The United States produces only 8 percent of the world's oil and yet is responsible for nearly 25 percent of the world's oil consumption.

Because of this dependency on imported oil, the United States has established the National Petroleum Reserve on the northern slope of Alaska. This 9.5-million-acre area is largely undeveloped and has been set aside in case of a national emergency. The nearby Arctic National Wildlife Refuge has been an object of contention for decades. Some want to open these lands for oil drilling, while others are fighting for the preservation of wildlife.

Outside of petroleum reserves, there is also potential for petroleum to be recovered from tar sands, hard oily substances mined from the ground. Although tar sands are abundant, the process of extracting oil from this resource is energy-intensive and inefficient. Therefore, tar sands are not presently considered a feasible source of fuel.

Several analysts agree that we have already depleted about half of the world's oil reserves. As oil reserves dwindle, we will need to switch to renewable energy sources.

Christo

FOR THE PAST FOUR DECADES, the husband-and-wife team of Christo and Jeanne-Claude (who, interestingly, share the same birthday: June 13, 1935) have wrapped or surrounded buildings and landscapes the world over—including a Roman wall, the Pont Neuf in Paris, and a stretch of the Australian coast—in addition to many projects that have nothing to do with wrapping. Their objective is to have people perceive an environment in an entirely new way. With the fabric billowing in the wind, reflecting the light, and seen amid the other elements of their setting, the projects achieve a stunning beauty and grace.

The couple's works are of short duration; they're usually in place from one week to a little over a month and then disassembled. This is in sharp contrast to the enormous amount of time that often goes into their realization. The scale and complexity of their projects mean that the artists need to obtain permission from the relevant authorities, a process that can take years. Their projects also involve vast sums of money. The expenses for this, as for all of Christo and Jeanne-Claude's projects, are borne by the artists themselves, paid for through sales of Christo's studies, drawings, and other works on paper.

Wrapped Reichstag, Berlin

Among the most difficult work for the artists to bring to fruition was *Wrapped Reichstag, Berlin* (1971–1995), requiring as it did that the artists obtain permission from the highest levels of the German government. After negotiations and meetings that occurred over the course of more than two decades, the couple finally received the go-ahead from the German Parliament in February 1994. For two weeks, the Reichstag—a building that was burned in 1933, almost destroyed in 1945, restored in the 1960s, and for the artists is a symbol of democracy—looked like a beautiful work of sculpture. The fabric created the effect of drapery on ancient Greek sculptures.

In *Surrounded Islands: Biscayne Bay, Greater Miami, Florida* (1980–1983), the artists surrounded 11 islands located amid the Greater Miami area with pink fabric. For the duration of the project (two weeks), the islands were transformed into a poetic vision that called to mind Monet's famous paintings of water lilies.

The Discovery of America

CHRISTOPHER COLUMBUS has long been popularly hailed as the discoverer of America. But ask almost any school child who *really* discovered America, and chances are they'll say, "the Vikings."

Historical and archeological evidence have persuaded scholars that Columbus was only one in what may have been a long succession of explorers and adventurers to "discover America." The world will probably never know who was first, but it was clearly not Columbus.

Christopher Columbus

Archeological evidence uncovered in northern Newfoundland during the early 1960s indicates that the Vikings arrived some 500 years before Columbus. Norse sagas also give evidence of the travels of Eric the Red and Leif Erikson into Greenland and beyond long before Columbus was even born.

Speculation about pre-Columbian explorers is nothing new and occurred even before the discoveries in Newfoundland. A study of the various theories published by Rasmus B. Anderson in 1891 under the title "America Not Discovered by Columbus" cites more than 300 sources. Most of the claims or theories lean toward the Norse, but other possible explorations include pre-Columbian visits by the Chinese, Arabs, Welsh, Venetians, Portuguese, and even the Poles.

Mysterious artifacts have only fueled speculation through the years. An old stone tower in Newport, Rhode Island, has been held forth as a Norse church and also dismissed as an old colonial windmill. A strange collection of stones in New Hampshire (now a popular tourist attraction somewhat ambitiously titled "America's Stonehenge") has been variously attributed to Phoenicians, Celts, or colonial smugglers.

A recent book claims that Chinese explorers landed in Massachusetts in 1421. Others have speculated that a Chinese explorer named Fusang arrived in the New World sometime in the fifth century.

There is no convincing archeological evidence for any of these theories—and until there is, the Vikings will retain top billing. Not that Columbus's contribution should be dismissed. It was, after all, his voyages and those of other intrepid mariners immediately afterward that were followed by the permanent settlement of the New World.

Edgar Allan Poe

"Quoth the raven: Nevermore."

ALMOST EVERYONE KNOWS that famous line from the pen of Edgar Allan Poe, one of the most influential American writers of the 19th century, father of the modern detective story—and a possible murder victim.

Poe was born in Boston on January 19, 1809, to struggling actors David and Elizabeth Poe. Both his parents died before he was three years old, and Poe was taken in by prosperous Scottish merchant John Allan. In his early teens, Poe began writing poetry. In February 1826, he entered the University of Virginia, where he began to gamble and drink. When Allan tried to get Poe to forgo literature for law, the two quarreled violently, destroying their relationship (and Poe's financial future) for life. Poe's first book of poetry was released in 1827, and two more followed in 1829 and 1831. He briefly flirted with the military from 1827 to 1831—he got himself court-martialed and dismissed from West Point—then moved to Baltimore to live with relatives.

In 1833 (around the time he started shifting his focus from poetry to prose) Poe's story *The Manuscript Found in a Bottle* won first prize from a local newspaper. He moved to Richmond, Virginia, in July 1835 to work as an editor on the magazine *Southern Literary Messenger*. In May 1836, the 27-year-old Poe married his 13-year-old cousin Virginia. Poe's insightful literary reviews for the *Messenger*, along with the publication of his own innovative short stories, increased his reputation as a writer.

Driven by his desire to found and edit a national literary magazine, Poe moved frequently, writing and taking editing jobs to stave off abject poverty. In April 1841, *Graham's Magazine* printed Poe's *Murders in the Rue Morgue*, considered the first modern detective story. In June 1843, Poe's *The Gold Bug* was so popular that the newspaper it was published in had to print a second edition. In January 1845, *The Raven*—perhaps the most popular poem in American history—was published to popular acclaim in the *Evening Mirror*.

Virginia Poe died of tuberculosis in January 1847. On October 7, 1849, Poe abruptly died in Baltimore. The cause of his death is still unknown, and speculations range from suicide to alcoholism to murder.

In addition to his many contributions to the American short story as an art form, Poe has become known as the classic "starving artist." Today, the man who struggled for a dollar has influenced writers the world over and is an icon of American popular culture.

Ronald Reagan (1911–2004)

T HE 40TH PRESIDENT of the United States, Ronald Reagan took an unlikely path to the White House—beginning as a motion picture actor and ultimately attaining the highest political office in the nation. In many ways, Reagan's rise to power reads like a classic American success story. He was born into a poor family in Tampico, Illinois, played football and acted in high school plays, and worked his way through Eureka College in Illinois where he was active in football and theater.

After college, Reagan became a radio sports announcer in Iowa. His career path changed in 1937 when he landed a screen test while visiting a friend in Southern California. His screen test was impressive enough to land him a role in *Love Is on the Air*, a B movie in which he played a radio reporter. Over the next 27 years, he acted in 50 movies, perhaps most famously in *Knute Rockne, All American*. In that movie, he played the terminally ill college football star George Gipp and uttered one of his most famous lines (and future political slogan), "Win one for the Gipper." From 1954 to 1962, he also served as host of television's *General Electric Theater*, which further enhanced his fame.

His first foray into politics came during the 1964 presidential election when he gave a televised speech for Republican candidate Barry Goldwater. Many observers saw the speech as a masterful piece of political genius, and although Goldwater lost, Reagan emerged as a popular new figure in the Republican Party. He was elected governor of California in 1966 and remained in office until 1975. As governor, he won recognition as a hard-nosed administrator who successfully tackled problems and articulated a conservative Republican ideology.

Reagan made a run for president in 1980 and easily defeated the incumbent, Jimmy Carter. He was reelected in a landslide vote in 1984 and left office as one of the most popular presidents in U.S. history. While in office, he oversaw an end to the crippling inflation and unemployment of the late 1970s. Even though the national debt grew significantly during his presidency—thanks to increased defense spending—consumer and business confidence rose and unemployment fell.

Perhaps his greatest accomplishment was opening a dialogue with Soviet premier and political reformer, Mikhail Gorbachev. Through their meetings, the two leaders negotiated a treaty that eliminated the use of certain intermediate range missiles. Most scholars today agree that Reagan's willingness to talk strengthened Gorbachev's reform movement and helped set the stage for the fall of the Soviet Union and the end of the Cold War.

Roman Games

THE MOST COMMON perception of Roman Games (Ludi Romani) is that of gladiatorial contests fought to the death in front of a large crowd of cheering spectators. While these bloody matches did become a part of Roman culture, the games actually began as religious festivals, celebrations of military victories, the passing of generations, or deliverances from crisis. Typically, the festivals would last for as long as three days and consist of sporting events or theatrical performances.

One of the most popular forms of sport at these events was chariot racing. The charioteer was carried on a small two-wheeled carriage pulled by a team of two to six horses. Hundreds of spectators would watch the races in long, narrow amphitheaters called *circuses,* the most popular being Circus Maximus in Rome.

Chariots were usually divided into teams designated by the colors white, red, blue, and green. Spectators would become avid fans of a particular color. The life of a charioteer was often short since an accident during the race frequently resulted in serious injury or death, but there were champions who profited handsomely from racing. Gaius Appuleius Diocles entered the arena at the age of 18 and finally retired at 42 after winning more than 1,400 races.

Gladiatorial contests were first performed in Rome during the funerals of public figures starting in 264 B.C. They proved so popular that by the time of Julius Caesar (the first century B.C.) and Emperor Trajan (end of the first century A.D.), thousands of gladiators fought in the Roman Coliseum over as many as 100 straight days. These contests were not limited to the citizens of Rome but were also held in coliseums in all corners of the Roman Empire.

Public executions, wild animal hunts, and even naval battles took place in the Roman Coliseum over the course of more than 600 years. Christian Emperor Constantine attempted to abolish these deadly games in A.D. 325, but they were reinstated by his successors. They were extremely popular with Roman officials because they kept the citizens' minds off more important political and economic issues.

POSTSCRIPT

▦ Not all gladiatorial matches ended in death. One famous gladiator, Flamma, had 21 wins, 9 draws, and 4 defeats before his death at the age of 30.

The History of Music Criticism

SOME PEOPLE INSIST that it is impossible to adequately describe one art form in terms of another—and suggest that music "speaks for itself." Be that as it may, a tradition of written commentary on the effects and qualities of music and its appropriate role in social activity dates at least as far back as the history of music in the Western tradition. Extended sections of the writings of Plato and Aristotle address contrasting perspectives on the nature and importance of music, and discussions on the role of music and worship have been crucial to the self-definition of every branch of Christianity.

The notion of music criticism—specific and regular commentary on the value of individual musical works and their place within an evolving set of traditions—is, however, arguably an invention of the 19th century, when increasing musical literacy among the growing middle-class public fostered the idea of collective and informed musical taste.

While he was not the inventor of the genre, composer Robert Schumann was perhaps the most prominent music critic in the early decades of the 19th century. In 1834, he founded the *Neue Zeitschrift für Musik* (*New Newspaper for Music*) in Leipzig. In addition to providing commentary on specific new works or performers, the *Neue Zeitschrift* also fueled the evolving 19th-century debate on the question of "program" versus "absolute" music. (Program music is meant to be enjoyed as a "representation" of an image or emotion. Absolute music does not have any meaning or agenda outside of itself.)

As the debates on musical aesthetics expanded in the mid-1800s, more and more nonmusic periodicals began featuring music criticism. While in some cases late 19th-century music critics were highly trained musicians and composers in their own right, the role gradually became specialized. This fact was controversial in the eyes of some composers, who felt they were not being judged by their peers and argued that critics were inherently unsympathetic to cutting-edge experimentation. However, 19th- and early 20th-century music criticism (both in Europe and in North America) was certainly a crucial factor in the establishment of a "canon" of great musical works that is largely accepted to this day.

POSTSCRIPT

■ A number of late 19th-century literary figures wrote music criticism. Walt Whitman wrote for the *Brooklyn Eagle* in the 1840s and '50s; George Bernard Shaw contributed to several London publications in the last quarter of the century.

The Biodiversity Crisis

ALL LIVING ORGANISMS—animals, plants, microorganisms—are a part of the world's biodiversity (biological diversity). Healthy biodiversity reflects a healthy ecosystem. There are three primary ways of measuring diversity: genetic (Are there a healthy number of different genes in the cheetah population?), species (How many types of monkeys remain?), and ecosystem (Are different habitats disappearing in Costa Rica from deforestation?).

These measurements help ecologists determine the relative health of particular ecosystems, as well as the health of our global ecosystem. In both respects, the news is grim. In particular, the world's "biodiversity hotspots" (regions with particularly high levels of species variations) are facing rapid losses in biodiversity. Brazil's Atlantic rain forests alone (a small fraction of the Amazon) contain 20,000 plant species, 1,350 animal species, and millions of insect species. Unfortunately, like many other biodiversity hotspots, this swath of forest is prime real estate for farmers, loggers, and developers.

Many people wonder why biodiversity should be considered a priority for conservation efforts. Perhaps the most immediate reason is that humans worldwide consume at least 40,000 different species of plants and animals each day. In the developed world, biodiversity helps introduce tougher varieties of domesticated crops. For instance, wild strains of rice can help inject greater resistance to bacteria and pests while providing higher nutrition value.

On a greater, more long-term scale, it is important to maintain the earth's biodiversity because different species depend on each other for survival. When biodiversity is threatened, cycles of life are interrupted; we may not fully understand the consequences of this interruption for generations to come.

Plants and animals currently face a variety of threats, from habitat destruction to the introduction of invasive species. Although predictions vary, some say that roughly 500 rain forest species become extinct every year. An entire field of study, *conservation biology*, seeks to help preserve biodiversity. For instance, researchers are studying ways to breed captive tigers and pandas to boost the wild populations.

To make matters even more pressing, recent studies indicate that global warming is exacerbating the decline in biodiversity. Rapid global warming can lead to the extinction of animals and plants that are not able to adapt to an Earth affected by an increased temperature.

The Builders of Rome

MODERN ROME IS largely the creation of Baroque artist Gianlorenzo Bernini (1598–1680). He designed the colonnade that embraces the Piazza San Pietro on the doorstep of St. Peter's Basilica. His marble angels ornament the Ponte Sant'Angelo that spans the Tiber River nearby. Bernini's fountains enliven squares throughout the city, and churches are rich with his sculpture.

Less well-known is the work of architect Francesco Borromini (1599–1667). In his buildings, light and dark along with concave and convex lines create the sensation of constant movement and growth. Sant'Ivo della Sapienza was meant to be a "chapel of wisdom." The structure, based on the geometry of two intersecting triangles, seems to be a metaphor for an unknowable divine.

Bernini was a child prodigy, producing work in his father's studio by the time he was 11 or 12. After an apprenticeship in Milan, Borromini was, by age 16, a respected designer and sculptor in Rome. Both men were famously temperamental, but Bernini was sociable and charming whereas Borromini was a loner often in the grip of depression.

The baldacchino

Bernini, however, owed much to the engineering knowledge and formal inventiveness of his chief rival, since his ambitious plans sometimes outstripped his technical skills. Borromini devised the engineering solution that allowed Bernini to create the towering bronze *baldacchino,* or canopy, that stands under the vast dome of St. Peter's. He also explained the structural failures of the bell tower Bernini was building at St. Peter's, stopping the work before disaster could occur.

In an era when artists and architects were celebrities, Bernini's and Borromini's respective works were closely scrutinized, analyzed, and interpreted. This fascination may be behind a story about Bernini's Four Rivers Fountain in the Piazza Navona. Large figures represent four rivers that are symbolic of the four corners of the earth. *Rio della Plata,* emblematic of the Americas, lifts his arm over his face. It is said that the he cannot bear to look at the church of Sant'Agnese in Agone opposite, the work of Borromini.

Churches by these remarkable competitors stand almost side by side on a quiet street in Rome. These exquisite buildings are an inspiration for modern architects and a magnet for visitors to the Eternal City.

The Creation of Israel

THE ANNOUNCEMENT by the Jewish Agency's Executive Committee on May 14, 1948, that the Jewish area of Palestine would now be the independent country of Israel caused reverberations throughout the Middle East and the entire world that are still felt today. Israel's creation was the culmination of decades of work by Jews called *Zionists*. Frustrated by the lack of a homeland, Zionists strived to re-create the biblical state of Israel.

After World War I, the League of Nations awarded to Great Britain a mandate over the territory called Palestine, with instructions to allow Jewish immigration and help create a Jewish homeland. Local Arabs opposed the plan, and there was unrest and sporadic fighting throughout Palestine. Britain clouded the issue further by trying to placate both Arabs and Jews, alienating both in the process. Adolf Hitler's rise to power in Germany led to increasing Jewish migration to Palestine. This increased even more after World War II, which resulted in escalating tension and violence.

The new United Nations tried to fix the problem after the British announced in February 1947 that they wanted to pull out of Palestine. The U.N. sent a commission to study the area and come up with a solution. This commission recommended that Palestine be divided into seven areas—three each for Arabs and Jews, with the greater Jerusalem area directly administered by the U.N. The Jewish Agency decided to accept this plan, but Arab governments loudly proclaimed that they would not abide by it. As violence increased, the British decided to withdraw their soldiers.

The result was the announcement of the creation of Israel on May 14, 1948. The next day, armies from all adjacent Arab nations invaded the new Jewish homeland, supplemented by volunteers from Saudi Arabia and Iraq. Although the Arab forces were more numerous and better-equipped, the Jewish troops were more unified—and they were fighting against annihilation. By the time the U.N. managed to enforce a ceasefire in January 1949, Israel had repelled the Arab attacks and established a viable country.

Thousands of Palestinian refugees had fled the fighting and were not permitted to return to their homes by the new country. Israel's borders remained as they did at the ceasefire until June 1967, when the Six-Day War expanded the Jewish state. The Palestinian refugee problem is still an issue today, with continuing violence in the Gaza Strip and on the West Bank, as a fledgling Palestinian state tries to establish its own nation.

William Shakespeare

DRAMATIST, THEATRICAL entrepreneur, and poet, Shakespeare is revered today by lovers of English literature. Although little is known for certain about the exact circumstances of Shakespeare's life, speculation about his personal dealings, his career, and the authorship of his plays has created a subgenre within Shakespearean studies.

Among the known facts are that Shakespeare was born in Stratford-on-Avon in the county of Warwickshire, England, in 1564. His father, a glover, was active in local affairs and became a bailiff and justice of the peace. At 18, Shakespeare married Anne Hathaway, eight years his senior. Their daughter Suzanna was born in 1583; twins Hamnet and Judith in 1585. Although when or how Shakespeare entered the theater is uncertain, a pamphlet printed in 1592 mentions him; by 1594, he was an active member of Lord Chamberlain's Men, a theatrical company.

London was the center for the burgeoning English theater at this time, and Shakespeare lived there during his active years, though he later acquired property in Stratford, where his wife and children remained. He probably retired from most theatrical involvement in 1613. He died in 1616 and was buried in Holy Trinity Church in Stratford. The monument to him on the north wall compares him to Socrates and Virgil.

There are 38 plays attributed to Shakespeare, along with a sequence of 154 sonnets and five longer poems. Only half of the plays appeared in print during his lifetime; the first nearly complete edition was the *First Folio*, published in 1623. Today, Shakespeare's plays are usually categorized as comedies, histories, tragedies, or romances. Among his most popular are *A Midsummer Night's Dream; The Merchant of Venice; Richard III; Henry IV, Parts 1 and 2; Julius Caesar; Macbeth; Hamlet;* and *The Tempest.* Throughout his working life, Shakespeare was popular and productive. Although doubts have been raised about the authenticity of his work, none have proved convincing.

The theater in Shakespeare's day was entertainment enjoyed by all classes of society. Although a huge body of scholarly writing about Shakespeare has accumulated over the years, he remains an iconic figure in popular as well as "high" culture. The reconstructed Globe Theatre in London—the original Globe opened in 1599 and burned down in 1613—attracts thousands of visitors each year. Shakespeare's plays, as well as film and television adaptations of them, are performed worldwide. Both the poetry of Shakespearean dialogue and the vast range of his characters possess a universal and enduring appeal.

Niccolo Machiavelli (1469–1527)

N ICCOLO MACHIAVELLI is today identified as a leading Renaissance thinker who was equally influential and notorious. However, the works that cemented his reputation were not published until after his death.

Beginning in 1498, Machiavelli spent 14 years as a high official in republican Florence. At that time in Italy, rival city-states schemed and fought for supremacy. When the Medici family returned to Florence with Spanish troops, they put an end to the republic, forced Machiavelli from office, and made him retire to his estate. For the rest of his life, he angled in vain for a new political position. He also wrote extensively. His writings included biographies, a study of Livy, seven treatises on the art of war, and several plays. In 1519, Pope Leo X commissioned him to write a political history of Florence.

Machiavelli's most famous book, *The Prince,* was written in the futile hope of gaining a political office from the Medicis. Advice books called "mirrors for princes" had long been written to counsel rulers on ideal methods of governing and outline the model Christian prince. *The Prince* broke ranks with previous works by completely separating politics from Christian ethics. For Machiavelli, winning—by any means necessary—was the all-important principle. He recommended lying, breaking treaties and promises, torturing opponents, and ruling through fear when necessary. He famously wrote that it was better to be feared than to be loved. Machiavelli also maintained that manipulation of the public was preferable to the use of open force. Yet, any moderation in violence was urged on practical, not ethical, grounds:

"… in seizing a state, the usurper ought to examine closely into all those injuries which it is necessary for him to inflict, and to do them all at one stroke so as not to have to repeat them daily … benefits ought to be given little by little, so that the flavor of them may last longer."

Although Machiavelli often protested that he was only describing politics as it was really practiced, *The Prince,* with its frank amorality, horrified many in Christian Europe, especially the clergy. Copies were publicly burned in several cities after its publication in 1532, and Machiavelli was posthumously denounced as an anti-Christ from many pulpits. To this day, the term "Machiavellian" refers to amoral scheming. Still, Machiavelli would prove to be a major influence on David Hume's political writings and many Enlightenment thinkers. In the years since the first scholarly edition of his works appeared in 1782, Machiavelli's place as a founder of modern political science has been assured.

Fibonacci Numbers:
The Mathematics of Nature

IF THE WORLD HAS come about by design, then the designer must also have been a mathematician.

Leonardo of Pisa, better known today as Fibonacci, was born around 1170 and died sometime after 1240. He was Italian by birth but grew up in North Africa. During his life, he traveled widely and learned a great deal about mathematics from scholars he met in Africa and the Middle East. From his studies, Fibonacci recognized the superiority of Arabic numerals (1, 2, 3, 4, 5, etc.) to Roman numerals (I, II, III, IV, V, etc.), which were used in Europe at the time. Through his writing, he introduced these numbers—and the numerical symbol for zero—to European mathematics.

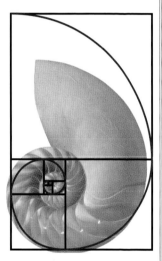

In a book about the use of Arabic numerals published in 1202, Fibonacci discussed an interesting numerical phenomenon. In a certain number sequence, each number is the sum of the two previous numbers (0, 1, 1, 2, 3, 5, 8, 13, 21, 34, 55, 89, etc.). What is particularly fascinating is that this sequence corresponds to many forms and patterns found in nature.

The diagram on this page shows squares assembled according to the Fibonacci series. The smallest square has a side one unit long, the next larger square has a side two units long, and the next one is a three-unit square, and so on. A curve divides each square and is equal to a quarter of a circle. When linked together, the curves create the same kind of spiral that is found inside a nautilus shell.

Fibonacci's spiral pattern also appears in the seeds of a sunflower and the scales of a pinecone. A surprising variety of flowers have petal counts that match Fibonacci numbers. For example, irises have 3 petals, buttercups have 5 petals, delphiniums have 8, many daisies have 13, and black-eyed Susans have 21. There are also many other flowers that have 34, 55, or 89 petals.

Stax and Motown

T HE YEAR 1959 MARKED the establishment of two groundbreaking independent record labels. Both Detroit's Motown and Memphis's Stax were successful at popularizing music by African American artists, each in its own way.

Detroit's Berry Gordy, Jr., was an amateur boxer and automobile assembly-line worker with an ear for commercial music. What he lacked in star power he more than made up for with vision and determination. His first efforts bore fruit when R&B crooner Jackie Wilson struck gold with a string of tunes Gordy had cowritten, among them "Lonely Teardrops."

The Supremes

But being a successful songwriter wasn't enough for the ambitious Gordy. He envisioned producing records by Detroit's local talent that he could pitch to a nationwide (i.e., white) audience as pop crossovers. Further, drawing upon his auto industry background, he decided the records would be generated assembly-line style: All aspects of production were handled in-house, as recording artists like Martha Reeves, Smokey Robinson, and Marvin Gaye helped with everything from answering phones to playing drums on the recordings of other musicians.

"Motown—the Sound of Young America" recording studio opened in a house dubbed "Hitsville U.S.A." on West Grand Boulevard in January 1959. Aspiring artists were schooled in decorum and presentation, then shuttled throughout the country on package tours that saw the likes of the Marvelettes, the Four Tops, the Miracles, and "Little" Stevie Wonder playing to theaters before black and white audiences. The label's two biggest acts, the Temptations and the Supremes, ruled the charts with classics like "My Girl" and "You Can't Hurry Love."

Meanwhile in Memphis, a white brother and sister, James Stewart and Estelle Axton, found success with a raw brand of gritty soul and blues that would prove to be more influential, if less commercially successful. Stax was set up in an abandoned movie theater on McLemore Avenue.

Their first major success came with a mostly instrumental tune called "Last Night," released by Stax house band the Mar-Keys. Later, organist Booker T. Jones would join; as Booker T. and the MGs (for "Memphis Group"), the ensemble produced a string of hits.

Carbon Dioxide and Global Warming

GREENHOUSE GASES ALLOW sunlight to enter and pass through the atmosphere freely. As solar radiation from the sun hits the earth, some of this radiation is reflected back toward the atmosphere. Greenhouse gases absorb this reflected infrared radiation and then warm the atmosphere by radiating heat originating from the absorbed radiation. Carbon dioxide is the most abundant greenhouse gas contributing to global warming.

Carbon dioxide is released into the atmosphere by the burning of fossil fuels, including coal, oil, and natural gas. Electricity generation is the largest source of greenhouse gases in the United States. Since coal-fired electric power plants alone account for 56 percent of the electricity produced in the United States, increasing our energy efficiency and switching to renewable energy sources such as solar or wind energy could drastically reduce greenhouse gas emissions.

Transportation is the second-largest source of greenhouse gases in the United States. Burning gasoline fuel not only releases particles that cause air pollution, but it also releases carbon dioxide. Increasing the use of public transportation and driving more fuel-efficient vehicles would help to reduce greenhouse gas emissions.

All in all, human activities have resulted in the highest levels of carbon dioxide in the earth's atmosphere in almost one million years. As a result, Earth's average temperature increased 1.0°F (0.6°C) during the 20th century. Due to our dependence on fossil fuels, carbon dioxide levels will only continue to rise, causing the earth's temperature to go even higher.

The effects of global climate change are far-reaching. Coastal regions and islands will be lost as melting ice caps release water into the oceans, increasing sea levels. Already, mountaintop glaciers have retreated in many parts of the world. Due to climbing temperatures, tropical diseases will spread into temperate latitudes. Droughts and water shortages will worsen to the point that five billion people are projected to have limited water supplies by 2025.

Ever-increasing greenhouse gas emissions and global temperatures are not inevitable, however. The U.N. Framework Convention on Climate Change has outlined a plan for reducing greenhouse gas emissions worldwide. From 1990 to 2003, Germany reduced its greenhouse gas emissions by 18.5 percent, and the United Kingdom reduced its emissions by 13 percent. Now other countries need to follow suit.

Surrealism

SURREALISM WAS AN OFFSHOOT of Dadaism but without that movement's inherent nihilism. It was also heavily influenced by psychotherapist Sigmund Freud, who believed that art could be a powerful means of self-revelation and catharsis. He posited the idea that the images that emerge from the subconscious are in some way more truthful because they have not been influenced by rational thought.

Writer André Breton officially launched the movement in 1924 when he penned the "Surrealist Manifesto," which declared the movement's aim to resolve the differences between conscious and unconscious realities by moving toward a *surrealite* ("super-reality"). Translating this aim into painting, the Surrealist artists tried to bring together both outer and inner reality in their compositions, just like fragments of real life can be found in the world of dreams.

The Surrealist artists were extremely diverse in their styles, ranging from Salvador Dali's hard-edged dream worlds to Max Ernst's ominous, moody canvases. Three contrasting approaches dominated the movement. Most widely discussed are those who advocated and used automatism to dictate their compositions, including Ernst and Andre Masson. Automatism, like the automatic writing practiced by Breton, involved drawing or painting without planning, without predetermination, and without thinking. The idea was to get down images and ideas directly from the subconscious because they were pure and truthful. Dali, René Magritte, and Giorgio De Chirico represent another approach to Surrealism with their scrupulously detailed styles that recall

The Persistence of Memory *by Salvador Dali*

hallucinations and dreamscapes, as in Dali's *The Persistence of Memory* and De Chirico's *The Delights of a Poet*. Finally, some surrealist objects, photographs, and paintings, such as the "rayographs" of Man Ray, used an irrational juxtaposition of images to suggest an alternative reality related to our own but just beyond our sensibilities.

Surrealism remained centered in Paris until World War II, when many European artists emigrated to the United States, making New York the new hub. Surrealism was widely disseminated around the world through major exhibitions and important art and literary journals.

Joseph Stalin

UNDER THE LEADERSHIP OF JOSEPH STALIN (1879–1953) the Soviet Union became a superpower—but at the cost of millions of lives.

In 1922, Vladimir Lenin appointed Stalin his party's general secretary. Instead of using the office to mirror Lenin's policies, Stalin embarked on his own course and removed party supporters of Leon Trotsky, his political rival. Although it had been Lenin's desire for Trotsky to become the next Soviet leader, Stalin joined forces with Trotsky's rivals and took over party leadership when Lenin died.

Stalin began his regime by defining agricultural policy. The *kulaks*, who were peasant farmers, owned their own land and were seen by Stalin as enemies of the state because they controlled the supply of their goods. When industrial workers complained of food shortages, Stalin confiscated the kulaks' property and included their land in the new collective farms the government had established.

Stalin and Trotsky continued to disagree over government policy. The differences were not resolved until Stalin had Trotsky removed from the government and banished to central Asia. Then Stalin began his program of modernizing the Soviet Union. His first Five-Year Plan focused on developing heavy industry. Unrealistic goals were set for increased coal, iron, and electric production; repressive measures were instituted when workers failed to meet government expectations. Opposition to Stalin's policies began to surface. Arrests, intense interrogations, executions, and assassinations were used to quell opposition. During Stalin's reign, millions of people were killed or died as a result of his policies.

Germany's intentions to extend its control over Eastern Europe caused Stalin to begin strengthening his armed forces. Germany invaded the Soviet Union in 1941. Over a period of two years, the Soviets battled fiercely and finally caused the Germans to retreat after their victory at Stalingrad. Stalin had become a key player on the international scene. He met with Winston Churchill and Franklin Roosevelt in Tehran, Iran, to discuss military strategy and postwar policy.

Stalin feared Britain and the United States would sign a peace agreement with Germany, withdraw from the war, and leave the Soviet Union on its own to fight Germany. He urged the Allies to launch a second European front to defeat Hitler. The D-Day landings in France on June 6, 1944, served as the second front of the war in Europe.

Stalin was hailed as a wartime leader within the Soviet Union, and he worked to spread Communism throughout Europe. He died in 1953.

Robert Frost's "Stopping by Woods on a Snowy Evening"

Whose woods these are I think I know.
His house is in the village, though;
He will not see me stopping here
To watch his woods fill up with snow.

Tʜᴇ ɪᴅᴇᴀ ғᴏʀ "Stopping by Woods on a Snowy Evening" came to American poet Robert Frost (1874–1963) near dawn in the winter of 1922 after a long night spent at his farmhouse in Shaftsbury, Vermont, composing another poem, "New Hampshire." He claimed to have written "Stopping by Woods" in just a few minutes. Both poems were published in a volume called *New Hampshire* (1923).

"Stopping by Woods" is composed entirely of words of one syllable (89) or two (16), except for the single three-syllable word "promises." The poem uses a rhyme scheme of a-a-b-a, with the next verse's "a" line rhyming with the previous verse's "b" line. Its iambic tetrameter meter (da DUM / da DUM / da DUM / da DUM) imitates the gentle clopping of a horse's hoofs—which is appropriate, since the occasion is that the speaker has stopped his horse-drawn sleigh to meditate on a dark woods during a snowy winter night.

Although the poem can be read and appreciated at its surface level, simply as a beautifully crafted meditation on a snowy winter night, it is often interpreted and taught as having two levels of meaning. The owner's "house" in the village could refer to either a human owner of the land the woods sits on or to a church, the "house" of God—the owner of the earth and everything in it.

The next-to-last line, "And miles to go before I sleep," is thought to refer to the literal sleep awaiting the poet at the end of the night's journey, while the repeat of this sentence in the last line refers to the sleep of death, which the speaker, finds a lulling, tempting prospect.

Although his poem "The Road Not Taken" is arguably just as well-known, Frost called "Stopping by Woods"—a mere 16 lines—his "best bid for remembrance." Bearing out his words, this poem is one of the most widely discussed of all Frost's work.

Genghis Khan (c. 1160–1227)

ORIGINALLY NAMED TEMUJIN, Genghis Khjan was the son of a tribal chieftain who was poisoned in an intertribal feud when Temujin was nine. Without an adult leader, the tribe drifted apart, leaving Temujin's family to fend for themselves.

Over the next two decades, Temujin reclaimed leadership of his tribe and built alliances with Toghril, a powerful Mongol leader who had been *anda* (sworn brother) with Temujin's father, and Jamuka, another ambitious young Mongol leader. As Temujin proved himself a powerful leader in battle, more tribes acknowledged him as their war leader. Soon, he began to systematically eliminate all rivals, including Toghril and Jamuka. In 1206, the assembled Mongol tribes recognized Temujin as their ruler and gave him the name Genghis Khan, "Universal Ruler."

Having unified Mongolia, Genghis Khan turned toward China, which had a long history of conflict with the Mongol tribes. His warriors captured Xi Xia and the Jin empire by 1211 and Zhongdu (now Beijing) in 1215. Leaving the further subjugation of northern China to his generals, Genghis Khan then marched west against Muhammad Ali Shah, emperor of Khwarezm, who had made the mistake of sending the severed head of Genghis Khan's ambassador in response to the Mongol's offer of peace.

In the West, Genghis Khan is remembered for his campaign against Khwarezm, which was condemned by contemporary historians for its savagery. Though Mongols did not usually partake in lavish displays of violence, they didn't hesitate to kill those who refused to surrender.

Despite his reputation for brutality, the fearsome Mongol was a liberal ruler and administrator. His legal codes made no distinction between conquered and conqueror, and he rebuilt the cities destroyed in the course of conquest. Trade routes and markets were protected by Mongol patrols. He chose civil administrators from the scholars and merchants of defeated nations.

In 1226, at age 66, Genghis Khan began a new campaign against the Chin and Sung empires. Early in the march, he fell from his horse while hunting, causing his stomach to hemorrhage. Although he grew steadily weaker, he refused to turn back. On his deathbed, in August 1227, he commanded that his death be kept a secret, and the campaign continued.

At the time of Genghis Khan's death, his rule stretched from Beijing to the Aral Sea, the largest empire ever conquered by a single commander.

Book of Revelation

WRITTEN IN GREEK between A.D. 68 and 96, the Book of Revelation is the last canonical book in the New Testament. The author identifies himself as a Christian named John living in exile on the island of Patmos in the Aegean Sea. While it is not precisely known who the author was, some believe it to be John the Baptist, who also wrote the fourth Gospel. Revelation is addressed to seven churches of Asia Minor (modern-day Turkey): Ephesus, Smyrna, Pergamon, Thyatira, Sardis, Philadelphia, and Laodicea.

In extravagantly symbolic and metaphorical language borrowed from the Old Testament books of Ezekiel and Zechariah, Revelation describes the events that will signal God's judgment on the world. Ultimately, it tells how Christ will return to Earth in glory at the end of the world, having triumphed over Satan to usher in the everlasting reign of God. The Book of Revelation consists of seven sections: the prologue; letters to the churches of Asia Minor; heaven's throne room, the seven seals and seven trumpets; beasts, war, seven plagues, seven bowls of wrath, and the Battle of Armageddon; the judgment of Babylon and a new heaven and Earth; a new Jerusalem; and an epilogue.

Revelation has been controversial through history, thanks to the difficulty of the text and varying interpretations of its message. This difficulty is manifested in the use of numerological symbols throughout the Revelation. In the book, the number four stands for the world, six indicates imperfection, seven signifies total perfection, and twelve references the tribes of Israel. One example of this deep symbolism occurs in the description of God and the Lamb (Christ) in the throne room of heaven. First, the Lamb is depicted with seven horns and seven eyes. When interpreted, this short description indicates that Christ has universal power (seven horns) and perfect knowledge (seven eyes).

Throughout history, the Book of Revelation has been called everything from canonical to nonsense written by a madman. Martin Luther even wrote that Revelation is "neither apostolic nor prophetic" and that "Christ is neither taught nor known in it." However, others have gone to the book in search of meaning. Some have attempted to arrange it chronologically, but that has proven difficult, as the structure of the book is nonlinear. Others view it historically, believing that it is a commentary on events from the time it was written. For example, references to Babylon in Revelation might actually pertain to the Roman Empire. To others, it is seen as prophecy, as they believe it reflects the condition of the world today.

Verdi's *Rigoletto*

IN MID-19TH-CENTURY Italy, during a time of absolute monarchies, it was unwise to create a story exploring a king's wrongdoings. This is why Verdi and his librettist Carlo Maria Piave had to change the setting of Victor Hugo's novella *Le roi s'amuse (The King Amuses Himself)* in order to appease the Austrian state censors. The resulting opera, *Rigoletto* (1851), is one of the most renowned and valued of Verdi's works. The mixture of beautiful solo showpieces and intense, gripping ensemble numbers (including a common theme for Verdi: the relationship between a pure daughter and a tortured father) make for a work that perfectly exemplifies the 19th-century Italian *bel canto* style.

The title character is a court jester, who serves the 16th-century Duke of Mantua, a womanizer. Rigoletto publicly mocks an old man whose daughter has been raped by the duke, and the old man curses him, to the jester's horror. As the story unfolds, we discover that Rigoletto has a young daughter, Gilda. When Gilda is also seduced by the duke, Rigoletto plots to have his master killed. Gilda, however, is both pure at heart and deeply in love with the duke. Sacrificing herself, she manages to be stabbed and put into a sack in place of the duke. Receiving the

Rigoletto

sack with his victim from the hired assassin, Rigoletto hears the duke's voice in the distance and opens the sack in panic, obtaining Gilda's blessing as she dies in his arms and he recalls the old father's curse.

The most famous song from the show—one of Verdi's most famous melodies overall—is the duke's signature cynical musing on women's fickleness, "La donna è mobile" ("Woman is fickle / like a feather in the wind / she changes her words / and her thoughts"). The song is not only deeply ironic in itself—it is the duke who is cruelly fickle, while Gilda, the heroine, is steadfast and brave—but it is also the offstage cue that later brings Rigoletto to the realization that the duke is still alive. Tradition has it that "La donna è mobile" was sung in the streets of Venice (then an Austrian territory) the day following the show's 1851 premiere; it certainly has been a showcase song for operatic tenors ever since.

Especially powerful is the quartet from Act III. The scene involves Rigoletto, Gilda, the duke, and the prostitute Maddalena ("sister" of the hired assassin). While the duke attempts to seduce Maddalena inside an inn, Rigoletto shows Gilda her "beloved's" betrayal. Each of the four characters expresses a different emotion, resulting in an intense musical texture.

Wetlands

THANKS TO CONSERVATION and restoration efforts, the rate of wetlands loss has slowed in the past two decades, but overall there are still more acres of wetlands lost each year than created by restoration efforts. Some wetlands are drained or filled in; others are suffering from chemical contamination and excess nutrient levels. Halting the destruction of our wetlands is important to both natural systems and the quality of human life on Earth.

The wetlands supply food and shelter for a diverse set of plants and animals. Dead plants break down in the water and form small particles of a nutrient-rich material called *detritus.* Detritus is the main food source for many shellfish, fish, and insects, which are in turn food for a variety of reptiles, birds, amphibians, and mammals. Ducks, geese, woodpeckers, and other migratory birds also use the wetlands as cover as they nest and raise their young. Since so many plants and animals depend on the wetlands, including more than one-third of the threatened and endangered species in the United States, preserving the wetlands is vital to prevent many species from becoming extinct.

These natural systems and wildlife also benefit humankind in a variety of ways. In the southeast United States, commercial fishing and shellfish harvesting largely depend on wetlands habitats. Wetlands also act as a sponge to trap and slowly release runoff water, protecting cities from floods. Furthermore, wetlands act as a last line of defense from surges during tropical storms. The wetland plants hold soil in place with their roots and prevent erosion. Many coastal areas are restoring these vital buffer zones of wetlands for this purpose.

This buffering zone of wetlands is also important near inland regions to improve water quality. The wetlands intercept runoff water from streets and farms before it reaches streams and lakes. This runoff water often contains pollutants and excess nutrients. The nutrients nitrogen and phosphorus are of special concern since they are found in fertilizers applied to field crops. The runoff water from agricultural fields dumps these excess nutrients into streams and eventually into oceans. These excess nutrients cause excessive algal growth, and the resulting algal blooms can poison and suffocate fish and other ocean life. This process can be prevented, however, by the filtering properties of wetlands. In the wetlands, excess nutrients are absorbed by plants and removed from the water or sediment to the bottom of the wetlands. Consequently, conserving and restoring wetlands near agricultural fields is especially important.

West African Masks

AT ALL PLACES and in all times, humans have disguised their appearance by wearing masks and costumes. Nowadays in the Western world, people wear masks primarily to amuse themselves—and they have no serious intention of personifying the man, woman, or imaginary creature depicted on their mask.

Conditions, both current and historic, are quite different in West Africa. Though most people in this part of the world are either Christian or Muslim, many follow traditional religions in which masks have a spiritual function. According to scholar Christopher Roy, West African masks embody spirits that are "supernatural, unseen, unknown, incomprehensible, so that the concrete forms that are carved to house them must also be invented." The masks, he continues, often depict spirits that people associate with the region's wild animals. When these masks are worn during dance rituals, they honor the animal spirits and summon their blessings.

Many of West Africa's traditional religions profess that human spirits live on after physical death and influence their descendants, along with the weather, crops, livestock, and more. In order to avoid misfortune and encourage prosperity, Africans seek to appease the spirits of the dead as they worship their gods.

Traditional religious rites can include prayers, songs, dances, and dramatic narratives called *masquerades.* Some rites are carried out before the entire tribe, but secret societies perform others in private. Different rites may celebrate festivals, solemnize marriages, or accompany funerals. Participants in masquerades typically dress in elaborately decorated masks and costumes that are believed to transform the wearer completely so that he or she ceases to exist and actually becomes the character (human or animal) of the mask.

The style and decoration of West African masks varies from one area to another, but many have male or female features with distinctive scarmarks on the forehead or cheeks that are associated with tribal membership or social rank. Color may suggest positive or negative characteristics. In some masks, white stands for beauty and serenity while black suggests a fierce warlike character. A half-white, half-black mask may mean that the character has one foot in the spirit world and one in the real world.

Most masks are carved from wood, often by master artists who have served for years as apprentices.

The Rosetta Stone

THE SLAB OF INSCRIBED black stone on display at the British Museum in London seems fairly unimposing. But it was this artifact, famed as the "Rosetta Stone," that permitted scholars to finally decipher the lost writing of the ancient Egyptians.

The stone might never have turned up if England and France had gotten along better. In 1798, Napoleon Bonaparte invaded British-controlled Egypt. The campaign proved ill-advised from a military standpoint, but it produced an archeological bonanza. In 1799, while working on an old fortress near Rosetta (present-day Rashid), southeast of Alexandria, a French officer, Captain Pierre-Francois Bouchard, uncovered a slab of black stone. Only 3′9″ long, 2′4½″ wide, and 11″ thick, it was inscribed with three different sections of writing dating to 196 B.C.

The top section contained hieroglyphics, which was the script used for religious or other important documents; the center section was Egyptian Demotic script, which was the common script of Egypt; and the bottom was ancient Greek, the language of Egypt's rulers at that time.

Immediately recognizing the significance of his discovery, Bouchard turned the stone over to a group of scholars accompanying the French expedition. But they didn't have it for long. In 1801, after defeating the French, the British took possession of the Rosetta Stone and sent it to England.

Scholarly interest was keen from the start. The three different texts presumably represented the same message, but only the Greek was immediately decipherable. The ability to read hieroglyphs had been lost for more than two centuries. Demotic script was also a mystery. The Greek text was translated in 1802 by the Reverend Stephen Weston, who determined the inscription was a decree by a council of priests to honor Ptolemy V.

That knowledge enabled French scholar and linguist Silvestre deSacy to make significant progress on decoding the Demotic script. Contributions were also made by Swedish diplomat Johann Akerblad and English physicist Thomas Young.

However, it was not until 1822 that French historian and linguist Jean-François Champollion was able to build on this previous study and truly crack the code. His revelation that the system used a combination of ideograms, phonetic signs, and determinatives provided the breakthrough needed to comprehend hieroglyphic writing.

Henry James

KNOWN IN HIS later years as "the Master," Henry James (1843–1916) created an innovative and substantial body of work: more than 20 novels, 20 volumes of novellas and tales, plus travel writing, autobiographies, art and literary criticism, and plays. He came from an exceptionally intellectual family: His father, Henry James, Sr., was a Swedenborgian philosopher; his brother, William, was a psychologist and philosopher; his sister, Alice, an accomplished diarist. Although born in New York, James lived in Europe from 1875 onward, residing for a time in Paris and in Italy, but living primarily in England. He became a British subject in 1915.

James moved easily in European circles, where he found material for his great international theme: the contrast between American and European manners and customs. Fascinated by interactions between relatively innocent and unsophisticated Americans and more cultured and sometimes decadent Europeans, James explored this subject from a number of vantage points.

Attitudes toward money and possessions were often a focus for James. In *Portrait of a Lady* (1881), for instance, his protagonist, Isabel Archer, suddenly becomes wealthy; a central question of the novel is what she will do with the freedom her money gives her. In *The Wings of the Dove* (1902), Milly Theale, a dying heiress, is surrounded by friends and associates hoping for a share of her wealth.

Always interested in the psychological complexity of his characters, James skillfully employs interior monologue in ways that anticipate the Modernist novelists who came after him. Especially in the three major novels written toward the end of his career—*The Wings of the Dove*, *The Ambassadors* (1903), and *The Golden Bowl* (1904)—he enters so deeply into his characters' minds, employing long sentences with many qualifying phrases and subordinate clauses, that some readers have complained that these works are "unreadable." Interestingly, however, all three of these novels, as well as a number of earlier ones, have been successfully adapted for television and film. For example, the 1972 television adaptation of *The Golden Bowl* used close-ups of actors' expressions to convey their inner struggles. The 1997 film *The Wings of the Dove*, starring Helena Bonham Carter as the scheming Kate Croy, won critical acclaim.

James's literary output, varied as well as vast, includes a memorable ghost story, *The Turn of the Screw* (1898), as well as a fascinating look at a dysfunctional family seen through the eyes of a child in *What Maisie Knew* (1897). James died in 1916 after suffering a stroke.

Mikhail Gorbachev (1931–present)

MIKHAIL SERGEYEVICH GORBACHEV was born March 2, 1931, in the small town of Privoolnoye, Russia. He was a hard worker and an excellent student; soon he earned a law degree at Moscow University. From the start, Gorbachev looked ahead with ambition and innovation. He joined the Communist party and became the secretary of the Young Communist's League. By 1961, he was a delegate to the Party Congress and was working to expand his education in economics and agronomy. From there, Gorbachev continued his political rise, becoming a full member of the Politburo in 1980 and the general secretary of the Communist Party of the Soviet Union.

Gorbachev went against tradition in many ways in his new position. He helped loosen the tight grip of Communism throughout Eastern Europe and eventually led millions of people to a better life of political and religious freedom. When his people wanted to move away from Communism, he did not fight it but instead gave them his blessing. He gave his people a truly unprecedented amount of freedom. His blueprints were known as *glasnost* (liberalization) and *perestroika* (reconstruction).

Gorbachev developed a relationship with President Reagan and worked hard on the arms reduction treaties. He also was instrumental in bringing an end to the division between the East and the West, as well as the destruction of the Berlin Wall. Gorbachev pushed hard for democracy in the Soviet Union and for free elections in Russia.

In 1990, Gorbachev was awarded the Nobel Peace Prize for his work. The following year, he left his position as general secretary and became president of the International Foundation for Socio-Economic and Political Studies, also known as the Gorbachev Foundation. In 2001, he founded the Social Democratic Party of Russia but resigned as their leader in 2004. In recent years, Gorbachev has made several trips to the United States. In October 2007, he went to New Orleans as part of the global environmental movement to visit the victims of Hurricane Katrina. While there, he stated, "If things haven't changed by our next visit, we may have to announce a revolution."

Radiocarbon Dating

DEVELOPED IN 1949 by a group headed by Willard F. Libby, a professor of chemistry at the University of Chicago, radiocarbon dating is a method for determining the age of organic materials. Radiocarbon dating can be consistently applied anywhere in the world, and is used to determine the age of wood, charcoal, bone, peat, soil, pollen, iron, textiles, paper, blood residues, and much more. Archaeologists, paleoclimatologists, anthropologists, Pleistocene geologists, geophysicists, and other scientists rely on radiocarbon dating. Today more than 130 radiocarbon dating laboratories worldwide provide crucial data to the scientific community.

There are three principal isotopes of carbon that occur naturally: carbon-12, carbon-13, and carbon-14. *Isotopes* are atoms of the same element with the same number of protons but differing numbers of neutrons. For example, all carbon isotopes have six protons, but carbon-12 has six neutrons, carbon-13 has seven, and carbon-14 has eight. Carbon-12 accounts for 98.89 percent of all natural carbon, carbon-13 comprises 1.11 percent, and carbon-14 constitutes 0.0000000001 percent.

Radiocarbon dating works thanks to the radioactive carbon-14 isotope, which is also known as radiocarbon. It is formed as neutrons of cosmic radiation enter the earth's upper atmosphere. These neutrons collide with nitrogen atoms to knock out and replace one of the protons from its nucleus, so that it has six protons and eight neutrons, which means it is now carbon-14. Oxygen atoms quickly attach to the carbon-14 and it oxidizes to form radioactive carbon dioxide (CO_2). This enters plants via photosynthesis and is passed along the food chain to all animals, including humans.

When an organism is alive, it continuously absorbs carbon-14, and levels of that isotope remain at equilibrium with levels in the atmosphere. Once the organism dies, it will no longer take in any carbon-14. From that point, the isotope begins to decay and loses half of its volume every 5,730 years. This predictable rate of decay is referred to as its *half-life*. By measuring the carbon-14 concentration, or residual radioactivity, of a sample whose age is unknown, it is possible to count the number of decay events per gram of carbon, calculate the number of half-lives, and estimate how long ago the sample organism died. The accuracy of radiocarbon dating is said to be plus or minus 200 years. In fact, when Libby and his team first tested radiocarbon dating, they were able to verify its accuracy using ancient Egyptian objects whose age was previously documented. The test dates matched.

Richard Wagner

VICIOUS ANTI-SEMITE and sensitive conveyor of the deepest musical emotions; megalomaniacal tyrant and immensely influential cultural icon—there are no half measures when it comes to describing Richard Wagner (1813–1883). Nor were there any half measures in his artistic vision, which he believed would redefine the scope not only of musical drama but of all musical expression. Even more broadly, Wagner aimed to renew the manifest destiny of Germanic cultural primacy—and in the process created a philosophical and aesthetic framework that was to feed the fuel of the drive toward German racial purity long after his death.

From a young age, Wagner dedicated himself to dramatic music, as director and arranger as well as composer. He gained an important mid-career appointment (partly on the strength of his third major opera, *Rienzi*, but also probably on recommendation from the prominent French Jewish composer Giacomo Meyerbeer, whom Wagner later viciously criticized), becoming royal court conductor for the Dresden court in the early 1840s.

But Wagner's tendencies toward philosophical radicalism led him to support the movement toward establishing a republic in Saxony during the pan-European uprisings in 1848. This ultimately caused him to flee Dresden in 1849, briefly staying with his mentor, Franz Liszt, and then moving to exile in Switzerland. There he wrote a systematic exposition of the "artwork of the future," a *Gesamtkunstwerk* (total art work) in which Wagner's overarching musico-dramatic vision could be achieved through his control of every creative aspect of a composition: text, scenery, action, and music. (In the process, he was laboring on the embodiment of this vision: his four-evening cycle *The Ring of the Nibelung*.)

As his grand vision started to take shape, Wagner found it necessary to condemn what he considered the dangers to the future of music: Italian and French operatic traditions and the "inferior race" of Jews, whose influence on German music Wagner found particularly insidious. These and other writings have made Wagner a controversial figure ever since. Many find it impossible to overlook his racial and national xenophobia, though his influence on 19th-century musical culture is hard to dismiss.

POSTSCRIPT

■ Wagner's worldwide popularity is reflected in his "American Centennial March," commissioned in 1876 by the city of Philadelphia on the occasion of the Centennial exposition commemorating the U.S. Declaration of Independence.

The Value of Pi

TAKE A CIRCLE and unroll it into a line. How long a line will you get? It's a far harder question than it seems. In fact, no one can answer it with complete precision.

If you're willing to settle for an approximation, the answer isn't so hard. For a circle that measures one foot across, the line will be a bit more than three feet long. To be more precise, it will be just over 3.14159 feet long. The length has a name: pi.

Nearly all of us know about pi, at least from having had to memorize in school that the area of a circle is πr^2. Yet no one knows exactly what the value of pi is, and no one ever will. That's because pi is irrational. If you try to write it out as a decimal, you'll have to keep writing forever, and the numbers will continue in an endless cycle, never repeating.

The ancient Greeks were familiar with the notion of irrationality, and around 300 B.C. Euclid proved that the square root of 2 is irrational. It took another 2,000 years to prove that pi is irrational.

Though the precise value of pi will never fully be known, mathematicians do know the value remarkably well. In 2002, three computer scientists computed more than a trillion digits of pi. Written in ordinary type, such a number would stretch to the moon and back—twice. The researchers found the value as a computational feat rather than from practical need. Just ten digits is enough to compute the circumference of Earth to within a fraction of an inch.

In the 1968 *Star Trek* episode "Wolf in the Fold," Spock exorcises an evil demon from the ship's computer system by ordering the computer to compute "to the last digit the value of pi." This kept the computer too busy for the demon to interfere. And pi is certain to keep scientists, mathematicians, and other numerical-minded people intrigued for ages.

POSTSCRIPT

■ Albert Einstein was born on March 14, or 3/14—"pi day."

■ In 2006, Akira Haraguchi recited the first 100,000 digits of π from memory, setting a world record. It took him more than 16 hours.

■ An urban myth says that a state bill legislates that pi is equal to 3. The story is apparently false, but it does have a germ of truth to it. In 1897, the Indiana State House of Representatives debated a bill that dictated varying incorrect values of pi, including 3.2. A mathematics professor from Purdue happened to be present and intervened, leading the lawmakers to kill the bill.

Rembrandt van Rijn

BORN IN THE SMALL DUTCH town of Leiden, Rembrandt van Rijn (1606–1669) settled in Amsterdam as an adult. There he mastered painting, drawing, and prints. His subject matter is wide-ranging, and his biography is filled with drama.

Rembrandt's early life was marked by prosperity and a happy marriage to Saskia van Uylenburg. His work during this period includes the group portrait *The Anatomy Lesson of Dr. Nicolaes Tulp* (1632), which shows the students and town notables viewing a dissection. His first history paintings exhibit dramatic, action-filled compositions and striking light-and-dark contrasts.

The critical turning point in Rembrandt's career is often said to be the negative reaction he received for *The Night Watch* (1642), a large group portrait depicting a civic guard organization in Amsterdam. Despite its title, the guards are shown in daylight. (As the painting's varnish darkened through time, the subject came to resemble a nighttime gathering.) Although it can be argued that the work breaks with tradition—for example, Rembrandt added numerous incidental figures—the claim that it launched the artist's downfall is not supported by evidence.

There was, however, a general change in taste during the later 17th century. Rembrandt's thickly textured paint handling, probing realism, and increasingly shadowed lighting schemes were at odds with a new, classically oriented French aesthetic. Declining sales coincided with the untimely death of Saskia in 1642 and a scandal involving Rembrandt's later affair with his housekeeper, Hendrijke van Stoeffels. Rembrandt was already at odds with the Calvinist moral code of his peers, and his relationship with Hendrijke, who bore him a child out of wedlock, further damaged his career. Moreover, poor money management led to bankruptcy.

Despite—or perhaps in response to—his reversal of fortune, Rembrandt imbued the figures in his late works with profound sensitivity and compassion. Late masterpieces from this period, such as *The Return of the Prodigal Son* (c. 1669), are noted for their thickly encrusted paint surfaces and softly glowing light, which emerges from a deep shadow.

Although Rembrandt's reputation was largely eclipsed in the century following his death, recognition of his genius eventually emerged.

The First Transcontinental Railroad

O N MAY 10, 1869, at Promontory Summit in Utah, a ceremonial gold spike was driven into the last rail of the first transcontinental rail line in the United States. This mammoth achievement was the culmination of years of dreaming and planning. The idea of linking America's east and west was first propounded by merchant Asa Whitney in 1845, but the concept foundered on the shoals of sectional discord and technological difficulties.

By 1862, engineer Theodore Judah determined that the Rocky Mountains could be traversed relatively easily through the Donner Pass. That year Congress passed a bill authorizing the construction of such a transcontinental rail line, with the Central Pacific building eastward and the newly chartered Union Pacific going westward.

As the Civil War wound down, serious work began on the project. The Central Pacific line hired several thousand Chinese workers to supplement their predominantly Irish workforce, while the Union Pacific used demobilized Civil War veterans and Irish immigrants to push into Nebraska by late 1866.

The project still faced a number of obstacles. In 1867, Union Pacific executives were implicated in the Credit Mobilier financial scandal, while Chinese workers went on strike against Union Pacific. A year earlier, a group of Sioux warriors, upset over railroad and associated military incursions into sacred hunting areas, ambushed an army contingent. In spite of these impediments, work continued, highlighted by a world record ten miles of track laid down by Central Pacific crews in one day on April 28, 1869. Less than three weeks later, the lines were joined as engine number *119* from the west and *Jupiter* from the east met at Promontory Summit in Utah.

The impact of this accomplishment was enormous. By 1880, the cross-country line carried $50 million worth of freight annually, as inefficient wagon trains gave way to the rails. Ultimately, the railroad system became the central spur that fueled the unparalleled economic growth in the United States during the last three decades of the 19th century. Beyond this, the building of the transcontinental railroad became a major American symbol.

George Orwell's *1984*

O NE OF THE MOST influential novelistic critiques of totalitarian societ- ies, George Orwell's 1949 dystopian novel *1984* gave us the term *Orwellian* as shorthand for nightmarish totalitarianism and oppression.

In *1984*, protagonist Winston Smith lives in Oceania, a future society divided into three groups: the tiny Inner Party of leaders, the Outer Party of state functionaries, and the majority Proles (proletarians or workers). In "Airstrip One" (part of Oceania that was once called England), all homes contain "telescreens" with two-way cameras and microphones that simultaneously monitor everyone and broadcast Party propaganda, dominated by the image of the all-knowing dictator, Big Brother.

Smith, an Outer Party official, works in the ironically named Ministry of Truth, falsifying historical records at the Party's direction to match politi- cal shifts. The action begins when Smith commits a "thoughtcrime" by beginning a personal diary (since personal expression is forbidden—in fact the Party's "Newspeak" has reduced all language to concrete words to avoid abstract thought). While remembering a recent propaganda session during which he felt an unspoken bond with O'Brien, an Inner Party member, Smith realizes he has written "Down with Big Brother" in his diary.

A woman named Julia initiates a secret meeting and says she is attracted to something in Smith's face that suggests he is against the Party. Smith and Julia begin an illegal affair, since sex for pleasure rather than repro- duction is forbidden.

O'Brien leads Smith to believe that he is secretly in contact with an underground anti-Party opposition. But O'Brien is actually a Party spy whose job is to sniff out any possible dissent. Smith and Julia have been monitored all the time, and each is eventually imprisoned and forced to betray each other. O'Brien breaks down Smith's resistance—especially his attachment to objective truth, as in his diary entry, "Freedom is the freedom to believe that two plus two equals four." Using torture and mind control, O'Brien finally transforms Smith into an internally loyal Party member who genuinely loves Big Brother and willingly says, and believes, that four fingers are really five.

POSTSCRIPT

▓ Orwell (born Eric Blair) got an up-close view of totalitarianism during his service on the Republican side in the Spanish Civil War (1936–1939), during which Soviet dictator Joseph Stalin purged the international Communist movement of perceived enemies.

Franz Liszt (1811–1886)

EVERY AGE HAS SEEN superstar musical performers, renowned and sought after and richly compensated for their ability to enthrall an audience. The image of a musician who holds a dangerous erotic spell over throngs of swooning young women is a more recent phenomenon, but it begins not with heartthrob crooner Rudy Vallee in the 1930s, nor with the Beatles in the 1960s, but rather with Franz Liszt in mid-19th-century Paris.

Liszt was a pioneer in several respects. He was one of the first musical artists to build a partnership with an instrument-maker designed to publicize that builder's products. From early in his career, Liszt made a show of playing only on pianos built by the Parisian company Érard. He was also a leader in the tradition of orchestral program music (music meant to evoke an image or emotion), championing the works of Hector Berlioz. He also encouraged and mentored the young Richard Wagner, who later married his daughter Cosima. But Liszt's most lasting contribution was arguably the establishment of the "piano recital," which is a central tradition in concert music to this day. Before Liszt's solo piano tours, even virtuoso pianists included a variety of works for different scorings on their concerts.

Liszt claimed that he was inspired by hearing a performance by the great violin virtuoso Niccolò Paganini (1782–1840), who tacitly encouraged rumors that he had been taught to play by the devil himself. Certainly Liszt developed his own style of dramatic showmanship, draping his tall frame in a cape and striding to the piano with great determination before attacking the keyboard with stunning dexterity. (Some of his works are still considered to be on the edge of physical impossibility, requiring extraordinary technique and stamina on the part of the performer.) Liszt certainly benefited from the "Lisztmania" in the early 1840s that saw young women throughout Europe fighting over the gloves and handkerchiefs he left behind on stage (and reportedly purchasing his hair-clippings and cigar stubs). He also increased his dramatic stature by insisting on complete silence during his performances—a relative novelty at the time—and was the first to play concerts entirely from memory.

Liszt's success and influence as a pianist is all the more remarkable since his most active concertizing lasted barely a decade. By the end of the 1840s, he had largely ceased touring, and while he continued writing and performing to the end of his life, his later works are considered to be more introspective (though in some cases equally technically challenging). His dedication to his Catholic faith came to the fore in his later years, when he took minor Franciscan orders, becoming known as the "Abbé Liszt."

The Tower of London

IN A.D. 1066, WILLIAM OF NORMANDY invaded England to claim the throne, which he believed had been promised to him. He defeated a defending Saxon army at the Battle of Hastings in October of that year and declared himself king of England.

One of William's first acts as king was to order the construction of a vast stone castle within the southeast walls of London. Located on the north bank of the Thames River, the structure was meant for defense and as a prison for William's enemies. The fortress, which eventually came to be known as the White Tower, had 100-foot-high ramparts that were up to 15 feet thick in some sections. This was later surrounded by a stone wall and a wide moat, both designed to keep prisoners in and enemies out. A series of additions were added over the centuries to complete all of the buildings collectively known today as the Tower of London.

In the 900 years since it was built, many famous men, women, and children have been imprisoned, tortured, and even executed in the Tower of London. However, not every person imprisoned in the Tower of London was executed. The first known prisoner was Ranulf Flambard, the Bishop of Durham, who was King William's tax collector. He was convicted of extortion in 1100 but managed to escape. One prisoner who was lucky enough to leave was Queen Elizabeth I. Sir Walter Raleigh was released from the tower once but was later imprisoned again and beheaded.

For those who were executed, the severity of the crime and the social standing of the condemned determined the manner and site of an execution. Some executions, such as that of Sir Thomas More, were carried out in public on Tower Hill. Other, private executions occurred behind the castle's walls on Tower Green. Two of the victims at this site include King Henry VIII's second and fifth wives, Anne Boleyn and Catherine Howard. The Tower of London was also the setting for political intrigue and murder. It is widely believed that the two young sons of King Edward IV were killed by order of King Richard III, their uncle, to avoid competition for the throne.

Today, the Tower of London is one of the most famous tourist destinations in Europe.

"Music of the Future"

IN THE DECADES FOLLOWING Beethoven's death in 1827, European musicians who were invested in symphonic and chamber repertories engaged in an endless debate about the future of instrumental music and the way to remain true to Beethoven's legacy of genius. One of the issues at stake was the claim of "succession" of creative prestige and visibility—an important consideration given that musical patronage was shifting from a court-based, retainer-driven model to a more free-market, public-sponsored setup.

A successful claim to the great composer's legacy was the ticket to public acclaim and (possible) financial success. Just as important, however, was the aesthetic consideration: Romantic writers proclaimed the potential of instrumental music over all the other arts to raise the soul to the much-desired sublime (an enlightened frame of mind often reached through nature or the supernatural). Defining the parameters of such a powerful art form was a heady and desirable prospect for mid-19th-century musicians.

While there were many individual attempts to "live up" to what was perceived as Beethoven's challenge to the future of music, there were two significant camps vying for basic definitions of the ground rules. One side (proponents of "program music") argued for flexibility of musical form and gesture, tied to the expression of specific images, stories, or emotions. Hector Berlioz's use of a specific descriptive narrative in his *Fantastic Symphony* (1830) was a prime example. Franz Liszt's pioneering "symphonic poems" (each associated with a particular poem, character, or picture) were the inspiration for an extended tradition of orchestral works designed to create specific images in listeners' minds. Prominent examples include Tchaikovsky's *Romeo and Juliet* (1870) and Mussorgsky's *Night on Bald Mountain* (1867).

The other side maintained that the "classical" formal and expressive resources that had been developed in the preceding decades by Haydn, Mozart, and especially Beethoven were the apex of musical expression. They believed the goal should be to adopt and further refine those resources. Prominent composers associated with the primacy of "absolute music" were Robert and Clara Schumann and especially Johannes Brahms.

A latecomer in the "music of the future" debate was Richard Wagner, whose concept of a "total art work" (such as his four-part *Ring of the Nibelung*) was designed to supersede the categories of "program" and "absolute" music and to provide the "true" fulfillment of Beethoven's vision.

What Is a Planet?

ASTRONOMERS USED to agree that our solar system had nine planets: Mercury, Venus, Earth, Mars, Jupiter, Saturn, Uranus, Neptune, and Pluto. True, Pluto seemed a little unusual. It was one-twentieth the size of the second-smallest planet, Mercury. Pluto had a moon called Charon with a diameter more than half of Pluto's. And while Pluto usually traveled farthest from the sun, its orbit occasionally took it inside Neptune's. Nevertheless most authorities accepted Pluto's planetary status.

However, in the 1990s, astronomers began to question what made a planet a planet. First, they discovered new bodies, called Kuiper belt objects, orbiting the sun far beyond Pluto. Then in 2002 and 2003, observers at California's Mount Palomar Observatory found three Kuiper belt objects—Quaoar, Sedna, and Eris—similar to Pluto in size and orbital shape. Finally, in 2006, precise measurements showed that Eris is actually larger than Pluto. If Pluto is a planet, astronomers reasoned, shouldn't Eris be one, too? Alternatively, did Pluto really deserve to be designated a planet at all?

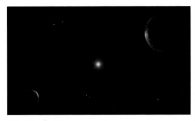

The Pluto-Charon system

The International Astronomical Union (IAU) quickly responded to these questions. It set up a committee to propose a formal definition of a planet. The committee first recommended two criteria for a planet: It must be a celestial body whose own gravity causes it to have a nearly round shape, and it must orbit a star but not *be* a star or a moon of another planet. That definition would have added at least three new planets to the solar system: Ceres, the largest asteroid; Pluto's moon Charon, making the Pluto-Charon combination a double planet; and Eris. Astronomers warned that many more Kuiper belt objects yet to be discovered might also fit the definition.

Facing that and other objections, the IAU committee devised an extra criterion for planethood: A planet must clear the neighborhood around its orbit. The committee proposed a new term for objects that meet the first criteria but do not clear their orbits and are not moons. They would be called *dwarf planets.*

That agreement makes Pluto, discovered in 1930, a dwarf planet. Our solar system now contains only eight planets. And the race is on to discover new dwarf planets beyond Pluto.

Marcel Duchamp

BY SUBMITTING AN ordinary bathroom urinal to the Society of Independent Artists' exhibition of 1917, Marcel Duchamp forever challenged the notion of what constitutes art. Signed with the pseudonym "R. Mutt"—a play on the name of the plumbing manufacturer—*Fountain* (as the urinal was titled) was the most notorious of Duchamp's "ready-mades," everyday objects given titles and placed in a gallery context. With the readymades, Duchamp asserted that art is not a matter of skill, and that the mere act of labeling something as "art"—even a men's urinal—*makes* it art.

Duchamp was born in 1887 in Blainville, France, to a family of artists, and he spent a substantial portion of his life in New York City, settling there permanently in 1942.

When Duchamp first arrived in New York in 1915, he was already famous because of the scandal surrounding the showing of his painting *Nude Descending a Staircase, No. 2* (1912) at the Armory Show of 1913. Presenting a nude woman whose figure is broken into a series of planes in the manner of Cubism, the painting was famously described as an "explosion in a shingle factory."

Nude Descending a Staircase, No. 2

While *Nude Descending a Staircase* challenged the grand tradition of the nude, another work by the artist, *L.H.O.O.Q.* (1919), attacked a sacred cow of Western art: the *Mona Lisa* (1503–1506). In this work—whose title is a French acronym for "she has a hot ass"—Duchamp painted a mustache on a reproduction of Leonardo da Vinci's famous painting. The following year Duchamp, who had a life-long interest in transsexuality, created his female alter ego, Rose Sélavy, and for the next 20 years used that name as a pseudonym.

During his first stay in New York, Duchamp was at the center of New York Dada, the New York wing of the international Dada movement, whose members sought to overturn artistic conventions and provoke society to self-awareness with shocking escapades. Upon his return to Paris in 1923, Duchamp pursued chess—one of his great passions—while continuing his artistic experimentation in secret.

Duchamp's influence on postwar art can be felt in countless ways, from the use of everyday objects in Pop Art to the emphasis on ideas rather than artistic execution in Conceptual Art, seen from the 1950s up to today.

The Signing of Magna Carta

IN 1199, PRINCE JOHN became the king of England after the death of his popular brother, King Richard I. King John continued some of his brother's policies, one of which was heavily taxing his subjects. Unfortunately, John did not have his brother's pleasing personality, and the wealthy barons began to resent the king's continual need for great amounts of money. Eventually, they planned a rebellion.

King John also angered Pope Innocent III, head of the Catholic Church in Rome. Traditionally, the king had selected, with the approval of the monks, the Archbishop of Canterbury. The selection had become controversial when the monks wanted input into the selection. In the early 1200s, a new archbishop needed to be named. The monks elected one of their own, and King John sent his choice to the pope. The pope selected neither person but elected his own choice. King John refused to accept the pope's choice. The pope responded by excommunicating King John from the Church. The king, in retaliation, taxed the Church and confiscated church lands.

Unsure of the barons' course of action, King John decided to get the Church back on his side. He accepted the pope's choice for Archbishop of Canterbury, compensated the pope for the Church's lands, and made England the pope's fief. To show his appreciation, the pope reversed his decision of excommunication for the king.

King John had long been planning to invade France, and he decided he needed more money to pay for the costs associated with this. Many barons refused to pay, and King John retaliated by attacking their properties. He proceeded with his army across the English Channel to invade France.

King John lost the war, returned home, and began making more financial demands upon the barons. They refused to comply, prepared for war, and demanded that they be granted certain rights. They presented their written demands to King John at Runnymede on June 15, 1215. A formal version called Magna Carta was drawn up on June 19, 1215. It consisted of more than 60 provisions. One of the most important was that the rule of law applied to the king as well as to his subjects. The document lessened the rights of the king and provided for expanded rights of citizens, including the writ of Habeas Corpus. It set the foundation for English law and eventually the U.S. Constitution.

Romanticism

ROMANTICISM IS THE LAST total cultural movement to have occurred in Western civilization. Originating in the mid-18th century and culminating in the early 19th century, the Romantic movement was a reaction against the European Enlightenment, which stressed balance, rationality, harmony, and rules in art, philosophy, and expression.

Romantic paintings showed isolated human figures in dramatic, sweeping landscapes and moody pictures of ruins. Romantic architects revived Gothic forms and even built deliberately "ruined" houses. In poetry, Romantics celebrated folk songs and fairy tales, produced by the anonymous *volk* (people). At the same time, Romantic writers like Goëthe exalted the individual artist.

Walter Scott's tales of medieval knights swept the world and defined Romantic fiction for a generation. William Wordsworth and Samuel Coleridge's *Lyrical Ballads* (1798) kicked off Romantic poetry in England, with John Keats, Percy Shelly, and William Blake emerging as the other foremost English Romantic poets.

In Romantic music, German composers dominated with sweeping chords and heavy emotion, often importing themes from peasant songs. Important Romantic composers include Ludwig van Beethoven; Franz Schubert; Frédéric Chopin; Franz Liszt; Carl Maria von Weber, the founder of Romantic opera; Frenchman Louis-Hector Berlioz; and opera composer Richard Wagner.

Politically, Romanticism had both "right" and "left" wings, a sign of its vast and far-reaching nature. Romanticism inspired intense nationalism in the 19th century among Russians, Swedes, Poles, Italians, Hungarians, and Czechs. After Napolean's invasions, at a time when Germany was divided into small principalities, Germans found their unity in the idea of a *volk* (people) and its anonymous productions, including folktales and peasant songs.

Romanticism in philosophy began with French philosopher Jean-Jacques Rousseau, whose idea of the "noble savage" changed attitudes toward "primitive" peoples. His novel *Emile: or, On Education* (1762), a deep influence on schooling to this day, argues that children are naturally good and that Nature is their best teacher. In *The Birth of Tragedy* (1871), Friedrich Nietzsche, perhaps the most renowned Romantic philosopher, argued that Western culture is in constant conflict between the spirit of Dionysius—god of wine, ecstasy, and madness—and Apollo—god of reason, harmony, light, and proportion.

Denis Diderot (1713–1784)

A FAMED FRENCH intellectual and man of letters, Denis Diderot helped shape the Enlightenment, part of a European cultural and intellectual movement marked by emphasis on reason, toleration, and expanded freedom from oppression.

Born the son of a successful knife maker, Diderot loved reading and was especially fond of works in Latin. He received a master's degree from the University of Paris and refused to study law or medicine, as his father wanted. Instead, he became a tutor and freelance writer, first gaining fame as a translator of English books.

In 1746, Diderot joined mathematician Jean D'Alembert as coeditor of what became *L'Encyclopédie (The Encyclopedia)*, one of the first attempts to create a compendium of useful knowledge. Published between 1751 and 1772 in 17 volumes of text and 11 volumes of illustrations, it created enormous controversy. Although *L'Encyclopédie* did contain a number of fairly innocuous factual articles on science, mathematics, and technology, many of its entries preached the virtues of religious tolerance and condemned religious oppression and censorship. Indeed, its publisher was arrested, and Diderot became an object of suspicion by both the Catholic Church and the French state.

Diderot wrote a number of other controversial works while compiling *L'Encyclopédie*. In his 1745 *Essai sur La Merite et la Vertu (Essay on Merit and Virtue)*, he argued that it was "only one step" from "fanaticism to barbarism." He anonymously published *Pensées Philosophiques (Philosophical Thoughts)* in 1746, only to see it burned by the French Parliament because of its alleged attacks on Christianity. In 1749, he was imprisoned for calling into question the existence of God.

Diderot continued his assault on intolerance until his death from emphysema. No doubt the work of Diderot and his friends such as Voltaire and Rousseau did much to sow the seeds of the French Revolution, as well as the growth of religious tolerance, especially in Europe and the United States. And his *Encyclopedia* became the prototype of similar works that did so much to bring the fruits of knowledge to a wide audience.

POSTSCRIPT

When Diderot's first wife said that she "would not touch a book which did not offer something spiritually uplifting," he tried to break her of this habit by reading "raunchy" books aloud.

Cassius Clay

WHEN A BRASH young boxer named Cassius Clay upset reigning heavyweight champion Sonny Liston in 1964, it marked a turning point for a man destined to become one of the most widely recognized people of the 20th century. Even before the bout with Liston, the Louisville, Kentucky, native had made a name for himself. Clay won an Olympic gold medal in 1960 and emerged victorious in his first 19 professional fights. Nicknamed the "Louisville Lip," Clay was a consummate showman who both entertained and infuriated fans with his loud mouth, incessant bragging, and poetic predictions of the round in which he would knock out opponents.

Clay was a heavy underdog when he challenged the reigning champ. Liston was a brutal fighter, winning 21 bouts between 1959 and 1964. All but two of his victories had come by knockouts within the first three rounds. Clay, it seemed to most observers and sports journalists, had no chance. However, the crafty Clay combined a footloose, almost dancelike style, constant verbal badgering, and a lethal series of jabs and counter-punches to thoroughly demoralize the champion. Claiming that he had injured his shoulder, Liston failed to leave his corner for the seventh round. Clay dashed around the ring in triumph, screaming at the boxing pundits in the crowd who had dared to doubt him.

Perhaps more significantly, at a press conference on the day after the fight, Clay revealed that he had joined the Nation of Islam, an organization of black Muslims. Soon afterward, he changed his name to Muhammad Ali. Ultimately, because of his new religious commitment, he refused to be drafted in 1966, at the height of the Vietnam War. Following his decision, he was stripped of his championship and criminally convicted for his refusal to serve. To many Americans, Ali became viewed as an unpatriotic villain, but to antiwar advocates in the United States and around the world, Ali became a hero. Ali was, of course, a great boxer, but also a major cultural and political figure in a turbulent era.

POSTSCRIPT

- Ali successfully defended his title against Liston in 1965.

- His conviction for draft refusal was overturned by the Supreme Court in 1971, and he ultimately regained his stripped heavyweight title.

- In 1996, he was the athlete chosen to light the Olympic flame for the Atlanta Games. This was considered a gesture of honor and redemption for a controversial individual.

The Rise of the Conductor and a Classical Repertoire

IN THE MID-1800s, the number and size of European orchestras grew significantly. Orchestras were no longer private ensembles at the disposal of a single rich patron but rather "public enterprises" patronized by the upper classes—and often competing for audiences. Ensembles of all sizes had long been coordinated by a designated leader, usually the keyboard player or the first violinist.

There was now an increasing tendency for composers to write for many simultaneous independent musical lines. (The practice of composers of the Mozart/Haydn generation was to write essentially melody-and-accompaniment textures.) That fact, along with the growing size of orchestras (from an average of 40 players at the beginning of the 1800s to close to 100 at the end of the century, reflecting Victorian-era fascination with artistic grandeur), made the need for a separate conductor increasingly crucial.

Initially, the role of the conductor was seen primarily as keeping everyone on the beat and ensuring attention to precision, but eventually conductors established the prerogative to make interpretative decisions as well. Composers such as Hector Berlioz and Felix Mendelssohn (and later Gustav Mahler) gained renown as conductors, but the two roles became more and more distinct, especially as some conductors became as well known and charismatic as the superstar performers of the time. By the first decades of the 20th century, the position of the conductor was firmly entrenched as fully separate (and arguably more prestigious) than that of the contemporary composer, establishing a tradition that has continued into the 21st century.

A concert of Hector Berlioz in 1846

The split between conductor and composer became ingrained as orchestras began focusing on a circumscribed and retrospective repertory. Around 1825, about three-quarters of orchestral works performed were by living composers, while 50 years later the percentages had switched, with the vast majority of orchestral performances featuring the music of Mozart, Haydn, Beethoven, and composers of the following generation (such as Schumann and Mendelssohn). This phenomenon combined with the evolving tradition of musical criticism to establish a repertoire of "musical classics" that forms the core of orchestral programming to this day.

Advances in Nuclear Fusion

"**N**UCLEAR FUSION," the old joke goes, "is the energy source of the future—and always will be." Ever since the 1950s, scientists have forecast that it would take about 20 years to tame the energy process that makes the sun shine and hydrogen bombs explode. Now, though, fusion power seems closer to becoming a reality.

A consortium from the European Union, Japan, the People's Republic of China, India, the Republic of Korea, Russia, and the United States plans to build a facility called ITER (*iter* is Latin for "the way") in Cadarache, France. Due to start up in 2016, ITER is designed to prove that nuclear fusion can produce more energy than it uses. If it works, it will open the way for the Demonstration Power Plant, a reactor intended to generate electric power continuously.

Fusion differs significantly from fission, the process that fuels present-day nuclear power plants. Fission obtains energy when large, unstable atomic nuclei such as uranium-235 split apart. Fusion occurs when two atomic nuclei "fuse" together. The most commonly used nuclei are deuterium and tritium. These are forms of hydrogen (the lightest of all nuclei) that contain extra particles called *neutrons*. When the two nuclei fuse, they create a nucleus of helium, a neutron, and vast amounts of energy.

Atomic nuclei naturally resist each other. So it takes a great deal of energy to force deuterium and tritium nuclei together. Gravity does the job in the sun. An atomic bomb provides the energy to set off a hydrogen bomb. Fusion reactors aim to achieve the same goal by heating a "plasma" of deuterium and tritium nuclei to temperatures of hundreds of millions of degrees while exposing the plasma to ultrahigh pressures.

To do that, ITER will use a process called *magnetic confinement.* An oval-shape vacuum vessel known as a *tokamak* contains the plasma. Coils and related equipment around the vessel will produce magnetic and electric fields to heat and compress the plasma. The reactor will need about 70 megawatts to start the fusion reaction. If it works, it will produce about 500 megawatts of power for five to eight minutes.

The National Ignition Facility (NIF) at Lawrence Livermore Laboratory in California is taking a different approach to producing sustainable fusion power. Due for completion in 2009, NIF will use inertial confinement: 192 high-power laser beams focusing from all directions on a pea-size plastic pellet that contains deuterium and tritium. The lasers will squeeze and heat the pellet enough to cause fusion for a millionth of a second. The process should generate more energy than needed to fire up the lasers.

Dada: Art or Anti-Art?

THE BRITISH WRITER and painter Wyndham Lewis (1882–1957) expressed this disillusioned perspective about World War I: "…and a war was started which has not ended yet: a 'war to end war.' But it merely ended art. It did not end war."

Disillusionment with civilization and Western culture set the stage for Dada. The movement was an assault on reason and the "rationality" that, in 1914, had resulted in a war of unimaginable horror. Dada emerged from the activities of an international group of artists, writers, and intellectuals who had retreated to the comparative safety of neutral Switzerland. Between 1916 and 1918, Dada groups would appear in New York, Paris, Cologne, Hanover, and Berlin.

There are various explanations for the name and conflicting statements of the group's goals. *Dada* is both a nonsense word and French for "hobby horse." It is likely that painter Richard Huelsenbeck (1892–1974) and writer Hugo Ball (1886–1927) found the word at random in a French-German dictionary. As Ball recalled, "It's just made for our purpose. The child's first sound expresses the primitiveness, the beginning at zero, the new in our art." The poet Tristan Tzara (1896–1963), however, declared, "The beginnings of Dada were not the beginnings of an art, but of a disgust. … Dada is a state of mind. … Like everything in life, Dada is useless."

Dada had no rules or restrictions; Dada "works" were more likely to be political statements and social criticism. Performances typically incorporated "bruitism," a sort of noise music compiled from all manner of sounds and generated in spontaneous outbursts. Accident was valued as a means of artistic process, and materials were more likely to be found in the trash than the studio. In fact, Dadaists generally avoided materials associated with the aesthetics of fine arts, although some did work in collage, sculpture, film, and photography.

Participants produced found objects (called *readymades*), documents, and performances that often were deliberately shocking, offensive, and incomprehensible. (One of the most famous was a urinal entitled "Fountain" submitted for exhibition by Marcel Duchamp in 1917.) Aesthetic qualities were largely irrelevant, and Dada objects and events were intended to make viewers reexamine their values and beliefs.

Dada fundamentally changed the definition of art and opened the door to the "Happenings" of the 1960s and the focus on the artist's concept that is central to contemporary art in the 21st century.

Two Great African Americans

BOOKER T. WASHINGTON was born into slavery in 1856. After the Civil War, his family moved to West Virginia, and he attended school while working in coal and salt mines.

Washington was instrumental in developing Alabama's Tuskegee Institute, recruiting black students to attend the teacher-training institute and creating programs for training students to learn useful trades and farming so they could become skilled workers.

W.E.B. DuBois was born in Massachusetts shortly after the Civil War. He attended integrated elementary schools, graduated from Harvard with a Ph.D., taught at an Ohio college, and directed a study of the societal conditions of black people in Philadelphia. He concluded that even the most educated blacks were hindered by discrimination.

Washington's experience at the Tuskegee Institute convinced him that blacks could advance in society through educational training programs such as the ones Tuskegee offered. In 1895, he addressed the Cotton States and International Exhibition in Atlanta, Georgia, and emphasized the need for blacks to be part of the South's economic progress. His remarks placed him in the national spotlight because he told his all-white audience that while the races could be socially separate, they needed to work together economically.

Washington accepted the fact that segregation was a reality. The white leaders looked to Washington as a leader of the black people, although some black leaders challenged his belief that the goal of ending segregation should be pursued at a later time.

Two years after Washington's Atlanta speech, DuBois proposed a program of educating an elite group of blacks to become leaders in order to advance policies of social change for their race. DuBois believed that industrial training programs such as those suggested by Washington would only further solidify the idea that blacks were second-class citizens. DuBois's goal for the "Talented Tenth" program was to have this highly educated group assist blacks in overcoming existing racial barriers.

The segregation issue became even more pronounced. By 1910, DuBois had helped to form the NAACP, and he approved of a more confrontational approach to resolve the problem of racial inequality. His approach fed into the Civil Rights Movement of the 1950s and '60s. By the time Washington, who was seen as being too accommodating to whites, died in 1915, his ideas for ways to eliminate the racial barriers were no longer appealing to many black leaders.

Miguel de Cervantes's *Don Quixote*

WRITTEN BY Miguel de Cervantes Saavedra (1547–1616), *Don Quixote* (the full title in Spanish is *El ingenioso hidalgo don Quijote de la Mancha*) is arguably the most influential work in all of Spanish literature. It regularly appears on lists of the best novels in Western literature.

The protagonist, a retired gentleman landowner, has read so many novels of chivalry that he loses touch with reality and sets out, believing himself to be a knight errant, to perform deeds of chivalry. He is accompanied by his commonsensical sidekick Sancho Panza and rides a horse called Rocinante, which he believes to be a noble steed but in reality is a skinny nag. Outfitted in rusty armor and wearing a helmet made partly of pasteboard, he is initially a ridiculous figure, laughed at by all he meets but oblivious to others' reactions.

The novel was published in two parts, the first in 1605, the second in 1615. The first part of the novel is primarily comical, as Sancho Panza tries to extricate his master from various complicated situations. In one of the most well-known episodes, Don Quixote charges a group of windmills, mistaking them for giants. The phrase "tilting at windmills," which is used to describe inept attacks on mistaken enemies, comes from this incident. Part two of the novel is darker and more philosophical, with the theme of illusion versus reality more subtly developed. Cervantes moves from the humorous episodes of part one to an exploration of his characters' humanity and an investigation of how to determine what is real and truthful.

The lasting influence of *Don Quixote* cannot be overstated. Artists, musicians, filmmakers, and writers have continued the "conversation" begun by Cervantes's often deceived and foolish but also courageous protagonist. In the visual arts, Don Quixote was depicted by Pablo Picasso and Salvador Dali. Operas, ballets, tone poems, and Broadway musicals have been inspired by the novel. *Man of La Mancha*, which premiered on Broadway in 1963 and became a film in 1972 (with Peter O'Toole playing both Don Quixote and Cervantes), is an excellent example of Cervantes's continuing influence on popular culture. In literature, authors as diverse as Henry Fielding, Charlotte Lennox, Charles Dickens, Gustave Flaubert, Fyodor Dostoyevsky, Graham Greene, Jorge Luis Borges, and Salman Rushdie owe a nod to Cervantes's writing.

Hans Bethe (1906–2005)

Hans Bethe was a giant of 20th-century science. His research covered almost every significant advance in theoretical physics from the early development of quantum mechanics to the most modern understanding of elementary particles. Along the way, he earned a Nobel Prize in physics and acted as a teacher and mentor to generations of young physicists. He played key roles in the development of the atom bomb and hydrogen bomb, and he subsequently joined fellow physicists in the efforts to limit nuclear weapons and promote the peaceful uses of atomic energy. Bethe also built up a world-renowned physics department at New York's Cornell University.

Born on July 2, 1906, in Strasbourg, a German city that has since reverted to France, Bethe received his doctorate in physics from the University of Munich in 1928. After fellowships abroad, he continued his research in Germany. But Adolf Hitler's rise to power in 1933 changed the course of his life. Because his mother was Jewish, Bethe lost his position at the University of Tübingen. In 1935, after two years in England, he moved to Cornell, which became his home for the rest of his life.

His theoretical research in the next three years revealed what causes the stars to shine. He identified two sets of nuclear reactions: The carbon-nitrogen cycle produces most of the energy in very bright stars, while the proton-proton reaction accounts for most of the power in our sun and fainter stars. Those findings earned Bethe the 1967 Nobel Prize in Physics.

When the United States started the Manhattan Project to develop an atomic bomb in World War II, Bethe became the head of the project's theoretical division. After the war, he took part in the successful effort to develop the hydrogen bomb—although he had originally joined the project in hopes of proving that the bomb could not be made. Bethe then involved himself in what he called "political physics." He helped to persuade the United States to ban atmospheric tests of nuclear weapons in 1963 and antiballistic missile systems in 1972. In the 1980s, he joined other physicists in opposing President Ronald Reagan's strategic defense initiative, otherwise known as the Star Wars defense.

At Cornell University, Bethe attracted several brilliant young physicists to work with him. His department became a global center for high-energy elementary particle physics. He retired from teaching at age 83, but he set out to learn about—and contribute to—the challenging field of lattice gauge theory, which deals with the most fundamental elements of all matter. He continued research in that field until he died in 2005 at the age of 98.

Mesopotamia, Ancient Agriculture, and Environmental Degradation

IN THE PUBLIC MIND, the idea of environmental degradation is often linked with modern industry, but this association can be misleading. Since ancient times, humans have transformed farmland into desert through poor farming practices and shortsighted leadership. An early example of negative human impact on the environment can be found in the area between the Tigris and Euphrates rivers in present-day Iraq, formerly known as Mesopotamia.

Archaeological evidence suggests that by 5000 B.C., people had established small farming villages on the banks of the Tigris and Euphrates. These people domesticated and bred farm animals and brought water to their wheat, barley, pea, and lentil fields using irrigation ditches. They erected houses and temples, devised a system of writing, developed specialized crafts, and fabricated useful objects from clay and copper. The population grew dramatically and independent city-states like Ur arose, inhabited by 30,000 to 50,000 people. By 3000 B.C., Sumer was comprised of 12 city-states believed to be history's first civilization.

To support the growing population, the Sumerians greatly enlarged earlier irrigation works, opening new fields to cultivation. However, this expansion had a price. Today, archaeologists believe that silt filled the slow-flowing Tigris and Euphrates until their levels rose higher than the farm fields. When floods came, the rivers overflowed their banks. Protective dikes gave way, and farm fields filled with water, which evaporated and left behind a layer of salt. Where the soil was more waterlogged, the water table rose and brought more salt from underground to the surface.

Still, all was not lost. The Sumerian farmers knew that salt levels would return to normal if the affected fields were left fallow for several years. However, instead of heeding the farmers' advice, Sumer's rulers insisted that cultivation continue at previous levels. Out of necessity, Sumerians replaced the wheat in their diets with barley, which is more salt-tolerant. Regardless, yields continued to fall, and food became scarce. Revolts, civil war, and a diminished food supply weakened Sumerian civilization, which was conquered by invading forces around 1940 B.C. At the same time, a significant population decrease—thought to be spurred by the increase in soil salinity—took place. Five hundred years later, agriculture in the area had ceased and Sumer was no more.

Melodrama Takes the Stage

THEATERGOERS ATTENDING the opening of Jean-Jacques Rousseau's play *Pygmalion* in Lyon, France, in 1770 experienced something new in live theater. Throughout the production, spoken dialogue was punctuated by short interludes of orchestral music that heightened the play's dramatic effect. What that opening night audience didn't know was that they were the first witnesses to a new genre of musical theater. This innovation would be labeled *melodrama,* a combination of the Greek word for song, *melos,* and the word *drama.*

At that time, this interplay of dialogue and orchestration was certainly innovative. Previously, dialogue in musical theater took two principal forms. Italian and French operas had dialogue that was sung either in rhythmic speech or in expressively melodic song with full-blown orchestral accompaniment. The other form was the English ballad opera and the German *singspiel* (literally, "singing play") in which dialogue was spoken, sometimes over music, and interspersed with short songs, ballads, or choral sections.

Rousseau's new style caught on, and by the end of the 18th century melodrama had become immensely popular. Audiences of early melodramas were drawn to the extravagant theatrical effects and progressively complex orchestrations. Music amplified the sense of drama in the charged emotions or actions of the play. Melodrama also appealed to composers, and pieces of the new genre soon found their way into classical opera. Most notably, Carl Maria von Weber used it to stunning effect in his wildly successful opera *Der Freischütz* in 1821. In one scene, he casts magic bullets while speaking devilish incantations—all the while accompanied by an increasingly expressive and gruesome musical score.

The halcyon days for melodrama as an art form soon passed. By the end of the 19th century, melodrama morphed into a genre of stage play that was considered lowbrow (albeit popular) entertainment. It became the refuge of B-list writers, composers, and actors. Melodramatic productions also began to follow a standard formula, featuring a plot full of emotional drama due to some violent or nefarious act. The characters were extremes of good and evil, and often a villain threatened a hero. However, the hero would later trump the villain, win the girl, and pave the way for the inevitably happy ending.

Still, the genre of melodrama has managed to adapt and endure through the years. Melodrama has found a niche in modern media in action films, detective shows, and soap operas.

Nanotechnology

NANOTECHNOLOGY DEALS with the behavior of materials on a very small scale—smaller than biological cells and roughly the size of molecules. The field involves items between roughly 1 nanometer and 100 nanometers in size. A nanometer is one billionth of a meter. A sheet of paper is about 100,000 nanometers thick. Strands of our genetic material, DNA, are roughly two-and-a-half nanometers in diameter.

Because of their ultrasmall scale, nanomaterials often behave in unexpected ways. For example, solids can turn into liquids when converted to nanoparticles. Opaque materials can become transparent. Insulating substances can become electrical conductors. For that reason, nanotechnology offers the prospect of new and entirely unexpected applications, ranging from tiny factories that manipulate atoms and molecules to build items from the bottom up, to stronger materials for aerospace. Other areas of application include medicine, environmental conservation, energy production, and computing.

Nanotechnology has already found practical applications—some of them quite mundane. For example, sunscreens that contain zinc oxide or titanium oxide nanoparticles appear invisible on the skin; sunscreens that contain normal-size oxide particles have a telltale white appearance. A thin layer of nanoparticles protects clothes from stains caused by water and ultraviolet radiation. Cleansers that incorporate nanodrops of oil can clean swimming pools more effectively. Nanoparticles embedded in glass can break down dust and dirt more effectively and help to keep automobile windshields clean. Liquid crystal displays that contain carbon nanotubes work more efficiently than those without them. Carbon nanotubes also make tennis rackets light in weight yet extremely strong.

In the future, nanotechnology offers the most promise to medicine. One day, analysts forecast, patients might drink fluids containing nanorobots programmed to hunt down and destroy cancer cells in the body. Tiny robots might also carry out surgery more accurately and effectively than the sharpest scalpel and would cause almost no scarring.

The environment also stands to benefit from nanotechnology. Visionaries imagine nanorobots will help purify the atmosphere and clean up oil spills as well as concentrations of heavy metals and other pollutants in oceans and waterways.

However, nanotechnology is not free of risk. Some scientists worry that nanoparticles used in medicine might harm patients. Because of their ultrasmall sizes, toxic particles could move rapidly through the body.

Leonardo da Vinci

F AMOUSLY DESCRIBED BY ONE biographer as "the most relentlessly curious man in history," da Vinci was many different things over the course of his extraordinary life. He was the man who painted *The Last Supper* and the *Mona Lisa* and was court artist to various royals and aristocrats. He was also a thinker and inventor whose interests extended to virtually everything: flight, human anatomy, mathematics, optics, weapons design, and mechanics.

Da Vinci's thirst for experimentation and knowledge went hand-in-hand with a tendency to start works but not complete them. This quality was noted in an early biography: "It is clear that Leonardo began many things and never finished one of them, since it seemed to him that the hand was not able to attain to the perfection of art in carrying out things which he imagined." Among the projects da Vinci left unfinished were two planned equestrian monuments and the *Battle of Anghiari,* a wall painting that was to have stood across from a painting by Michelangelo—thus pitting the two giants of the Renaissance (who reportedly disliked each other intensely) against each other.

One of the equestrian monuments in question was commissioned by Ludovico Sforza, da Vinci's first important patron. While the monument did not make it beyond the clay model, another commission from the family made the artist famous: *The Last Supper* (c. 1495–1498). Among the most celebrated aspects of this painting is its variety of gestures and facial expressions—something of great concern to da Vinci, who combed Milan in search of expressive facial types and models for the apostles' hands.

Several years after completing *The Last Supper,* da Vinci began the *Mona Lisa* (1503–1506). A portrait of Lisa Gherardini commissioned by her merchant husband to celebrate the birth of their son and their acquisition of a new house, the *Mona Lisa* has inspired endless fascination and speculation, largely stemming from the subject's famously inscrutable smile. King Francis I of France bought the painting for 4,000 gold florins (equal to $1,470 today) and brought it to France, where it later entered the Louvre.

Da Vinci spent the final years of his career in the service of the French monarch, where he was involved with the design of court festivities, an irrigation project, and drawings for a royal palace.

U.S. Declaration of Independence, Constitution, and Bill of Rights

IN JUNE 1776, Richard Henry Lee of Virginia presented a resolution to the Second Continental Congress, expressing the idea that the American colonies should be free and independent from Britain and that political connections between them should be dissolved. The Lee Resolution was not immediately voted upon. A five-member committee was appointed to draft a document that presented the colonial position on independence.

Thomas Jefferson was the primary author of this document—the Declaration of Independence—and was heavily influenced by Thomas Paine's *Common Sense*. The Declaration states that people have certain inalienable rights and lists the acts that Britain had committed to make separation between the colonies and Britain necessary. Lee's resolution passed on July 2, and on July 4, the Declaration of Independence was adopted.

A year later, the Articles of Confederation became the governing document of the new nation. Leaders recognized weaknesses in the Articles, so they agreed to meet in Philadelphia to make revisions. Once they met, they decided to write a new document rather than revise the old one. Federalists favored a strong central government, and Anti-Federalists and delegates who represented smaller and less populated states wanted the states to have more power. James Madison's Virginia Plan ultimately served as the basis for the new government. The resulting document, the Constitution, was a compromise of economic, political, and geographic interests represented at the Convention. The Constitution provided for three branches of government and a system of checks and balances for each branch.

After the Constitution was signed, Alexander Hamilton, James Madison, and John Jay wrote a series of essays to explain the philosophy of the newly proposed system of government and to promote ratification of the document in the state of New York. Each of the 85 essays, known together as the Federalist Papers, was published in several newspapers and signed with the pseudonym "Publius."

The Constitution, as drafted, did not provide protection of individual rights. The Founders realized that without provisions to protect individual rights the Constitution had a poor chance of being ratified. Twelve amendments were presented to the states for approval; ten were ratified. These first ten amendments to the Constitution are called the Bill of Rights.

Leo Tolstoy's *War and Peace*

War, peace, love, rejection, life, death, aristocratic society, people's choices, history's effect, time's passage—Leo Tolstoy's epic 19th-century Russian novel contained all this and more in a story considered one of the all-time greatest works of literature.

Tolstoy originally planned to write about another chapter in Russian history, the Decemberist Revolt, but his background research led him to Napoleon's 1812 invasion of Russia, which ultimately became the backdrop for this sweeping novel. Published between 1865 and 1869 in four books and two epilogues, much of *War and Peace* was written in Russian. However, Tolstoy also wrote significant portions of the dialogue in French, since most of the Russian nobility spoke that language fluently.

The novel contains an incredible 580 characters. Two of the main ones include nice but socially awkward Pierre Bezukhov and his friend, the intelligent and caustic Andrei Bolkonsky. Critics have said that these two characters represent different sides of Tolstoy. Another main character is Nikolai Rostov, a gambler whose debts bring his family to the brink of ruin. On the female side, Natasha Rostova is first introduced as lively and fun-loving; she undergoes a spiritual change that complements that of Pierre, whom she ultimately marries. There is also Andrei's sister Marya, and the beautiful but emotionally bankrupt Elena.

Another memorable Tolstoy creation is one-eyed General Kutuzov, who, although not as dashing as Napoleon, manages to defeat him in battle. Several aristocratic families are also central to the story, including the scheming Kuragins and the noble Rostovs. Throughout the story, society life in Russia whirls madly onward as the country is gripped by the war. Although the characters try to live as if there is no conflict, Napoleon's invasion ultimately influences their lives.

The novel demonstrates Tolstoy's view of history: People do not cause events but can take advantage of them, such as Napoleon taking advantage of the French Revolution to rise to power. Although there is much violent imagery in *War and Peace,* Tolstoy also explores romance, particularly the implications of those relationships that characters undertake without much thought.

POSTSCRIPT

■ Tolstoy turned increasingly spiritual in later life, sparking many quarrels with his wife.

Charlie Chaplin (1889–1977)

CHARLES SPENCER CHAPLIN was born in London, England, and was the son of music hall performers. Sadly, his father died from the effects of alcohol abuse and his mother went insane. Because of these circumstances, Charlie and his brother Sidney spent their youth in orphanages or on the streets of London.

At age 20, Chaplin caught a break when he joined the Fred Karno Pantomime Troupe, an acclaimed music hall act. On their second tour of America, a representative of Mack Sennett, the owner of the famed Keystone Studio, saw Chaplin perform. This resulted in a job offer, and Chaplin went to work at Keystone in January 1914. By the end of that year, he had appeared in 35 one- and two-reel comedies. He also created his signature comic character—a tramp with baggy pants, bowler hat, toothbrush mustache, and cane. The character made his debut in the film *Kid Auto Races at Venice,* but his persona developed over several films. The tramp was small, which made him vulnerable, but he was also agile and resourceful, making it possible for him to prevail in a cold, cruel world. He longed for the girl, whom he often rescued, but he was frequently rejected because of his inadequacies.

Chaplin's rise in the industry coincided with his growing popularity. He joined Essanay Film Company in 1915. He wrote, directed, and starred in 14 comedy shorts for Essanay before moving on to the Mutual Film Corporation. There, he made even more money, built his own studio, and enjoyed increased creative control. For Chaplin, total creative control was essential to fully utilize his tramp character and comedic artistry for social commentary. The Little Tramp became a representative of the disenfranchised, the homeless, immigrants, and orphans—who lived at the fringes of society thanks to rigid class distinctions or social conventions.

Chaplin added a touch of pathos to the Little Tramp when he began making feature-length films in the 1920s. Films such as *Modern Times, The Gold Rush,* and *City Lights* illustrated the socio-political ramifications of the Tramp. Amazingly, Chaplin was the only silent film performer who was not forced into making talking films at the end of the silent era. Such was his popularity that he did not make a sound film until *The Great Dictator* in 1940, 13 years after their debut. Chaplin moved to Switzerland for political reasons in 1953, and directed his last feature, *A Countess from Hong Kong,* in 1967.

Noir Literature

Today, noir is associated with books and films that originated in 1920s America and offer a dark, gritty view of crime and evil. French literary critics were the first to apply the term *noir* to American crime fiction. This came after the publisher Gallimard began releasing French translations of those works in the *Série Noir,* or noir series, in 1945.

In the 1920s and 1930s, American literary critics had labeled the crime novels of Dashiell Hammett and Raymond Chandler "hardboiled," because of their tough detective protagonists, such as Hammett's Sam Spade and Chandler's Philip Marlowe. The term *hardboiled* came to be used for the crime fiction featured in such popular magazines as *Black Mask* and *Dime Detective.*

Not all of these stories revolved around detectives, however. The novels of James M. Cain, who is also considered a founder of noir fiction, do not feature detectives. Consequently, not all detective novels are necessarily noir, but the line can be hard to draw. Some critics make a distinction between hardboiled detective novels and noir novels, or those in which the nondetective protagonist is directly connected to the crime or act of violence. One example of this type of character is the corrupt insurance salesman Walter Huff in Cain's famous book *Double Indemnity.*

Noir novels are often preoccupied with fate, expressed in imagery of gambling and casinos, such as dice and roulette wheels. Their plots link the American dream of material success with fraud, crime, and violence. San Francisco and Los Angeles are frequent settings of early noir novels, partly because California was seen as a land of opportunity during the Depression era. Their protagonists are typically men who are morally compromised or flawed in some way. These men usually come into contact with women whom they seek to rescue or help. However, the women often turn out to be femme fatales, literally "disastrous women," who seduce them or lie to them. Internal guilt and confession are also frequent themes, often occurring in the context of police or court proceedings.

Besides Hammett, Chandler, and Cain, other famous noir writers include William Burnett, Lou Cameron, James Ellroy, Patricia Highsmith, Chester Himes, Dorothy Hughes, Elmore Leonard, Ed McBain (real name, Evan Hunter), Horace McCoy, Ross Macdonald (real name, Kenneth Millar), John D. MacDonald, Mickey Spillane, Jim Thompson, and Cornell Woolrich. While these writers' novels were once considered trashy, some are now viewed as serious literary works.

Mussorgsky's *Pictures at an Exhibition*

INSTRUMENTAL PROGRAM MUSIC has often been adopted as a resource by composers who wish to provide a specifically "regional" or "nationalistic" character to their works. This became a trend in the second half of the 1800s as political reconfigurations on the European subcontinent led to an increased awareness of "nationhood" as a desirable quality to unite individuals of all walks of life under a commitment to a political framework, especially in opposition to other nations. Artistic creativity was thus often directed at creating national cultural icons and identifying (and elaborating on) authentic elements of a people.

One example of a specifically nationalistic set of program music is *Pictures at an Exhibition* (1874), created by Russian composer Modest Mussorgsky (1839–1881). *Pictures* is a set of works written to celebrate the posthumous exhibition of selected paintings by Viktor Hartmann, a friend and colleague of Mussorgsky's. It consists of a series of "musical images" inspired by Hartmann paintings, several of which concern specifically Russian topics. For example, "The Hut on Fowl's Legs" evokes a mythical Russian witch; "Cattle" actually uses a Polish word and is probably linked to a Hartmann painting showing a Polish ox-cart; and "The Great Gate at Kiev" is clearly a response to a sketch of a gate designed by Hartmann (but never built) to commemorate Russian Tsar Alexander II. (Note that while these are "Russian" topics, they encompass the "Greater Russia" of the Tsars rather than the nation as it is known in the present day.)

Among the resources Mussorgsky uses to "paint" these images are rhythms and melodies that appear to be derived from Russian folk musical traditions. The various self-contained images are introduced and linked by a recurring melody that Mussorgsky called the "promenade"— intended to describe the viewer's walk through the gallery.

Mussorgsky composed *Pictures* for the piano, but it was later orchestrated by a number of other musicians, including Frenchman Maurice Ravel (1875–1937) in 1922. It is the Ravel orchestration of *Pictures* that has made the work a longtime favorite and a staple of symphony orchestras worldwide.

POSTSCRIPT

■ Ravel's arrangement is the most famous but by no means the most recent. The English progressive rock band Emerson, Lake & Palmer created a version in 1971 later released as an album named (appropriately) *Pictures at an Exhibition*.

The Hubble Telescope

Earth's atmosphere distorts light from objects in space. Even telescopes on high mountains, with little air above them, record somewhat fuzzy views of the heavens. Ideally, astronomers want their telescopes completely above the atmosphere. They got their wish in 1990, when the space shuttle *Discovery* launched the Hubble Space Telescope into orbit 350 miles above Earth.

Named for Edwin Hubble (1889–1953), the American astronomer who first showed that the universe is expanding, the telescope has become an astronomical wonder. It has surveyed everything from the solar system to the edge of the universe. In the process, it has produced discoveries that have changed astronomers' understanding of the cosmos.

The Hubble Telescope faced a difficult start. Soon after its launch, scientists at NASA realized that its 94-inch mirror had been ground incorrectly. Hubble had what astronomers called a *spherical aberration*. In 1993, space-walking astronauts acted like celestial optometrists: They fitted Hubble with corrective lenses.

Almost immediately, the telescope proved its value. A few months after the correction, Hubble took extraordinarily sharp pictures of a comet colliding with Jupiter—an extremely rare event. Hubble has taken high-precision images of objects at the edge of our solar system, such as Pluto and its moon Charon and the newly discovered dwarf planet Eris. Beyond the solar system, the telescope has confirmed that disks of dust from which planets might form surround stars. And it has identified atmospheres on planets that orbit other stars.

Hubble's greatest contributions to astronomy, however, involve the nature of the universe. The telescope has spotted black holes at the centers of some galaxies. It has peered back in time, seeing stars and galaxies created at the dawn of the cosmos. By measuring the distances to certain stars more accurately than before, Hubble provided a precise measure of the rate at which the universe is expanding. Its observations of distant supernovas proved, to astronomers' amazement, that the universe's rate of expansion is increasing rather than decreasing. Finally, Hubble has found evidence of dark energy, the mysterious repulsive force that may be causing the faster expansion.

Astronauts have made regular service visits to Hubble. A shuttle mission planned for August 2008 will set Hubble up for several more years of observation. By the time Hubble stops working in about 2013, the James Webb Space Telescope will have started its own work of discovery.

Grant Wood's *American Gothic*

*A*MERICAN *G*OTHIC IS MORE than just Grant Wood's most famous painting. This portrait of an expressionless Midwestern couple in front of a white farmhouse has become a recognizable icon of Americana even to those who know little about art. As such, it has been parodied, spoofed, and caricatured—none of which has diminished the impact of the original painting.

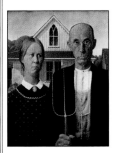

Wood was one of the Regionalist painters of the 1930s who rejected European modernism and abstraction in favor of local American subject matter in an accessible style. The subject matter of *American Gothic* was in keeping with Regionalist sensibilities and reflective of Wood's own childhood on a Quaker farm near Anamosa, Iowa.

Wood found the farmhouse used in the painting in Eldon, Iowa. He did a quick sketch and then photographed the white house with the wide porch, pointed roof, and Gothic window to use as aids in creating the painting. Wood's sister Nan and a local dentist, Dr. B. H. McKeeby, served as models for the two sober-looking figures in the foreground. The vertical lines of the farmhouse are echoed in the stripes in the farmer's shirt as well as in the stiff, straight posture of both figures, who exude Midwestern strength and stoicism.

The painting was done on beaverboard, a type of fiberboard used in building the interior of houses. Wood applied several thin layers of pigment and glaze to the board to create a smooth finish.

Wood developed his distinguished style after a trip to Munich in 1928 to supervise the production of stained glass for a window he had designed for the Veterans Memorial Building in Cedar Rapids. While there, he became enamored with the work of the 15th- and 16th-century Dutch masters, particularly Hans Memling. Wood saw a stylistic similarity between the hard-edged, detailed style of these painters and the visual quality of American folk art and American decorative arts from the 19th century. All of these influences came to bear on Wood's subsequent style.

In 1930, *American Gothic* won the bronze medal at an exhibit at the Art Institute of Chicago (where it is currently housed), setting off a controversy regarding Wood's treatment of the figures. Because of the plain, rigid look of the man and woman, many saw the painting as an insult to rural folks and their lifestyle, a charge Wood vehemently denied.

Franklin Delano Roosevelt

WHEN FRANKLIN D. ROOSEVELT (1882–1945) took the reigns of national leadership from Herbert Hoover in March 1933, he had a monumental crisis to overcome. The Great Depression had devastated the United States: Factories had closed, banks had failed, and massive numbers of people were unemployed.

To help restore the country, Roosevelt, with the help of congressional legislation, implemented the New Deal. Banks were closed to stop depositors from removing their savings, and agencies were established to hire the unemployed. The Civilian Conservation Corps (CCC) utilized young unemployed men to help reforest the country's diminishing timber areas and fight soil erosion. The Agricultural Adjustment Administration (AAA) was an attempt to balance agricultural supply and demand by paying farmers to take some of their land out of production in order to maintain farm prices at a higher level. The Works Progress Administration (WPA) was an ambitious New Deal program that used the unemployed to construct and repair bridges, roads, and parks.

In addition to work programs, the New Deal included cultural programs. The Public Work of Arts Project (PWAP) employed artists to paint murals in the interiors of public buildings such as schools and museums. The Treasury Art Program focused on having unemployed artists paint murals in post offices throughout the nation.

Although Roosevelt's New Deal policies helped restore the nation's economy, they were criticized because they required the government's direct involvement in the lives of the country's citizenry.

Roosevelt had been involved in politics for more than 20 years before he became president. His political career was derailed briefly after he was stricken with polio in 1921. Roosevelt courageously fought the disease and, although he never regained the use of his legs, he reentered the political arena in 1928. He used a wheelchair but was careful to always be seen standing (even if supported) in public.

Throughout Roosevelt's political career and illness, his wife, Eleanor, encouraged and supported him. She was the first First Lady to hold press conferences, give lectures, and express her opinions. Because of Franklin's extramarital affairs, Eleanor eventually moved into her own residence, but the couple never divorced.

FDR was elected to the presidency an unprecedented four times (1933–1945), serving from the Great Depression through World War II. He died in 1945 and was succeeded in office by Harry S. Truman.

Marcel Proust's
Remembrance of Things Past

REMEMBRANCE OF THINGS PAST is a portrait of the French upper classes and their social and sexual involvements at the beginning of the 20th century. Among its themes are the human ability to recover past time, the loss of innocence, the emptiness of love and friendship, and the triumph of sin. On the hopeful side, Marcel Proust sees life as being filled with beauty and joy, which can be lost but also recovered.

Proust's semiautobiographical novel in seven volumes was published between 1913 and 1927. Written in French, the novel was first translated into English in 1922 as *Remembrance of Things Past*. A recent translation renders the title literally as *In Search of Lost Time.*

Remembrance of Things Past is a major example of Modernist literature in French that has influenced subsequent literary and popular culture. It is particularly noted for episodes of "involuntary memory," a phrase created by Proust to describe situations in which everyday stimuli evoke the past so intensely that these events come alive again for characters who don't consciously recall them.

Proust was born on July 10, 1871, in a Paris suburb to a physician and his Jewish wife. Though he suffered from asthma all his life, Proust served in the military and earned degrees in law and literature. As a young man, he went to soirées with the French nobility where he met many of the people who became characters in *Remembrance of Things Past.*

Proust started his career by contributing short fiction to literary magazines. After publishing a volume of his stories in 1896, he worked on *Jean Santeuil,* an (unfinished) autobiographical novel, until 1899. Proust publicly defended Alfred Dreyfus, the Jewish army officer who was falsely accused of treason and sent to Devil's Island. Disillusionment with the anti-Semitism of the French elite was to become a background theme in *Remembrance of Things Past.*

In January 1909, a childhood memory was revived in Proust by the taste of tea and a biscuit. Six months later, he started on the first volume of *Remembrance of Things Past.* Thanks to the large inheritance he received after his mother's death in 1905, he was able to focus solely on his writing. Several publishers turned down the first volume *(Du côté de chez Swann),* but it was finally published at the author's expense—and to good reviews—in November 1913. He continued to work on the novel, writing six more volumes before his death from pneumonia in 1922. The last three volumes were published posthumously.

Evelyn Waugh (1903–1966)

NOVELIST, JOURNALIST, and travel writer, Evelyn Waugh is known for his satiric novels that hilariously reveal the shallowness of how the so-called Bright Young Things lived during the time between the World Wars. In *Vile Bodies* (1930), he captures the frivolity of London's smart set, who were determined to escape the sense of futility engendered by World War I. Other works of social comedy in the same vein include *A Handful of Dust* (1934) and *Scoop* (1938).

For the general reader, however, Waugh's most well-known work is probably *Brideshead Revisited* (1945), which he wrote during World War II while on extended leave from the Royal Marines. Different from his social satires, *Brideshead* is a nostalgic evocation of Waugh's time at Oxford, as well as a description of the years leading up to World War II. Protagonist Charles Ryder is a student at one of the less fashionable Oxford University colleges (as Waugh himself had been). Entranced by the beauty and the careless grace of the more aristocratic Sebastian Flyte, Ryder enters a social milieu that is initially foreign to him but very seductive. Autobiographical elements include the lure of Roman Catholicism (Waugh had converted in 1930) and the continuing hold on Ryder of associations from university days. The 1981 television adaptation of *Brideshead Revisited,* which was hugely popular, created renewed interest in the novel.

Waugh's World War II experiences provided background for a highly regarded trilogy titled *Sword of Honour* (1965), a narrative about civilian and military life that is both humorous and emotional. Protagonist Guy Crouchback, like Charles Ryder from Brideshead, displays characteristics of Waugh.

A social satirist who aspired to enter the world he mocked, Waugh gradually transformed himself into an English gentleman who held increasingly conservative views and lived in the country (he bought Combe Florey in Somerset in 1956). Damaged by drink and haunted by depression, he indulged in self-caricature in *The Ordeal of Gilbert Pinfold* (1957), in which a famous Roman Catholic novelist drinks heavily and has a general disdain of modern life.

Today, Waugh is considered one of the great comic novelists of the 20th century. His son Auberon was also a man of letters, and the tradition is now being carried on by grandson Christopher, who has written *Fathers and Sons* (2007), an account of five generations of Waugh males.

Early Photography

THE PRACTICE OF CREATING permanent images of objects began in ancient times. However, it was not until 1826 that Joseph Nicéphore Niépce of Chalon-sur-Saône, France, was able to create the first photograph.

Niépce combined two well-known discoveries to create photography. The first was a device called the *camera obscura,* or "dark chamber," which had existed for hundreds of years. It was a box, which could be as large as a room, that worked by projecting an image through a small hole onto a flat surface. Artists began using this device in the 16th century to trace an image onto a wall or other surface to permanently capture it.

The second part of Niépce's process came from a discovery made by Johann Heinrich Shulze in 1727. He found that sunlight could produce a permanent image on silver halide. Niépce cleverly used a camera obscura to project an image onto a pewter plate covered with silver halide. He captured the view outside his window and produced the world's first photograph. Niépce's new process, called *heliography,* or sun drawing, required an exposure of at least eight hours to get a dark enough image.

Niépce partnered with Louis-Jacques-Mandé Daguerre in 1829 to further refine the process. By 1837, Daguerre had devised a way to capture detailed images on silver and copper plates. He called his images *daguerreotypes.* They immediately became popular but were very fragile and difficult to reproduce.

Independent of Daguerre's work, Englishman William Talbot developed a photographic process in 1835. First, paper was soaked in solutions of salt and silver nitrate. When exposed to light, the paper would produce a negative image. By exposing

Louis-Jacques-Mandé Daguerre

another soaked piece of paper to light while it sat on top of the negative, a photograph could be produced.

Various inventors refined the photographic process, but it still remained the domain of professional photographers. However, in 1888, American George Eastman invented a small hand-held box camera that almost anyone could use. It held a 100-exposure roll of paper negatives. When all the pictures were taken, the user sent the camera to the Eastman Kodak Company. The photos were then developed and returned to the customer, along with the reloaded camera. In fact, the Kodak company motto was, "You press the button, we do the rest."

John Philip Sousa

BRASS BANDS HAD PLAYED a crucial role in the cultural life of soldiers in the American Civil War, and their popularity—which had already taken hold in the decades preceding the war—expanded dramatically in the latter part of the 19th century. The figurehead of this expansion was John Philip Sousa (1854–1932), a prominent bandleader who composed arguably the most recognizable and widely known American musical works.

After wide-ranging musical training (and reputedly just as he was about to join a circus band), Sousa was enlisted in the U.S. Marine Band by his father at the age of 13. His career was not exclusively connected to that group; he left at the age of 20 and built a parallel career connected to musical theater, predominantly in Philadelphia, through the 1870s. However, upon becoming the conductor of the Marine Band in 1880, he dedicated himself increasingly to band repertory, writing a string of increasingly popular marches. (*The Gladiator* was the first to sell more than one million copies in sheet music.)

Sousa left the Marine Band in 1892 to form his own ensemble, Sousa's Band, which made four European tours and one year-long world tour (in addition to many North American appearances) by 1910. During World War I, Sousa brought his talents to the navy, organizing ensembles and continuing to compose wartime marches. Sousa's Band reformed after the war and continued its success (eventually performing more than 15,000 concerts) until the Great Depression, when its touring schedule decreased and eventually fell off. By 1931, radio was becoming a crucial medium for music distribution, and the Sousa Band performed for radio broadcast until Sousa's death.

In the later decades of his life, Sousa was recognized as an American cultural giant and became increasingly concerned with his legacy. He worked to increase music education in the schools and campaigned strenuously against the rise of recorded sound distribution, which he felt was damaging both to working musicians' livelihoods and to the musical education of young Americans. Sousa died in the practice of his craft: He had just completed a rehearsal for one of his most famous marches, *The Stars and Stripes Forever,* when he collapsed of a heart attack.

The Doppler Effect

IF YOU STAND in a railroad station when an express train passes through while blowing its whistle, you will hear changes in the sound. As the train approaches, the pitch increases. Then, as the train passes through, the pitch suddenly drops. This happens because the sound waves from the whistle are squeezed as the train approaches and stretched out as it moves away. Scientists call this phenomenon the *Doppler effect* after Christian Doppler, an Austrian physicist who explained it mathematically in 1842. Doppler's legacy appears in everything from astronomical observatories to police speed traps to hospitals.

The Doppler effect applies to more than just sound. When astronomers study stars' spectra, they see lines characteristic of the chemical elements in the stars. In 1848, French astronomer Armand-Hippolyte-Louis Fizeau noticed that the spectra of some distant stars looked unusual. They contained the expected lines but in the wrong positions. All were shifted toward the longer-wavelength red end of the spectrum. The Doppler principle meant that the light waves from the stars were stretched out. So the "red shift" indicated that the stars were moving away from Earth. In the 1920s, American astronomer Edwin Hubble realized that the large red shifts of distant galaxies meant that the universe was expanding.

Today, astronomers apply the Doppler effect in several sophisticated ways. The sizes of the farthest galaxies' red shifts indicate their distances from Earth. Those distances help to calculate the age of the universe. Astronomers also use the effect to measure the temperatures of gases in stars and galaxies.

On Earth, the Doppler effect is often combined with radar. Doppler calculations applied to reflections of a radar beam from a moving target indicate the target's speed. Police officers point Doppler radar systems at automobiles to identify speeders. Doppler weather radars fire radio waves at raindrops and other objects in the air. They then convert the reflected waves into images that show the location, speed, and intensity of the storm or other weather condition.

On a smaller scale, doctors use the Doppler effect to diagnose disease. They apply the effect to ultrasound images to calculate the speed at which blood flows through the body. Speeds that differ from normal can indicate medical problems, such as leakage of blood through heart valves or blockages of veins or arteries.

Sir Christopher Wren

O**N THE NIGHT** of September 2, 1666, a small fire started in a London bake shop. In a city built largely of wood, the windblown sparks found fuel everywhere. Five days later, when the blaze was finally extinguished, 430 acres in the city's center had burned. Gone were 13,000 homes, 89 churches, and 52 guildhalls. Following the fire, London was rebuilt as a modern city with wide streets and brick buildings. Christopher Wren (1632–1723) designed 51 new churches, including St. Paul's Cathedral.

Wren had not been trained as an architect. The son of a Wiltshire clergyman, he studied astronomy at Oxford University. Wren spoke of arithmetic and geometry as the only human truths "void of all uncertainty." He saw mathematics not only as key to the science of astronomy but to all intellectual pursuits. His other interests included anatomy, mechanics, optics, and the design of meters and gauges.

By 1657, Wren knew the work of Vitruvius (active 25 B.C.), whose *Ten Books on Architecture* had exerted a profound influence on artists and architects of the Renaissance. Wren's first design was for a small chapel at Cambridge University. Success at this and subsequent commissions quickly made him England's top architect. In 1669, King Charles II made Wren the Surveyor General of the King's Works. In 1673, he honored Wren with knighthood.

Wren's masterpiece of church architecture, St. Paul's Cathedral, the largest cathedral in England, was built between 1675 and 1710. The dome is modeled after the dome that Michelangelo designed for St. Peter's in Rome. On the west facade, porches, columns, pediments, and towers provide contrasts of carved marble, soaring columns, and deep shadows. The dome, supported by a circle of pillars—the "drum"—rises 366 feet above the pavement. This cylindrical drum is famous as the "whispering gallery." The acoustics are so perfect that words whispered against the wall are completely audible on the opposite side.

Sir Christopher Wren's London churches include Saint Clement Danes, Saint Mary Le Bow, Saint Stephen's Walbrook, and Saint James. His other buildings include the Royal Observatory at Greenwich, hospitals for retired soldiers and sailors, and Trinity College Library at Cambridge University, as well the south front of Hampton Court Palace.

Sir Christopher Wren is buried in St. Paul's Cathedral. The Latin inscription on his gravestone reads, "If you seek his memorial, look about you."

The Spanish Armada

IN MAY 1588, a great fleet of ships set out from Lisbon, in Portugal, and headed north toward England. Known to history as the Spanish Armada, its purpose was to overthrow Queen Elizabeth I and establish Spain's Philip I as regent of a Catholic England.

Philip had a litany of grievances against the Protestant queen. He was also determined to halt English aid to the Protestant Dutch who were resisting his reign over what was then called the Spanish Netherlands.

After two years of preparations, the "Invincible Armada," which included 130 ships and 30,000 men, set sail under the command of the Duke de Medina Sidonia. According to the Spanish plan, the Armada would sail to Flanders, pick up an army commanded by the Duke of Parma, and then proceed across the Channel to England.

Storms delayed the fleet until July, depriving the invaders of any hope of surprise. As the Spaniards entered the English Channel, the alarm was raised. According to accounts, Sir Francis Drake nonchalantly insisted on finishing his game of lawn bowls before sallying forth to do battle.

Initial attacks on the Spanish fleet had little effect. Medina Sidonia, who had been directed to proceed straight up the Channel to pick up the invasion army, had arranged his ships in a protective crescent formation and was able to fight off the faster but smaller English vessels. However, on August 6 he was forced to anchor near Calais to await the arrival of the Duke of Parma's ground troops. Stationary and without the protection of their moving crescent formation, the Spaniards were now vulnerable.

On the night of August 7, the English sent eight fire ships—appropriately called "Hell Burners"—into the enemy anchorage. Frantically trying to avoid destruction by the flaming ships, the Armada broke in all directions.

Taking advantage of the disarray, the English attacked on August 8. They inflicted severe damage on the scattered Spanish fleet before a sudden wind shift allowed the surviving Spanish ships to flee northward. This would turn out to be less fortuitous than it appeared.

Unable to return back down the Channel because of the English, the much-battered Armada attempted to sail home around Scotland and the west coast of Ireland. Storms soon dispersed the ships. Provisions ran out. Many of those who landed or were shipwrecked in Ireland were killed by English troops. More than 20,000 Spanish sailors and soldiers perished. The English did not lose a single ship.

John Milton

JOHN MILTON (1608–1674), famous for the epic poem *Paradise Lost*, was born to a prosperous scrivener (a combination legal secretary, notary, and real estate agent) in London. Milton grew up comfortably and was educated by tutors in the Latin and Greek classics, as well as French, Italian, and Hebrew. He attended Christ's College, Cambridge, intending to be an Anglican priest. He worked hard but quarreled with his tutors and was briefly suspended in 1626 after a fistfight with one of them. After earning his master's degree *cum laude*, Milton embarked on a six-year period of further intensive study in literature, theology, and philosophy.

Milton toured Europe in 1638 and met scholar Hugo Grotius in Paris and the astronomer Galileo in Florence. But unrest in England brought Milton back in 1639, a year before the Civil War erupted between Charles I's Royalist supporters and Oliver Cromwell's Puritan "round-head" republicans. Milton, a passionate, if eccentric, Puritan, was appointed secretary of Foreign Tongues by Cromwell's Commonwealth and spent much of Cromwell's 11-year Interregnum ("between kings") writing propaganda pamphlets and responses to scholarly attacks on the Puritan cause and Charles I's execution.

A poet who had published since his Cambridge years, Milton worked throughout his life on his long poem about the creation and fall of humanity, *Paradise Lost*. After the Restoration of the monarchy in 1660, Milton—who had written political treatises and proposals—was imprisoned by the Restoration government and lost much of his money in fines. Once freed, he retired from public life, giving him time to complete his great epic. It first appeared in 1667.

An ambitious work, *Paradise Lost* aims to "justify God's ways to man" by retelling the story of humanity's fall as a blank-verse epic poem that both draws from and challenges classical models such as Homer's and Virgil's epics. Told from the point of view of the rebel angel Satan, it begins *in medias res* ("in the middle of things") and employs flashbacks as in Homer's *Iliad* and *Odyssey*. The poem received immediate and lasting success, establishing Milton as one of the most renowned English poets.

POSTSCRIPT

■ Milton lost his eyesight to illness and dictated the lines of *Paradise Lost* to his daughter.

■ Controversially, in *Paradise Lost* Milton showed Adam and Eve working in Eden, although in the Bible work is the punishment for Adam's sin.

Joni Mitchell (1943–present)

BORN ROBERTA JOAN ANDERSON in Alberta, Canada, Joni Mitchell is one of the most influential singers and songwriters of the 20th century. As a student in commercial arts at the Alberta College of Art, she performed in local coffeehouses. Following a short-lived marriage to folk singer Chuck Mitchell in Toronto, she eventually settled in Los Angeles in 1968.

Her first commercial success was as a songwriter. Judy Collins's recording of Mitchell's "Both Sides Now" reached the number eight spot on the national music charts in 1968. Mitchell's first album, *Song to a Seagull,* received some play, but her second album, *Clouds,* won the Grammy Award for best folk performance in 1969. Her fame grew with the release of each succeeding album, including: *Ladies of the Canyon* (1970); *Blue* (1971), her first million-copy seller; *Court and Spark* and *Miles of Aisles* (1974), which both reached number two on the American charts; *The Hissing of Summer Lawns* (1975); and *Hejira* (1976), her last top 15 hit.

"As a songwriter," a Detroit reviewer once wrote, "she plays Yang to Bob Dylan's Yin, equaling him in richness and profusion of imagery and surpassing him in conciseness and direction." Throughout her career, Mitchell has not been afraid to experiment in various musical genres from folk, pop, and jazz, to the classics. "I looked like a folksinger," she has stated, "even though the moment I began to write, my music was not folk music. It was something else that had elements of romantic classicism to it."

Since the 1980s, music and visual arts have shared Mitchell's interest. While she has used both mediums to further her stances on political and social issues, such as the Ethiopian famine ("Dog Eat Dog," 1985), she has not lost sight of music as a means of expressing personal emotions and passions, as seen in the album *Turbulent Indigo,* which won the 1994 Grammy Award for Pop Album of the Year.

POSTSCRIPT

▦ Mitchell taught herself to play guitar using a Pete Seeger instructional record.

▦ Mitchell contracted and recovered from polio when she was nine years old, which is also the age at which she began to smoke.

▦ In February 1965, Mitchell gave birth to a daughter, Kelly Dale Anderson. whom she gave up for adoption. Years later, Kelly, renamed Kilauren Gibb, began the search for her birth-mother, which led to a very emotional reunion in 1997.

The Seven Wonders of the Ancient World

Aᴺᵀᴵᴾᴬᵀᴱᴿ ᴼꜰ Sᴵᴰᴼᴺ, a writer during the second century B.C., listed seven wonders (literally "must-sees") of the ancient world:

- Pyramids of Egypt, located along a 50-mile stretch of the Nile Valley near ancient Memphis. The Pyramids of Khufu, Khafre, and Menkäure were constructed around 2500 B.C. and still survive today.

- Hanging Gardens of Babylon, irrigated roof gardens on terraces in present-day Iraq. Built around 600 B.C., probably by Nebuchadrezzar II, they were destroyed in an earthquake after the first century B.C.

- Temple of Artemis at Ephesus, in present-day Turkey. Built by Croesus, king of Lydia in 550 B.C., the temple was destroyed by fire in 356 B.C., rebuilt, and then destroyed for good by the Goths in 262.

- Statue of Zeus at Olympia, erected in 435 B.C. in present-day Greece, was more than 30 feet high and plated with gold and ivory. Destroyed by fire in the fifth century A.D.

- Mausoleum of Halicarnassus, in present-day Bodrum, Turkey, was constructed about 315 B.C. by king Mausolus' widow, Artemisia, to house his remains. Looted and vandalized through the years, it was destroyed by an earthquake in the 15th century A.D.

- Colossus of Rhodes, a 100-foot iron-reinforced bronze statue of the sun god, was built in present-day Greece between about 292 and 280 B.C. Destroyed by an earthquake around A.D. 225, its remains were sold for scrap some 400 years later.

- Pharos of Alexandria, a 440-foot lighthouse, was built on the island of Pharos, near Alexandria in present-day Egypt for Ptolemy II around 280 B.C. It was destroyed by an earthquake in the 12th century.

Since only one of the seven ancient wonders has survived, many alternative lists have been compiled. Wonders of the Middle Ages include Stonehenge and the Great Wall of China. The American Society of Civil Engineers lists seven modern wonders such as the Panama Canal (1914) and the Channel Tunnel (1994) between England and France. Howard Hillman, a travel writer, made lists of man-made wonders, natural travel wonders, and underwater wonders. Other lists include the Seven Wonders of Wales and the Seven Blunders of the World (compiled by Mahatma Gandhi).

The Rise of Atonal Music

Writing music in a key and arranging harmonies in a systematic, logical order—a concept known as *tonality*—has been one of the basic organizing principles of Western music since the 17th century. This mattered little to Arnold Schoenberg (1874–1951). In the opening decades of the 20th century, he redefined musical composition by devising a new method known as *atonality*.

Tonal music is organized around a certain key, and notes and chords are chosen to be in harmony with that key. Keys can change throughout a piece, but tonal compositions will begin and end with the key's main chord, called the *tonic*. Additionally, there are certain "rules" that tonal music must follow: Harmonies are ordered in progressions that move away from and then back to the tonic; and dissonance, which is the use of two or more contrasting notes, can be used to create a harsh sound to cause feelings of tension. Dissonance is contrasted by *consonance*, pleasing sounds more closely related to the tonic chord. Using these rules, composers are able to create a musical narrative where there is a sense of resolved tension with the return of more pleasing sounds.

Rules, however, are meant to be broken—and Schoenberg did just that. He was influenced by the expressionist movement in art, with its tendency to distort reality to evoke stronger emotion, and he hoped to apply this to music. Schoenberg believed a greater intensity of feeling could be achieved in music by expanding the harmonic language of composers such as Wagner, Mahler, and Debussy who had rejected the idea that dissonance always leads to consonance. Following their lead, Schoenberg revolutionized musical organization by using notes, harmony, and dissonance in a non-systematic manner dubbed "the emancipation of the dissonance."

Between 1907 and 1913, Schoenberg spearheaded the emergence of atonal expressionist music, definitively demonstrated in his signature composition, *Pierrot Lunaire* (1912). Having challenged the conventions of harmony, Schoenberg took aim on the other pillar of tonality—the notion of key. In the early 1920s, he invented a 12-tone technique of music writing in which each of the 12 tones of a chromatic scale were referenced to *each other* instead of a specific key. Using this technique, music radically separates itself from the tonal norm, as it has no key.

Schoenberg's innovations were tremendously influential, as atonality became a prominent part of the work of many 20th century composers. His work also inspired composers to experiment with atonality to create politically resistant works in the aftermath of totalitarianism and world war.

Randomness

Astatistician has a nose for the flavors of randomness, just like an oenophile has a nose for the flavors of wine.

Gaussian, Levy, exponential, Laplace, gamma, Pareto, Cauchy, uniform—the kinds of randomness go on and on, and each one has its own special characteristics. A process is random if its outcome cannot be determined in advance. But that doesn't necessarily mean that there's no order of any kind.

The kind of randomness you probably think of initially is called *uniform*. If you have ten different marbles in a jar and you shake it up, close your eyes, and draw one out, there is, at least in theory, the same chance of drawing each marble.

That's not the only kind of randomness, though. Suppose someone was chosen at random from your office building, and you were asked to predict the height of whoever would be chosen. You couldn't say for sure, of course, because it's random. But still, you probably wouldn't just choose any arbitrary measurement, like one foot or ten feet. Instead you'd probably pick a height close to the average, which in the United States is about 5 feet, 6 inches.

In statistical terms, that's a good choice because height has what's called a *normal distribution*. Normal distributions form the classic bell-shape curve. Suppose, for example, that you drew a graph showing the number of people of each height in your office building. The curve would probably look like a bell, with the highest spot around 5 feet, 6 inches and falling off in both directions from there. Only a few people would be very short or very tall.

But there are many other kinds of randomness, too. For example, say that a telephone operator ordinarily gets a phone call about every five minutes. She wants to know the chance that a telephone call will arrive within a given amount of time. That's yet another flavor of randomness. The chance that the phone will ring within one second is pretty small. The chance that it will ring within a minute is a bit larger, and the chance that it will ring sometime in the next hour is very large indeed. A graph of these probabilities would look a bit like a ski jump, starting fairly flat and getting steeper and steeper. This is called an *exponential distribution*.

So, the next time you say, "'That's so random," you might want to consider just what kind of random it might be.

Frank Gehry and the Guggenheim Museum

O PENED TO THE PUBLIC in 1997, the 258,330-square-foot (24,000-square-meter) Guggenheim Museum Bilbao has become one of the world's best-known art museums and most recognizable buildings. This huge, sculpturelike structure is situated along the Nervion River that runs through the center of Bilbao in northern Spain's Basque country. Intended to suggest a ship and thus to symbolize Bilbao's maritime history, the museum's walls are made from titanium reflective panels, glass, and limestone.

The Guggenheim Museum Bilbao is a branch of New York's Solomon R. Guggenheim Museum, which was founded in 1937 by Solomon Guggenheim and Hilla Rebay. In the late 1980s, the Basque administration created a redevelopment plan for Bilbao that included a museum of modern and contemporary art. In 1991, Basque officials approached the Solomon R. Guggenheim Foundation and invited it to build a branch there. The Foundation agreed, and Frank Gehry was chosen as the architect. The museum has been a tremendous success, drawing thousands of tourists and art lovers to the region.

Gehry, who is sometimes labeled a "deconstructionist" for the way he plays with architectural shapes and textures, designed the Guggenheim Bilbao as a juxtaposition of fragmented volumes with regular forms. This makes it seem chaotic at first, but the building is organized as a collection of interconnected blocks around a huge atrium, which is lit by daylight that floods in through a skylight set high in its dome. From this central point, visitors proceed to exhibition galleries, an auditorium, a restaurant, administrative offices, and a museum store by curved walkways, glass elevators, and staircases.

Gehry designed the Guggenheim Bilbao's striking interior and exterior curves using computer assisted drafting, a technology not available to earlier architects. Designed for flexibility, the museum interior has 19 exhibition galleries, many of which are square or rectangular, though some have unusual shapes. This flexible interior can accommodate numerous types of art exhibitions.

The Council of Nicaea

EARLY CHRISTIANITY HAD no formal or universal creed. As a result, there were scores of conflicting viewpoints, and church leaders tried with varying results to form core beliefs about God and Jesus Christ and humanity's relationship with them.

In the early fourth century, Arius, a bishop in the Egyptian city of Alexandria, advocated a theory that became widely accepted in Egypt and Palestine. He wrote that there is only one God, who created the Son (Jesus). Thus, Jesus must be subordinate and not of the same substance as God, his creator. Arius essentially questioned the divinity of Christ. His views inflamed some church leaders, and the arguments threatened to split the young church.

To fix this growing problem, the Roman Emperor Constantine convened a church council in the city of Nicaea. More than 300 church leaders attended. Constantine himself opened the two-month-long council and attended many of its sessions. Eusebius of Caesarea, a future church historian, offered a preliminary version of a creed that included the essential beliefs of the church. His draft was vague enough to make everyone happy, but those who opposed Arius did not like it. Eventually, an amended version was placed before the council and accepted as orthodox faith. Jesus was declared to be consubstantial and coeternal with God. Arius was branded a heretic and excommunicated.

The Nicene Creed, as this document came to be called, was further amended at the Council of Chalcedon in 451 and remains much the same today (with some variations among different denominations). It is the official declaration of faith subscribed to by much of the Christian world. The following is an excerpt from the Nicene Creed:

We believe in one God, the Father, the Almighty, of all that is, seen and unseen.

We believe in one Lord, Jesus Christ, the only Son of God, eternally begotten of the Father, God from God, Light from Light, true God from true God, begotten, not made, of one Being with the Father.

Through him all things were made.

We believe in one holy catholic and apostolic Church.

We acknowledge one baptism for the forgiveness of sins.

We look for the resurrection of the dead, and the life of the world to come. Amen.

George Eliot's *Middlemarch*

Fᴵʀꜱᴛ ᴘᴜʙʟɪꜱʜᴇᴅ ɪɴ 1871–1872, *Middlemarch* is the crowning achieve-ment of English novelist George Eliot, pseudonym of Mary Ann Evans (1819–1880). Popular in its day, *Middlemarch* continues to delight and intrigue readers, who consistently vote it one of the best books in English literature.

The story's focus is on interwoven lives in the fictional Midlands town of Middlemarch, modeled on Coventry, England. The complex plot involves interrelated sets of characters who, despite the large cast, are fully developed. Eliot treats even the least appealing of her characters with understanding and compassion.

Set shortly before the passage of the Reform Bill of 1832, the novel examines the need for change on both personal and societal levels. One of the novel's main concerns is the need to reform common attitudes toward women and their circumstances. Eliot's "Prelude" to the novel compares Saint Theresa, reformer of a religious order, with more recent "Theresas" who, because of "meanness of opportunity," are unable to realize their full potential.

One of these "Theresas" is Dorothea Brooke, the main female character, who marries Edward Casaubon, an elderly scholar, believing that she will be able to assist him with his great work in progress, a "Key to all Mythologies." But after a miserable honeymoon in Rome, she realizes that she will never be happy with this man and that his "great" work is futile pedantry. Later, as a widow, she tries again to find an outlet for her desire to improve society. Mr. Casaubon is probably the most famous failed scholar in literature; to call someone a "Casaubon" is to say that he has expended great effort on a worthless project.

The most important male character in *Middlemarch* is Tertius Lydgate, an idealistic young doctor who comes to Middlemarch eager to reform medical practices. Sadly, his view of women is less progressive than his view of medicine. He courts and marries the lovely, but materialistic and cold-hearted, Rosamond Vincy, whom he comes to regard as his "basil plant—a plant which had flourished wonderfully on a murdered man's brains." Through this story line, Eliot makes reference to class distinctions and implications, exposing how a desire to rise in society can trump a genuine romantic connection.

Virginia Woolf called *Middlemarch* "one of the few English novels written for grown-up people," and part of the appeal of the novel resides in the voice of the omniscient narrator, often identified with Eliot herself.

Iris Murdoch (1919–1999)

BORN IN DUBLIN and raised in England, Iris Murdoch—one of the most learned minds of her generation—is known for her moral philosophy and for her novels. After attending the Badminton School in Bristol, she went on to Somerville College, Oxford, where she studied "Greats" (classics). In 1942, she left Oxford with a first class honors degree and began working in London at the Treasury (1942–1944) and as a relief worker for the United Nations (1944–1946). After the war, she returned to academic life. She was a Fellow at St. Anne's College, Oxford, as well as a university lecturer from 1948 to 1963. Her first six novels were published during this time, after which she retired to devote more time to writing.

As a philosopher, Murdoch was a Platonist who believed that most humans view things imperfectly and only occasionally have glimpses of the truth. As a writer, Murdoch created characters who exhibit many of her preoccupations: the difficulty of being good (rather than simply nice), the nature of evil, the complications of human sexuality, the difficulties of religion, the moral as well as aesthetic power of art. In *A Fairly Honourable Defeat* and *The Black Prince,* these themes receive particularly complex treatment.

In Murdoch's world, seeing clearly is of utmost importance: Paying careful attention to the world and to other people can bring about moral improvement. Her novels, especially those set in London, lovingly describe the parks, statues, bridges, and other landmarks that connect her characters. Music and art powerfully affect them. In *The Bell,* for instance, Dora Greenfield experiences an epiphany while looking at a portrait in The National Gallery: "She looked at the radiant, somber, tender powerful canvas … and felt a sudden desire to go down on her knees before it, embracing it, shedding tears."

Murdoch's novels are often epic in scope, richly symbolic, and highly allusive. As many have noticed, Shakespearean references abound. *The Sea, the Sea,* which won the prestigious Booker Prize in 1978, has a number of connections with *The Tempest.* References to *Hamlet* are central to the plot of *The Black Prince.*

While writing *Jackson's Dilemma,* her twenty-sixth and final novel, Murdoch became afflicted with Alzheimer's disease. Until she entered a nursing home, she was cared for by her husband, John Bayley, who was also a writer and literary scholar. Bayley wrote two accounts of her last years, *Iris* (1998) and *Iris and Friends* (1999). The film *Iris,* based primarily on the first memoir, helped to create interest in Murdoch's life and work.

Citizen Kane

FREQUENTLY HERALDED as the best film ever made, *Citizen Kane* (1941) has repeatedly landed the number one slot on *Sight and Sound*'s international critics' poll, which is only conducted once every decade. With its complex narrative structure and unique visual style, *Citizen Kane* is unlike any Hollywood film created before it.

Orson Welles

Directed by the iconoclastic Orson Welles (1915–1985), *Citizen Kane* is the tale of wealthy newspaper baron Charles Foster Kane. His character was partly patterned on newspaper magnate William Randolph Hearst—this connection has become part of the film's legend. While similarities can be found between the fictional Kane and the real-life Hearst, Welles maintains that Kane was a composite of several industry barons, and the character was meant to expose the pitfalls of capitalism and enterprise.

The movie tells the life story of Kane and unfolds in a series of flashbacks from people who knew him. While flashbacks were a common device in Hollywood, no previous film had used them in such a complex manner. The flashbacks are not structured chronologically. Instead, they overlap, jump back and forth in time, and leave out significant portions of his life. Each character had a different relationship with Kane, so each story reflects varying biases and perspectives. On one occasion, the same event is recounted, with several key differences, by two separate characters. As a result, the viewer learns more about the storytellers' personalities and foibles than about Kane, whose personal motives and inner thoughts remain a mystery.

For *Citizen Kane*, Welles took full advantage of Hollywood's premier cinematographer, Gregg Toland, who became legendary for his use of deep focus photography in the film. Instead of dividing key scenes into a series of long shots, medium shots, and close-ups, Welles and Toland let certain scenes unfold in single, continuous shots. These shots tended to be long and maintained a great distance between the subject and the camera. The foreground, middle ground, and background all remain in sharp focus. This technique is considered one of the film's crowning achievements, because of its incredible difficulty. In addition, the chiaroscuro lighting, experimental use of sound, and extremely low angles gave the film an unusual look that put it outside the norms of contemporary Hollywood.

The Brass Band

FROM PARADES TO political rallies, brass bands have long played a part in public social gatherings. Some suggest that they arose from the French Revolution, as egalitarian-minded leaders organized musical extravaganzas for their citizens. Orchestras of wind instruments were assembled to perform republican anthems, as they were best suited for these outdoor events. However, another theory contends that brass bands emerged from the Industrial Revolution in Britain, when downtrodden laborers formed factory bands as a diversion from the trials of their work.

The prevalence and popularity of brass bands were cemented by two innovations in brass instrument design—the emergence of valve technology in the 1820s and the invention of the saxophone in the 1840s. Combined, these advances gave brass ensembles a more voluminous, appealing sound, and made brass instruments more accessible. This sparked a proliferation of brass ensembles throughout Europe.

As masses of European immigrants came to the United States in the latter half of the 19th century, brass bands also became an integral part of American culture. Brass band music was first introduced to the eastern United States in the 1850s through public concerts given by the Germania Serenade Band and the French conductor Antoine Jullien, who led brass bands in New York's Castle Garden. At the same time, brass bands began to spring up in the Gold Rush towns of the West Coast. In South Carolina, an all-slave brass ensemble, called the Juvenile Brass Band, formed and toured the nation.

The American brass band phenomenon exploded during the Civil War as regimental ensembles marched alongside Union and Confederate troops to entertain and provide moral support. Often, bands from opposing sides would engage in musical competitions. After the war, Patrick S. Gilmore, the man responsible for training the Union bands, organized huge peace concerts. In doing so, he showcased the great American concert band and established himself as America's preeminent bandleader.

Following the Reconstruction era, brass bands became entrenched in New Orleans society. The African American community in the city organized lavish funeral marches in which brass bands played an integral part. In the late 19th and early 20th centuries, the American brass band movement entered its golden age. During that time, the legendary composer John Philip Sousa created stirring marches, most famously, "The Stars and Stripes Forever." His compositions helped to establish brass band music as the first form of American popular music.

Stephen Hawking

H E HOLDS THE PROFESSORSHIP at Cambridge University once graced by Sir Isaac Newton. He has made key contributions to understanding the basic laws that govern the universe. He authored *A Brief History of Time,* a global best seller. He has received honors from numerous scientific societies and universities. And he is feted as a modern genius wherever he goes.

Stephen Hawking is a man who has it all—except his health. In 1963, he learned that he had amyotrophic lateral sclerosis (ALS), also known as Lou Gehrig's disease. ALS attacks the motor cells in the body and causes increasing paralysis. It usually proves fatal within five years of diagnosis.

Hawking's case has defied the odds: He has survived ALS for almost 45 years. However, the disease has taken a huge toll on his body. Hawking gradually lost the strength of his muscles and has used a high-tech wheelchair for several years. He has a personal staff that takes care of all his needs. His power of speech has deteriorated to the point that he can no longer talk. Instead, he uses his fingers to control a system that translates his thoughts and words into understandable speech. But none of this has detracted from his theoretical studies of astrophysics and cosmology.

Hawking majored in physics at Oxford University, where he was a bright but somewhat lazy student. He moved to Cambridge for a Ph.D. in cosmology and stayed on to conduct further research into black holes. Astrophysicists at the time believed that no light or matter could escape from these incredibly dense remnants of dead stars. Hawking suggested that, in some circumstances, black holes could emit subatomic particles. Cosmologists now accept the idea and call the emissions "Hawking radiation." Hawking also realized that to understand the universe fully, cosmologists would need to combine Einstein's theory of general relativity and quantum mechanics. His research since then has focused on this "Holy Grail" of science.

The scientific community quickly recognized Hawking's genius. At the young age of 37, he was appointed to Isaac Newton's old chair at Cambridge, becoming the Lucasian Professor of Mathematics. By then, Hawking was already a member of the Royal Society, Britain's premier scientific organization. In 2006, the Society awarded him its Copley Medal, the world's oldest award for scientific achievement.

Caravaggio

BY 1600, THE PAINTER Caravaggio (1571–1610) had radically altered the course of Italian painting and laid the foundation for the Baroque art of the 17th century. Born in the small Italian town of Caravaggio, Michelangelo Merisi (his given name) produced early works in Rome showing boys and young men playing music, cheating at cards, or getting their fortunes told.

The Conversion of Saint Paul

But it was in Caravaggio's religious paintings, such as *The Conversion of Saint Paul* (1600–1601) and the *Death of the Virgin* (c. 1606), that his revolutionary style was clearly revealed. First, he enveloped his figures in darkness and illuminated them with a bright beam of raking diagonal light. He featured common-looking, proletarian figures, rejecting heroic models while simultaneously eliminating supernatural elements, such as flying angels or clouds from heaven. Caravaggio's St. Paul, blinded and knocked to the ground by the force of God, was said to resemble a drunken soldier who had fallen from his horse. His model for the Madonna on her deathbed was purportedly a drowned prostitute with a swollen belly and feet, dragged from the River Tiber.

The artist's unorthodox approach has been linked to the Counter-Reformation movement of the Catholic Church, which insisted on art as a tool to reinforce the worshiper's religious fervor against Protestantism. By appealing to the common people with his aggressively democratic and dramatic mode, Caravaggio fulfilled the proselytizing objectives of the Church.

The chaos that fills Caravaggio's personal biography offers a fitting counterpoint to his startling paintings. By the age of 33, he'd been involved in numerous acts of violence, including stabbings and miscellaneous assaults climaxing in a brawl in 1606 that left a man dead. Forced to flee Rome, Caravaggio's final years consisted of an odyssey from Naples to Malta and Sicily, often one step ahead of the law. At age 38, he died suddenly of malaria during his return to Rome. The artist's far-reaching influence included schools of followers ("Carvaggisti") in both Italy and Northern Europe.

Thomas Jefferson

THE THIRD PRESIDENT of the United States, Thomas Jefferson (1743–1826) was born into a prominent Virginia plantation family. Well educated, he began studying law after graduating from the College of William and Mary in 1762.

Jefferson practiced law and served in the Virginia legislature. In 1775, he and four others were selected to write the Declaration of Independence. Considered to be the best writer of the group, Jefferson wrote the first draft and is recognized as the primary author of the document.

Jefferson served as the governor of Virginia from 1779 to 1781 and as minister to France from 1785 to 1789. Because of this diplomatic assignment, he was not able to attend the Constitutional Convention that took place in 1787. James Madison corresponded with Jefferson during this time to keep Jefferson advised of the progress of the Convention.

Jefferson served as America's first secretary of state for President George Washington. He opposed the Bank of the United States and other Federalist fiscal policies because he was a fierce proponent of republicanism and states' rights. Jefferson cofounded the Democratic-Republican Party and in 1796, became a Republican candidate for president. John Adams won the electoral vote; Jefferson became vice president.

In 1800, Jefferson and Aaron Burr were presidential candidates. Electoral college votes were evenly divided for the two men, and the election had to be decided by the House of Representatives. The Federalists dominated the House but eventually elected Jefferson president when some of the Federalists shifted their votes from Burr to Jefferson.

Jefferson's presidency left the United States with the legacy of land. In 1803, the purchase of the Louisiana Territory from France doubled the size of the country. In 1804, Jefferson selected Meriwether Lewis and William Clark to lead an expedition to explore the newly acquired land and to report their findings.

Throughout his life, Jefferson assumed many roles. In addition to being a political leader, he was an architect, inventor, and writer. He expressed the political belief that a limited federal government was best for the United States, and he supported separation of church and state. Jefferson used his architectural skills to plan the campus of the University of Virginia and designed many of the classical-style buildings on the campus. He also designed his beloved Virginia home, Monticello.

Jefferson died on July 4, 1826, and is buried on the grounds of Monticello.

The Irish Renaissance

ALSO CALLED THE Celtic Revival or Celtic Renaissance, this revival of interest in Ireland's Gaelic heritage began in the late 19th century and continued into the 1920s. There was a distinct nationalistic element in the Irish Renaissance, as writers sought to create work in the spirit of Irish, rather than British, culture.

Standish O'Grady's *History of Ireland* (1880) retold legends of Ireland's past and inspired writers to translate these works, produce a self-consciously Celtic literature, and sometimes to write verse whose rhythms followed those of Irish Gaelic. Leading authors of the Irish Renaissance were novelist George Moore; playwrights Lady Gregory, John Millington Synge, and Sean O'Casey; and William Butler Yeats, who wrote poetry, plays, and essays. Some of the authors, Yeats in particular, produced political essays and became active in political affairs.

Yeats profoundly influenced the course of 20th-century literature in English. An aesthete, mystic, and nationalist, he studied English poet and artist William Blake, as well as mystical traditions. He was deeply interested in magic and the pagan beliefs of Ireland. Yeats's unrequited passion for Irish beauty Maud Gonne was what first led him to national-ism, for she was very committed to Ireland's cause. Many of his poems, essays, and plays embody ideals of the Irish Renaissance. The bulk of his poetry explores the creative life of the imagination. He was awarded the Nobel Prize for Literature in 1923.

Accompanying the literary Irish Renaissance was an international revival of interest in traditional Irish art, such as Celtic crosses, among painters and ecclesiastical interior decorators. Traditional Irish music and step dancing were also revived and performed.

Dublin's Abbey Theater was a key center of the Irish Renaissance. Founded in 1904 by the English art patron Annie Horniman in asso-ciation with Yeats and Lady Gregory, the Abbey was intended to be a "people's theater." Yeats wrote plays (such as *Cathleen Ní Houlihan*) for the Abbey that were beautiful but difficult to stage. Lady Gregory wrote many comedies for the Abbey and worked in management for the theater.

The 1907 premiere of J. M. Synge's satirical play *The Playboy of the Western World* resulted in a riot at the Abbey when audience members objected to his treatment of the Irish peasantry. The theater subsequently went through numerous artistic and financial ups and downs until the early 1920s, when Sean O'Casey's plays revived it. The Abbey still oper-ates today under Irish government ownership.

Richard Nixon (1913–1994)

RICHARD NIXON WAS born in Yorba Linda, California, to Quaker parents. He was an excellent student, graduating from Whittier College and Duke University Law School. After a brief tenure in a Whittier, California, law office, Nixon accepted a job in the office of price administration in Washington, D.C. During World War II, he served as an officer in the navy. Following the war, Nixon would represent his home state of California in Washington. He was elected to the House of Representatives in 1946 and the Senate in 1950. Two years later, he successfully ran as Dwight D. Eisenhower's vice president and was reelected along with Eisenhower in 1956.

Nixon's meteoric rise in politics halted when John F. Kennedy defeated him in the 1960 presidential race. Another attempt to reenter the political arena was quashed in 1962 when he lost the California gubernatorial race to Pat Brown. On the day following his defeat, Nixon called an impromptu press conference where he laid much of the blame for this loss on negative media coverage and revealed that he had decided to retire from public office, telling the press, "You won't have Nixon to kick around anymore."

However, Nixon's retirement would be short-lived. He became an active campaigner for Barry Goldwater during the 1964 presidential race and was once again thrust into the national spotlight. By appealing to the "silent majority" of American conservatives who were tired of the liberal handling of the Vietnam War and antiwar protests, Nixon became the 37th president of the United States in 1968.

The year 1972 was the last of Nixon's first term in office and a monumental time for the president. Through the efforts of Secretary of State Henry Kissinger, Nixon achieved major successes in foreign affairs. In February, he opened diplomatic relations with Communist China by visiting that country and meeting with Chairman Mao Tse-tung. Nixon followed this up with a visit to the Soviet Union three months later. Thanks in part to these diplomatic triumphs, the year ended with his reelection.

However, in 1972, another event occurred that would ultimately lead to the downfall of Nixon's presidency. At 2:30 A.M. on June 17, 1972, five men were caught breaking into the Democratic National Committee office in the Watergate Hotel in Washington, D.C. Within four months, the FBI traced the break-in to Nixon's reelection campaign, and in May 1973, a Senate committee began nationally televised hearings regarding the scandal. Testimony from a number of witnesses close to Nixon and the release of previously secret presidential tapes eventually led to his resignation on August 8, 1974.

The Real Dr. Seuss

A RGUABLY THE MOST RENOWNED author of children's books in the 20th century, Ted Geisel is better known as Dr. Seuss. The son of a successful German immigrant brewer, he had a penchant for drawing cartoons and writing humorous poems. His childhood hobbies were nurtured and expanded when he became editor of Dartmouth College's humor magazine. For his work there, he began using his mother's maiden name, Seuss. By 1931, he was a contributor to major magazines, such as *Life,* and wrote advertising copy for Standard Oil. His first children's book, *And to Think that I Saw It on Mulberry Street* was published in 1937. For over half a century, he wrote and illustrated more than 50 other books for children. During World War II, Geisel also drew influential, pro-American political cartoons for *PM* magazine.

Geisel's unique stories combine appealing, singsong rhythms with colorful, quirky cartoon drawings. His art is whimsical, often featuring goofy-looking creatures of indeterminate species. Some of his books, such as *The Cat in the Hat* (1957), seem to be composed of silly nonsense rhymes; however, Seuss intended them as hymns of praise to the beauty of children's imaginations and the power of fantasy. Moreover, several of his books have serious moral subtexts, usually involving themes of social justice. *Yertle the Turtle* (1958), for example, can be read as an antifascist allegory and *The Sneetches* (1961) is a thinly veiled condemnation of racism. *How the Grinch Stole Christmas!* (1957) tells of the importance of love, community, and forgiveness. Perhaps Geisel's most controversial work, *The Butter Battle Book* (1984), is an attack on the nuclear arms race between the United States and the Soviet Union that assigns blame to both Cold War superpowers.

From delightful flights of fantasy to cautionary tales, the works of Dr. Seuss have become massively popular all over the world. At the time of his death in 1991, Ted Geisel's books had sold an astonishing 200 million copies and been translated into 15 languages. With their unique visual style and captivating language, there is little doubt the stories of Dr. Seuss will continue to enchant and enlighten for years to come.

POSTSCRIPT

■ *How the Grinch Stole Christmas!* has been a holiday television favorite since it was first aired on December 23, 1966.

■ *The Lorax* (1971), a dark parable about the degradation of the environment through corporate greed, was the first Dr. Seuss book to prompt calls for its removal from school libraries.

Mbube and *Isicathamiya* Song Traditions

O NE OF THE FIRST South African songs to gain worldwide exposure was "Mbube" (Zulu for "Lion"), a song by Solomon Linda that was taken up by the Weavers in the early 1950s as "Wimoweh/The Lion Sleeps Tonight" and later "covered" by many other North American and British groups. Highly successful in Africa in the decades following its first recording by Linda and his ensemble in 1939, Mbube gave its name to a Zulu musical tradition characterized by loud and powerful singing.

Related to but contrasting with Mbube is *Isicathamiya*, a more nuanced song style (still, however, relying primarily on choral part-singing) generally accompanied by choreographed dancing involving steps that seem to stalk (the Zulu root—*cathama*—means "to stalk like a cat"). Isicathamiya ensembles are almost always all male and tend to feature a lead singer in the tenor range, a couple of higher-range vocalists, and a number of bass-range singers. These groups often wear coordinated uniforms and sometimes gloves and spats, which may indicate the deep roots of the tradition in (paradoxically) American blackface minstrelsy. Although the first documented Isicathamiya performances took place in the 1920s and '30s, a cappella harmonizing has been a long-standing practice among the Zulu, Xhosa, and Swazi peoples of Eastern South Africa.

The most prominent Isicathamiya ensemble is Ladysmith Black Mambazo, which gained worldwide renown for their work on Paul Simon's 1986 *Graceland* album. Simon's incorporation of South African practices was controversial at the time, in part because of debates over the breaking of the cultural boycott of the apartheid regime and also because of perceptions that the styles were distorted to appeal to North American audiences. The ensemble, however, has had an influence far before and beyond that particular collaboration, leading the revival of Mbube and Isicathamiya traditions within South Africa (partly through a foundation the group has established). They work as semiofficial cultural ambassadors for the post-apartheid South African government and have become involved in fair-trade advocacy.

POSTSCRIPT

■ The song "Mbube/Wimoweh/The Lion Sleeps" was incorporated into Disney's *The Lion King*. This led to a lawsuit between Solomon Linda's estate and Disney, since Linda had never been able to claim royalties for the worldwide distribution of his song. In February 2006, a settlement was reached in favor of Linda's estate.

Ethanol

CARS HAVEN'T ALWAYS run on gasoline. Henry Ford's wildly successful "Model T," which was launched in 1908, was able to run on ethanol, a renewable fuel produced by fermenting plants rich in starch or sugar—such as corn and sugar cane—to create alcohol. But as the price of oil plummeted, the market for ethanol vanished.

Today, ethanol is making a comeback as an environmentally friendly alternative to gasoline. Ethanol is not only renewable, it's also relatively clean-burning. Vehicles that run on ethanol produce less carbon monoxide, volatile organics, and nitrogen oxides than those that run on fossil fuels. And the corn used to produce ethanol can be grown in the United States, reducing the country's dependence on imported oil.

Most cars already run on fuel blends that contain up to 10 percent ethanol. In 2006, ethanol plants produced 4.89 billion gallons, but lawmakers and the White House are pushing for even more production. In January 2007, President George W. Bush called for production of 35 billion gallons of alternative fuels by 2017.

In the United States, ethanol comes primarily from corn. But researchers disagree about whether corn-based ethanol is efficient. Some have found it takes more energy to produce the fuel than the end-user gets out of it. And manufacturing and transporting ethanol consumes large quantities of fossil fuels. Furthermore, opponents point out that putting more farmland into corn production could mean negative environmental impacts. In some regions, corn requires irrigation, which could deplete aquifers, as well as substantial amounts of fertilizers and pesticides, which could contaminate wells, rivers, and lakes.

Environmentalists aren't the only ones concerned about the ethanol boom. As production has increased, the price of corn has skyrocketed. Ranchers and dairy farmers, who rely on corn to feed their livestock, worry that they'll be driven out of business.

Most experts acknowledge that corn based ethanol is, at best, a short-term fix. New technologies are currently under development to turn the cellulose fibers in wood chips, grasses, or corn stalks into a new form of ethanol. Many experts say producing cellulosic ethanol is easier on the environment and more sustainable. But the procedure still needs to be refined before the fuel can be mass-produced.

Domenico Ghirlandaio's Frescoes

DOMENICO GHIRLANDAIO (1449–1494), an artist of the early Italian Renaissance, was a master of fresco, which is a complex, multistep mural painting process that requires careful advance planning and support from assistants. Ghirlandaio primarily painted religious scenes, but unlike other artists of his day, he placed biblical figures in secular settings and accompanied them with recognizable portraits of his contemporaries.

Ghirlandaio was born Domenico di Tommaso Bigordi in Florence, the son of a goldsmith. He acquired his name because of his father's skill in making garlands. By the early 1470s, he had completed his first fresco, and in 1475, he made his first major fresco, the *Life of Saint Fina* for the church at San Gimignano near Florence. In 1481, the Vatican

Calling of Saints Peter and Andrew

commissioned Ghirlandaio to paint a fresco in the Sistine Chapel of the calling of the first Apostles. Included in this work are members of Rome's Florentine colony, who are shown witnessing the biblical events.

Fresco (*pintura alla fresca* or *buon' fresco*), one of the oldest and most durable painting techniques, dates from Crete's Middle Minoan Period (c. 1750 B.C.) to the end of the Late Minoan Period (c. 1400 B.C.). Ghirlandaio was one of many Renaissance artists who made extensive use of this technique.

Fresco involves design of the mural itself and preparation of the wall surface by applying three coats of lime plaster. When the third coat had dried, Ghirlandaio traced a full-size drawing of his mural (called a *cartoon*) onto the plaster in red-earth pigment. Next, he applied a final coat of wet plaster, thin enough so he could see the cartoon through it, and then painted the final image on top in dry-powder pigments that he had ground and diluted in water.

As the colors dried and set with the plaster, they became part of the wall. At a later time, Ghirlandaio might have painted on the dry surface of the wall to touch up his picture or intensify the color. Frescoes are large, and the paint must go on fast, so Ghirlandaio employed assistants and only applied as much wet plaster as he expected to paint in a day's time. Since he had many commissions for frescoes, Ghirlandaio kept a team of workers busy. One of them was Michelangelo Buonarroti (1475–1564), who apprenticed in Ghirlandaio's workshop as a boy.

The Battle of Vicksburg

Virtually every American has heard of Gettysburg, scene of the famous Civil War battle in July 1863. Fewer are familiar with another crucial battle that took place the same summer at Vicksburg, Mississippi.

Gettysburg may have the fame, but many historians say the Union victory at Vicksburg was the true turning point in the war. Located on the Mississippi River, the Confederate-held city was invaluable because it controlled traffic on the river—a crucial supply artery—and provided a gateway to resources in the West.

By the summer of 1863, Union forces under General Ulysses S. Grant were closing in on Vicksburg. Grant captured Mississippi's state capital, Jackson, in mid-May. Subsequent maneuvers forced Confederate General John Clifford Pemberton back into Vicksburg, which had been transformed into one of the war's great strongholds. Though their troops were outnumbered, Pemberton expected Confederate General Joseph E. Johnston to send help. Instead, as Grant's forces closed in on May 18, Johnston sent a message advising Pemberton to abandon the city. Pemberton refused.

Grant launched his first attack—a frontal assault from the landward side of the city—on May 19. The assault collapsed under heavy Confederate resistance. Subsequent attacks also failed, so Grant turned to siege warfare. The city, with its mixed military and civilian population, was subjected to heavy bombardment as Union infantry and engineers trenched their way toward the Rebel lines. Federal gunboats sealed off any retreat across the river.

Boxed in, Vicksburg's defenders ran short of food. Scurvy, dysentery, and other illness ravaged Pemberton's troops. Horses and dogs disappeared as soldiers and civilians sought to fill their empty stomachs. As artillery fire turned the city into rubble, civilian refugees moved into dugouts scooped out of a nearby ridge, soon dubbed "Prairie Dog Village."

By July 3—the day of the disastrous Pickett's Charge at Gettysburg—Union infantrymen and pioneers were on the verge of breaking through the Confederate's defense. That same day, Pemberton asked Grant for terms, and on July 4, Vicksburg formally surrendered.

The victory gave the Union control of the vital Mississippi River and effectively split the Confederacy in half. The Confederate presence in the West was largely neutralized, allowing the Federals to focus on the war in the East.

Sophocles

SOPHOCLES (C. 496–406 B.C.) WAS ONE of three great ancient Greek playwrights (along with Aeschylus and Euripides), although his reputation is based on a small surviving fragment of his suspected overall work.

Not much is known about Sophocles' personal life. He is thought to have been born in the mid-490s B.C. about a mile or so outside Athens. His father was a wealthy manufacturer, so Sophocles was able to indulge his passion for studying the arts. At the age of 16, he was already so highly thought of that he led a song of praise celebrating a Greek military victory over the Persians.

In 468 B.C. Sophocles' theater career got off to a rousing start when he beat the legendary Aeschylus in the city of Dionysia at the annual playwright festival and competition dedicated to the god Dionysus. After Aeschylus' death in 456, Sophocles took first place 18 times and never failed to at least finish second. Besides his literary output, Sophocles was a well-respected figure in Athens' political circles, and he held several important governmental posts during his lifetime.

Sophocles' reputation rests on seven intact plays out of an estimated 123 or so that he is thought to have written. At the time, Greek theater was changing from employing just a chorus to stories featuring two actors. This shifted the bulk of the action and character development to the actors. Sophocles was the first to add a third actor to the cast. (Toward the end of his life, Aeschylus used a third actor as well.) Another innovation of Sophocles'pπ was to abandon the practice of using three plays to tell a story and instead telescope the action by making each play a single story. He is also credited by some with inventing the art of "scene-painting" (though the exact meaning of this is unclear).

Of Sophocles' recovered plays, The Theban Plays, a.k.a. The Oedipus Cycle, are the most famous. The cycle consists of *Antigone, Oedipus the King* (*Oedipus Tyrannus*)*,* and *Oedipus at Colonus.* Written over a 40-year span, the three plays tell the story of a single family. The story of Oedipus, a man who discovers that he has killed his father and married his mother, was familiar to Greek audiences. Sometimes considered a perfectly structured play, *Oedipus* was cited by Aristotle as the consummate example of tragedy. Although tortured by his actions, Oedipus finds some measure of peace in *Oedipus at Colonus. Antigone* features a woman who struggles against a male power structure. It is one of the first examples of a heroine in literature.

Muhammad (A.D. 570–632)

THE PROPHET MUHAMMAD was born in the city of Mecca, located in present-day Saudi Arabia. His father, a trader, died before Muhammad was born, and his mother died when he was only six years old. Muhammad was raised by one of his uncles and found work in Mecca's thriving caravan trade. In Muhammad's day, Mecca was a prosperous commercial center located at the crossroads of the trade routes linking the Indian Ocean and the Mediterranean Sea.

When he grew up, Muhammad became the commercial agent for a wealthy widow named Khadija, and the two were eventually married. Muhammad began to retreat to a cave a few miles north of Mecca to meditate and pray. During one such retreat in 610, he received the first of many revelations from God through the angel Gabriel, who instructed him to recite religious verses. At first, Muhammad feared that he had become possessed and tried to kill himself. However, the angel stopped him and declared, "O Muhammad! You are the messenger of God and I am Gabriel." Encouraged by Khadija and a handful of trusted friends, Muhammad embraced his new role as God's messenger, having been sent to bring men back to the religion of Abraham, which he called Islam. Muhammad continued to receive revelations for the next 22 years, which were collected into the Koran, Islam's main scripture.

In the first few years, serving as God's messenger proved difficult for Muhammad. Although he gained a handful of followers, most people in Mecca rejected his message. The oligarchy of Mecca, in particular, saw Islam as a challenge not only to their traditional religion but also to their social, economic, and political interests. In 619, the Umayyad clan, who were the keepers of the Ka'bah, escalated their opposition of Muhammad and his followers into active persecution.

A major turning point for Muhammad occurred in 622, when he was invited to the city of Medina to arbitrate a dispute between its Arab tribes. Muhammad and 200 of his followers moved to Medina between July and October of that year. Following this migration, known as the *hejira*, Muhammad established an Islamic community-state at Medina and was able to pressure Mecca to convert to Islam through a combination of force and diplomacy. At the same time, he also began to expand Muslim rule over other Arabic tribes. In the two-year period following Mecca's surrender, so many tribes sent delegations to negotiate with the new Islamic community that this time is now marked as the "time of deputations." By Muhammad's death in 632, all of Arabia had been converted to Islam.

French Salon Culture

A SALON IS A PRIVATE GATHERING, typically in the home of an aristocratic or wealthy hostess or host. Guests may converse on serious subjects such as literature, philosophy, or political affairs, or just laugh and gossip. Many salons include literary readings or musical performances.

Though salon-type gatherings have been held for centuries in many parts of the world, the term *salon culture* is associated with 17th- and 18th-century France—specifically with aristocratic women, who used salons to escape from their limited lives and educate themselves in feminism, politics, and culture. At some salons, the hostess selected a subject for discussion and asked each visitor to comment. Male authors, artists, and musicians attended salons hoping for patronage and intelligent company. Some men called the experience rewarding, but others considered it a waste of time.

During the early 17th century in Paris, rival salons were dominated by Madame de Rambouillet and Madeleine de Scudéry. The women at these gatherings were nicknamed "blue stockings," a term that evolved from the casual atmosphere of the gatherings. In such salons, women were free to complain about their lives and advocate greater freedom for their sex.

During the 18th century, Jean-François Marmontel, the poet and dramatist, attended the salons of Julie de Lespinasse in Paris. According to him, she invited people from different levels in society who did not know one another. Through her conversation, she harmonized the group and elicited a variety of views. Jean-Jacques Rousseau, the philosopher whose ideas influenced the French Revolution, attended salons but did not think much of them. Some women at salons enthusiastically endorsed the Revolution.

Musicians and artists benefited from salon culture. Frédéric Chopin, the composer and pianist, was already known when he came to Paris from his native Poland in 1831. Salons multiplied Chopin's contacts in Paris and expanded the audience for his music. At a party hosted in 1836 by Countess Marie d'Agoult, Chopin met George Sand, the French writer and feminist. Sand came from an aristocratic family and was married with two children, but she had left them to lead an independent life. She shocked society by dressing in men's clothing and taking a series of lovers. Chopin did not care for Sand at first, but she pursued him. Their affair lasted from 1837 until shortly before his death in 1849.

Wagner's *Ring of the Nibelung*

FRUSTRATED WITH WHAT he felt was insufficient attention to the dramatic aspect of musical theater in the operatic writing of his contemporaries (and scoffing at the Italian *bel canto* tradition as insipid and crowd-pleasing), Richard Wagner (1813–1883) set out to reinvent the music-drama tradition through his notion of the "Total Art Work" (*Gesamtkunstwerk*), in which all aspects of a multimedia production (music, dance, staging, text, etc.) would be created and coordinated by Wagner himself.

Wagner even envisioned (and convinced a rich sponsor, King Ludwig of Bavaria, to bankroll) a specially designed theater to accommodate his new vision. This theater, in Bayreuth, Germany, is still dedicated exclusively to Wagner's works and administered by the Wagner family. The crowning glory of Wagner's new model of Total Art Work is his four-part *Ring of the Nibelung*, composed in the course of more than two decades in the mid-1800s and first performed in its entirety at the Bayreuth Festival Theatre in 1876.

The *Ring* tells the story of Norse/Germanic mythology over the span of more than 15 hours and was designed to be spread over four days. The story revolves around Brünnhilde, leader of the Valkyries (who ride to bring heroes from their deaths on the battlefield to fight for the gods), and daughter of the chief of the Norse gods, Wotan. Brünnhilde rebels against Wotan's plan to rule the world through a magic ring, and Wotan places her in a magic sleep, foretelling the arrival of the hero, Siegfried, who will rescue her and win the ring of power. This comes to pass, but Siegfried is vanquished, and Brünnhilde returns the ring to the Rhine River from which it came, bringing about the destruction of the gods.

More than any of Wagner's other stage works, the *Ring* exemplifies his technique of *leitmotiv,* through which key elements of the story—individuals, objects, even concepts—are associated with noteworthy musical ideas. These are not static; they change and "develop" along with the dramatic circumstances of the action on stage. Many 20th-century film composers have acknowledged Wagner's influence in their use of "commentary" music; foremost is John Williams, whose scores for the *Star Wars* films has been characterized by many as "Wagnerian."

POSTSCRIPT

■ The magic ring in Wagner's opera may have been the source of inspiration for the "one ring" in J.R.R. Tolkien's *Lord of the Rings.*

Gene Therapy

HUMANS HAVE MORE than 4,000 genetic disorders, which are caused by one or more abnormalities in DNA. Consider the genetic disease adenosine deaminase (ADA) deficiency. The disease results from mutations in nucleotide sequences that encode ADA enzymes. The mutated genes produce defective ADA enzymes, resulting in the accumulation of deoxyadenosine in the blood. Deoxyadenosine kills white blood cells, thus impairing the function of the immune system. Children born with ADA deficiency can suffer severe infections that may prove fatal.

For about two decades, scientists have been working on an experimental approach to treat or prevent genetic disorders: gene therapy. Depending upon the particular disorder, gene therapy aims to add a normal gene into a patient's chromosomes where the patient has an abnormal, nonfunctional gene; repair an abnormal gene; or deactivate a gene that cannot function properly.

Recombinant viruses are the most common vehicle for delivering a therapeutic gene. To perform gene therapy, researchers alter a virus's genetic material by adding the therapeutic gene and removing the genes required for the virus to reproduce itself. The recombinant virus conveys the therapeutic gene to the patient's cells, where the gene can insert itself into chromosomes.

On September 14, 1990, a young girl with ADA deficiency became the first gene therapy patient. Scientists removed white blood cells from the girl, exposed the cells to recombinant virus DNA that had a normal ADA gene, and reinfused the treated cells back into the patient. The process had to be repeated about a dozen times over the next two years. Eventually, the young patient's body did produce enough ADA enzyme to enhance the immune system and improve her health.

During the ten years following this victory, physicians around the world initiated more than 400 gene therapy clinical trials. Unfortunately, few proved successful. Clinical studies have uncovered some unexpected barriers to gene therapy. One problem arises from the use of recombinant virus DNA, which inserts into human chromosomes at random places. In one gene therapy trial, two children developed a leukemia-like condition after receiving cells treated with recombinant virus DNA. The new DNA had inserted into the patients' chromosomes in a way that promoted the growth of cancer cells.

Recent years have seen slow but steady progress in gene therapy trials. Gene therapy has improved the quality of life for a number of patients.

Las Meninas:
Velázquez's Portrait of a Family

DIEGO RODRÍGUEZ DE SILVA Y VELÁZQUEZ (1599–1660) spent most of his career as the official painter to the court of Philip IV of Spain. *Las Meninas (the Maids of Honor),* 1656, is his most famous painting.

Originally titled *The Family,* this portrait was a work of radical modernism in its time. The towering space of the setting, the elegance of the costumes, and the glow of light around the little girl create a sense of awe. The feeling of chatter and movement momentarily stilled give the painting a candid air, like that of a snapshot.

Velázquez shows a picture gallery in the Alcázar palace in Madrid. The five-year-old Infanta Margarita Teresa (1651–1673) seems restless as her maids attend to her. Two dwarves in her entourage wait off to the right; a boy nudges the sleepy mastiff with his foot. The Infanta's *duenna,* or chaperone, is a few feet away in the shadows. The painter behind his immense canvas holds his palette and brushes.

What initially seems to be just another painting hanging at the back of the room turns out to be a mirror reflecting the faces of King Philip IV (1605–1665) and Queen Mariana (1634–1696). Suddenly a narrative falls into place. The royal couple poses as the painter works on their portrait. The princess arrives, presenting herself with a willful look and adamant posture, followed by the various persons responsible for her care and amusement.

By 17th-century rules for art, everything is wrong with this painting. The king and queen, the ostensible subjects of the portrait, are obscured. Figures are arranged in a wavelike line across the bottom of the canvas rather than in a solid, pyramidlike form in the middle. The upper two-thirds of the canvas is merely an empty, shadowy space.

By all standards, however, this painting is a masterpiece. *Las Meninas* shows the scene through the eyes of the king and queen. Everything, from the blurred figures of painter and courtiers to the light-enveloped form of the Infanta replicates both the optical experience of the royal couple and their psychological focus on an adored daughter.

Napoleon Bonaparte

Napoleon di Buonaparte (later changed to Bonaparte) was born in 1769 on the Mediterranean island of Corsica, which had just been acquired by France. After graduating from a French military academy in 1785, Napoleon quickly rose through the ranks and was sent to Italy, where his troops won a series of small battles against the much larger Austrian army. In 1798, Napoleon led a French invasion of Egypt, which, though victorious on land, was ultimately unsuccessful because of the British Royal Navy's powerful defense.

After returning to Italy, Napoleon participated in a coup that toppled the revolutionary government and earned him the title of First Consul. He then won another victory over Austria.

A few years of peace followed. It was during this time, in 1803, that Napoleon engineered the sale of the Louisiana Territory to the United States to raise money for his government.

Napoleon became emperor in 1804 and embarked on a series of campaigns to protect France from invasion. He showed himself to be a great general, a master of tactical battlefield maneuvers and strategic planning. The French Grand Armée defeated the Austrians, Russians, and Prussians from 1805 to 1807. However, the British Royal Navy kept that nation safe from invasion.

Napoleon soon committed two major mistakes. In 1809, he toppled the Spanish king, resulting in a guerrilla war that the French were unable to quell. Then in 1812, Napoleon invaded Russia with a massive army of 600,000 men. Although he won battles and occupied Moscow, Napoleon could not bring the Russians to the peace table and had to retreat in the face of a bitter Russian winter. Fewer than 50,000 soldiers survived the retreat.

The Russian debacle encouraged an alliance against France, and in 1813 and 1814, the allies gradually whittled down Napoleon's army, eventually forcing his abdication on April 6, 1814. Napoleon went into exile on the island of Elba. In March 1815, he returned to France with a hero's welcome. Louis XVIII fled, and Napoleon gathered a new army. However, on June 18, the Duke of Wellington, with Prussian assistance, defeated Napoleon at the Battle of Waterloo. Napoleon was exiled again, this time to the island of St. Helena in the South Atlantic, where he died in 1821. Although Napoleon was defeated militarily, his campaigns spread the ideals of the French Revolution across the continent.

Wordsworth and Coleridge's *Lyrical Ballads*

T HE POETRY COLLECTION *Lyrical Ballads, with a Few Other Poems* (1798) by William Wordsworth (1770–1850) and Samuel Taylor Coleridge (1772–1834) was vital in inaugurating the Romantic movement in English poetry.

At the time, *lyrical* meant short poems expressing deep feeling arising from personal circumstances. Ballads were longer narrative songs or poems in folk tradition, often telling stories of the supernatural. Combining the two terms signaled the desire of Wordsworth and Coleridge to do something new in poetry. Rejecting the overwrought poetic language of the 18th century, these poets wrote in a new style and with a new subject matter: humanity's primal connection with nature, a connection that had been torn apart by societal influences.

The two then-unknown poets left their names off the first edition. But the book proved popular and appeared in three more editions through 1805. In a preface he added to the 1802 edition, Wordsworth explained that he was trying to show "incidents and situations from common life . . . in a selection of language really used by men, and, at the same time, to throw over them a certain colouring of imagination . . . ." His definition of poetry as "the spontaneous overflow of powerful feelings" expressed in common, everyday language, free of poetic diction, became founding statements of Romantic poetic practice. Wordsworth's poems are often in unrhymed iambic pentameter, a meter also used by Shakespeare and Milton that closely follows the rhythms of English speech.

The first poem in the 1798 edition, once taught to generations of schoolchildren, was Coleridge's long ballad "The Rime of the Ancient Mariner," describing supernatural events at sea. Among Wordsworth's many famous poems in this book, "Lines Composed a Few Miles Above Tintern Abbey, on Revisiting the Banks of the Wye During a Tour. July 13, 1798" (often called simply "Tintern Abbey"), a meditation on a ruined monastery, shows the Romantic tendency to find religious significance in nature. His long ballad "Michael: A Pastoral Poem," describing the desperate labors of a shepherding family to hold onto their little plot of land, is both an English modern pastoral and an "anti-pastoral," in that it breaks the old rule of poetic pastoral about avoiding the unpleasant side of shepherding life.

In these poems and others, the focus was on emotion and memory, the dignity of humanity, and the idea that poetry should be pleasurable for all—groundbreaking ideas that ushered in a new era of Romantic writing.

Maria Callas (1923–1977)

PRAISED BY MOST and condemned by some, Maria Callas was certainly the most widely known and publicized female opera singer of the 20th century. Born to Greek immigrant parents in New York City, she often spoke of an unhappy childhood marred by fights between her parents and jealousy of her slimmer sister. She did, however, love to sing to her friends.

After Maria's mother and father separated in 1937, Maria's mother moved the family back to Greece. At 14, Maria won a scholarship to the National Conservatoire in Athens, where she excelled. She made her debut at the Athens opera when she was 19 and returned to the United States in 1945. She failed to secure a place at the Metropolitan Opera, and thus moved to Italy in 1947, where she sang in the Verona Opera. Here, she was deeply influenced by noted conductor Tullio Serafin.

Over the next seven years, she gained the reputation of being a brilliant, if sometimes mercurial, singer and actress. She sang the lead in several major operas, including Verdi's *Aida* and Bellini's *Norma,* which became her signature role. She also toured successfully in South America and appeared at London's famed Royal Opera House. She made her United States debut at Chicago's Lyric Opera, and by the time she finally sang at the Metropolitan in New York in 1956, she was so popular that crowds lined up for tickets.

Although her voice declined in the late 1960s, she continued to sing in most of the great opera houses of the world. Her specialty was *bel canto,* literally "beautiful singing" in Italian. This style featured great vocal agility and a sweetness in tone, both of which Callas displayed. Although some critics complained that she shrieked at the higher registers, her ability to sing descending scales and her tonal richness won audiences over, as did her passionate acting.

Callas was probably as famous off the stage as on—she was the subject of well-publicized tantrums, feuds, and romances. She refused to return to the Chicago Lyric Opera after she was served with a lawsuit there, publicly fought with fellow soprano Renata Tebaldi (they reconciled only late in their careers), and most famously had an affair with Greek shipping magnate Aristotle Onassis that was featured almost daily in the tabloid press. But her art was ultimately her legacy. At her final appearance in Carnegie Hall, a patron yelled from the balcony, "You are opera!" Callas was truly a diva for all ages.

Jack the Ripper

IN THE FALL OF 1888, a serial killer terrorized London, viciously murdering several prostitutes in the poverty-stricken area of Whitechapel. First referred to as the "Whitechapel Murderer" or "Leather Apron," the killer was renamed after a letter arrived at the Central News Agency signed "Yours truly. Jack the Ripper." Whether as a harbinger of modern sex crimes, a reminder of the price of urban poverty, or the ultimate whodunit, the case of Jack the Ripper has haunted the industrialized world ever since.

Despite decades of investigation by amateur sleuths called Ripperologists, the Ripper has never been identified, and his exact number of victims has never been determined. The case first stirred the imaginations of the press and public when a prostitute named Mary Ann (Polly) Nichols was discovered with her throat cut on August 31, 1888, in Buck's Row. Annie Chapman was found similarly slain on September 8, and the double murders of Elizabeth Stride and Catherine Eddowes followed three weeks later, on September 30. These four killings took place in courtyards and back alleys, but the fifth (and some say the Ripper's last) occurred indoors—in the room of Mary Kelly, whose body was mutilated beyond recognition. Ripper folklore generally posits these five as the primary case, but recent research has suggested that the murders may have started earlier, perhaps with the knifing of Martha Tabram on August 7. It is also possible they continued weeks after Kelly's death, with as many as nine total victims.

Both Scotland Yard and the City of London Police worked the case; the Yard had jurisdiction over Whitechapel, and the City Police over Mitre Square, where Eddowes was murdered. Neither force could make a case against their primary suspects: a teacher named M. J. Druitt, wife-poisoner Severin Klosowski, Michael Ostrog (a Russian-born physician and criminal, who had been placed in an asylum), and a Polish Jew named Aaron Kosminski (who was later committed to an asylum).

Ripperologists have proposed a number of other possibilities. In 1929, the first book on the case, *The Mystery of Jack the Ripper* by Leonard Matters, suggested a tragic young surgeon named Dr. Stanley as the famous killer. One of the most notorious theories surfaced in 1970, when Dr. Thomas Stowell's article in *The Criminologist* named Duke of Clarence, Prince Albert Victor (Queen Victoria's grandson) as Jack the Ripper. Later, the royal physician, Sir William Gull, was suspected. However, recent allegations by crime novelist Patricia Cornwell have resurrected past hunches that point to English painter Walter Sickert as the primary suspect.

Jubilee and Ragtime

AFRICAN AMERICANS left little in the way of written records about their music-making before the Civil War, given slaveholders' reluctance to allow literacy among the slaves. With emancipation came the opportunity for some African American musicians to gain more visibility and financial or artistic prominence. Some examples may seem paradoxical today, such as the practice of "African American blackface" minstrelsy— troupes of African American singers and actors who modeled their depictions of stereotypical plantation scenes on those of white minstrel troupes—though there is some evidence that their approach was indeed more "authentically" reflective of slave musical practices.

One striking example of verifiably African American traditions in the late 1800s is provided by the primary choral ensemble of historically black Fisk University. The Fisk Jubilee Singers (taking their name from the common term *jubilee,* used to describe sacred singing in African American Christian traditions of the time) toured the northern United States and Europe in the decades following the Civil War. They astounded audiences who had never heard African American sacred music, which by this point had assimilated both Anglo American hymn singing and African-derived textures and vocal ideals.

Europeans were especially taken by the "new" soundscapes presented by the Fisk Singers and other African American musicians, who brought their dance hall "ragtime" style across the Atlantic at the turn of the 20th century. The term *rag* initially described a way of performing rather than a specific compositional type. The basic structure of the music was essentially the same as the dance hall marches and jigs that were common in North American band repertories, but the performer enlivened that structure through emphasis on rhythmic "off-beats."

Scott Joplin (1867/1868–1917) was the preeminent ragtime composer. Records of his early life and career are sparse and varied, but we do know that he studied classical piano and later worked as a traveling musician. He composed various styles of music but eventually made a name for himself through his "rags," such as the "Maple Leaf Rag," which he sold in 1899.

The rise of ragtime was accompanied by dance crazes that swept both sides of the Atlantic up to the beginning of the World War I. The most popular was the foxtrot, originally a controversial dance because of its close-contact style. At the close of the Great War, the massive presence of American troops on the European continent cemented the cultural power of the African American dance music tradition, which by that point had become known as jazz.

Water on Mars

IN THE LATE 1870s, Italian Giovanni Schiapparelli was studying Mars through a telescope when he spotted what he called *canali* (channels). Some English-language reports mistranslated the word as *canals.* That persuaded American amateur astronomer Percival Lowell to build an observatory in Arizona. His observations convinced him that Mars was a dying world whose intelligent inhabitants had built a vast network of canals to conserve the planet's dwindling supplies of water.

Nobody today believes that Mars harbors intelligent beings. But scientists know that the red planet is desperately short of water. For more than 40 years, spacecraft have searched for evidence that Mars contains—or once contained—liquid water. Early results were disappointing. Now, though, astronomers know that ice and water vapor do exist on the planet. They also have indirect evidence that liquid water once flowed on the Martian surface.

Why bother to investigate? Liquid water is critical to all forms of life, from microorganisms to humans. If astronomers can prove that Mars has—or had—liquid water, the planet might also have supported life. Understanding how life developed beyond Earth could provide clues to the nature of life. Just as important, learning how Mars evolved from a wet planet to the arid object it is today may help scientists find ways to avoid the same fate for Earth.

The first close-up pictures of Mars sent back by uncrewed spacecraft in the 1960s showed a dry surface blistered by craters. It looked more like the moon's surface than Earth's. And there were no signs of water. In 1975, two robotic craft that landed on the surface and tested the Martian soil had equally disappointing results. They showed no evidence of life.

Astronomers now accept that any liquid water on the Martian surface today would freeze or evaporate. However, certain geological formations indicate that water once flowed freely on the planet. Images show deep channels, canyons, and sediment-filled gullies on the surface of Mars. The most likely reason for their appearance is that water once flowed through them. Analyses carried out by *Opportunity* and *Spirit,* two robotic chemical laboratories that travel around the Martian surface, indicate that rocks there were once soaked in liquid water. Recent evidence also suggests that a "greenhouse effect" much stronger than any on Earth could have caused the surface water to disappear. While no water now exists on the surface, astronomers believe that Mars contains sources of water. They have already detected ice around the planet's north pole. And they expect that much more ice, or even liquid water, is trapped beneath the surface.

Intaglio Prints: Art Under Pressure

THE WORD *INTAGLIO* comes from the Italian *intagliare,* meaning "to cut" or "incise." The technique is thousands of years old. Artisans in Mesopotamia carved designs into gems. Greeks and Romans incised decorations onto metal objects. Medieval metalworkers added ornate patterns to suits of steel armor. During the 15th century, artists began to ink intaglios and transfer the images to paper. Soon, intaglio prints had become an important art form.

In printmaking, intaglio is the opposite of relief. In a relief print, like a woodblock print or even a common rubber stamp, ink adheres to the highest areas of the block. Those inked areas are then transferred to paper. In intaglio prints, however, ink is rubbed into the lines of the design, and the surface of the plate is wiped clean. When the plate and a dampened sheet of paper are put through a printing press, weight forces the paper into contact with the inked lines. The edge of the plate also leaves a telltale mark or embossing on the paper. In intaglio, as in relief prints, the design on the plate is printed in reverse on the paper. Copper, steel, and zinc are the metals most commonly used for intaglio plates.

Engraving is the oldest and most durable intaglio technique. In an engraving, the artist incises lines directly into metal with a tool called a *burin.* This difficult technique requires an artist who is nearly ambidextrous. The artist holds the burin in the dominant hand and pushes it through the metal. With the other hand, he or she must simultaneously adjust the angle and direction of the plate.

Engraving plate

A similar method is called *drypoint.* In drypoint, however, the instrument used to scratch into the plate is handled more like a pen or pencil. The movement of the drypoint needle raises a rough edge or burr that collects ink, making a rich, luxurious line in the final print. Lines produced in drypoint are fragile and break down more easily than engraved lines.

In etching, the plate is first covered with a material impervious to acid. Lines scratched through the coating, or "resist," are bitten into the plate when it is submerged in acid. The longer the plate remains in the acid, the deeper the lines become. The process of making an etching plate can involve repeated immersions in acid and reapplications of the resist. Drypoint is frequently used to add detail and emphasize lines.

The Unifications of Germany and Italy

BEFORE 1870, Germany and Italy were made up of several independent states. In Germany, Prussia was the largest and most powerful state.

In 1863, Denmark claimed the northern state of Schleswig. Prussia's prime minister, Otto von Bismarck, challenged the Danish claim and asked Austria to help Prussia regain the territory. This conflict, called the Second War of Schleswig, ended in Danish defeat. The land in question went to Prussia and Austria. But disputes over the administration of Schleswig led to Prussia's demand that Austria return it. Austria refused and enlisted other German states to fight Prussia. The Austro-Prussian War resulted in Schleswig and another Danish-held state being returned to Prussia. After the war, a confederation of northern states was formed. King Wilhelm I of Prussia became president of the new confederation and appointed von Bismarck as chancellor.

France feared that Prussia's victory over Austria would upset the balance of power in Europe, so they declared war on Prussia. The remaining independent German states supported Prussia, and together they quickly defeated France. At the conclusion of the Franco-Prussian War, the French territories of Alsace and Lorraine were ceded to Prussia. Bismarck negotiated with the southern German states, and a new German empire of 25 states was formed. King Wilhelm became emperor, and von Bismarck was named imperial chancellor.

During the same time period, independent states in Italy were divided among several European powers. Austria dominated northern Italy because it occupied Lombardy and Venice. Central Italy was controlled by the pope. Separate monarchs ruled southern independent states. A few independent states also existed near the French border in the northwest.

In the 1830s, Giuseppe Mazzini, who was a Genoese living in Marseille, France, organized Italian exiles and promoted the unification of Italy. Their planned uprisings were discovered and repressed by military troops. But Giuseppe Garibaldi, an Italian seaman who supported Mazzini's idea of unification, offered his backing and led campaigns in southern Italy against the French.

In 1849, Victor Emmanuel II became king of Piedmont-Sardinia, which worked to engineer Italy's unification. Prime Minister Camillo di Cavour enlisted France's aid to unify much of northern Italy.

Italy finally became united in 1860 when the pope gave up Rome in exchange for a separate territory that would become the independent Vatican state. Victor Emmanuel II became the first king of unified Italy.

Johann Wolfgang von Goethe

NOVELIST, POET, PLAYWRIGHT, critic, theater manager, musician, scientist, administrator, and lawyer, Johann Wolfgang von Goethe (1749–1832) was perhaps the last universal genius of Western culture. The precocious, mostly home-schooled child of a prosperous lawyer, Goethe already knew some Greek, Latin, Italian, and French by the age of eight, and he later learned English, Hebrew, and some Persian.

Goethe first earned recognition for his play *Götz von Berlichingen* (1773), the story of a medieval robber baron that he turned into a metaphor of rebellion against established order. This work helped define the literary style known as *Sturm und Drang* ("storm and stress"), an early form of Romanticism.

Goethe's first novel, *The Sorrows of Young Werther* (1774), further defined the Romantic movement in literature. This semiautobiographical story of a young man who commits suicide because of his unrequited love for a young girl inspired a rash of adolescent suicides throughout Europe. Goethe's life was marked by passionate attachments to young women, both platonic and carnal. His 1796 novel *The Apprenticeship of Wilhelm Meister* became the prototype of the bildungsroman, or novel detailing the education and moral development of a young man. During this period, Goethe began a lifelong study of plant and animal morphology that resulted in many scientific publications.

In 1775, Karl August, Duke of Saxe-Weimar, invited Goethe to his court, where he spent the rest of his life. Goethe served as chief minister for ten years, supervising everything from the court theater to the province's mines, roads, and finances. Later he gave up all but the directorship of the state theater and scientific institutions.

In 1810, Goethe published a 1,400-page treatise on color theory, part of which anticipates later findings that human color perceptions are determined by our nervous systems rather than simply the properties of light.

Goethe's masterwork was the two-part epic poem *Faust,* on which he worked for 57 years. Based on a medieval legend about an alchemist who sells his soul to the devil in exchange for knowledge, Goethe's version makes Faust a positive representation of human striving, embodying the Romantic artist as well as the Promethean scientist. Goethe finished the second half just months before he died at age 82.

Martha Graham (1894–1991)

NO DOUBT THE MOST well-known and innovative American dancer of the 20th century, Martha Graham was born into an upper-class family. Her father was a doctor and her mother a descendent of Miles Standish. Graham joined the Denishawn Dance Company in Los Angeles—one of the few American companies that emphasized non-balletic dance—two years after her father's death in 1914. She made her concert debut in New York City in 1926 and then gave private lessons. In 1927, she formed a company of female dancers (with men added in 1938) and began to choreograph. Initially, she focused on American themes and produced such ballets as *Appalachian Spring* (1944), which won a Pulitzer Prize for composer Aaron Copland.

While working with her company, she also took on individual dancing roles, like that of the Chosen One in Stravinsky's *Rite of Spring* (1930). But her main interest was always choreography. After World War II, she turned to classical themes—especially Greek and Hebrew—and produced a series of stunning works, most notably *Clytemnestra* (1958). She also turned to historical figures, like Joan of Arc for *Seraphic Dialogue* (1955). Ironically, she always considered herself a dancer first, and when she simply couldn't perform any more, stepping down as a dancer at the age of 75, she still went on overseas tours with her company into her 90s.

Her major contribution to dance was her belief that the movements of the human body could express a variety of emotions. She wanted dance to provide "visible substance to things felt" and to "chart the graph of the heart." Her style emphasized jaggedness, dynamic tension, and unexpected moves, a clear departure from carefully patterned classical ballet. In a sense, she did for dance what Picasso did for painting and Stravinsky for music, as she opted for bodily movement that often appeared to be dislocated and distorted, revealing an inner reality. She broke the mold. Not surprisingly, one of the most consistent motifs in her art was an indomitable defense of the world's unconventional nonconformists—much like herself.

POSTSCRIPT

■ In 1962, two U.S. congressmen saw her *Phaedra* in Bonn, West Germany. Unaware that the Greek legend featured a queen's passion for her stepson, they proclaimed that the production was too racy to be an appropriate American cultural export.

Cultural Patrimony and Repatriation

CULTURAL PATRIMONY is one of the most tangled and divisive international issues of our time. Nearly every group of people in the world places importance on the religious or artistic objects that it views as uniquely its own. In past times, many such objects were taken in the name of science or archaeology and came into the possession of institutions and individuals.

Many years ago, objects were openly looted from archaeological sites across the world, and to a large extent, this looting continues today. Stolen goods might become part of private collections only to be sold and resold later, eventually ending up in museums. In recent years, national governments have employed diplomatic and legal pressure to reclaim these objects. In some cases, museums voluntarily return artifacts, particularly after a strong case has been made to do so. However, other times museums will claim to have exercised due diligence during acquisition and refuse to give objects back. The process of repatriation can thus be very slow, as claims are generally evaluated on a case-by-case basis.

Perhaps the most famous example of this issue is the controversy surrounding the Elgin Marbles. The marbles are a collection of sculptures created in ancient Greece during the fifth century B.C., which once decorated the Parthenon in Athens. Between 1801 and 1812, Lord Thomas Elgin, the British ambassador to the Ottoman Empire, removed roughly half of the surviving sculptures from the Parthenon with permission from the Ottoman authorities ruling Greece at that time. Elgin then shipped the marbles to London where, following a parliamentary debate, the British government purchased them in 1816. They were placed in the British Museum, where they remain to this day.

Even in Elgin's time, some people in Britain protested the removal of the marbles from the Parthenon, and over the past 40 years, an intense international campaign has sought their return to Greece. While Elgin had permission and technically broke no laws, many believe he defaced a beautiful building and an important symbol of Western civilization.

While Greece has not been successful in brokering the return of the Elgin Marbles, other cultural groups have made important gains. Today, many people demanding the return of cultural artifacts are members of indigenous tribes. During the 19th century, anthropologists disinterred funerary and cultural objects from these groups and placed them in museum collections. Since 1990, many tribes have been able to reclaim such sacred objects under the Native American Graves Protection and Repatriation Act.

The Operas of Giacomo Puccini

T HE DEATH OF COMPOSER Giuseppe Verdi in 1901 was perceived as a
deep blow to the Italian operatic tradition—indeed, to Italian culture
as a whole. But Verdi had been writing very little in the last two decades
of his life, and a new generation of operatic composers had already tried
its hand at becoming worthy successors of the iconic master. Most prominent among these was Giacomo Puccini, who is widely acknowledged
as the leader in a tradition often called *verismo:* the depiction of "true
stories" and realistic characters (as opposed to grand or historical themes
and "larger-than-life" protagonists), in the context of what Puccini himself once called "great sorrows in little souls."

Puccini's operas are sometimes comic, but his most popular characters
are his tragic heroines: Mimì in *La Bohème* (arguably Puccini's most
popular work) and the title characters in *Tosca* and *Madama Butterfly,*
women who are undone by their male partners and whose elaborate,
climactic death scenes seem predestined from their first appearance
on stage. Mimì in particular is an almost achingly stereotypical tragic
heroine: A cold-handed, warm-hearted seamstress in a Paris garret, she
falls in love with the Bohemian playwright Rodolfo, but their relationship is tormented because he is afraid that he cannot provide for her in
her illness. (She is sick with "consumption"—tuberculosis, the archetypal
19th-century sensitive-artist's disease.) The rest of the opera chronicles
their deep but doomed love. In the closing scene, Rodolfo convinces a
friend to pawn his overcoat to buy a fur muff to warm Mimì's hands, and
she dies happily—it seems—in his arms.

Puccini's musical treatments are lush, with instruments often reinforc-
ing intensely powerful vocal lines. Listeners can still identify "set piece"
songs, which are characteristic of the Italian operatic tradition since its
earliest roots. However, many elements of Puccini's musical landscape
(the use of developing ideas to represent emotions or characters, the
almost unbroken musical flow, the interplay between characters, and
the vocal demands of the roles) take strong inspiration from Wagner's
musico-dramatic approach.

POSTSCRIPT

■ Puccini's success can largely be attributed to the music publisher Giulio Ricordi,
who had long been Verdi's publisher. Ricordi was frustrated by the older
composer's "dry spells" In the 1880s, so he took the young Puccini under his wing
and encouraged him through his early efforts. Ricordi then reaped the financial
rewards of having the exclusive rights to the composer's most successful mid-
career operas at century's end.

Pollutants in the Environment

MANY TOXIC CHEMICALS, such as pesticides and heavy metals, are released into our air, soil, and water. Depending on the type of chemical, the toxin may degrade quickly and become harmless, or it may remain in the environment for years. Toxins that take a long time to degrade have the greatest potential for harming humans and wildlife. For example, the pesticide DDT has been of special concern because it degrades very slowly. These types of persistent toxins can move through the environment and sometimes become dangerously concentrated.

Pollutants in the air can be distributed far from the original source. For example, the airborne spread of pesticides can cause health problems in people who live throughout agricultural regions. Even Arctic polar bears and Antarctic penguins have accumulated surprisingly high levels of toxic chemicals in their tissues, due to the atmospheric patterns that move air toward the poles.

Water can also move toxins from one place to another. Water carries toxins from contaminated land and concentrates them in surface water. Chemicals in the soil can also seep down into groundwater. In either case, drinking-water supplies can become contaminated. And aquatic organisms, such as fish and frogs, can drink or absorb the toxins through their skin.

Organisms may quickly excrete chemicals they have been exposed to through the air, water, or soil. However, a few especially dangerous toxins are not excreted. For example, DDT is fat-soluble and is stored in animals' fatty tissues. Other toxins, such as methylmercury, can build up in muscle tissue.

When toxins accumulate in living organisms (a process called *bioaccumulation*), they are transferred to animals higher in the food chain when predators consume contaminated prey. As a predator continues to hunt, it takes on all the stored toxins from each prey. So with each higher level of the food chain, the level of toxins in the organisms increases. Top predators, like hawks or osprey, end up with the highest concentration of pesticides because the toxins have been magnified as they move from water to algae to zooplankton to small fish to large fish and finally to the birds.

A primary example is the bioaccumulation of DDT in bald eagles, which brought this bird to the brink of extinction. DDT was causing eggshells to grow thinner and break more easily. Since DDT was banned in 1973, the population of bald eagles has recovered, and these birds are no longer considered endangered species.

Édouard Manet's *Olympia*

*O*LYMPIA RECLINES ON the pillows stacked on her couch. An African servant presents a bouquet of flowers, pulling back the florist's wrapping. Olympia, though, ignores them. She is unclothed yet has a fashionable air, with her bracelet and satin slippers, the ribbon bow that holds a pearl at her throat, and the pink flower tucked behind her left ear. At the foot of the bed, a black kitten hisses, its back arched and its tail upright.

When this painting was first displayed at the Salon, Paris's premier art exhibition, in 1865, it was greeted with shock and anger. The critic Jules-Antoine Castagnary reviled the painting as an "ugly portrait of a disgusting whore." Another critic described the main figure as "a rotten corpse resurrected from the dead." Édouard Manet had appropriated the composition of Titian's *Venus of Urbino* (1538) for his *Olympia* but transformed it from an allegory of idealized femininity into a statement of modern beauty and sexuality.

It was obvious to most viewers that the artist had reduced Venus to a "working girl" and had surrounded her with details that proved the point. The black cat? The French word was slang for prostitute. The coral-colored camellia behind her ear? An obvious reference to Alexander Dumas' 1848 novel about a Parisian courtesan, *The Lady of the Camellias.*

Yet Manet's art also found its champions. The writer Émile Zola saw beyond the nominal subject matter of this nude. He called *Olympia* a "great painting" because it confirmed the purpose of painting as an expression of "the verities of light and shade, the realities of persons and things."

Manet (1832–1883) was a key figure in modern art. He challenged the values of the official art academy by taking as his subject modernity itself: city scenes, nightlife, and popular recreation. Manet also made pure color and the materiality of paint the focus of his art. His creative daring and dazzling brushwork inspired the younger painters who came to be known as the "Impressionists" in the 1870s.

Today, Manet's painting is an icon of modernism. His Olympia coolly appraises the client, and she presents her confident self for his appraisal. What was—and perhaps still is—so terribly shocking is that Manet's composition places the viewer in the role of the client. Olympia's eyes meet the viewer's, and she will not be the first to look away.

Adolf Hitler

BORN IN AUSTRIA IN 1889, Adolf Hitler moved to Germany in 1913 and served in the German Army during World War I. He was wounded and gassed while fighting on the Western Front.

In 1919, Hitler joined a small right-wing party, which was renamed the National Socialist Workers', or Nazi, Party the following year. A gifted orator, Hitler steadily rose to party prominence, and—though they didn't hold a majority—the Nazis gained enough influence to be included in any coalition government.

Hitler published his autobiography, *Mein Kampf,* in two volumes in 1925 and 1926. In it, he espoused Nazi party ideology and his own beliefs, including the supremacy of "Aryans" over other races, most notably the Jews.

Hitler officially became a German citizen in 1932. In January 1933, President Paul von Hindenburg appointed Hitler chancellor of Germany. Hitler used his power to quickly destroy German democracy by rigging local elections and ensuring Nazi dominance. In July 1933, the Nazi Party became Germany's only legal party.

With the Nazis in total control by 1935 and any political opposition suppressed, Hitler began rearming the German military (in violation of the Treaty of Versailles), which put people back to work and gave Hitler immense popularity. He improved Germany's infrastructure, placed an emphasis on new architecture, and gave hope to a nation that had been wracked by economic depression, often under the guise of "racial cleansing."

Hitler was violently anti-semitic, blaming the Jews for Germany's military defeat in 1918. As soon as he rose to power, Hitler began herding Jews into concentration camps and forced labor camps, eventually beginning the "Final Solution," a systematic mass murder of what Hitler considered an inferior race. More than six million European Jews perished at the hands of the Nazis. Millions of others were murdered as well. All told, Hitler and the Nazi party were responsible for the deaths of up to 11 million people.

In 1938, Germany annexed Austria and most of Czechoslovakia. In September 1939, Hitler attacked Poland and thereby precipitated World War II. By June 1941, the Nazis had overrun Denmark, Norway, Belgium, the Netherlands, France, Yugoslavia, and Greece. At the same time, Hitler's armies faltered. They surged into the Soviet Union, but the Russian winter stopped the eastward march. Britain and the United States later opened a second front, and the Allies steadily drove the Germans back. On April 30, 1945, as Soviet troops battled only blocks from his underground bunker in Berlin, Hitler committed suicide.

Walt Whitman

WALT WHITMAN, one of America's most important poets, spent his final years overseeing the building of his own tomb—and reading scraps of his poetry to the laborers as they worked.

The second of nine children, Whitman was born on May 31, 1819, on Long Island, New York. Whitman had only six years of formal education but inherited a liberal and free-thinking independent streak from his father, Walter, a Quaker carpenter. Early in his professional life, Whitman worked as a reporter, a teacher, and an editor, including a stint as the editor of the newspaper the *Brooklyn Daily Eagle* from 1846 to 1848. In 1855, Whitman published the first edition of his signature work, *Leaves of Grass,* which contained just 12 poems. Although essentially ignored by reviewers and the public, it did generate a congratulatory letter from poet Ralph Waldo Emerson. Whitman reprinted the letter in the next edition of *Leaves,* which he increased by 20 poems. By 1860, *Leaves* contained more than 150 poems.

In 1861, Whitman became a nurse, caring for sick and wounded Union soldiers in the Civil War. Deeply affected by the suffering and misery he experienced, Whitman wrote *Drum Taps* in 1865, a volume of poetry about the war. He later incorporated *Drum Taps* into *Leaves of Grass.* The assassination of Abraham Lincoln inspired one of Whitman's most famous poems: "Oh Captain! My Captain!"

Leaves of Grass was a sensation in France, where its intense feelings and graphic descriptions touched a chord. But it was received quite differently in the United States. Whitman was fired from a job in the Department of the Interior when it was discovered that he was the author of the sexually explicit *Leaves.* He wrote graphically about the body and sex. Lines such as this from "Once I Pass'd Through A Populous City" shocked American sensibilities: "I remember I say only that woman who passionately clung to me."

Whitman is seen as a bridge between transcendentalism and realism because he provided both points of view. His use of free verse had a liberating effect on American poetry. He suffered a stroke in 1873, and thereafter his health was poor. He moved to Camden, New Jersey, where he bought a small house and stayed for the remainder of his life. In the early 1890s, realizing he didn't have long to live, Whitman produced the "deathbed" edition of *Leaves of Grass,* which contained poems dealing with old age. Arranging for his tomb to be built in Camden's Harleigh Cemetery, Whitman would journey to the site to check on its progress. He died in March 1892.

Jacques-Yves Cousteau (1910–1997)

JACQUES COUSTEAU IS probably best remembered as a diver of the oceans' deep waters and a producer of documentary films. Cousteau, who was born in France, always loved the water; when he graduated from boarding school, he entered the French naval academy. After graduation, he joined the French navy and worked as part of an underwater research team.

Cousteau was seriously injured in an automobile accident when he was about 25 years old. Several months passed before he regained mobility in his arms and was again able to devote time to the undersea world. The following year, Cousteau combined his love of water and his interest in photography when he filmed an underwater movie using a movie camera with waterproof housings.

In 1950, Cousteau purchased a former mine-sweeper, converted it to a vessel equipped to scientifically explore the waters of the world, and took the vessel to study reefs in the Red Sea. Cousteau and his ship, the *Calypso,* explored the depths of the oceans, coral reefs, river systems, and marine life throughout the world for many years. As he explored, he filmed footage for more than 100 documentaries that he produced.

The Undersea World of Jacques Cousteau television series was launched in the late 1960s and continued to introduce people to fascinating underwater life for about eight years. In the 1980s, Cousteau began an around-the-world exploration of waterways and oceans, filming throughout the journey.

Cousteau was also an inventor. During World War II, he and an engineer perfected a device that gave divers the ability to go deeper into ocean waters and dive for longer periods of time. The device has been referred to as an aqualung and is considered to be the first self-contained underwater breathing apparatus (SCUBA). The apparatus is thought to be Cousteau's greatest contribution to the scientific world.

Throughout his life, Cousteau's goal was to explore and protect the world's environment. To further this endeavor, he established the Cousteau Society in the United States and the Foundation Cousteau in France. Two of his documentary films received Academy Awards. He was also awarded the Medal of Freedom in the United States and given membership in the highly esteemed French Academy.

Art Theft: Nazi-Looted Art and Issues of Ownership

ONE OF TODAY's most tangled issues in international law concerns ownership of artwork looted by the Nazis during World War II from Jewish people who subsequently died in concentration camps. American and Soviet troops also took artwork from homes and churches during their wartime occupation of Europe—some was stolen from museums.

Whatever its origin, the art was sold through public and private channels to museums and collectors who later claimed no knowledge of the works being stolen. Often these parties had documented provenance for the artwork. Dealers who sold the art also had documentation.

When some of the looted artwork appeared on the market, descendants of the rightful holders claimed ownership and asked courts to restore their property. They provided proof of ownership, such as bills of sale or photographs of the works hanging in the homes of their forebears.

It is said that as much as $30 billion in art was stolen or looted during World War II. In 1999, an international commission was established to deal with the problem. Since then, the commission has not had an idle moment. Even now, after years of litigation and international negotiations, cases are decided one at a time, and the outcome always varies.

For example, on October 19, 2007, a California judge dismissed a challenge to the Norton Simon Museum's ownership of two paintings by Lucas Cranach the Elder, a 16th-century German artist. Marei von Saher of Greenwich, Connecticut, said that the paintings were seized by the Nazis from her father-in-law, an art dealer in Amsterdam, Holland, during 1940 and never returned.

In 2001, two 18th-century landscapes by Bohemian artist Norbert Grund appeared at auction in Vienna, consigned by a party in Germany. When their provenance was questioned, the auction house withdrew the works from sale and prepared to return them to the consignor. Instead, after investigation, discussion, and an agreement with the Commission for Looted Art in Europe, the paintings were returned to the claimants.

In a 2005 case, actress Elizabeth Taylor won a judgment to retain a Van Gogh painting that had been claimed as Nazi-looted art because the statute of limitations had expired. However, museums and private parties have quietly returned many looted works to descendants of their owners—this story is far from over.

Aaron Copland's *Fanfare for the Common Man* and Joan Tower's *Fanfares for the Uncommon Woman*

AARON COPLAND'S (1900–1990) most famous and widely performed work is probably *Fanfare for the Common Man* (1942). It was written to honor the men and women who served in World War II. The work was enthusiastically received and its themes were later used in the fourth movement of Copland's *Third Symphony.*

One particularly interesting response to Copland's work is a series of compositions called *Fanfares for the Uncommon Woman*, written by Joan Tower (1938–present), one of the most prominent female composers of the late 20th century. Tower, who has specialized in orchestral composition throughout her career, won the prestigious Grawemeyer Award for Music Composition in 1990 with her work *Silver Ladders.* She has since garnered a number of other honors, including being selected as the first composer commissioned for the "Ford Made in America" program, a collaboration of the American Symphony Orchestra League and Meet the Composer. This program is designed to give smaller-budget orchestras the opportunity to collaborate in soliciting a new composition from a prominent individual. Tower's composition for this program, *Made in America,* was premiered by the Glens Falls Symphony Orchestra in October 2005 and was then performed by 65 small orchestras throughout the United States (with at least one performance in every state) during the following two years, providing exceptional outreach for a new 20th-century work.

The first work in Tower's *Fanfares for the Uncommon Woman* series, composed in 1986, uses the same orchestration (brass and percussion) as Copland's *Fanfare,* and the opening musical idea resembles Copland's opening theme. Tower conceived it both as a tribute to Copland and, in her words, "a tribute to women who are adventurers and risk-takers," dedicating it to Marin Alsop, who was at the time the director of the Colorado Symphony Orchestra (one of a small handful of women in the orchestra-directing field).

Tower followed this first *Fanfare* with four additional works composed in the early 1990s for varying instrumentation, all drawing on similar musical ideas. All five of Tower's *Fanfares* were recorded by Alsop and the Colorado Symphony on Koch International Records in 1999 and have become increasingly popular since that release, inspiring performances by more than 500 ensembles.

Functional Magnetic Resonance Imaging

A NERVE CELL IS LIKE a person; when active, both require large amounts of oxygen. Energy-burning neurons greedily consume oxygen molecules delivered by hemoglobin proteins of red blood cells. The oxygen-feasting process changes blood circulation in the brain and gives clues about brain function.

When a part of the brain becomes particularly active, blood in the region can be depleted of oxygen. Within seconds, the body responds by increasing the flow of oxygen-rich arterial blood to oxygen-poor areas. Local concentrations of oxygen-bearing hemoglobin and oxygen-free hemoglobin rapidly shift. The loss of oxygen from its iron atoms alters the magnetic properties of hemoglobin. A magnetic resonance imaging scanner can detect these minute changes in magnetic fields and locate those areas of the brain that have become activated. In a nutshell, this is the most commonly used method of functional magnetic resonance imaging, or fMRI.

The ability to observe changes in the activity of brain structures has launched a new era of investigations into brain function. Brain mapping, just one area of basic fMRI research, identifies the parts of the brain responsible for speech, movement, perception of sensations, and even thought. Neuroimaging provides insights into many neurological disorders, including seizures, schizophrenia, major depression, and Alzheimer's disease. One recent study indicates that fMRI may offer a prognosis of preclinical Alzheimer's disease and may identify people with mild cognitive impairment, who are at greatest risk for a progressive decline in their condition.

A brain tumor can change the location of a normal function or may grow in a part of the brain that has an uncertain function. Neurosurgeons can use fMRI to map a patient's brain before operating on a tumor. In one ongoing study, researchers scan subjects who take tests designed to localize areas of the brain responsible for language, sensory perception, movement, and vision. Such studies have proven useful when planning neurosurgery in a way that minimizes postoperative neurological damage.

Neuroimaging has also proven useful in studies outside the field of medicine; one such example is the discovery of brain regions associated with a religious experience.

Louis Comfort Tiffany
and the Art of Stained Glass

ALTHOUGH LOUIS COMFORT TIFFANY (1848–1933) worked in an astonishing array of media, it was his work in glass that consumed much of his creative energy and led to his most notable achievements. Tiffany's stained-glass windows breathed new life into this once-stagnant art form, while his hand-blown Favrile glassware raised the decorative arts to new heights.

The son of the founder of the New York City jewelry store Tiffany & Co., Louis developed an early appreciation for the finer things in life. He decided to pursue a career in the fine arts rather than enter the family business, starting out as a painter in the mid-1860s. Later, inspired by the Roman and medieval glass he saw on his travels to Europe and Africa—especially the great stained-glass windows of Europe's cathedrals—he changed his focus to glass.

Tiffany acorn lamp

Following his return to New York, Tiffany became part of a move-ment to restore stained glass—an art form that had declined for several centuries—to its former glory. Dissatisfied with the range of colors then available to commercial artists, Tiffany set out to develop a technique that would allow a more varied palette. The result was opalescent window glass, in which several colors were combined to create an unprecedented array of hues and textures.

Tiffany's *Four Seasons* (designed in 1892) reflects his signature window style, with its brilliant colors, unabashed celebration of nature, and use of leading as an integral design element. The window was one of his celebrated works, earning him the gold medal at the 1900 Exposition Universelle in Paris.

Tiffany wanted to incorporate electric light into his artistic designs, and in 1899 he introduced his first table lamp. Essentially, the covering for the electric bulbs was a stained-glass window in the form of a lamp shade. These luxurious lamps cost between $30 and $750 in the early 20th century. As an artist, Tiffany struggled with the idea of having his designs mass-produced, so he always had mixed feelings about his lamps.

For some, Tiffany's true genius lay in his Favrile glass pieces, which mixed up to seven colors. With their free-flowing forms, Favrile glass objects are seen as precursors of Abstract Expressionism.

Aztec and Incan Societies

THE AZTECS INHABITED Mexico's central valley and, in 1325, founded Tenochtitlán near where present-day Mexico City is located. The Aztecs had a barter economy but also used a form of money for trade.

Deities were important to the Aztecs, and Quetzalcóatl was the most important. *Quetzalcóatl* means *feathered serpent,* and the Aztecs believed Quetzalcóatl and his twin created the world. The Aztecs worshipped him as their religious deity and regarded him as the patron of the Aztec priests. They carried out human sacrifices for religious purposes.

The Aztecs had a highly advanced civilization. Their well-developed road system connected villages that would otherwise have been isolated and provided a network of communication for foot travelers. The Aztecs maintained a class structure that included educated nobility as well as artisans, traders, and warriors who provided sources of income for the Aztec economy. They also had slaves, who could own possessions, including other slaves.

Montezuma became leader of the Aztecs in 1502 and is considered to be the primary architect of the Aztec empire. When Cortez, the Spanish conquistador, arrived in Mexico to defeat the Aztecs in 1521, Montezuma believed Quetzalcóatl had returned. Under Spanish rule, the Aztec traditions and culture were phased out and eventually forbidden.

While the Aztecs were living in central Mexico, the Incas were developing a highly sophisticated civilization in South America. The Incan dynasty is said to have begun in Lake Titicaca, a lake that divides present-day Peru and Bolivia. According to legend, after the Sun caused Manco Capac and his sister to emerge from the lake on the Island of the Sun, they founded the Inca Empire (in the early 13th century). The city of Machu Picchu, built around 1450, provides an excellent example of Incan architecture.

In the 1470s, Topa Inca became ruler of the Inca nation. He led troops into battle, captured numerous tribes, unified his nation, and enlarged the Incan empire to include land between present-day northern Ecuador and central Chile. The Incas built a network of roads that connected coastal areas with remote mountain valleys, developed irrigation systems, and built cities high in the Andes where centers of government were located. Cuzco, the Incan capital, is one example.

The Spanish conquistador Pizarro arrived in 1526, about the same time the Incas were hit with a smallpox epidemic, presumably from Central America, and were fighting a civil war. The Incan Empire officially came to an end in 1572.

Ernest Hemingway

KNOWN FOR ITS crisp and lucid style, the fiction of Ernest Hemingway (1899–1961) had a significant influence on the works of many 20th-century writers. Hemingway led a very public life, and his numerous adventures and relationships were often the thinly veiled subjects of his stories.

Born into an upper-middle-class family in Oak Park, Illinois, a suburb of Chicago, Hemingway developed his love for writing in high school. Upon graduation, he was hired as a reporter for the *Kansas City Star*. He remained at the paper for only six months before joining the American Red Cross as an ambulance driver during World War I. Wounded shortly after arriving in Italy, Hemingway was hospitalized in Milan, where he met Agnes von Kurowsky, a Red Cross nurse. He later fictionalized the account of their relationship in his novel *A Farewell to Arms* (1929).

Hemingway worked for various newspapers in the United States and Canada before eventually relocating to Paris in the early 1920s where he joined other American expatriate writers, including F. Scott Fitzgerald, Ezra Pound, and Gertrude Stein. His first book *In Our Time* (1925), a collection of short stories, was quickly followed by *The Torrents of Spring* (1926) and *The Sun Also Rises* (1926), an account of the aimless lives of disillusioned Americans, members of the postwar "Lost Generation."

The focus of many of Hemingway's novels and stories fell on strong male figures. The protagonist of his most critically acclaimed novel *For Whom the Bell Tolls* (1940) is Robert Jordan, an American who volunteers to fight against fascists during the Spanish Civil War. The account of Jordan's heroic actions in Spain, punctuated by a number of flashbacks, explores the themes of proactively confronting and giving one's life for social causes.

Hemingway's sparse use of adjectives and adverbs in his fiction and non-fiction, including *Death in the Afternoon* (1932) and *A Moveable Feast* (1964), was heavily influenced by his journalistic background. He also experimented with the use of nouns and verbs in a rhythmic cadence, such as in his short story "A Clean, Well-Lighted Place." His short, tight, rhythmic style influenced many post-World War II authors, including Jack Kerouac and J. D. Salinger.

An alcoholic who suffered from bipolar disorder, Hemingway committed suicide on July 2, 1961.

Sir Edmund Hillary (1919–2008)

Edmund Hillary was born in 1919 and grew up near Auckland, New Zealand. He was an avid reader and dreamed of a life of adventure. Hillary became interested in climbing during a school trip to New Zealand's Mount Ruapehu when he was 16. Even though he was lanky and somewhat uncoordinated, Hillary found that he had greater stamina for climbing than many of his schoolmates. Following his own schooling, Hillary worked as an assistant in a school near Auckland for a short time, but his focus shifted toward climbing. To free up the winter months for climbing, he found work as a beekeeper during the summer.

When he was 20 years old, Hillary completed his first major climb in New Zealand's Southern Alps, the longest and highest range in the country. However, World War II would interrupt his climbing pursuits. Hillary joined the Royal New Zealand Air Force as a navigator and served on floating aircraft.

Following the war in 1951, he joined a British reconnaissance climbing expedition to the world's highest point, Mount Everest, and in 1953 he joined another British expedition in an attempt to reach the summit. Because the approach from Tibet was barred by China, the expedition began its assent through Nepal. Base camp was established in April 1953, and the group began its long climb, reaching the final camp before the summit at the end of May. At this point, most of Hillary's support team retreated because of the effects of the high altitude. Hillary and Tenzing Norgay, a Sherpa (a native people of the Himalayas), were paired to assault the peak. The pair reached the summit on May 29.

Conditions on the summit only permitted a few minutes for the two men to stand, take photos, and leave small personal offerings. Their descent was complicated because snow had covered the tracks of their ascent. News of the successful expedition was sent to Britain, reaching the country a day before the coronation of Queen Elizabeth II.

Because of his achievement, Hillary was knighted. After reaching the top of Everest, he would climb other Himalayan peaks, reach the North and South poles, and lead an expedition to the source of the Ganges River. However, even with all of his achievements, he was proudest of his humanitarian work. Throughout his life, he continually devoted time and funds to help the Sherpa people by building schools, clinics, and hospitals throughout Nepal. In 2003, thanks to his charitable work, he became the first foreigner to receive honorary citizenship from the Nepalese government. Hillary died in January 2008 of heart failure. He was 88.

The T-and-O Map: Spiritual Geography

FROM ANCIENT TIMES until the beginning of the Christian era, cartographers produced increasingly accurate representations of the known world. By the seventh century A.D., however, mapmaking skills had declined. As the Catholic Church came to dominate scholarly life in Europe, it discouraged scientific investigation that contradicted information about the universe set forth in scripture. Medieval cartographers no longer focused on the measurement of real space. Instead, their maps of the world, called *mappamundi,* depicted a conceptual truth. They created a representation of the world in keeping with prevailing religious beliefs.

T-and-O maps evolved from ancient Roman models. The term "T-and-O" describes the format in which an all-encompassing ocean bordered the circular form. Inside this circle (the "O") were the three known landmasses, Europe, Africa, and Asia, which formed a rough T-shape. Christian scholars embraced this three-part representation of the world, as it seemed to confirm religious beliefs. In the Old Testament book of Genesis, it said that God had divided the world among the sons of Noah. Shem received Asia, Ham got Africa, and Japheth acquired Europe, hence the three continents.

The earliest T-and-O maps often were oriented with east at the top, where north is located on a modern map. This directional orientation also resonated with theological truth. In the medieval church, the east was a metaphor for salvation. The sun, which brought light and warmth each day, rose in the east, and the Holy Land, where Jesus of Nazareth had been born, was in the east. Physical movement toward the east implied a journey that would take one nearer to God. Thus, east was placed at the top of the map, occupying an exalted place above all of humankind.

Even the measure of distance took on a religious connotation. In most mappamundi, the distance from the Holy Land was equated with the distance from God's influence. The central part of the map was considered to be a state of grace as much as it was a particular geographical place. Lands remote from the Christian world at the center of the map were portrayed as wildernesses occupied by violent, deformed creatures.

With the emergence of secular humanism in the late 15th century and the dawning of a new scientific age, Western culture began to form a different view of their surroundings. Additionally, the exploration of the Americas almost doubled the size of the world known to Europeans. An individual's place in the world once again became a matter of physical location rather than spiritual condition.

The Institution of Public Concerts in the 1600s

UP TO THE LATE 1600s, European musical performances in a non-sacred context were almost always by invitation only. Monarchs or aristocrats would hire professionals to create elaborate musical works for special events and would invite their friends to be the audience. Alternatively, amateurs at different social levels would make music among themselves, but such activities were designed to be communal, without a separate audience, much less a paying one.

Economic and social circumstances came together in England in the 1660s to create a new scenario: Tavern-keepers and enterprising musicians supplemented their income by arranging for performers to gather at eating establishments, and they charged admission to those who wanted to hear the musicians play. These concerts were open to all who could pay a shilling for the event (food and drink were extra, of course). Musicians were often advertised as being connected to the royal establishment, thus giving the middle classes the opportunity to enjoy the kinds of musical luxuries that had long been associated only with the nobility.

The earliest such concert series for which there are surviving advertisements was organized at the Mitre Tavern on London's Fleet Street in December 1772 by John Bannister, the director of a prominent string ensemble established by King Charles II in the early 1660s. The ensemble was directly modeled on the highly fashionable and renowned "twenty-four violins" of King Louis XIV of France, so Bannister was able to draw not only on royal prestige but also on the international renown of the French instrumental style of the time, which he had studied in Paris.

Bannister's enterprise was successful enough to serve as a model for a number of "pub concerts" and more formal public-admission events, not only in England but gradually throughout northern Europe in the early 1700s, resulting in a significant increase in performing opportunities for instrumental musicians. This in turn led to the remarkable flourishing of instrumental musical genres—particularly the orchestral symphony—that characterizes the European musical tradition in the mid and late 18th century.

As concerts shifted from private to public, composers, as well as musicians, gained more freedom and opportunity. They did not have to be tied down to one patron and could present public concerts of their own musical works. As public audiences grew increasingly interested in orchestral concerts, composers broadened their work to accommodate the new demand.

The Golden Ratio

CALLED BOTH "the divine proportion" and "a precious jewel," the golden ratio may be the most storied number in mathematics. Through the ages, it has inspired mathematicians, artists, physicists, biologists, musicians, architects, painters, and even mystics. The golden number is approximately 1.618, and the golden ratio is simply the proportion of the golden number to 1. Shapes and designs, such as the so-called "golden rectangle" are constructed with sides or proportions in the ratio of 1 to 1.618.

The golden ratio has been known for some time. Euclid studied the golden ratio extensively around 300 B.C. and first demonstrated how it could be calculated. Amazingly, the golden ratio also pops up in several surprising places in the natural world. For example, the pattern of seeds on a sunflower and the spines on a cactus form "golden spirals" whose shapes match the golden ratio. The golden ratio can also be found in the spiral arms of the Milky Way galaxy.

A near cult has developed around the ratio, with devotees in a variety of fields. During the Renaissance, Luca Pacioli wrote a treatise arguing that the golden ratio had religious significance. While Pacioli did not ascribe any aesthetic significance to the ratio, his work nevertheless inspired many artists and architects to use the golden ratio in their work. In the 20th century, the Swiss architect Le Corbusier, for example, incorporated the ratio into his influential modern designs, and artists Salvador Dalí and Piet Mondrian used it in some of their paintings.

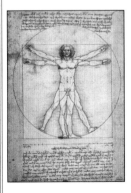

While many have found significance in the golden ratio, the science behind claims of its special aesthetic appeal is somewhat lacking. For example, a rigorous 1966 study found that, aesthetically, people seem to prefer rectangles with a ratio of about 1 to 1.9, rather than 1 to 1.618. In the past, many have also claimed that the golden ratio exists in a variety of classic buildings and artwork including the Parthenon, the Great Pyramid of Khufu, and the *Mona Lisa*. However, careful measurement has shown that the proportions found in these works are, in fact, not very close to the golden ratio. There have also been claims that the golden ratio exists in the proportions of the human body, but this is difficult to prove. Regardless, the golden ratio has proven to be unquestionably useful in mathematics.

Johannes Vermeer

JOHANNES VERMEER (1632–1675), a 17th-century master of Dutch painting, depicted the world of Delft, his hometown, with such convincing precision that his works strike the casual viewer with their uncanny—almost photographic—realism. Typically, Vermeer depicted women in private living spaces, usually in prosperous middle-class homes and engaged in activities such as performing domestic tasks, reading letters, or playing musical instruments. Daylight enters from windows above, bathing the women in its soft glow. The special light, combined with carefully balanced compositions, creates a timeless world in which the figures seem forever suspended.

The Artist's Studio

Part of the visual fascination of these interiors resides in Vermeer's tendency to deliberately blur portions of his figures, highlight details with white lines, and dot various parts of his compositions with tiny spots of white paint. These resemble many of the effects of photographs; for example, "discs of confusion," or unfocused spots of light that occur when taking pictures in direct sunlight.

It is possible that Vermeer used a camera obscura for his interior scenes, including the famed *Girl with the Pearl Earring* (c. 1665–1675), as well as his cityscape, the panoramic *View of Delft* (c. 1660–1661). It is known that camera obscuras, ancestors of the modern camera that did not yet preserve images on film, were available to Vermeer. Moreover, one of his distinguished friends, Antonie van Leeuwenhoek, a pioneer in developing the microscope, experimented with such devices. It is noteworthy that Vermeer's *The Astronomer* (c. 1668), showing a scientist with a globe of the stars, is believed to be a portrait of Van Leeuwenhoek himself.

Vermeer's late paintings included religious allegories promoting allegiance to the Catholic faith, to which he had apparently been required to convert at the time of his marriage in 1653. This put Vermeer in the religious minority in predominantly Protestant Holland. Despite a change in subject as well as technique—toward a harder-edged and more classically conceived style—evidence of Vermeer's reliance on the camera obscura is still evident in these late efforts. His enduring interest in the scientific properties of light remains evident, even though his themes and certain elements of style had shifted.

Winston Churchill

A s England's high-profile prime minister during World War II, Winston Churchill (1874–1965) led his nation, inspired his people, and helped reshape postwar boundaries.

After attending boarding school, Churchill embarked on a military career. While serving his country, he also pursued his love of writing and submitted articles to London newspapers as a war correspondent. When he concluded his military service, Churchill sought a political career in Parliament. His defeat did not discourage him from running in later elections. In 1900, Churchill was elected to Parliament and began his governmental career. He held a variety of political and cabinet positions and served with the British army in World War I. He became Chancellor of the Exchequer, wrote books and articles (he would go on to receive the Nobel Prize for Literature in 1953), and was active in a variety of political causes, such as the fight to maintain British control of India.

When Neville Chamberlain resigned as prime minister in 1940, Churchill was asked to form an all-party government and serve as the wartime prime minister. Throughout World War II, Churchill refused to negotiate with Germany and provided encouragement and hope to the people through his speeches. The famous "blood, sweat, tears, and toil" speech was the first he gave as prime minister. He also rallied the British as they faced the Battle of Britain.

Churchill met with President Franklin Roosevelt several times during the war. They convened on a battleship in the waters of the North Atlantic to discuss strategy, and they met with Chinese leader Chiang Kai-shek in Cairo to discuss military operations against Japan. Churchill and Roosevelt also flew to Tehran to confer with Russian leader Joseph Stalin regarding war plans against Germany, Russia's participation against Japan, and the formulation of a postwar policy.

Churchill met with Roosevelt and Stalin in Yalta in 1945, and it was at this monumental Crimean meeting that the three men agreed on the division of Germany, war reparations, and the creation of the United Nations.

Churchill, a conservative, lost his bid for prime minister to the Labour Party shortly after the war, although he served again in that capacity from 1951 to 1955. When he resigned from office because of failing health, he continued to pursue his pastime of painting. His work has been displayed in galleries throughout the world. Churchill died in 1965, and he was given the illustrious honor of a state funeral.

F. Scott Fitzgerald's *The Great Gatsby*

PUBLISHED IN 1925, *The Great Gatsby* looks at an American generation wallowing and decaying in excess—and also provides insight into author F. Scott Fitzgerald himself.

Set against the frenetic background of the Roaring '20s, *The Great Gatsby* is a story of the people during that hedonistic time, as well as of America's descent as a nation into the moral decay brought about by easy money. The narrator is Nick Carraway, a young man from Minnesota who goes east to learn the bond business. Arriving on Long Island in 1922, Carraway moves in next door to Jay Gatsby, who throws a grand party every Saturday night. Carraway's neighbors and friends are *nouveau riche,* and they act with vanity and moral bankruptcy.

One night, Nick has dinner with his cousin Daisy and her husband, Tom, who is having an affair with a woman named Myrtle. Eventually, Nick is invited to one of Gatsby's legendary parties. He learns that Gatsby has been desperately in love with Daisy for years, and he throws his lavish parties to impress her. Gatsby has Nick arrange a meeting with Daisy, which results in her starting an affair with Gatsby. Eventually, her husband finds out and is furious. Daisy chooses Tom over Gatsby. But while driving back to Long Island with Gatsby, Daisy accidentally hits Myrtle with her car and kills her. Gatsby tells Nick that he will say he drove the car to spare Daisy. Tom tells Myrtle's husband, George, that Gatsby was the driver. George has already decided that whoever was the driver was Myrtle's lover. He goes to Gatsby's mansion and shoots him, then kills himself. A disillusioned Nick has a funeral for Gatsby and then returns to the Midwest.

Like Nick, Fitzgerald was originally from Minnesota and went east, in Fitzgerald's case to Princeton University. He had to show his beloved fiancée, Zelda, that he could financially support and spiritually maintain the wild, lavish lifestyle she demanded before she would agree to marry him, just as Gatsby desperately tries to impress Daisy with his parties.

The success of Fitzgerald's first novel in 1920, *This Side of Paradise,* and his second in 1922, *The Beautiful and Damned,* made him a literary star. Some people believe that once he attained those heights, he drank and partied excessively to keep up with Zelda—to the detriment of his writing. The single-minded pursuit of wealth sapped him—Fitzgerald might have written—as it sapped a once-vital America.

John Cage (1912–1992)

Hᴉѕ ᴄᴏᴍᴘᴏѕɪᴛɪᴏɴѕ ᴀʀᴇ ʀᴀʀᴇʟʏ performed nowadays and even more seldom recorded; yet John Cage was probably the most influential American musical thinker of the 20th century. He was a pioneer in a number of different areas of avant-garde music, notably the use of turntables and other electronic sounds, extended percussion resources, "prepared" or modified instruments, and "chance" compositional or performance operations.

Cage studied with some of the most prominent musicians of the early 20th century, most notably Arnold Schoenberg and Henry Cowell. From the 1930s onward, he developed novel ways of employing percussion in conjunction with electronically generated sound (through turntables, radio signals, and other electrical media). Early on he also developed a strong connection with dancer Merce Cunningham, who would become his lifelong companion. The two collaborated on a number of ground-breaking music-dance projects.

Cage developed a compositional system based on the additive combination of small musical units. He also expanded the use of the "prepared piano," a technique invented by his mentor Cowell in which a variety of objects (screws, bolts, felt strips) are overlaid on piano strings to create novel percussive and resonant effects.

As he became interested in East Asian philosophical traditions in the 1940s, Cage began to experiment with the Chinese *I Ching* system of divination, in which random numbers are generated to consult specific sections of an oracular text. Cage used the *I Ching* to craft his *Music of Changes* (1951), in which a series of musical ideas are arranged using random number generation. The resulting work is thus partly shaped by chance rather than by the composer's control, and Cage built on the principle of chance music (keeping some parameters under his control and relinquishing others) for the rest of his career.

Probably the most famous (or infamous) of Cage's chance compositions is *4'33"* (1952), in which he instructs any number of musicians to sit quietly on the concert stage for exactly four minutes and thirty-three seconds. The sounds generated by the audience during this silence, as well as the air-conditioning system of the hall, outside noises, and so forth, are the focus of the "work." The opening of musical activity to what Cage termed *indeterminacy* was enormously influential to his contemporaries, especially as a response to a movement toward absolute precision and control that had dominated much of "art" music for the first half of the century.

The Reform Act of 1832 and Chartism

AT THE BEGINNING of the 19th century, England was in state of political, social, and economic turmoil. With the end of the Napoleonic wars came falling prices, an unstable currency, and widespread unemployment. At the same time, the industrial revolution had changed the nation's population patterns, leaving new cities in the north and west unrepresented in government and large landowners in control of under-populated "rotten boroughs." Also, a newly wealthy middle class now demanded the voting rights traditionally denied to them. Working-class radicals and middle-class manufacturers alike agitated for free trade and electoral reform.

Thanks to growing unrest and violent demonstrations, the Whig government headed by Lord Grey responded by proposing a reform bill in March 1831. However, the Tory-controlled House of Lords defeated the measure twice. A third attempt passed only after King William IV threatened to create enough new peers to override the opposition. The resulting Reform Act of 1832 disenfranchised most "rotten boroughs," redistributed seats to previously unrepresented boroughs, and increased the electorate in England and Wales by 57 percent. It also expanded the right to vote to the middle class; however artisans, the working class, and some sections of the lower middle class were still not granted suffrage. In the next election, despite Tory fears that the expanded electorate would result in revolution, the new House of Commons looked much the same as the one it replaced.

Since the reform act failed to address important working-class concerns, it was inevitable that protests would resume. In the late 1830s, working-class resentment rose in the face of continued economic distress and the suppression of trade unions. Drafted in 1838 by labor organizer William Lovett, the *People's Charter* enumerated the demands of working-class people. The document demanded six political changes: annual Parliamentary elections, universal male suffrage, equal electoral districts, an end to property qualifications for members of Parliament, secret ballots, and a salary for members of Parliament. The movement soon became known as Chartism.

Between 1839 and 1848, several petitions calling for the enactment of the Charter were presented to Parliament, but Parliament refused to act.

Still, the spirit of the movement lived on. By 1918, Parliament had enacted all but one of the measures called for in the *People's Charter;* only annual Parliamentary elections did not become a feature of the British electoral system.

Philip Glass and *Einstein on the Beach*

PHILIP GLASS (1937–PRESENT) is arguably the best-known "serious" composer of our time, partly through his collaborations with artists in many different traditions (including Ravi Shankar, Aphex Twin, and David Bowie) and through his extensive work in multimedia and movies. Glass's first opera, *Einstein on the Beach* (1975), exemplifies his revolutionary approach to multimedia composition.

Einstein was Glass's first substantial collaboration with playwright Robert Wilson, with whom he has since produced a number of musical-theater works. In retrospect, Glass labeled *Einstein* as the first of three loosely connected "portrait" operas—the others being *Satyagraha* (1980) and *Akhnaten* (1983). Each of the three works concerns an individual who had a quasi-mythological impact well beyond his immediate cultural situation. Especially in the case of *Einstein*, the opera is not about *Einstein* as a person but rather about the social impact of his scientific arguments. It is thus not narrative but evocative.

Einstein was designed to be performed without an intermission, and in its first round of performances, it took approximately five hours to complete. Wilson expressly intended for the audience to come and go during the performance; accordingly, Glass specifically designed his score to be heard in a nonlinear fashion. The musical ideas are short and consonant, repeated at length with very gradual process-based change and expansion. The effect is not one of traditional "development" but rather a paradoxical alternation of stasis and continuous flow, resonating with *Einstein*'s theoretical formulations about time. Instrumental sections often feature a violinist dressed as Einstein, who is placed between the orchestra proper and the stage action. In his notes for *Einstein,* Glass characterized the violin as providing "the most important musical material" in the work, lending "a musical touchstone to the work as a whole."

While Glass's compositional approach has often been characterized as "minimalist," he rejects that term for all but his earliest work. Indeed, Glass maintains that his approach to music took a drastic turn specifically with *Einstein*.

There are two CD recordings of *Einstein* on the market. (Unfortunately, there is no DVD.) The original version was released in 1979; an updated version was rerecorded in 1993. The latter has been characterized as more polished and better recorded, while some feel the former is more faithful to the edginess of the original production.

The Human Genome Project

OCTOBER 1990 MARKED the formal launch of the Human Genome Project (HGP), a massive international effort to determine the sequence of the three billion base pairs that make up human DNA. Scientists had planned to complete the project in 15 years, but advances in technology accelerated the progress. A working draft of a human genome—the complete genetic material of a human—became available in June 2000, and a finished nucleotide sequence was released in 2003. The colossal endeavor captured the public's imagination and raised expectations about an imminent new era of genetics-informed medicine. However, things haven't really changed that dramatically—yet.

The project revealed that the human genome contains 3.1647 billion nucleotide bases, the chemical building blocks of DNA. Around the globe, people share an identical order of 99.9 percent of their nucleotide bases. That is, human genetic variation resides in 0.1 percent of the genome. Gene size varies greatly. The average gene has 3,000 nucleotides; the largest, 2.4 million nucleotides. Before the HGP, scientists estimated that humans had 80,000 to 140,000 genes. Computer analyses of DNA sequence data indicate that the human genome boasts a mere 20,000 to 25,000 genes.

The HGP brought other surprises as well. Less than 2 percent of the human genome encodes proteins. Human chromosomes contain gene-dense oases surrounded by vast regions of DNA desert that lack identifiable genes. The reason for the existence of genetic deserts is unclear. In the traditional view, a gene provides a template for the synthesis of ribonucleic acid (RNA), which directs the synthesis of a protein. Yet researchers have discovered that many RNA molecules do not encode proteins; their function is unknown.

Although the HGP did not usher in an array of new medical treatments, the process of gene mapping has helped to expand our understanding of the causes of disease. Genome maps have helped researchers find genes associated with many diseases and disorders, including familial breast cancer, inherited colon cancer, Alzheimer's disease, deafness, and blindness. These discoveries should inform new diagnostic tests and aid efforts to devise therapies that target the cause of a disease.

The HGP also generated low-cost and efficient technologies that enable ongoing investigations into human genetic differences. The International Haplotype Map Project, for instance, has charted patterns of genetic variation that contribute to common diseases. Another group, the Genetic Association Information Network aims to identify genetic risk factors.

Claude Monet's *Water Lilies*

IN 1890, IMPRESSIONIST painter Claude Monet (1840–1926) purchased a small farmhouse in the village of Giverny in Normandy, France. The setting consumed Monet's attention, as both painter and gardener, for the rest of his life. He expanded the property to include a pond and stream, planted flowers near the house, designed an arched bridge to span the stream, and introduced exotic water lilies—*nymphéas*—to the pond. He even placed easels throughout the property so that he could easily begin work when struck by a special quality of light or color.

By the late 1880s, Monet was refining the style that had inspired the term *Impressionism.* Each change of light or atmosphere inspired a new picture; by 1900, Monet might paint a dozen canvases in a single session. As he said to a fellow artist, "When you go out to paint, try to forget what objects you have before you—a tree, a house, a field, or whatever. Merely think, 'Here is a square of blue, here an oblong of pink, here is a streak of yellow,' and paint it just as it looks to you, the exact color and shape, until its gives your own naive impression of the scene before you." Monet later reworked his paintings inside his studio to develop color harmonies and more fully express each particular moment of inspiration.

In the paintings of water lilies, rosy flowers seem suspended in an atmosphere that is both water and air. Reflections of trees and clouds intermingle and confound the viewer's sense of space and direction. During the last three decades of his life, Monet painted nearly 250 scenes of water lilies.

In 1914, Monet began the magisterial series of water lilies that he would donate to France in 1918. He arranged the easels in his studio in such a way as to suggest a curved wall. Monet envisioned an oval installation for these paintings so that the viewer would literally be surrounded by water, clouds, and water lilies.

On May 16, 1927, five months after Monet's death, the public saw the "water lilies decoration" for the first time. Monet's son, Michel, bequeathed the house and gardens in Giverny to France's Academy of Fine Arts in 1966. The refurbished house and gardens were opened to the public in 1980.

The Battle of Stalingrad

THE WORLD WAR II BATTLE of Stalingrad began with the German army sweeping through Russia in a seemingly invincible tide. It ended with Hitler's legions dead or in retreat, demoralized and defeated.

Widely viewed as the turning point of the war in Europe, the battle for Stalingrad came about almost by accident. Two German army groups were pushing toward the oil-rich Caucasus in southwest Russia in the summer of 1942 when Hitler ordered a pause to seize Stalingrad. Despite its limited military worth, Stalingrad's symbolic value prompted both Germany and Russia to pour men and materiel into the struggle.

The German Sixth Army, under the command of General Friedrich Paulus, advanced on Stalingrad in September. They encountered fierce resistance from Russian troops fighting house to house, street to street, and block to block. The rubble of buildings destroyed by bombs and artillery fire provided ideal defensive positions. German advances were often counted in mere yards, with each small gain the target of near-suicidal counterattacks by Russian troops. Much of the combat was hand to hand.

The struggle continued as severe winter weather arrived. Already faced with fierce Russian resistance, German soldiers now found themselves ill-equipped to deal with the bitter cold. Many men froze to death as temperatures plunged. A German soldier reported that his right hand was so frozen that he was forced to shoot with his little finger.

Meanwhile, Russian commander General Georgi Zhukov was preparing a trap for the 250,000 to 300,000 Germans bogged down in Stalingrad. While continuing the fight in the city, Zhukov surrounded Stalingrad with six armies numbering one million men. General Paulus recognized his peril, but Hitler forbade him to break out of the city while escape was still possible.

With his troops cut off from supplies and help, starving and freezing, Paulus disobeyed Hitler. "I have no intention of shooting myself for that Bohemian corporal," he declared. Paulus surrendered his southern sector on January 31. The northern group surrendered two days later.

Defeat cost the Germans a complete army group. Total Axis casualties were around 550,000, including 91,000 Germans taken prisoner. Most would never return home. Russian casualties are believed to have exceeded one million.

The German Army would never regain the initiative on the Eastern Front. "The God of War has gone over to the other side," lamented Hitler.

Henry David Thoreau

POET, NOVELIST, PHILOSOPHER, advocate of nonviolent resistance, nature-lover...Henry David Thoreau (1817–1862) packed many different talents into a life cut short.

Thoreau was born on July 12, 1817, in Concord, Massachusetts. His brother John, to whom he was close, taught school to pay for Thoreau's Harvard tuition. In 1835, Thoreau caught tuberculosis, which would periodically plague him throughout the rest of his life. In 1838, he and John opened a school in Concord, but John died of lockjaw in 1842. Meanwhile, Thoreau had met Ralph Waldo Emerson (1803–1882). Taking a fatherly interest in Thoreau, Emerson introduced him to local writers such as Nathaniel Hawthorne and Margaret Fuller. Thoreau even lived with Emerson for three years, working as a handyman and tutor. Thoreau also periodically worked in his father's pencil factory.

On July 4, 1845, Thoreau moved into a house he had built on land owned by Emerson on the shore of Walden Pond in Massachusetts. During this period he walked, observed nature, and wrote a book entitled *A Week on the Concord and Merrimack Rivers* about a rafting trip he and John had taken. At Emerson's urging, Thoreau published the book at his own expense. Its commercial failure seriously damaged their relationship.

In 1846, Thoreau was jailed overnight for refusing to pay poll taxes because of his opposition to the Mexican War and the extension of slavery. That led to his 1849 essay *Resistance to Civil Government* (also called *Civil Disobedience*). The essay advocated nonviolent resistance and disobedience to a government with which one does not agree. Its message of nonviolent protest influenced such prominent social leaders as Mahatma Gandhi and Martin Luther King, Jr. "I ask for, not at once no government, but at once a better government," wrote Thoreau.

After leaving Walden Pond in September 1847, Thoreau spent the next several years working to pay debts and continually revising his book about Walden. Published in 1854, *Walden: or, Life in the Woods* celebrated the joys of nature and the simple tasks in life. The book is often misunderstood as a rejection of civilization and an embrace of nature. But Thoreau advocated a balanced life in harmony with both. He died in 1862 at age 44.

POSTSCRIPT

■ Thoreau's Walden cabin was not in the wilderness; it was located on the outskirts of town. It cost $28 to build.

Martin Luther

MARTIN LUTHER (1483–1546) WAS BORN into a peasant family in what is today central Germany. His father eventually became more successful and was able to send his son to school to prepare for a legal career. However, Luther was far more interested in matters of religion. He entered an Augustinian monastery in 1505. He earned a doctorate degree in divinity in 1512 and began teaching at Wittenberg University.

Luther intently studied the Bible and came to the conclusion that the Catholic Church was wrong on a number of points. The church advocated that man could find salvation through good works, yet Luther believed that man could be saved simply by faith alone, aided by the grace of God. He also reasoned that people did not need priests to act as intermediaries with God.

Another practice that Luther disliked was the sale of indulgences by the church. An indulgence was a monetary payment by which a person's temporal punishment for sins would be lessened in both life and in purgatory. When papal representatives began selling indulgences to fund the building of St. Peter's Basilica in Rome, Luther vigorously objected. On October 31, 1517, he nailed a list of 95 theses on the church door in Wittenberg, detailing his attack on the selling of indulgences.

As news of Luther's list spread, he became famous throughout Europe. In his theses, Luther had claimed that the pope was not infallible and that scripture was the final authority, not the word of the pope. Additionally, he believed that of the seven sacraments, only two, the Lord's Supper and baptism, were relevant. Hearing this, the pope insisted that the German assembly convene and investigate Luther's writings. After much argument and debate, the assembly issued an edict in 1521 that branded Luther a heretic, ordered his arrest, and mandated that his writings be burned.

However, by that time Luther had stirred feelings of German nationalism against the church and many German leaders sided with him. As a result of his new ideas and powerful allegiances, the Protestant Reformation was underway, and Lutheranism became a major religion in Germany. Unlike their Catholic counterparts, Lutheran priests were allowed to marry. Also, Lutheran church services were carried out without the pomp of Catholic masses. To bring religion to the masses, Luther translated the Bible into German in 1534 and penned many prominent Lutheran hymns before his death in 1546.

Biological Weapons

THE 2001 ANTHRAX ATTACKS in the United States and the suspected pursuit of biological weapons by Saddam Hussein focused world attention on these potential weapons of mass destruction. But the use of biological weapons, such as a viruses or bacteria, to cause illness, death, and destruction in an enemy population is not new.

Bioterrorism is the contemporary term for a type of warfare that was used centuries ago. In the sixth century B.C., for example, Assyrians poisoned enemy wells with rye ergot, a toxic mold that grows on grasses. In 1346, the Tartar army catapulted the bodies of plague victims over the walls of the city of Kaffa, infecting its citizens and causing it to surrender. In colonial America, the British attempted to infect Native Americans with smallpox by bringing them blankets that had been used by victims of the illness. It has even been suggested that the use of biological weapons dates to biblical times. A *Jeopardy* question on the subject might read: "What were the plagues?"

Biological weapons may date to ancient times, but modern technology has increased their number as well as their capabilities. The infective agents can be loaded into bombs or artillery shells and exploded over large population centers. They can be powdered and sent in the mail, sprayed from a boat offshore, dispersed from moving vehicles, and even released from dropped lightbulbs. People can become infected through a variety of means, including inhalation, absorption through the skin, and ingestion.

Biological weapons are odorless, tasteless, and invisible, so their presence is not immediately detectable. And their effect continues long after they are released, as infection may take time to cause illness—and some can be transmitted from person to person, increasing the range of impact.

Acknowledging the worldwide devastation that biological weapons could have, 162 countries have signed the Biological and Toxic Weapons Convention (BTWC), and 144 of these have ratified it. The BTWC outlaws the development, production, stockpiling, or acquisition of biological agents as weapons of war. It also bans weapons, equipment, or means of delivery designed to use the agents or toxins for hostile purposes or in armed conflict.

Interestingly enough, the BTWC does not outlaw the use of biological weapons. Countries that signed the BTWC are allowed to pursue peaceful research, such as the development of antidotes and vaccines against biological weapons.

Banjo

T HE FIRST BANJOS appeared in the Caribbean and the American South during the 18th century. African slaves in those regions used gourds, wood, and animal skin and gut to re-create a four-stringed instrument commonly used in West Africa. In the 1830s, the instrument found its way into wider use in America with the popularity of minstrel shows. For these shows, white performers wearing blackface makeup and outrageous costumes provided a caricature of plantation tradition. The banjos used in minstrel shows were fretless, five-stringed instruments. They were played with a picking technique now known as *clawhammer,* in which players move their wrists or elbows but keep their fingers and hands rigid in a claw shape.

Banjo music grew in popularity and even became the subject of popular satire. In 1865, Mark Twain wrote, "When you want genuine music—music that will come right home to you like a bad quarter, suffuse your system like strychnine whiskey, go right through you like Brandeth's pills, ramify your whole constitute like measles, and break out on your hide like pin-feather pimples on a plucked goose—when you want all this, just smash your piano and invoke the glory-beaming banjo!" By the 1870s, the banjo had moved out of the minstrel show and into the parlor. Banjo arrangements became available for American folk songs, marches, polkas, popular songs, classical music, and later, a new musical craze called *ragtime.*

As American musical styles developed during the first half of the 20th century, the banjo played an important role. Dixieland jazz bands incorporated banjo into their sound. As they needed more volume, the tenor banjo was developed. It was a four-stringed instrument with a shorter neck, steel strings, and a tuning style that facilitated rapid single-note passages. In 1945, banjo player Earl Scruggs introduced a distinctive three-finger picking style, which today is referred to as *Scruggs style.* The sound of his banjo playing helped define a new form of acoustic country music called *bluegrass.*

Today, there are three basic types of banjo: the five-string banjo, the plectrum banjo, and the tenor banjo. The five-string banjo has four long strings tuned for picking and a shorter top string, which is used to create a drone. Both strummed and picked, the five-string is the banjo of choice for traditional bluegrass and folk music. The plectrum and tenor banjos have four strings and are played with a flat pick, called a *plectrum,* or a finger covering called a *thimble.* These four-string banjos are traditionally used in vaudeville, jazz, ragtime, and swing bands.

The Sun's Electromagnetic Spectrum

THE SUN IS A TREMENDOUS source of electromagnetic radiation, which includes radio waves, microwaves, infrared, visible light, ultraviolet, X-rays, and gamma rays. These waves of radiation constantly bombard Earth and its atmosphere. The sun's electromagnetic activity can best be seen during magnetic storms, with solar flares and coronal mass ejections that produce highly energetic particles. In turn, these particles travel to Earth and react with our planet's magnetic field. Most particles ejected from the sun come from sunspot groups (called *active regions*) and typically reach Earth one to five days after leaving the sun.

If one of the Sun's particle ejections is directed at Earth, the high-energy particles may disrupt the planet's magnetosphere, further compressing it on the side facing the sun and stretching it out on the side facing away. The stretched portion is called the *magnetotail.* This part of the magnetosphere is quite dynamic, and ions and electrons often become energized in that area. Where the magnetotail converges, it creates trillions of watts of power, which can then be directed back toward the planet's upper atmosphere.

Aurora borealis

As the highly charged particles are drawn toward Earth, they collide with the atoms and molecules of Earth's upper atmosphere, about 50 miles (80 kilometers) above the ground. This activity frequently creates auroras—also called the *northern lights,* or *aurora borealis,* in the Northern Hemisphere, and the *southern lights,* or *aurora australis,* in the Southern Hemisphere. These atmospheric light displays range from shimmering curtains and ribbons to bright rays. They can vary greatly in color depending on the type of particle in the atmosphere. For example, oxygen yields a green and red aurora, while nitrogen produces a red, blue, or violet display.

POSTSCRIPT

▪ Even though auroras occur some 50 miles (80 kilometers) above the surface of Earth, some people believe that they can hear sounds from auroras, such as whistling or hissing. This may or may not be true, but the aurora has been known to produce audible interference in devices such as telephones.

▪ Auroras occur more often between September and October and March and April.

Edvard Munch's *The Scream*

IN 1893, NORWEGIAN PAINTER Edvard Munch (1863–1944) added *The Scream* to a series he called the *Frieze of Life,* a set of paintings about love, sexual anxiety, and death.

In the painting, a figure stands on a bridge or dock along a coast, not unlike the shoreline near Oslo where Munch lived at various times. The dark figure, who stands in the foreground with his hands over his ears, appears to be screaming. Heavy bands of bright colors echo across the landscape like sound waves and merge into a blood-red sky.

The impetus for the painting was Munch's personal experience. One evening, as he walked along a path at sunset with friends, he grew increasingly melancholic. The sky turned deep red as flame-colored clouds floated over a blue-black fjord, which frightened him. He claimed that he then felt a "loud, unending scream piercing nature." While most assume "the scream" of the title comes from the figure in the foreground, it is also nature that is shrieking.

The Scream was completed during Munch's most prolific and symbolically explicit period—the 1890s and early 1900s. During this era, his style was characterized by bold, deep colors and sinewy, curving lines that create the illusion of movement or vibration. While *The Scream* depicts a moment of universal pain, many of the paintings in the *Frieze of Life* revolve around sexual anxiety, sickness, and death.

Munch had lived with death and madness most of his life. His mother died of tuberculosis in 1869, and a favorite sister died of the disease in 1877. His father was driven to the edge of insanity by grief and died in 1889. Munch himself was touched with both tuberculosis and mental instability exacerbated by destructive love affairs and drinking. His paintings from this time in his life portrayed themes of sickness, sexually voracious women, and death, reflecting Munch's fear of women and marriage that might result in passing his physical and mental illnesses to eventual offspring. In 1908, he suffered a complete mental breakdown. After eight months in a clinic in Copenhagen, Munch returned to Norway and altered his artistic style.

Despite its basis in Munch's personal experiences and issues, *The Scream* has become a universal symbol of modern angst and alienation.

Peter the Great

Without a doubt, Peter the Great (or Peter I) was aptly named, for most historians consider him the greatest of all Russian tsars. When Peter was born in 1672, Russia was centuries behind western Europe. Russia had missed the Renaissance and Reformation, was largely illiterate, and its peasants (called *serfs*) were essentially without rights and tied to their land. When Peter's father, Tsar Alexis, died in 1682, Peter was one of several sons by two wives who were considered for the throne. After years of turmoil and intrigue, Peter emerged as the sole ruler in 1694.

Once Peter was in control, he set out to modernize Russia. In 1697–1698, Peter and his entourage took an 18-month trip across western Europe, visiting several counties to learn all about their technical skills and crafts, armies, and other relevant information. He recruited more than 700 foreigners to go to Russia to teach his subjects Western ideas and skills.

Peter also began to modernize Russia's army and navy. He fought two wars with the Ottoman Empire as Russia's southern boundary pushed toward the Black Sea. During the Great Northern War (1700–1721), Peter fought against Charles XII and the superbly equipped Swedish army. He defeated the Swedes at the Battle of Poltava (July 8, 1709), and when peace was finally declared, Russia acquired land adjacent to the Baltic Sea. Peter founded the new city of St. Petersburg in 1703, which replaced Moscow as the capital.

Peter created a series of colleges (ministries) to run the government, established a Senate, reorganized the Russian Orthodox Church, and tried to modernize local government. In 1722, he created the Table of Ranks, a series of 14 ranks in the court, military, and civil services, designed to promote men by merit and thus create more qualified government servants. He modernized the calendar, simplified the Russian alphabet, and encouraged the publication of newspapers. He also founded the first Russian university.

Peter died on February 8, 1725, before he was able to name a successor, though his second wife, Catherine, was quickly named empress of Russia.

POSTSCRIPT

▨ Among his many decrees, Peter stipulated that Russian men should shave their beards, wear Western clothes, drink coffee, and take up smoking. He wanted the aristocracy to mimic what he saw during his tour of western Europe.

▨ In 1718, Peter put Alexis, his son by his first wife, on trial for treason. Alexis was found guilty but died from torture before he could be executed.

Shakespeare's Sonnet 18: "Shall I Compare Thee to a Summer's Day?"

THIS, THE OPENING LINE of William Shakespeare's often-quoted sonnet 18, develops a theme that recurs in a number of his sonnets: the beauty of youth and its transience versus the "eternal summer" of the beauty preserved in the "eternal lines" of the poem.

The imagery of the first two stanzas displays youth's beauty as superior to that of the natural world. In contrast with summer, the poet says that "Thou art more lovely and more temperate." Thus, the beautiful youth avoids the extremes often seen in nature: "Sometime too hot the eye of heaven shines,/And often is his gold complexion dimmed."

The third stanza proclaims that the young man's perfectly "temperate" beauty will live forever as immortalized in the lines of the sonnet: "Nor shall Death brag thou wand'rest in his shade/When in eternal lines to time thou grow'st." These sentiments are underlined in the final couplet: "So long as men can breathe or eyes can see/So long lives this, and this gives life to thee."

This sonnet, like the others in Shakespeare's sequence of 154 sonnets, exemplifies the rhyme and meter of the so-called English, or Shakespearean, sonnet. The rhyme scheme is abab, cdcd, efef, gg—that is, there are three stanzas of four lines each, followed by a final couplet. The meter is iambic pentameter: Each line has five "iambs"—an unstressed syllable followed by a stressed one, the most common meter in English.

Shakespeare's sonnets flow musically when read aloud. The "I" of the sonnets (all are written in the first person) speaks to readers across the centuries of love and its related emotions—longing, jealousy, frustration, and loss—as well as of the enduring power of the art that captures these emotions. The sonnets have been variously interpreted; undoubtedly they do, when read in sequence, unfold a narrative that in part depicts the triangular relationship among the "I" whom we hear, the fair young man addressed in sonnet 18 and in many others, and the "dark lady" loved by both men.

An esteemed literary genre since it developed in Italy in the 13th century, the sonnet remains an elegant and enduring form of lyric poetry. Sonnet 18, along with the rest of Shakespeare's sequence, was first published in 1609. Still popular with readers today, the sonnets have also been a source for other works, including musical interpretations.

Mother Teresa (1910–1997)

IN HIS EULOGY TO Mother Teresa following her death in September 1997, former U.N. Secretary-General Javier Perez de Cuellar stated, "She is the United Nations. She is peace in the world." During her 70 years as a missionary, Mother Teresa and her religious order, the Missionaries of Charity, touched the lives of hundreds of thousands of poor, dying, and homeless people around the globe.

Mother Teresa was born Agnes Gonxha Bojaxhiu in what is now Skopje, Macedonia. At age 12, she decided that she wanted to be a missionary, and at 18 she joined the Sisters of Loreto, an Irish order with missions in India. In Calcutta, she taught in a high school for approximately 17 years before receiving a "call within a call," which she attributed to God, to minister to the poor and sick of the city. She received permission in 1948 to leave the cloistered life of the Sisters of Loreto to pursue her calling in the slums of Calcutta. Two years later, the Vatican gave her the authority to form her own order, the Missionaries of Charity.

Within two years, Mother Teresa opened her first hospice in Calcutta. "A beautiful death," she declared, "is for people who lived like animals to die like angels." Her order opened a leper colony and a number of centers throughout the city to administer to the needs of orphans, the disabled, and the elderly. As her order grew, Mother Teresa opened more homes for poor, sick, and dying people across the world. Later, as the AIDS epidemic spread around the world, it also became a focus of her ministry. Mother Teresa would go on to win many humanitarian awards for her works of mercy, including the Nobel Peace Prize in 1979. She donated her prize money to the poor in India.

She continued her ministry even after two heart attacks and bouts of pneumonia. However, a serious fall and the onset of pneumonia in 1996 forced Mother Teresa to step down as the head of the Missionaries of Charity in March 1997. She died six months later. By the time of her death, her order had grown to include more than 4,000 sisters and one million lay followers, as well as missions in more than 90 countries. Her legacy continues to this day with the works of her many followers around the world.

Birth of a Nation

THE 1915 FILM *Birth of a Nation* by producer/director D. W. Griffith has been hailed as an American masterpiece. But it has also been decried for its racist and vicious portrayal of African Americans. So virulent is its message that the film has been used as a recruitment tool by the Ku Klux Klan.

Based on a play called *The Clansman: An Historical Romance of the Ku Klux Klan* by North Carolina Baptist minister Thomas Dixon, Jr., the film romanticizes slavery, the Old South, and the KKK. Klan members are heroes, while blacks are denigrated by the most offensive stereotypes; they are portrayed either as criminals and rapists or as faithful "darkies."

The three-hour film—the longest film produced up to that date—covers the events leading up to the pre-Civil War era through the postwar rise of the KKK. It concludes with the KKK successfully protecting white society from the insidious black threat. Adding to the insult, whites in blackface were given the major black roles in the movie. Only minor roles were played by African Americans.

Despite its racist theme, *Birth of a Nation* is an important film in American movie history because of its many pioneering technical achievements. The film was the first to use night photography, parallel action, the still-shot, fade-outs and cameo profiles, a color sequence, elaborate and authentic costuming, and its own musical score. These and other technical innovations laid the groundwork for future generations of filmmakers.

Originally budgeted at $40,000, the movie cost $110,000 to make, but it became one of the biggest box office smashes in history. It remained the top moneymaker until 1937, when it was finally eclipsed by Disney's *Snow White and the Seven Dwarfs.*

The film's depiction of race relations brought an immediate outcry from the newly formed National Association for the Advancement of Colored People (NAACP). The movie sparked riots in Boston and Philadelphia. Some cities banned the film outright, and it was picketed by protestors in other locations. Ironically, this attention only enhanced the film's box office appeal.

In an attempt to answer the film's critics, D. W. Griffith subsequently made a sequel called *Intolerance,* which chronicled prejudice through the ages. *Birth of a Nation* was voted into the National Film Registry in 1993 and was voted one of the "Top 100 American Films" by the American Film Institute in 1998.

Mozart's *Le Mariage du Figaro*

WOLFGANG AMADEUS MOZART (1756–1791) became accustomed to being treated as the darling of the European aristocracy during his international travels as a child prodigy. Having seen the great capitals of Europe and enjoyed their exciting cultural life, the younger Mozart was seriously disappointed when his father—sensibly—suggested that he settle down in Salzburg, their hometown, to a respectable position in the employ of the ruler of that provincial capital.

While the exact circumstances of Mozart's departure from Salzburg are subject to debate—was he let go because of his lack of commitment to the job, or did he quit?—it's certain that his goal was to try his luck in the imperial capital, Vienna. Although he had some success displaying his extraordinary keyboard skills, Mozart resolved to make a splash with Italian comic opera, which he knew was well loved by the Viennese upper classes and especially the imperial family.

Collaborating with Italian librettist Lorenzo Da Ponte (with whom Mozart went on to create *Don Giovanni* in 1787 and *Così Fan Tutte* in 1790), he settled in 1784 on a reworking of a play by Beaumarchais, *Le Mariage du Figaro*. The Beaumarchais play was rife with provocative statements about the misdeeds of the nobility and the equality of men, and its performance was banned in Vienna because of its potentially seditious nature.

In his memoirs, Da Ponte claims that Emperor Joseph of Austria himself asked him and Mozart to create an operatic *Figaro*. While Da Ponte was notoriously self-aggrandizing, there may be an element of truth to his story, since the opera transforms what was originally a play about class conflict into a romantic comedy of errors, thereby making it "safe for public consumption."

While there are a number of *set pieces* (arias) for each of the lead characters, Italian comic opera in Mozart's day was characterized by ensemble numbers in which two or more characters (sometimes up to five or six in the final scene of an act) sing simultaneously about conflicting emotions. Mozart was especially intrigued by the musical and dramatic opportunities provided in these scenes, and he applied marvelous care and tremendous skill to create ensembles that were both hilarious and deceptively complex.

Le Mariage du Figaro was well received at its Vienna premiere in 1786 and was an even greater success later that year in Prague. It had a revival in Vienna in 1789 and has gone on to be one of the most popular and often performed operas of all time.

Transgenic Crops

IN OCTOBER 2007, Monsanto Company announced that the South African government had granted permission to begin field trials of a type of drought-resistant maize. A product of genetic engineering, these corn plants have a "drought gene" that increases the efficiency of water use and enhances tolerance to the absence of water. Drought-resistant maize is one example of a transgenic crop.

A genetically modified crop is called a *transgenic crop* because scientists have added at least one foreign gene—the *transgene*—to the plant's normal genetic material. Farmers initiated the first significant commercial planting of transgenic crops in 1996. A decade later, farmers planted more than 252 million acres of genetically engineered crops in 22 countries.

The first generation of transgenic crops had traits that improved production. Many early efforts focused on engineering crops that synthesized their own insecticidal proteins, eliminating the need for farmers to spray hazardous and costly chemical insecticides. One approach took advantage of toxin genes from the bacterium *Bacillus thuringiensis*. These Bt toxins typically target a limited number of insect species and do not directly affect other animals, such as humans.

Early types of transgenic crops also addressed the problem of weed infestation, which causes the loss of about 10 percent of the global production of conventional crops every year. This occurs despite an investment of $10 billion on more than 100 different chemical herbicides. Researchers designed transgenic crops for tolerance to the herbicide glyphosate, a chemical that readily degrades to nontoxic compounds in the soil. Farmers can limit herbicide application to treat weeds as needed without concerns about destroying their glyphosate-tolerant crops.

Some of the more recent types of transgenic crops have genes that enhance flavor, nutritional value, and other qualities for consumers. Golden Rice is such a crop. This engineered plant produces provitamin A in the grains, thus providing a valuable nutrient through an inexpensive and plentiful type of food.

Risks accompany the benefits of transgenic crops. In 2007, scientists revealed an unintended effect of transgenic corn that produces a Bt toxin. Byproducts of a transgenic corn crop, such as pollen, entered nearby streams. Laboratory studies showed that the Bt toxin kills nontarget insects that live in streams. Since fish and other animals eat these stream insects, the transgenic crop may produce an unexpected effect on the ecosystem.

The Pre-Raphaelite Brotherhood

IN 1848, THE PAINTERS William Holman Hunt (1827–1910), John Everett Millais (1829–1896), and Dante Gabriel Rossetti (1828–1882) formed a society they called the "Pre-Raphaelite Brotherhood." Over the next decade or so, a number of other artists and writers, including Rossetti's sister, poet Christina (1830–1894), would come to be identified with the group. The eminent Victorian writer John Ruskin (1819–1900), who called for "truth" in the depiction of nature, became their most ardent champion. By the end of the century, however, the Pre-Raphaelite style would be dismissed as sentimental and moralizing. But today these artists are enjoying renewed interest.

Initially, the aim of the brotherhood was to restore authentic expression and spiritual conviction to British art. These were the qualities the artists believed had been lost with the advent of the Renaissance at the end of the 15th century. The term "pre-Raphaelite" was a common designation for Italian artists working at the end of the Middle Ages. The founding members modeled their society on a fanciful sense of the medieval craft guild. When their paintings were first shown in 1849, all were signed with the initials "PRB." Journalists tried to guess the meaning of this mysterious acronym: "Please Ring Bell" was one suggestion; others were more colorful and often indecent.

At first, the artists of the Brotherhood favored strong, clear contours, traditional symbolism, and iconic gestures. Authors from Dante Alighieri (1265–1321) to William Shakespeare (1564–1616), John Keats (1795–1821), and Alfred Lord Tennyson (1809–1892), as well as Arthurian legends, fairy tales, and biblical stories provided their sub-

Ophelia *by John Millais*

ject matter. Painstaking technique rendered all details in the same sharp focus. A commitment to accurate optical effects often led to dangerous practices. When Millais painted his masterpiece, *Ophelia* (1851–1852), he put his model, Elizabeth Siddall, fully clothed into a tub of water to more accurately portray Shakespeare's drowned heroine. Millais became so absorbed in his work that he failed to notice that the oil lamps that warmed the water had gone out, and Siddall, thoroughly chilled, fell ill.

Never a stylistically coherent group, the artists quickly directed their energies into highly individualized approaches. By 1854, the original group had largely disbanded.

Queen Victoria

Q UEEN VICTORIA (1819–1901) WAS THE longest-ruling monarch in British history, serving as queen of the United Kingdom from 1837 and as empress of India from 1876 until her death in 1901. During her reign, Britain became the world's greatest imperial power.

Raised in isolation from the Hanoverian court, Victoria took the throne in 1837 when she was only 18 years old.

The political power of the British monarchy was already in decline, but Victoria had received a political education in the letters of her uncle, King Leopold of Belgium, and had a clear understanding of both her constitutional role and her prerogatives. She quickly confounded politicians who expected to dominate an inexperienced young woman. From her accession to her death, Victoria confidently exercised the power of appointing government ministers and what constitutional theorist Walter Bagehot described as "the right to be consulted, the right to encourage, the right to warn."

Victoria's relationships with her prime ministers were often personal as well as political. This was particularly true with the two great political rivals of the era, Benjamin Disraeli and William Gladstone. She adored Disraeli, who charmed and flattered her, and disliked Gladstone, who she complained addressed her as if she were a public meeting.

Victoria found a new political mentor in 1840, when she married Prince Albert of Saxe-Coburg and Gotha, with whom she had nine children. She was so strongly influenced by her husband that Albert was king in all but name, and the two worked closely together. Victoria read the official documents, discussed them with Albert, and corresponded with her ministers. Albert often drafted her responses. When Albert died in 1861, the "Widow of Windsor" went into deep mourning and lived in virtual seclusion. She continued to read and respond to state documents, as she had when Albert was alive, but she neglected her ceremonial duties and rarely went to London.

Popular criticism of the monarchy grew through 1871, fueled by her son Edward's (the prince of Wales) playboy reputation as well as the queen's isolation. In 1872, Edward suffered a serious attack of typhoid. Bullied into attending a service of thanksgiving on his recovery, Victoria was surprised and pleased by the enthusiasm with which she was greeted by the London crowds. She gradually reentered the ceremonial life of the nation, though she continued to wear mourning clothes until her death. From 1872 on, her popularity steadily increased.

Charlotte Brontë's *Jane Eyre*

*J*ANE EYRE, THE MONUMENTAL novel by Charlotte Brontë (1816–1855) published in 1847, contains Gothic and romantic elements and complex psychological realism. This bildungsroman (novel of development) follows the orphaned Jane Eyre into maturity and eventually marriage. Small and plain, Jane is also bright and courageous; the novel depicts her need to break through the restraints imposed on her by class, gender, and societal hypocrisy.

The novel's first sentence—"There was no possibility of taking a walk that day"—moves the reader immediately into the claustrophobic world inhabited by Jane. She lives with her Aunt Reed, who resents her late husband's injunction to care for his niece. When Jane rebels against the cruelty of her cousins, she is unjustly punished and later sent to Lowood, a charity school where the girls are neglected, underfed, and preached to by Mr. Brocklehurst, the self-righteous headmaster.

The novel contains certain autobiographical elements. Lowood is modeled on the Clergy Daughters School at Cowan Bridge, a school where two of Charlotte's sisters died of consumption, circumstances evoked in the novel by the death of Jane's friend Helen Burns. Brontë herself was briefly a governess, as is Jane, who leaves Lowood as a young woman to take a position at Thornfield, a manor belonging to the darkly mysterious Edward Rochester.

Thornfield, despite the frightening and unexplained events that occur there—such as screams in the night and bedclothes set on fire—becomes a place of increasing happiness for Jane, who is fond of her pupil, Adele, and treated respectfully by her employer. The story of Jane and Rochester's growing love for each other is remarkable for its delineation of the psychological needs of women. In an often-quoted passage, Jane insists that women "need exercise for their faculties, and a field for their efforts as much as their brothers do; they suffer from too rigid a restraint, too absolute a stagnation, precisely as men would suffer."

When Rochester is forced to admit that he has a wife—a madwoman kept confined to the attic at Thornfield—Jane leaves rather than living with him as his wife, as he has urged her to do. The ensuing narrative, often melodramatic, nevertheless allows Brontë to explore the status of women in the 19th century. Eventually, the widowed Rochester and Jane are reunited as equals, a necessary condition for their happiness, according to Brontë.

One of the best-loved English works, *Jane Eyre* is studied today in schools and universities and has often been adapted for film and television.

Martin Luther King, Jr. (1929–1968)

IN A 1967 SPEECH, Martin Luther King, Jr., proclaimed: "Discrimination is a hellhound that gnaws at Negroes in every waking moment of their lives to remind them that the lie of their inferiority is accepted as truth in the society dominating them." Beginning with the December 1955 Montgomery bus boycott until his death 13 years later, King devoted his life to freeing not only African Americans, but all people from all forms of discrimination.

While a student at Morehouse College in Atlanta, Georgia, King originally intended to break with family tradition and become something other than a Baptist minister. However, he changed his mind during his senior year and entered the ministry. After completing a doctorate, King and his wife, Coretta Scott, moved to Montgomery, Alabama, in 1953. He became pastor of the Dexter Avenue Baptist Church. His popularity in the church led to his election as president of the Montgomery Improvement Association, which was formed following the arrest of Rosa Parks, who had refused to surrender her bus seat to a white passenger. King led a city bus boycott that lasted for more than a year and ended with the desegregation of Montgomery buses.

In 1957, King also became a founding member of the Southern Christian Leadership Conference. The group united African American churches throughout the South in a nonviolent movement to secure the civil rights of their members. As a student of the nonviolent philosophy of India's Gandhi, King tirelessly worked to spread his belief that peaceful resistance was the only way for the oppressed to gain freedom. He attracted many charismatic African American leaders, such as Ralph Abernathy and Jesse Jackson, to his cause.

King led a series of nonviolent protests throughout the South during the 1960s. Although jailed on numerous occasions, he never faltered in his quest to bring civil rights to African Americans. During the historic March on Washington on August 28, 1963, more than 250,000 people heard King's famous "I Have a Dream" speech. He spoke of his longing for the day when all of humankind would join together and proclaim, "Free at last! Free at last! Thank God Almighty, we are free at last!"

King made his last public appearance on the night of April 3, 1968. In his speech, he said, "I've seen the promised land. I may not get there with you. But I want you to know tonight that we, as people, will get to the Promised Land." The next day, he was assassinated by James Earl Ray.

Adam Smith's *Wealth of Nations*

ADAM SMITH'S *An Inquiry into the Nature and Causes of the Wealth of Nations,* published in 1776, was the first comprehensive treatment of political economy.

Smith was an important figure in what is now called the Scottish Enlightenment, a movement that included such luminaries as David Hume, John Home, Lord Hailies, and Principal Robertson. He was educated at the University of Glasgow and Oxford University. In 1751, he was elected chair of logic at the University of Glasgow and then became chair of moral philosophy the following year. He traveled to Europe in 1754, while tutoring the young Duke of Buccleuch. During his travels, he met notable European intellectuals, including Voltaire and Rousseau. He also met Francois Quesnay, founder of the school of economics known as physiocracy, which proposed that a nation's wealth could only come from agriculture or land use.

In 1776, Smith published *Wealth of Nations,* which he intended to be the first volume of a complete theory of society. Originally delivered as lectures at Glasgow, Smith's work examined in detail the division of labor, the function of markets, and the law of supply and demand. In addition, he examined the nature, accumulation, and use of capital and the implications of a free economy. His work was also filled with side excursions into subjects as diverse as the manufacture of pins, the opulence of the Abbasid Caliphate, and statistics of the herring catch.

Importantly, in *Wealth of Nations,* Smith attacks the concept of mercantilism, with its elaborate system of regulations, tariffs, and monetary controls. He also rails against the belief of the French physiocrats that land, not labor, is the basis of wealth. In place of mercantilism, Smith proposes a system of "natural liberty," in which the "invisible hand" of the marketplace is left unimpeded by government interference. According to Smith, self-interest drives people to produce what society needs. He contends that self-interest also provides the competition that regulates pricing, supply, and quality to the benefit of the community as a whole. Coining the phrase "nation of shopkeepers," Smith created a newly democratic vision of wealth, in which the market, left to regulate itself, would bring prosperity to all. He claimed, "No society can surely be flourishing and happy, of which by far the greater part of the numbers are poor and miserable." Smith's principles would ultimately lead to the more extreme 19th-century policies of free trade and laissez-faire, which promoted government noninterference in economic affairs.

Giuseppe Verdi

IF OPERA IS quintessentially and stereotypically Italian, the individual who personifies opera in the Italian imagination is, without question, Giuseppe Verdi (1813–1901). Every Italian town has a street named after Verdi, and it's usually a central thoroughfare. His works are the most frequently performed operas throughout the world. In fact, most pop-culture depictions of opera (with the exception of the fat lady with horns, a Wagnerian icon) are derived from either Verdi's music or imagery.

Indeed, Verdi is still celebrated as a hero of Italian national identity, and in his own lifetime he was lionized as the greatest living Italian artist. His funeral became a national event, with hundreds of thousands of people lining the streets and huge ensembles performing excerpts from his most popular operas. Verdi's early career belies this end-of-life grandeur: Born in a small town far from the centers of operatic activity, he was refused admission to the Milan conservatory because his keyboard technique was poor. This perhaps contributed to Verdi's mystique, since he became a self-made composer.

Following a couple of early successes, he wrote the opera *Nabucco* (1842), in which the customary love story is set during Jewish captivity in Babylon. A memorable chorus of Israelites pining for their lost homeland ("Va pensiero") was swept up into political and cultural efforts to create a unified Italian nation, and this became one of Verdi's most performed works.

As his career began to take off, Verdi struck up a relationship with one of the star singers for whom he was contracted to write: Giuseppina Strepponi, who initially was a much more successful professional than Verdi and who helped him build his reputation. The two lived together unmarried for almost a decade to the shock of many of Verdi's contemporaries. (They married in 1859.) By this point, however, Verdi's popular and financial success allowed him to scorn what he considered small-minded public opinion.

Verdi built his success partly through the mass marketing of excerpts and arrangements from his operas as sheet music. His tendency toward catchy songwriting (both in solo/duet "set pieces" and in choral numbers) facilitated this practice, and he was the first operatic composer to forge contracts that would bring him percentages of music-sales revenue. Eventually, Verdi's works (such as *Rigoletto,* 1851, and *La Traviata,* 1853) became so popular that they passed into regular repertory. He began writing less and less new music and had to be coaxed by his friend (and publisher/producer) Ricordi to write his last two operas, *Otello* and *Falstaff,* which many consider his most sophisticated works.

Insulin Resistance

INSULIN, A HORMONE SECRETED by the pancreas, plays a vital role in regulating the body's use of glucose, its main energy source. Glucose must enter cells before it can be used, and this is where insulin comes in. Insulin binds to receptor proteins located on the surfaces of cells, initiating changes that allow glucose to travel from the blood into the cell's interior. Once inside a cell, glucose can be used for energy or stored in another chemical form.

In some people, the immune system destroys the pancreatic cells that produce insulin. The loss of insulin production eliminates the body's ability to regulate blood glucose, resulting in Type 1 diabetes (formerly called juvenile diabetes).

In other people, the pancreas produces insulin, but cells cannot respond to the hormone even if they carry insulin receptors. Blood glucose levels rise. The body's regulatory mechanisms sense abnormally high glucose concentrations and signal the pancreas to secrete more insulin proteins, which accumulate in the bloodstream. This is a condition known as insulin resistance syndrome.

Insulin resistance usually fails to produce outward physical symptoms. However, the condition is far from benign. People who have abnormally high blood glucose levels risk the development of the most common form of diabetes mellitus, Type 2 diabetes. With this form of diabetes, people must closely regulate and manage their blood sugar levels to prevent serious complications, such as heart disease, kidney disease, or foot problems.

While the cause of insulin resistance remains unclear, studies have revealed a genetic susceptibility to the disorder. One or more genetic mutations may alter the cellular mechanism that translates insulin-receptor binding into a signal to allow an influx of blood glucose. In 2007, researchers at the University of Alabama at Birmingham identified two genes that appear to boost insulin sensitivity in muscle cells. This discovery suggests that one day insulin resistance may be treated by gene therapy.

Meanwhile, two low-tech approaches can help those who have insulin resistance syndrome: exercise and improved diet. Excess weight contributes to insulin resistance, and obesity is a factor that paves the road to Type 2 diabetes. Researchers have found that a low-fat, low-calorie diet coupled with increased physical activity can lower blood glucose concentrations to a normal level.

Vincent van Gogh and Paul Gauguin in Arles

DUTCH ARTIST VINCENT VAN GOGH (1853–1890) worked as a preacher and missionary before devoting himself to art in 1880. He preferred to work from nature. "I cannot work without a model," he wrote. "I am too afraid of departing from the possible and the true."

Paul Gauguin (1848–1903) lived in Peru with his maternal relatives as a child, worked briefly as a hand on a cargo ship, and enjoyed financial security as a stockbroker in Paris before devoting his life to art. In contrast to van Gogh, Gauguin based his work in imagination, and he advised a fellow artist, "Do not paint too much after nature. Art is an abstraction."

In the spring of 1888, van Gogh traveled to Arles in Provence, France, to establish a "Studio of the South." He envisioned a community of modern artists who would share their lives and ideas and create masterpieces of modern art. The companion he most desired was Paul Gauguin. Van Gogh begged and nagged Gauguin to join him. He even offered a bribe of sorts, persuading his brother Theo van Gogh, an art dealer in Paris, to guarantee living expenses in return for the pictures Gauguin would paint.

Van Gogh Painting *by Paul Gauguin*

Eventually, Gauguin agreed to come, after repeated delays and much foot-dragging. His tumultuous sojourn in Arles would last only nine weeks, ending on Christmas Day. Gaugin left Arles after the unstable van Gogh tried to attack him with a razor, then cut off part of his own ear.

Despite their differences—or because of them—van Gogh and Gauguin produced an important body of work during their short time together in Arles. They visited the same locales, including the Alyscamps, a medieval avenue lined by tomb fragments and church ruins. They painted portraits of the same people. They recorded the crowds at the Roman arena in Arles and women washing clothes in the canal. Their constant proximity also helped clarify their distinctive visions.

The relationship between van Gogh and Gauguin ultimately inspired some of their most important work.

Nelson Rolihlahla Mandela

THE 1990s WERE MARKED by a series of remarkable liberation move-ments, including the collapse of the apartheid system in South Africa, a rigid and often violent program of racial separation of the black majority from the white minority that had been in place since 1948. Nelson Mandela (1918–present) was one of the most important black figures associated with the end of apartheid.

Mandela was born into relative comfort; his father was the chief of the Tembu tribe in Transkei. Mandela was educated at the prestigious University of Witwatersrand and became a lawyer in 1942. Two years later, he joined the African National Congress (ANC), a largely black organization dedicated to the support of black rights in South Africa. After the first apartheid laws were passed in 1948, the ANC increasingly resisted the ruling National Party's separation policies. Mandela was acquitted of treason charges in 1961, a year after the government banned the ANC, but was later arrested after setting up a military wing of the organization and urging violent resistance to the regime. He was convicted of conspiring to overthrow the government by violence in 1964 and sentenced to life in prison.

Over the next quarter century, Mandela's stature grew as a symbol of resistance to oppression. While he was in jail, other opponents of apartheid, especially Bishop Desmond Tutu, continued their support of Mandela and the resistance movement. Mandela himself consistently refused freedom in return for a renunciation of violence, arguing that such a threat was regrettably the only way such an evil and entrenched system could be confronted.

A number of powerful nations, including the United States and Great Britain, condemned the system of apartheid and applied economic sanctions on South Africa. By 1990, world opinion had so turned against South Africa that F. W. De Klerk, the newly elected head of the Nationalist government, began the process of dismantling apartheid. He lifted the ban on the ANC, unconditionally released Mandela from prison, rescinded separation laws, and opened the way for a drafting of a new constitution that was based on the principle of universal voting rights.

Mandela and De Klerk jointly won the Nobel Peace Prize in 1993, and in 1994 Nelson Mandela became the first democratically elected president in the history of South Africa. He served as president until 1999, when he retired from public life. He has traveled extensively since then, giving speeches and consulting with world leaders. Mandela lives in Qunu, the village in which he was born.

Beloved

BELOVED (1987) IS A NOVEL by Toni Morrison. It won the Pulitzer Prize in 1988, and in 1993 Morrison became the first African American woman to win the Nobel Prize for Literature. In 1998, a movie version of *Beloved* was filmed with Oprah Winfrey as the protagonist, Sethe.

Stylistically experimental, *Beloved* is told in fragments and has a supernatural quality. Morrison writes in this manner because her subject matter—the long-term psychological effects of the slave experience—is too intense and horrifying for a traditional telling.

Beloved is inspired by the true story of Margaret Garner, an American slave woman who escaped a Kentucky plantation with her husband. She fled to Ohio, was caught, and consequently killed her baby to save it from a life of slavery. In *Beloved,* Sethe tries to kill several of her children to keep them from becoming slaves but only succeeds with her unnamed infant. When the infant is buried, its tombstone reads "Beloved" because Sethe does not have enough money to pay for the phrase "Dearly Beloved."

Other characters in *Beloved* include Sixo, who "stopped speaking English because there was no future in it" and Baby Suggs, who makes her living with her heart because slavery "had busted her legs, back, head, eyes, hands, kidneys, womb, and tongue."

At one point in the story, Sethe is living with her teenaged daughter, Denver, in a house haunted by Beloved's ghost. A man named Paul D., with a rusted metal box for a heart, visits Sethe and drives the ghost from the house. Sethe and Paul D. become lovers. Sethe eventually becomes so violent that Denver abandons her. Later, Sethe is found at the house with the naked, pregnant body of Beloved. The spell breaks, Beloved vanishes, and Paul D. returns to care for Sethe.

Daughter of a welder who fled the South for greater freedom, Toni Morrison was born Chloe Anthony Wofford in Ohio on February 18, 1931. She was educated at Howard and Cornell universities, changing her first name to Toni because it was easier to pronounce. After graduating, she taught college and worked as a book editor, marrying Harold Morrison in 1958 and having two children. She began writing fiction in the late 1960s and published her first novel, *The Bluest Eye,* in 1970. To date, she has written eight novels and several volumes of essays, including her Nobel Prize acceptance speech.

Sigmund Freud (1856–1939)

ONE OF THE MOST IMPORTANT thinkers of the 20th century, Sigmund Freud helped change the way we think about ourselves, our motives, and our minds. He was born into a relatively prosperous Jewish family in Moravia. His mother, only 21 when he was born, was 20 years younger than his father, a successful wool merchant. His family moved to Vienna in 1860, mainly because the city had rescinded many of the laws discriminating against Jews. A bright young man, Freud studied medicine at the University of Vienna.

Working at Vienna's General Hospital, Freud became interested in psychiatry while studying the effects of hypnosis on the treatment of women suffering from hysteria. He opened a private practice in 1886 and by 1896 had found what he saw as the key to his work—the use of free association to delve into the mysteries of the unconscious mind, especially through the analysis of patients' dreams. In 1900, he published his first major work, *The Interpretation of Dreams,* which spurred the spread of psychoanalysis. Over the next 39 years, Freud continued to refine his work while teaching, writing, and lecturing, in addition to keeping up his private practice. When the Nazis came to power in Germany (and burned his books as subversive), he migrated to London, where he died of throat cancer in 1939.

Freud's most lasting accomplishment was the refinement and popularization of the concept of the unconscious. In contrast to the idea that human action was the product of rational decisions, Freud argued that the desires and instincts existing beneath consciousness determined much of human behavior—and mental illness. He saw sexual desire as the most powerful of all human instincts and the refusal to recognize this desire as the root of much mental illness.

Since his death (and even before), many of his theories have come under attack—especially his focus on sexuality. Also, the growth of cognitive psychology and the discovery of the importance of the brain's electrical and chemical activity have called into question Freud's method of analyzing mental illnesses. Whereas Freud primarily used talk therapy, many mental illnesses today are treated with drugs. Perhaps his most lasting impact has been on culture, as psychoanalytic approaches to biographical, historical, and literary production and analysis blossomed in the 20th century. Freudian terminology has also influenced popular culture, with terms like *Oedipus complex, penis envy,* and *phallic symbol* gaining widespread acceptance. It is a different world because of Sigmund Freud.

Honoré Daumier: Politics and Art

POLITICAL UPHEAVAL was a fact of life in 19th-century France, with periods of relative calm under republican leadership alternating with oppressive, nearly tyrannical administrations. Following the reign of Napoleon I, a series of constitutional monarchs ruled France. In 1830, the "July Revolution" brought Louis-Philippe, the so-called "citizen king," to power. Initially, the new regime seemed like an improvement. Soon enough, however, the government began restricting the freedom of the press and deployed military forces to unruly areas of Paris.

Following these crackdowns, artist Honoré Daumier (1808–1879) responded with a series of devastating lithographs that were published in popular newspapers. In the most notorious picture, Daumier portrayed Louis-Philippe as the giant Gargantua, swallowing up the nation's wealth and excreting it as honors and favors to a privileged few. For this and other works, Daumier was sentenced to six months in prison.

In 1834, inspired by real events, Daumier created an image that, with its sobriety and realism, was even more shocking than his previous work. While attempting to quell a demonstration by poor workers in Paris, a member of the civil guard was shot by an unidentified sniper. Believing that the shot had come from an apartment block where many workers lived, police raided the building and massacred the inhabitants.

Rue Transnonain

Simply titled *Rue Transnonain, le 15 Avril 1834* to name the location and date of the event, Daumier's work is visually powerful. Looking into the image is almost like adjusting to darkness after coming in from a sunny day. Illuminated by a bright light that shines into the room, a man in a bloodied nightshirt lays sprawled on the floor next to a bed. An overturned chair next to his body suggests that a violent struggle has occurred. Lying in the shadows on either side of the man are the bodies of a woman and an old man. Perhaps the most gruesome figure is a toddler, lying under the illuminated man's body in a puddle of blood.

Daumier's work also uses strong symbolism. The man's form, with his straight legs and outstretched arm, evokes images of the crucifixion of Christ. By alluding to that event, Daumier essentially casts Paris's poor as modern-day martyrs. Although Daumier did not personally witness the event, his deeply evocative scene proves to be more eloquent than his most scathing caricatures.

Music and the French Revolution

THE REVOLUTION IN FRANCE (1789–1799) had crucial and long-lasting political and social effects, and its influence on music was just as dramatic. Musical life in France had officially revolved around the king for almost two centuries; as the Revolutionary government attempted to cleanse society of royalist influences, musicians had to quickly disassociate themselves from the practices and traditions that had defined court music.

Musical theater continued to flourish, but both themes and musical styles were modified to suit the narratives of equality and simplicity that were at the root of the revolutionary effort. The so-called "rescue opera" genre—in which a heroic "commoner" male character, assisted by his comrades, would save his beloved from the clutches of an oppressive powerful nobleman—became quite popular, and its musical and emotional intensity was influential well outside of France. The one opera that Beethoven completed, *Fidelio* (1805), is in the mold of a "rescue opera."

Musicians who had been employed by the Catholic Church—long the most widespread patron of music, and now outlawed by the revolutionary government—retooled their approach for the new celebratory humanistic hymns. Indeed, the notion of a "national hymn"—a grand musical resource to celebrate the power and righteousness of the collective government—was created in this circumstance as a reconfiguration of "God Save the King," which had long been used to celebrate the union of royal and divine power. "La Marseillaise," written in 1792, is still the national anthem of France.

More importantly, the revolutionary government wished to establish its legitimacy through collective musical celebrations in which hundreds or thousands of French citizens would unite to praise their solidarity. This meant that there was a need for basic training in music (both singing and instrumental) for the masses. For this purpose the government established the Paris Conservatory in 1795, which provided free music education through a standard curriculum.

While the Revolution met an unhappy end, the Conservatory flourished and became a model for many such institutions both in France's territories and abroad. It still stands as a dominant force in French musical and artistic life. Additionally, the emphasis on collective and public music-making through amateur or semiprofessional bands led to a widespread commitment to innovation and mass marketing in instrument manufacturing, bringing about the popularity of band music in both Europe and North America throughout the 1800s and to the present day.

Meteors

WHY DID THE DINOSAURS die out? Many scientists blame meteors. These chunks of rock travel through space and occasionally collide with planets and moons. Scientists believe that 65 million years ago a huge meteor created the vast Chicxulub crater in Central America's Yucátan Peninsula. Similar craters in other parts of the earth date from the same time. That happens to be the era during which the dinosaurs disappeared. Scientists speculate that dust sent up by the meteor impacts changed Earth's temperature. Dinosaurs became extinct because they were less able to adapt to the new conditions than mammals were.

You can see the devastation that meteors cause by looking at the moon or Mars through a telescope. Craters cover their surfaces. Those stark landscapes differ greatly from the gentle contours of much of Earth's surface. Earth's atmosphere protects it from the impact of meteorites and other objects careening through space.

Most of the billions of objects that enter our atmosphere each day burn up long before they reach the surface. We see them as shooting stars. However, larger objects flying in from space don't burn up entirely. The Chicxulub crater provides one such example. Geologists believe that a meteor the size of Mount Everest caused a crater in Northwest Australia that killed off 90 percent of the species on Earth 251 million years ago.

Meteor collisions didn't happen only in the distant past. In June 1908, an explosion above the Siberian region of Tunguska flattened trees over an area of 800 square miles. Scientists believe that the breakup of a meteor caused the explosion. However, we don't need to worry about this happening again. NASA has a Near Earth Object Program that continuously watches out for approaching meteors or other objects. It would identify a threat in time to take action to divert it.

POSTSCRIPT

- In October 1992, fragments of a burnt-up meteor fell through an automobile in a driveway in Peekskill, New York.

- Records from throughout the world show that no human has died because of a meteorite impact for 500 years. But falling rocks that might have been caused by the descent of a large asteroid killed several thousand people in China's Shanxi province in 1490.

Abstraction as Realism: Cubism

CUBISM IN ART IS SOMETHING of a paradox. On the one hand, a cubist painting often conveys a great deal of information about the subject. On the other, the artist presents the subject in a way that looks unrealistic and abstract. Cubism was the most common style among the modern artists working in Paris from 1910 to 1920 and has remained an important method in painting—and other art forms—since then.

Cubism is practically synonymous with artist Pablo Picasso (1881–1973), but it was actually named for the paintings of "little cubes" made by Georges Braque (1882–1963) around 1907. Cubism freed painters from the rules of composition that had been in place for almost 500 years. For centuries, artists had defined a picture as an "illusion of space." The surface of the painting was supposed to be a transparent plane, like a glass window, that separated the real space of the viewer from the imaginary space inside the picture. This approach seemed truthful, even scientific, because it matched the empirical experience of the view. In other words, the more a picture resembled visual experience, the better it expressed reality.

At the beginning of the 20th century, however, discoveries in science supported artistic experiments that led painters away from traditional representation. Among these discoveries was *Relativity: The Special and General Theory* published in 1905 by Albert Einstein. Special relativity linked time and space together, making each dependent on the other. Thinking about time and space as a continuum led to the equally astonishing idea that matter and energy are different but equivalent conditions.

What does this have to do with the way artists make a picture? It suggested that what the eyes see may not be the truth about the way things are. Space is not the neat, geometric cube of Renaissance thinking. Space, moreover, is not separate from the things—people and buildings, fruit bowls and musical instruments—that it contains. Space can penetrate volumes; parts of an object can be disconnected from the whole; objects can be seen from many points of view at the same time.

In early Cubist paintings—in the phase known as "Analytic Cubism," in which the subjects were "analyzed"—the subject could usually be clearly seen. By around 1910, the images had become almost complete abstractions. This phase was known as "Synthetic Cubism."

Cubist ideas and theories were also seen in sculpture, poetry, architecture, and even music. They heavily influenced later art movements such as Dadaism and Surrealism.

Julius Caesar

Thanks to William Shakespeare, much of the English world knows about Julius Caesar and his assassination on the Ides of March in 44 B.C. When Caesar was born in 100 B.C., Rome was in turmoil as generals and politicians struggled for supremacy in the dying Republic. Although Caesar's family was an old and respected one, he had no real political connections. As a young man, Caesar served in the military in Asia Minor, then he began his slow rise as an orator of note and a crafty politician.

Caesar's political dealings landed him deeply in debt, and he also made numerous enemies in Rome. To further his career, he allied himself with Crassus and Pompey, two powerful men whose ambitions matched his own. As a result, in 58 B.C. Caesar received the governorship of three provinces whose territory bordered northern Italy. With four legions, Caesar enlarged his territory by conquering Gaul (modern France and Belgium) by 51 B.C. His memoir of the campaigns, *De Bello Gallico (The Gallic War),* has since become a Latin classic, read by students around the world.

Fearing Caesar's rising popularity, the Senate ordered him to return without his army when his appointment expired. Knowing that his life was in danger, Caesar refused and crossed into Italy with his troops in 49 B.C. Pompey fought against Caesar but was defeated and killed. The war ended in 45 B.C. with Caesar as the head of Rome.

Caesar then began a series of reforms. He settled army veterans in colonies throughout Roman territory, extended citizenship to more people, planned municipal reforms in the cities, and drew up plans for a massive public building program. He also carried on a lengthy relationship with Cleopatra, the Queen of Egypt, whom he had met while fighting in Alexandria.

It was members of Caesar's own Senate who would eventually assassinate him, stabbing him at a meeting on March 15, 44 B.C. Caesar's death resulted in another power struggle that destroyed any hope for survival of the Roman Republic and led to the formation of the Roman Empire.

POSTSCRIPT

- Caesar was the first and most famous recorded caesarian birth; in fact, this type of birth is named after him.
- Caesar also reformed the Roman calendar. While doing so, he added a month that was named after himself (July). With minor adjustments, this calendar is still in use today.

Modernism

T HE TERM *MODERNISM* has been used to describe visual and applied arts, architecture, music, and literature. As used here, it refers to literary movements that originated in the first part of the 20th century. Modernist authors, including James Joyce, Virginia Woolf, and William Faulkner, employed the "stream of consciousness" method to depict the flow of thought in the waking mind. In poetry, the key figures are William Butler Yeats, Ezra Pound, and T. S. Eliot. These poets used what Eliot called the "mythical method": Allusions to fragments of myth, history, art, and literature imply—but do not make explicit—a "whole" meaning.

Yeats, Pound, and Eliot were close friends and read each other's work prior to publication. For several months, Pound and Yeats even shared the same house. In addition, Pound was particularly influential to Eliot, editing his most famous poem, *The Waste Land.*

Yeats steeped himself in Celtic mythologies; he wrote modern English translations and based poems and verse plays on them. Pound, who was once called "a man in love with the past," translated ancient Greek, Chinese, Anglo-Saxon, Provençal, and Italian Renaissance poetry. While his translations are often textually inaccurate, he brought dead authors to life more vividly than any other scholar. Pound published his translations separately and incorporated many fragments into his *Cantos,* an unfinished life's work that was to be 120 long poems commenting on history, literature, economics, and political affairs.

Eliot's *The Waste Land* (1922) contains references to Greek literature, as well as ancient rites and mythology as described in Sir James George Frazer's *The Golden Bough: a Study in Magic and Religion.* While the subject of this poem is civilization's decline following World War I, many see hints of Eliot's failed marriage to a woman who spent much of her life in mental hospitals.

The most famous Modernist author was James Joyce, whose *Ulysses* (1922) describes a single day in Dublin, Ireland. The protagonist, Leopold Bloom, travels through a series of scenes and encounters, some quite bawdy. *Ulysses* takes the reader inside Bloom's mind and presents the chaos of thoughts, memories, and emotions that run through a human head all day. *Ulysses* is loosely based on Homer's epic poem the *Odyssey.*

Virginia Woolf and William Faulkner also made use of the Modernist approach. Woolf used stream of consciousness to depict people who were going mad, and William Faulkner employed the technique in his novels about the Deep South.

Gandhi (1869–1948)

MOHANDAS GANDHI, known as Mahatma ("Great-Souled") Gandhi, was the most famous leader of India's independence movement. His methods of nonviolent resistance and civil disobedience to enact change earned him followers in India and admirers worldwide.

Gandhi's first efforts at political activism occurred in South Africa, where he took a job after training as a barrister in London. In 1906, the Transvaal government passed an ordinance requiring registration of the Indian expatriate population. Under Gandhi's leadership, Indians protested by disobeying the ordinance and suffering the subsequent penalties without fighting back. Gandhi called his new technique of civil disobedience *satyagraha* (devotion to truth).

In 1914, Gandhi returned to India. Traveling throughout the country, he witnessed the British destruction of the once-famous Indian textile industry and the poor conditions suffered by Indian workers. He became involved in politics and led satyagraha campaigns against the mistreatment of peasants by indigo planters and the exploitation of textile workers. Rooted in the Hindu concept of *ahimsa,* Gandhi's actions were based on nonviolent noncooperation. Thousands followed him on a march to the sea to protest the salt tax. Many were arrested in each campaign, including Gandhi himself.

With the outbreak of World War II, Indian nationalism entered its final stage. Nationalists of all parties refused to support the war without a British commitment to Indian independence, and they protested India's involvement in the war. Instead of mass marches, satyagraha now took the form of individual acts of civil disobedience. Within eight months, 60,000 satyagrahis had been arrested.

When Japan declared war, India became an important base for the Allies. In March 1942, the British offered India dominion status at the end of the war in exchange for nationalist cooperation. Gandhi described the offer as "a post-dated cheque on a bank that was failing" and introduced a new campaign, the "Quit India" movement. The British responded by arresting the Congress leadership.

The Labour Party victory of 1945 changed Britain's relations with India. For two years, the British government negotiated the terms of independence with nationalist leaders. The final result was the creation of the separate dominions of India and Pakistan. Disappointed, Gandhi spent his last months trying to heal the scars of communal conflict. On January 30, 1948, Gandhi was assassinated by a young Hindu fanatic.

Mary Wollstonecraft

MARY WOLLSTONECRAFT (1759–1797) was the daughter of a London master weaver who squandered his income through speculation. Because of her family's financial difficulties, Wollstonecraft was largely self-educated. Still, she was able to open a school with her sister in 1784 and subsequently spent several years as a governess in Ireland. In 1788, she returned to London, where she worked for publisher Joseph Johnson as a translator and reviewer. At this time, Wollstonecraft became acquainted with a radical group known as the English Jacobins whose members were sympathetic to the French Revolution.

Wollstonecraft published her first feminist essay in 1787, entitled *Thoughts on the Education of Daughters.* In 1790, in response to Edmund Burke's conservative work *Reflections on the Revolution in France,* she published *A Vindication of the Rights of Man,* which defended the ideologies of the French Revolution. She followed that work in 1792 with a book that made her both famous and infamous, *A Vindication of the Rights of Women.* In her book, Wollstonecraft refuted Jean-Jacques Rousseau's argument that girls should receive a different education than boys. She believed that this separation was designed to train women to be more submissive. The book reached a wide audience for its day, going into two editions and becoming available in England and America.

Wollstonecraft's work was important for a variety of reasons. It was the first to make the feminist argument that the dominant social system forced women into a subordinate position, not any biological difference between the sexes. She advocated a society in which women received the same education as men and worked beside them as equals. While most of her contemporaries considered Wollstonecraft's life scandalous and her works subversive and unwomanly, her writings would endure and become part of the foundation of the suffragette and feminist movements of the 19th and 20th centuries.

Threatened because of her support of the French Revolution, Wollstonecraft moved to Paris in 1792 to observe and write about the Revolution, arriving just one month before Louis XVI was executed. While in Paris, she became involved with an American timber merchant named Gilbert Imlay. When Imlay deserted her and their 18-month-old daughter Fanny in 1795, Wollstonecraft followed him back to London. When he rejected her, she twice attempted to commit suicide.

Following her recovery, she went to live with philosopher William Godwin. The two married in 1797 after she became pregnant. Wollstonecraft died later that year from complications following the birth of a daughter.

American Blackface Minstrelsy

THE TRADITION OF Euro-American fascination with African American musical culture had its first flowering in the early 1840s, when a group that called itself the Virginia Minstrels began its performances in New York City. The group was led by Dan Emmett (1815–1904), who composed a number of popular songs in the mid-1800s, most notably "I Wish I Was in Dixie's Land," also known as "Dixie."

The white Virginia Minstrels blackened their faces with burnt cork and played "plantation" instruments such as the banjo and "bones" (a simple percussion instrument that probably came to North America with Irish immigrants). Through songs and skits, they portrayed plantation slaves as two-dimensional happy-go-lucky simpletons. While the group's musical instruments and mannerisms (and use of nonstandard English "dialect") were meant to evoke images of African American practice, the melodies and harmonies of their songs were entirely based on Euro American models. Through the Virginia Minstrels' performances, European American audiences could fantasize about the "exotic" slave populations in their land while enjoying familiar, "safe" musical numbers.

Hugely popular in the American northeast and even in European tours all through the mid-1800s, groups modeled on the Virginia Minstrels changed their shows in the years following the Civil War. They incorporated additional sketches and songs that depicted the new immigrant Irish, Italian, and Jewish populations, in most cases in ways that modern audiences would find stereotypical and offensive. Just as in early minstrelsy, the goal was to "frame and tame" the unfamiliar, strange population by using humorous or poignant songs that would secure the cultural superiority of the Anglo American audience.

After emancipation, freed slaves began assembling their own minstrel troupes, which began to incorporate more authentic African American musical traditions (though African American performers often wore blackface as well). By the end of the 19th century, the more ethnically diverse "variety show" began to predominate throughout North America, though blackface minstrelsy continued in amateur theatrical practice well into the 1900s. The occasional furor over present-day blackface performances "just for fun" shows that the legacy of minstrelsy in American culture is deep indeed.

Cell Receptors

HORMONES, WHICH ARE produced by the endocrine glands, have diverse and substantial effects on the body. These chemical substances shape an individual's growth and development, alter the levels of salts and sugar that circulate in the blood, govern the use and storage of energy, modify the ability to respond to infections, and regulate many other vital functions.

In this coordination of biological activities, hormones act as messengers. When certain hormones arrive at a target cell, they bind with receptor proteins embedded in the cell's surface. The binding between a hormone and its receptor resembles the interaction between a key and lock—with one crucial difference: Hormone-receptor interaction causes the receptor protein to change its shape. From its hormone-binding segment on the surface of the cell to a segment that lies within the cell, the receptor protein contorts and, in doing so, transfers a signal from the cell's exterior to its interior. This signal stimulates the action of small chemicals—"second messengers"—that alter the physiologic state of the cell by triggering a cascade of molecular interactions.

Some hormones affect cells of only one or two organs, whereas other hormones influence cells throughout the body. The brain's hypothalamus, for example, creates the protein hormone *corticotrophin releasing factor* (CRF), which travels in a small blood vessel system to the pituitary gland. Here, the factor binds with its receptor and stimulates the pituitary gland to release *corticotrophin,* a protein hormone that travels through the general blood circulation. When it reaches adrenal gland cells, corticotrophin stimulates the synthesis and release of *cortisol,* a steroid hormone. Like corticotrophin, cortisol moves throughout the body in the general circulation. But unlike corticotrophin, cortisol can affect most cells in the body. Among its many effects, cortisol stimulates liver cells to synthesize glucose, muscle tissue to block the uptake of glucose, and adipose tissue to break down fat. It also suppresses functions of immune system cells.

Not all hormones bind with receptors located at the cell surface. For instance, cortisol and other steroid hormones slip inside cells and bind with intracellular receptors. Hormone binding incites a conformational change in the receptor that enables it to attach to DNA and alter gene expression.

POSTSCRIPT

▓ The human nasal cavity can harbor a thousand different receptor proteins that bind odor molecules.

Ukiyo-e Prints (Japanese Woodblocks)

*U*KIYO-E, WHICH MEANS "visions of the floating (i.e., transient) world" is a genre of Japanese woodblock prints and paintings made in the 17th to the 20th centuries. Ukiyo-e style, which originally followed Chinese models, combines the decorative with the realistic and narrative.

Beginning in the 17th century, this art appealed to the rising merchant and artisan classes in Japan's cities, who purchased illustrated books and later single sheet prints and posters. The prints were mass-produced for people who could not afford paintings. Thousands of Ukiyo-e prints were published between 1658 and 1858.

Thirty-Six Views of Mount Fuji *by Hokusai*

While many of the most famous Ukiyo-e images depict Tokyo's geishas and prostitutes, there are also numerous landscapes and prints of actors, sumo wrestlers, and ordinary people. Ukiyo-e shows a Japan of another time, but the style has had such influence on Western art that it still seems fresh today.

Hishikawa Moronobu, the first major Ukiyo-e artist, made single-color woodblocks using India ink in the 1670s. Artists soon began to color the prints with brushes. In the 18th century, Suzuki Harunobu created a technique that permitted polychrome color printing with woodblocks. Some of the best-known Ukiyo-e artists—Kitagawa Utamaro, Katsushika Hokusai, and Ando Hiroshige—were active in the mid-18th century. Hokusai's famous *Thirty-Six Views of Mount Fuji* was published in 1831.

After the Meiji Restoration in 1868, Japan opened up to foreign influence and trade. Ukiyo-e prints found their way to Europe, often as wrappings and paddings for export goods, and began to show up in the art market at very low prices. As artists discovered them, the prints had a decisive influence on European painting, beginning with Édouard Manet and continuing through the Impressionist, Post-Impressionist, and Cubist periods.

French artists abandoned academic rules and clichés under Ukiyo-e influence. Edgar Dégas discovered that he could paint without narrative and crop out part of an image instead of showing an entire scene. Other artists who adopted Japanese perspective, flatness, and cropping include Vincent van Gogh, Claude Monet, and Mary Cassatt.

September 11, 2001

O N September 11, 2001, at 8:45 A.M. Eastern Daylight Time, a hijacked plane, American Airlines Flight 11 originating in Boston, crashed into the north tower of the World Trade Center in New York City, leaving a gaping hole filled with flames. At 9:03 A.M., a second hijacked plane (United Airlines Flight 175) slammed into the south tower, while 40 minutes later, a third plane (American Airlines Flight 77) struck the Pentagon. Both towers at the World Trade Center collapsed within a few minutes of each other (at 9:59 A.M. and 10:28 A.M.).

At 10:03 A.M., a fourth plane (United Airlines Flight 93) crashed in rural Pennsylvania. It was later discovered that courageous passengers, aware of the other attacks, stormed the cockpit and prevented their airplane from reaching its intended target, probably the White House or Capitol.

According to *The 9/11 Commission Report,* "More than 2,600 people died at the World Trade Center; 125 died at the Pentagon; 256 died on the four planes." In fact, the *Report* noted, "The death toll surpassed that at Pearl Harbor in December 1941." Among the dead were 60 police officers (NYPD and Port Authority) and 343 firefighters and paramedics. One investment firm within the World Trade Center lost 658 employees.

It soon became clear that the 19 hijackers of the four planes were sponsored by al Qaeda, a fundamentalist Muslim terrorist organization led by Osama bin Laden, whose hatred of the American presence in the Middle East and its support for Israel was well documented. Americans overwhelmingly supported President George W. Bush's decision to invade Afghanistan, whose oppressive Taliban government was providing shelter to bin Laden. The first strikes of Operation Enduring Freedom occurred on October 7, 2001. Although bin Laden was not captured, the oppressive Taliban forces were easily defeated, which most Americans saw as a triumph for freedom. Americans also generally supported costly enhanced security measures to prevent future terrorist attacks.

For the most part, this sense of unity carried over through the early days of the U.S. invasion of Iraq in March 2003. Operation Iraqi Freedom was undertaken in large part because of alleged connections between Iraq's dictator, Saddam Hussein, and various anti-American terrorist organizations, including al Qaeda, and the fear that Saddam might give Iraqi weapons of mass destruction to terrorist groups.

Although the Iraqi military was easily defeated, many Americans became disillusioned when internal violence required the continued presence of U.S. troops, and no firm evidence of weapons of mass destruction was found.

Crime and Punishment

CRIME AND PUNISHMENT, a novel by Russian author Fyodor Dostoevsky, was first published serially in 1866 and later as a single volume. With the crime occurring at the beginning of the work and the punishment arriving at the very end, the novel's true subject is the psychological effect of a criminal act upon its perpetrator. *Crime and Punishment* is generally viewed as the first of the cycle of Dostoevsky's great novels, which culminated in *The Brothers Karamazov.*

The protagonist of *Crime and Punishment* is Rodion Romanovich Raskolnikov, a Russian student heavily in debt to his landlady. He murders Alyona Ivanovna, a repulsive pawnbroker, partly for her money, but also because he thinks she is evil and should be destroyed. Lizaveta, Alyona's younger sister, catches Raskolnikov committing the murder, and he ensures her silence by killing her, too.

Raskolnikov wants to be similar to Napoleon and believes he can walk away from a murder without consequences. However, he is delirious after killing the two women. He tries to clean himself up and then escapes with some of the money as visitors arrive. Overcome with paranoia and guilt, he manages to bluff his way through a conversation with the police but has episodes of illness and delusion.

Semi-irrational, Raskolnikov stumbles through encounters with different people and almost confesses to a police officer. The novel is a series of such episodes, showing the protagonist being slowly destroyed by his own guilt. One of the characters, Sonya Semyonovna Marmeladov, a woman who prostitutes herself in order to feed her family, later falls in love with Raskolnikov.

In the end, Raskolnikov admits what he has done to the police and is sentenced to eight years in Siberia. Sonya follows him there. The novel ends as Raskolnikov becomes aware of his love for Sonya. He has progressed from criminal acts to realizing love.

Crime and Punishment is divided into six parts and contains an epilogue. The first three parts have key episodes, as do the second three parts, creating a dualistic structure. Furthermore, the names of many of the characters have symbolic meanings in the Russian language. Overall, *Crime and Punishment* is notable for its psychological and moral insight, as well as its revealing descriptions of slum life in St. Petersburg, Russia, during the mid-19th century. Many novelists have been influenced by the dark, furtive quality of the story and its presentation.

Eleanor Roosevelt (1884–1962)

ELEANOR ROOSEVELT BEGAN life as a shy and awkward child and ended it as one of the most respected and loved women in American history.

She was born into a life of privilege—her father was Theodore Roosevelt's younger brother. In 1905, she married Franklin Delano Roosevelt, a distant cousin. They had six children in eleven years, and Eleanor seemed well on her way to becoming, in her words, "a fairly conventional, quiet, young society matron."

Politics and devotion to her ambitious husband would take her on a very different path. Franklin served in the New York State Senate for three years, then in Washington, D.C., as assistant secretary of the navy. Stricken with polio in 1921, he rebounded to win the governorship of New York in 1928 and was elected president of the United States in 1932. Eleanor came to serve as his partner and confidante, representative and eyes and ears—a relationship that is perhaps most closely resembled in recent times by Bill and Hillary Clinton. (Ironically, it was the discovery in 1918 that her husband was having an affair with another woman that pushed Eleanor to become stronger and more independent.)

As First Lady, Eleanor understood the politics of Washington and wasn't shy about airing her own ideas. She held her own press conferences, traveled widely, gave lectures and radio broadcasts, and penned a daily syndicated newspaper column, "My Day." Deeply dedicated to social reform, she spoke out on behalf of civil rights, equality for women, the abolition of child labor, the implementation of a minimum wage, and legislation to better protect workers. She helped secure the first government funds for childcare centers.

Stunned by the discrimination against blacks, she persuaded Franklin to bar discrimination in New Deal projects. While attending the Southern Conference for Human Welfare in Alabama in 1938, she refused to sit in the whites-only section. A year later, she resigned from the Daughters of the American Revolution after the organization denied black singer Marian Anderson entry to its auditorium.

When Franklin died of a cerebral hemorrhage in April 1945, Eleanor returned to their estate at Hyde Park, New York. She told reporters, "The story is over." But it wasn't. Less than a year later she became a U.S. delegate in the United Nations and remained a prominent figure worldwide until her death in 1962 in New York City. She is buried next to Franklin at Hyde Park.

A Dictionary of the English Language

SAMUEL JOHNSON, often referred to as "Dr. Johnson," was the son of a bookseller. As a young man, he was forced to drop out of Oxford University because he was unable to pay tuition. From there, he made his way to London, where he began to make a living as one of the earliest professional writers.

In 1747, a group of London booksellers responded to a perceived need for a canon of correct usage of the English language and commissioned Johnson to compile what would be called *A Dictionary of the English Language.* At that time, the English language had no equivalent to the dictionaries produced for French and Italian by the great academies in those countries. English dictionaries were usually lists of technical vocabulary or other difficult words. In response, Johnson hoped to produce "a dictionary by which the pronunciation of our language may be fixed and its attainment facilitated; by which its purity may be preserved, its use ascertained, and its duration lengthened."

Johnson issued the prospectus for the dictionary project in 1747. He estimated that it would take him three years to complete the project, regardless of the fact that it had taken 40 scholars in the French Royal Academy 55 years to compile their dictionary. In the end, it took Johnson, working with six assistants, eight years to create *A Dictionary of the English Language.*

As the project progressed, Johnson's conception of his job changed. In the prospectus, he presented himself as a defender of the language against barbarisms and impurities. However, in the preface of the completed work, he abandoned that role, saying that his task was not to reform English but to record it. He wrote, "It has been asserted that for a law to be known, is of more importance than to be right." Still, Johnson was quite opinionated when it came to the English language. In one case, he warned against importing words from other languages, claiming that would be "naturalizing foreigners to the injury of the natives." His definitions often reflected his own opinions. For instance, he wrote that a patron was "one who countenances, supports, or protects. Commonly a wretch who supports with indolence, and is paid with flattery."

A Dictionary of the English Language was a monumental task. Ultimately, Johnson defined 42,773 words, from the estimated 200,000 words used in the English vocabulary at that time. The first edition had 2,300 pages and weighed 22 pounds. Five editions of Johnson's dictionary were published in his lifetime, and it remained the definitive English language dictionary until the publication of the *Oxford English Dictionary* in 1928.

Hector Berlioz's *Symphonie Fantastique*

THE ARTISTIC MOVEMENT of the early 1800s called *romanticism* had a number of colorful exponents, and on the musical front perhaps no one was more colorful than Hector Berlioz (1803–1869). Berlioz successfully established himself primarily as a composer rather than as a performer. He was perhaps the first "master orchestral conductor" and the first true expert in the subtle use of the wide variety of sounds available in a large ensemble with many different kinds of instruments—what musicians call the *art of orchestration.* Indeed, Berlioz wrote a remarkable "how-to" manual on orchestration that is still a crucial teaching tool for music professionals today.

Like many orchestral composers of the mid-1800s, Berlioz felt compelled to "respond to" the creative genius of Beethoven. But unlike most of his contemporaries, Berlioz thought himself fully up to the task. In Berlioz's view, the way to take the symphony to the next level after Beethoven was to build on the notion of program music—music that is associated with specific visual or poetic images. (Beethoven had called his Sixth Symphony the "Pastoral" and had given brief descriptive titles to each of the four movements. In his Ninth [and final] Symphony, Beethoven even added vocal soloists and a chorus, associating the final grand set of musical variations with a poem by Schiller, the now-famous "Ode to Joy.")

Berlioz found inspiration for his first and most famous program symphony in his own biographical situation. At the premiere of the *Symphonie Fantastique* in 1830, Berlioz distributed a narrative to the audience: Each of the five movements of the work, he explained, was intended to "depict" (through sound alone) various stages in the "life of an artist." Obsessed with a young woman, the artist sees her in a variety of dreamlike situations; he takes opium to dispel his obsession and dreams that he has killed her and is then executed for the murder. Finally, he hallucinates a witches' Sabbath, in which his beloved is revealed as an ugly hag.

Berlioz made it known that he was the artist protagonist, and the beloved woman was Harriet Smithson, an Irish actress who was then performing Shakespeare—in English—on the French stage. Berlioz didn't speak a word of English, but that didn't stop him from being swept away both by the power of Shakespearean drama and by the intensity of Smithson's acting. He fervently pursued Smithson, asking her to marry him. The *Symphonie Fantastique* was, in a way, "their song."

Francis Crick

DURING AN INTERVIEW, Francis Crick (1916–2004) credited the *Children's Encyclopedia* for sparking his early passion for science. He decided to become a scientist, but he worried that everything would be discovered by the time he grew up. His mother reassured the young boy; there would be plenty left for him to discover. She was right.

Francis Harry Compton Crick was born in Northampton, England. Following World War I, his family moved to London. Crick studied physics at University College in London. He earned his degree in 1937 and started his graduate work when World War II broke out. Throughout the war, he worked at the British Admiralty Research Laboratory, designing magnetic and acoustic mines for naval warfare. He remained there for two years after the war, working as a scientific civil servant.

In 1949, Crick joined the Medical Research Council at Cambridge University. There he examined protein structure with X-ray crystallography. Once again, his graduate studies took a detour, and this time a new scientific pursuit intervened.

American scientist James Watson joined the Medical Research Council in 1951. Like Crick, Watson was supposed to use X-ray crystallography to examine protein structure. After the two scientists met, however, they discovered that they shared an interest in discovering the structure of DNA.

About 50 miles away at King's College in London, Rosalind Elsie Franklin and Raymond Gosling were investigating DNA structure using X-ray diffraction in Maurice Wilkins's laboratory. As Crick and Watson learned about Wilkins's lab studies, they developed their own ideas regarding the structure of the DNA molecule. The April 25, 1953, edition of the journal *Nature* included their proposal for the double helix. In 1962 Crick, Watson, and Wilkins shared a Nobel Prize (for Physiology or Medicine) for their elucidation of DNA structure.

Crick's interests moved on from structure to function, as he considered how DNA encodes genetic information. His inquiries helped to crack the genetic code and lay the foundation for modern molecular biology.

In 1976, Crick joined the Salk Institute for Biological Studies in San Diego, California, where he studied brain function and the nature of consciousness.

He died in July 2004 from colon cancer at the age of 88.

Rodin's *Gates of Hell*

IN 1900 AT THE Universal Exposition of Paris, there was no more famous or successful artist in France—or likely in the world—than François Auguste René Rodin (1840–1917). It had not always been so. Rodin failed three times to win a place at the prestigious School of Fine Arts in Paris, so he trained as an apprentice, designing furniture, jewelry, ceramics, mantelpieces, and other architectural ornaments.

Rodin despised the artifice of the neoclassical style promoted by the French Academy and admired the monumentality and vigor of the Renaissance masters Donatello (1386–1466) and Michelangelo (1475–1564). He sought to achieve a realism and emotional expression in his art that, he said, had disappeared from modern sculpture. Eventually his work began to attract attention, and in 1880 he was commissioned to create a set of doors for a new Museum of Decorative Arts. The museum was never built. But Rodin's monumental doors—his *Gates of Hell*—included motifs that became his best-known sculptures.

The *Gates of Hell* were inspired by Dante Alighieri's epic poem *The Divine Comedy* (1320), in which the author is guided by the Roman poet Virgil through the realms of the dead. Rodin's main interest was the poem's first section, *Inferno* or "Hell." Rather than illustrate Dante's narrative, however, Rodin chose episodes that focus on passions expressed through love, violence, and treachery. A few of the images come from the symbolist poetry of Charles Baudelaire (1821–1867). The turmoil and emotion of the subjects infuses the material of the doors. Figures seem both to rise up and sink into the bronze as light flickers over the shapes, gleaming off some details and casting others into deep shadow.

The story of the adulterous lovers Francesca and Paolo, for instance, became the basis for Rodin's sensuous composition known as *The Kiss*. Dante himself was transformed into *The Thinker*. Rodin imagined Dante as a heroic nude, and this brooding figure, his chin supported by his hand, has become an iconic image as well as Rodin's most famous work. Rodin said of this sculpture, "What makes my Thinker think is that he thinks not only with his brain, with his knitted brow, his distended nostrils and compressed lips, but with every muscle of his arms, back and legs, with his clenched fist and gripping toes." On the day of Rodin's funeral in 1917, *The Thinker* was placed above his grave.

The Attack on Pearl Harbor

PRESIDENT FRANKLIN ROOSEVELT called December 7, 1941—the day the Japanese attacked Pearl Harbor—a "date which will live in infamy."

The attack—launched without benefit of a formal declaration of war—sank or heavily damaged 18 warships, destroyed nearly 200 aircraft, and killed 2,400 U.S. servicemen. It also aroused the fury of a nation.

The brainchild of Japanese Admiral Isoroku Yamamato, the attack on Pearl Harbor was intended to remove the U.S. Pacific Fleet as a threat to Japanese expansion in the east. By the time the United States recovered, it would be too late. Faced with a fait accompli, the Americans would agree to a negotiated peace. That, at least, was the plan.

Although American intelligence realized war with Japan was imminent, it was believed that any attack would fall first on the Philippines. Neither of the commanders at Pearl Harbor, Army General Walter C. Short nor naval commander Admiral Husband Kimmel, anticipated a carrier raid on Hawaii. The Japanese approach went undetected.

Under the command of Vice Admiral Chuichi Nagumo, the Japanese carrier strike force launched its aircraft at 6:00 A.M. from 275 miles out. The first bombs fell at 7:55 A.M. as the Japanese achieved complete surprise.

Fortunately, the U.S. aircraft carriers, a top Japanese target, were at sea and escaped the attack. Nevertheless, the 30-minute raid damaged or sank all eight U.S. battleships in the harbor, along with ten other vessels. Among the losses was the USS *Arizona,* which remains on the harbor's floor. Almost 1,200 crew members were killed in the attack.

A second strike came moments after the first but achieved little damage due to the pall of smoke hanging over the harbor. Urged to make a third strike, Nagumo, worried about the threat from the unlocated U.S. carriers, refused. The Japanese turned for home.

While considered a great victory, the attack on Pearl Harbor proved to be an even greater miscalculation. Within months, many of the sunken and damaged vessels had been repaired and were back in action. American industry geared up to produce an unending stream of tanks, planes, and ships, while the Japanese were unable to replace their own losses. Less than eight months after the surprise attack, U.S. carriers won a decisive victory at Midway and seized the initiative in the Pacific.

Yamamato was killed in 1943 when his plane was shot down over the island of Bougainville (part of Papua New Guinea). Nagumo died less than a year later during the American invasion of Saipan.

Samuel Beckett

ONE OF THE 20TH CENTURY's most lauded writers and the author of perhaps the finest example of a play for the so-called "theater of the absurd," Samuel Beckett was such an intensely private person that when he won the Nobel Prize for Literature his wife called it a "catastrophe" for the public acclaim it would bring him.

Beckett was born on Good Friday (April 13) in 1906 in Foxrock, a suburb of Dublin, Ireland. He attended the same school as Oscar Wilde and was an unhappy, morose child. After studying at Trinity College in Belfast, Beckett went to Paris, where he met celebrated Irish author James Joyce. The two became close, and Beckett wrote an essay defending Joyce's work against the reading public's need for easy comprehension. But the relationship between the two cooled when Beckett rejected Joyce's daughter Lucia.

Beckett won his first literary prize (ten pounds) for a quickly written poem entitled "Whoroscope." But after returning to Trinity College as a teacher, he decided that habit and routine were the "cancer of time," so he resigned at the end of 1931. He then wandered through Europe. Whenever he was in Paris he visited Joyce, although it was rumored that the two depressed men mainly sat together in silence.

In January 1938, after the publication of his novel *Murphy,* Beckett was stabbed on the street in Paris and nearly killed. When he asked his attacker why, the man replied: "I do not know sir. I'm sorry." Words to this effect would repeatedly turn up in Beckett's subsequent writing, as his characters tried to explain their actions.

After fighting with the French underground in World War II, Beckett returned to Paris at war's end in 1945. The next five years were his most prolific as a writer. He wrote the plays *Eleutheria, Endgame,* and the classic *Waiting for Godot,* as well as several novels, including *Molloy* and *Malone Dies,* two books of short stories, and more. *Waiting for Godot* has been called a play in which nothing happens—Godot never appears—yet it keeps the audience utterly enthralled. The play touches a universal chord in demonstrating that life and existence are primarily about killing time and desperately hoping that something will happen to make the future better. This feeling of merely existing, of inching through life while overcome by its futility, is a signature theme of much of Beckett's work.

In 1969 Beckett won the Nobel Prize for Literature. His later writings became increasingly minimalist. He died on December 22, 1989.

Meredith Monk (1942–present)

IN THE DECADES FOLLOWING American composer John Cage's experiments with chance music, many musicians and performance artists developed Cage's principles to establish a tradition of *process music*, in which subtle changes in sound structure were brought to the foreground to make the listener especially aware of the process of change. Some results of this movement are now labeled *minimalism*, but not all artists influenced by the process music approach claim the "minimalist" label.

An outstanding example is Meredith Monk, who has been leading ensembles dedicated to what she has called "an interdisciplinary approach to performance" for more than four decades. Monk considers her work to be "at the intersection of music and movement, image and object, light and sound in an effort to discover and weave together new modes of perception." Particularly noteworthy is her focus on the voice and its "extended" possibilities through unconventional singing techniques. Her performance-compositions are difficult to categorize using standard genre labels. While she herself has claimed "traditional" genres for her work (one of her major compositions, *Atlas,* is called an "opera"), she has used those labels more to play with listeners' expectations of the genre than to fulfill standard historical criteria. Her multimedia productions tend to include dance, vocal and instrumental resources, and occasionally film.

Monk's wide-ranging influence came to light in 2005 during the 40th-anniversary celebration of the start of her career. Included in the festivities was a Carnegie Hall concert with performances by popular musicians Björk and DJ Spooky; prominent experimental composers Terry Riley and John Zorn; the new music ensembles Alarm Will Sound and Bang on a Can All-Stars; along with the more "traditional" Pacific Mozart Ensemble.

Monk's many awards include a MacArthur Foundation "genius" grant, several honorary Doctor of Arts degrees from art institutes and conservatories, and most recently the ASCAP Concert Music "Bessie" award for Sustained Creative Achievement.

POSTSCRIPT

■ Monk credits her focus on the power of the voice (she claims that singing was her "first language") to her family background, which includes four generations of professional vocalists: Her mother sang for radio commercials in the 1940s; her grandfather was a professional singer; and her great-grandfather was a synagogue cantor.

Betty Freidan

BETTY FRIEDAN, author and feminist, is considered the mother of the contemporary women's movement. In 1963, she launched what has been called "feminism's second wave" with the publication of her book *The Feminine Mystique*. The book traces the changing role of the American woman, from the independent working woman of the post-suffrage era to the domesticated housewife of post-World War II. In describing their discontent and dissatisfaction, Friedan gave voice to the growing number of women who felt unfulfilled in their primary role as wife and mother. Friedan exploded the myth of suburban women's domestic fulfillment in what became known as "the feminine mystique."

Friedan had never planned to become one of the most important feminists of the 1960s and '70s. She graduated *summa cum laude* from Smith College in 1942 with a degree in psychology, and she initially pursued graduate work at the University of California, Berkeley. She had a fellowship to study with Erik Erikson, the developmental psychologist who coined the term *identity crisis.* Turning down a second fellowship, she moved to New York and worked as an editor and reporter. In 1947, she married Carl Friedman (they dropped the "m" sometime after their marriage) and shortly thereafter settled into a life as a housewife and mother with a part-time job as a freelance journalist to supplement her husband's income. *The Feminine Mystique* grew out of a survey she conducted among fellow alumni of Smith College at their fifteenth class reunion in 1957.

The success of *The Feminine Mystique* propelled her to the top of the growing women's movement. Friedan helped found the National Organization of Women (NOW) in 1966, and she served as its first president until 1970. She also cofounded the National Association for the Repeal of Abortion Laws (NARAL) in 1969. NARAL is now known as Naral Pro-Choice America.

Liberal feminists, such as Susan Brownmiller, criticized Friedan for being "hopelessly bourgeois" for placing too much focus on the plight of middle-class white homemakers and not enough on minorities, the poor, and lesbians. Others, such as feminist leader Germaine Greer, believed that Friedan "changed the course of human history almost single-handedly."

Later in life, Friedan turned her attention to ageism and published *The Fountain of Age* in 1993. She died in 2006 at the age of 85.

Italian Opera in an Age of Superstars

EARLY IN HIS CAREER, Giuseppe Verdi (1813–1901) wrote a significant amount of new music on commission, calling himself a "galley slave" at the service of theatrical producers. This was, in fact, the model under which Italian-style musical theater ("opera") had functioned for almost two centuries prior to Verdi's first productions in the early 1840s. Audiences paid to hear specific singers; composers were hired to write music that would "suit" those singers most readily. Indeed, Verdi was both the beneficiary and a key architect of the change in priorities that led to the increasing importance of the composer and the standardization of a "reper- tory" of great operatic works that are performed around the world to the present day.

Giuseppe Verdi

By the early 1800s, proponents of Italian opera had long been referring to their tradition as one of "beautiful song" (*bel canto* in Italian). This term has now come to be associated with the style of singing and composing that emerged in the first few decades of the 19th century. The most esteemed composer in the early stages of the bel canto tradition, both then and now, is Gioacchino Rossini (1792–1868). Rossini was one of the first composers to be given "billing" almost on a par with the star singers of his day. While in the late 1700s audiences rarely knew (much less cared about) who had written the music sung by their favorite artists, by the 1810s opera-goers looked forward to a Rossini opera because they valued Rossini's deft touch with comic situations. (*The Barber of Seville,* 1816, is the most popular of a half dozen of his comic operas still in repertory.) Having made good money early in his career, Rossini retired to France early, leaving the "field" wide open.

By the 1820s, a change in dramatic ideals—from comic high jinks to intense, even tragic love stories—also provided an opportunity for com- posers to take on a "tortured intense artist" persona. Gaetano Donizetti (1797–1848) and Vincenzo Bellini (1801–1835) were successful in exploiting the new ideals, and some of their works (for example *Lucia di Lammermoor,* 1835, by the former, *Norma,* 1831, by the latter) began to gain the kind of multiple-performance runs that Rossini had established. These two composers died young at the height of their success, however, and the thirst for novelty was greater than the demand for "classics." It took the immense popularity of Verdi's music to establish the notion that a particular opera was worthy of being performed year after year around the globe.

Marie and Pierre Curie

MARIE CURIE (1867–1934) and Pierre Curie (1859–1906) were the power couple of science at the turn of the 20th century. The pair explored the newly discovered phenomenon of radiation, uncovered two new elements, and shared the Nobel Prize for Physics. When her husband died, Marie continued their research, earning a second Nobel Prize.

Born in Warsaw, Poland, Maria Sklodowska showed little indication that she would excel in science. After high school, she worked as a teacher and governess, and she used some of her earnings to fund her older sister Bronia's medical studies in France. In 1891, she joined Bronia in Paris and set out to earn a physics degree from the Sorbonne. She also changed her first name to Marie. In 1895, she gained a new surname when she married Pierre Curie, a chemist with an established scientific reputation for studies on the electrical and magnetic properties of crystals.

In 1896, Henri Becquerel discovered that uranium emitted strange radiations. Marie began to study those radiations, which she called *radioactivity,* using a meter built by her husband. She found that the strength of radiation that uranium compounds emitted was proportional to the amount of uranium. Compounds of the element *thorium* followed the same pattern. Then, in 1898, Marie discovered that the minerals *pitchblende* and *chalcocite* emitted four times as much radiation as their uranium content indicated. She concluded that the minerals contained an unknown new element that caused the extra radiation.

At that point, Pierre gave up his studies and joined Marie's research. They quickly discovered two new radioactive elements: polonium, named for Marie's native Poland, and radium. That achievement earned them a share, with Becquerel, of the 1903 Nobel Prize in Physics.

In 1906, Pierre died after being hit by a horse-drawn carriage. Although grieving deeply, Marie continued their research. The Sorbonne gave her the posts of lecturer and then professor that Pierre had previously held, making her the first woman to hold either position at the university. In 1911, Marie won an unprecedented second Nobel Prize. This one, in chemistry, recognized her isolation of pure radium.

For the rest of her career, Marie concentrated on the application of X-rays to medicine. She died of leukemia, almost certainly caused by constant exposure to radiation during her pioneering research.

The Curies's daughter, Iréne Joliot Curie, and her husband, Frédéric Joliot, won the 1935 Nobel Prize in Chemistry for their production of new radioactive elements.

Fauvism

T HE FIRST ARTISTIC MOVEMENT of the 20th century, Fauvism spear-headed the major avant-garde movements of pre-World War I Europe that represented an unprecedented experimentation in the arts. Fauvism was characterized by scorching, vivid colors, a lack of traditional perspective, and a rich surface texture. Bringing color to new levels of intensity liberated painting from its traditional descriptive functions. The Fauvists used color to suggest space, to create a decorative effect, and, most importantly, to communicate or express personal emotion.

The Fauvists were never an organized group but rather a loose association of friends and acquaintances interested in overturning academic conventions. Several artists exhibited together in the Salon d'Automne in 1905, which prompted critic Louis Vauxcelles in *Gil Blas* to refer to them as *les fauves,* or wild beasts. Though the Fauvists received some ridicule and criticism, they defiantly adopted the name.

The Red Room *by Henri Matisse*

The dominant figure in the group was Henri Matisse (1869–1954), who had begun using vividly contrasting colors around 1899. But it wasn't until the summer of 1904, while working in the bright light in southern France, that Matisse fully realized the emotional effect of color. The following summer, he was joined by French artist Andre Derain (1880–1954) on a painting expedition to the Mediterranean coast, and Derain discovered the use of color to create light by eliminating shadow. Other Fauvists included Maurice de Vlaminck, Raoul Dufy, Albert Marquet, and Kees Van Dongen.

The Fauvists were directly influenced by the paintings of Vincent van Gogh (1853–1890), who had used color to convey his troubled emotions, and Paul Gauguin (1848–1903), who had disregarded perspective. Indirect influences included Gustave Moreau—an instructor to several of the Fauvists whose liberal teaching methods opened a door for them—and the newly discovered exotic arts from Africa, Polynesia, and Central and South America.

Fauvism peaked as a movement at the Salon d'Automne in 1906 when all the leading participants exhibited. Shortly thereafter, the artists drifted apart to pursue individual creative paths.

Emperor Augustus

BORN IN 63 B.C. WITH the Roman name of Gaius Octavius, the future Roman emperor's father died when Octavius was four. He probably would have never been famous except that his mother was the daughter of Julius Caesar's sister. Because Caesar himself never had a son, he adopted young Octavius and prepared him for a political career. When Caesar was assassinated in 44 B.C., Octavius was only 18 years old.

Octavius secured an uneasy alliance with Mark Antony and Aemilius Lepidus and defeated Caesar's assassins in the battle of Philippi (in Greece) in 42 B.C. Two years later, the three Triumvers divided Rome among them, Lepidus going to Africa, while Octavius took the West and Antony the East. But Antony, who had married Octavius' sister, dallied in Egypt with Queen Cleopatra, giving Octavius the chance to have the Senate declare war on Antony. Octavius won the naval battle of Actium in 31 B.C. Antony and Cleopatra both committed suicide the next year, leaving Octavius in control of Rome.

In 27 B.C., Octavius shrewdly announced that he was restoring the Republic and offered to resign all of his posts and titles. But he retained control of the three provinces in which most of the army was stationed, ensuring his ultimate success. The Senate voted Octavius the title of "Augustus" (revered); he was also retained as commander of the army. In effect, Octavius was Rome's "Princeps" (first citizen) and the de facto emperor. Augustus treated the Senate with respect but was also firm, allowing the Senate to continue in its traditional role but always with the knowledge that Augustus had the final word in any major legislation. In effect, Augustus created the position of Roman emperor.

Augustus' generals completed the conquest of Spain and Egypt, extended the empire's boundaries to the Danube River, and finished occupying Asia Minor. The army's successes helped create what has been called the *Pax Romana* (Roman peace), which led to economic and social calm throughout the empire for almost 200 years.

Augustus created a massive road-building project across the empire, revised the empire's tax structure, and built many new public buildings in Rome. To maintain his personal safety, Augustus created the Praetorian Guard. He also began a permanent Roman naval force in the Mediterranean. His reign saw the growth of Latin literature, with Virgil, Ovid, Horace, and Livy leading a host of talented writers. Augustus died in A.D. 14 and was succeeded as emperor by his adopted son, Tiberius.

Thomas Hardy's
Tess of the d'Urbervilles

*T*ESS OF THE D'URBERVILLES: *A Pure Woman Faithfully Presented* by Thomas Hardy (1840–1928) was first published in 1891. Hardy's themes—Victorian hypocrisy, the beauty of the natural world, and its destruction by the soulless and mechanical era—make *Tess of the d'Urbervilles* a work of transition between the 19th and 20th centuries.

Tess Durbeyfield is the daughter of peasants, but her father discovers that his name is a corruption of an extinct Norman family called d'Urbervilles. He begins to put on airs and sends Tess to stay with a family called d'Urberville, who had bought the extinct name and title. While staying with the family, Tess is courted and raped by the son, Alec. After a halfhearted affair with Alec, Tess returns home, where she hides in her bedroom and eventually gives birth to a son who lives only for a week.

Two years later, Tess leaves her village and encounters Angel Clare, a minister's son whom she had known in the past, and becomes romantically involved with him. He proposes marriage, and she cannot decide whether to tell him about her past. She remains silent, and soon after their wedding he confesses to a past indiscretion. She then tells him about her rape, but he cannot reconcile himself to it. The two separate. Tess returns home and eventually finds work at another area farm. Secretly, Angel goes to Brazil to start a new life.

Later, Tess encounters Alec, who has become a Christian. Now contrite, he wants to marry her, but she is still married to Angel. Tess's family loses its homestead, cannot find lodging, and spends a night in a churchyard. Meanwhile, Angel has failed in Brazil, regrets his treatment of Tess, and heads for England. By the time he arrives, Tess has become Alec's mistress. Angel and Tess converse, and she sends him away. Alec discovers this, and she tells him she's lost the only man she ever loved. After a quarrel, she murders Alec and runs away to find Angel. The two have a few days together before the police find them and she is taken away to trial and execution.

Tess of the d'Urbervilles contains many pagan and neo-biblical references that allow for multiple interpretations. The book has been adapted for the stage (including a Broadway play), television, and film. The most famous adaptation was by Roman Polanski, who directed the movie *Tess,* starring Nastassja Kinski, in 1979.

Sergei Eisenstein (1898–1948)

DURING THE YEARS OF revolutionary fervor following the creation of the Soviet Union, another revolution took place in the new nation, this time in the arts. Filmmaker Sergei Eisenstein was among the most important figures of this artistic time. His innovative use of film editing and montage has had an enormous impact on the art of filmmaking.

Eisenstein was born in Riga and was educated as a civil engineer. However, after serving in the Red Army, he turned his attention to experimental theater. He soon fell under the influence of theatrical director Vsevolod Meyerhold, who had broken with the naturalist traditions of the stage. Eisenstein sought to create a new theater experience in which the masses became the collective hero, conventions were broken, and social issues were explored. Many Soviet artists of the time easily moved from one art form to another, and Eisenstein soon switched to film.

For his films, Eisenstein expanded on the ideas and experiments of other filmmaker-theorists and saw montage editing as a visual equivalent to Karl Marx's dialectical theory. This stood in contrast to Hollywood's use of continuity editing. In that method, films generally progressed in a linear fashion, and one shot continued where the previous shot left off, creating the illusion of smooth, continuous action. Conversely, montage relies on the juxtaposition of differing shots. The cumulative power of this succession of shots agitates, moves, or manipulates the viewer. Eisenstein pushed montage further, creating "intellectual montage," in which two unrelated shots were juxtaposed to suggest meaning not inherent in either.

His first feature film, *Strike* (1925), was also Eisenstein's first chance to employ his new ideas of montage editing. However, his masterpiece, *The Battleship Potemkin,* also released in 1925, is considered the compendium of his ideas on editing. In particular, a famous sequence on the Odessa steps features a collage of disjointed cuts, extreme close-ups, rhythmic editing, and the compression and expansion of time. The sequence ends with an intellectual montage in which Eisenstein cuts between images of stone lions and the destruction of the Odessa Opera House. In doing so, he suggests that the rise of the powerful masses, or the lions, will result in the fall of the old social order, represented by the ruined opera house.

The Battleship Potemkin was the last film for which Eisenstein was granted total creative control. Eisenstein's later films, *Alexander Nevsky* and *Ivan the Terrible I* and *II,* are significant efforts but lack the daring experimentation of his 1920s films.

Andrew Carnegie and His Libraries

IN HIS 1889 ESSAY "The Gospel of Wealth," American industrialist Andrew Carnegie (1835–1919) wrote, "a rich man should, after acquiring his wealth, distribute the surplus for the general welfare." The best known of Carnegie's many philanthropic projects was the funding, design, and construction of 2,509 public libraries between 1883 and 1929. The majority of the libraries, totaling 1,689, were built in the United States, but Carnegie also funded numerous libraries in Britain, Ireland, Australia, New Zealand, and even Serbia and Fiji.

Books and libraries were always important to Carnegie. As a weaver's son in Scotland, he borrowed books from the Tradesman's Subscription Library, which his father had helped to create. In 1848, at age 13, he emigrated to the United States. As a boy, he found work with a telegraph company in Allegheny, Pennsylvania. During that time, Carnegie borrowed books from Colonel James Anderson, an individual who regularly opened his personal library to laboring people.

Carnegie's path to wealth began in 1873 when he left a job with the Pennsylvania Railroad Company and founded the Keystone Bridge Company, which specialized in the manufacture of steel. Fifteen years later, he owned a huge steel mill, coal and iron mines, a 425-mile-long railroad, and a line of lake steamships. In 1901, he sold his company to the United States Steel Company and devoted the rest of his life to philanthropy.

His most famous philanthropic projects were his libraries. Most were funded according to the "Carnegie Formula." This required the recipient town to demonstrate the need for a public library, provide a site, and furnish 10 percent of the cost of construction annually to support library operation. Each town determined the appearance of its library, and most incorporated innovative features like open stacks (to encourage browsing) and children's rooms. One of the important aspects of the libraries was the staircase leading to the entrance, which made visitors rise to their encounter with knowledge.

As years passed, some of the libraries were demolished, gutted, or converted to other uses. However, historical preservationists have managed to save many with architecturally distinctive interiors and exteriors. In fact, many Carnegie libraries are still in use today, with alterations to accommodate computers and the needs of the disabled. In addition to libraries, Carnegie funded the Carnegie Institute of Technology, now part of Carnegie-Mellon University in Pittsburgh, the Carnegie Institution of Washington, D.C., and the Carnegie Foundation for the Advancement of Teaching in New York City.

Stephen Foster's "Old Folks at Home"

IN THE FIRST DECADES of the American Republic, a market quickly grew for sheet music for the entertainment of the new nation. Parlor songs for voice and piano accompaniment were the most widespread musical resource in print. These songs were mainly reprints and adaptations of European songs, capitalizing on a sense of nostalgia for the Old Country that was shared by recent immigrants and third-generation Yankees alike.

The first native-born Euro-American to earn a living (though a precarious one) as a song composer was Stephen Foster (1826–1864). A native of Pittsburgh, Pennsylvania, Foster was a self-taught musician. He mostly wrote his own texts, shaping a musical style that synthesized several European and Euro-American traditions (Italian opera, Anglo-Irish folk song, German art song, and English upper-class parlor song). Foster was truly skilled at creating simple, memorable melodies. His songs quickly became successes (the first was "Oh, Susanna" in 1848), though the chaotic sheet music market and lack of copyright protection meant that little of the profit on song sales found its way back to Foster, who died destitute in a hotel in Manhattan at the age of 37.

Foster wrote most of his songs on contract for blackface minstrel shows, and as a consequence many were originally in "Negro dialect" and dealt with subject matter related to the "idealized plantation" (for example "Camptown Races," "My Old Kentucky Home," "Old Dog Tray," and "Hard Times Come Again No More"). Other songs were more squarely in the European-modeled wistful/nostalgic mode that was so popular in the mid-1800s (for example, "[I Dream of] Jeannie with the Light Brown Hair").

Even the "plantation" songs had essentially no connection with actual African American musical practices. For example, one of Foster's most popular and famous songs, "Old Folks at Home" is musically indistinguishable from conventional British parlor song melodies, even though the text (in its original "dialect" spelling) tells us "Way down upon de Swanee ribber/Far, far away/Dere's wha my heart is turning ebber/Dere's wha de old folks stay."

Many of Fosters's songs (including "Old Folks") have since been brought into the sphere of "popular" or even "folk" music. But in their day they were not separated from other traditions (for example, the German art songs or Italian operas that served as inspiration for Foster) that we now think of as "high art."

Walter Reed

IN 1867, 16-YEAR-OLD WALTER REED entered the University of Virginia and, two years later, earned his medical degree. He still holds the record as the youngest graduate of the university's medical school.

Reed moved to New York, where he earned another medical degree at Manhattan's Bellevue Hospital Medical College in 1870, and he interned at New York City hospitals. For a while, Reed served as the assistant sanitary officer for the Brooklyn Board of Health. His experience there kindled an enduring interest in public health problems.

In 1875, Reed joined the medical department of the army as an assistant surgeon with the rank of first lieutenant. The army not only offered Reed unique professional opportunities but also the financial stability to support his marriage to Emilie Lawrence. After their wedding, Walter Reed and Emilie began an 18-year expedition from one posting to the next in Arizona Territory, Dakota Territory, Minnesota, and Nebraska. As he toured the American West's frontier outposts, Reed gained a proficiency in the investigation of the causes of epidemic disease.

Major Reed returned to the east coast in 1893, where he accepted the position of professor of bacteriology and clinical microscopy at the Army Medical School in Washington, D.C. For the next five years, he researched and taught in the new discipline of bacteriology. His interest in microorganisms placed Reed on the cutting edge. At the time, scientists and physicians still debated whether microscopic organisms or foul air spread infectious disease.

The Spanish American War began in 1898, and typhoid fever plagued volunteers at crowded army training camps. Headed by Reed, the Typhoid Board discovered how typhoid bacilli spread between humans, from contaminated flies, and by impure drinking water.

After the war, Reed was appointed president of a board tasked with the investigation of yellow fever and other tropical diseases that killed American soldiers in occupied Cuba. In 1900, Reed traveled to Cuba following the death of Dr. Jesse W. Lazear, a board member. In Lazear's notebook, Reed found the key to understanding yellow fever: A mosquito acts as an intermediate host for the biological agent that causes the disease. Further studies by Reed and his colleagues uncovered details about disease transmission, which led to a yellow fever eradication strategy.

In November 1902, Reed's appendix ruptured. He died from peritonitis on November 23. The Walter Reed National Army Medical Center in Washington, D.C., named in his honor, opened in 1909.

Piet Mondrian

THE PAINTINGS FOR WHICH Dutch painter Piet Mondrian (1872–1944) is best known are unmistakable: Constructed solely of straight lines, rectangles, and primary colors, they exemplify pure abstraction, containing no images or references to the physical world. The mature paintings of Mondrian and the artists who worked in a like manner are known alternately as De Stijl ("The Style") and Neo-Plasticism.

Mondrian's path to extreme pictorial reduction, which emerged by 1919, involved earlier experimentation with a variety of painting styles. These ranged from a freely brushed, earth-toned realist mode to a mystically inspired, abstract approach to form, often used to portray women in trances.

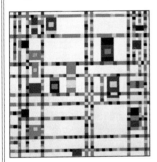
Broadway Boogie Woogie

Only after Mondrian felt the serious impact of Cézanne's late style and Picasso's Cubism, both of which stressed flattened space and geometric form, did his familiar style begin to take shape. As certain themes such as trees or still-life objects were painted and repainted over time, greater emphasis was placed on lines and grids suggested by natural shapes, until only geometric forms remained.

To Mondrian, after 1919, true art consisted only of the purest, simplest formal elements: straight lines and primary colors. With these deliberately limited means, he created endless compositional variations using square and rectangular shapes. The expression of universal balance was dependent, he felt, upon adherence to his strict aesthetic principles. When one of Mondrian's compatriots, Theo van Doesburg, introduced diagonals in his painting, the two had a falling out and parted ways.

De Stijl also extended to architecture and interior design in the Rietveld-Schröder House in Utrecht, designed by Gerrit Rietveld and Truus Schröder in 1924. Here the sliding doors and windows, primary-hued walls and severe, angular furniture constitute a translation of Mondrian's aesthetic into three dimensions.

In 1940, Mondrian traveled to New York to escape World War II. Inspired by the dynamic environment of Manhattan, he produced works such as *Broadway Boogie Woogie* in which his normally black lines take on checkered shapes of primary colors. Mondrian remained in New York until his death following a bout with pneumonia in 1944.

Karl Marx

A REVOLUTIONARY AND A HISTORIAN, Karl Marx (1818–1883) influenced political thought with his theory that "the history of…society is the history of class struggles." He believed capitalism would give way to communism.

Georg Hegel was a German philosopher and professor at universities in Heidelberg and Berlin during the early 1800s. His teachings dominated philosophical thinking in Germany, and he published major works in the area of philosophy.

Karl Marx, the son of a lawyer, was born in Trier and graduated from the local Gymnasium. He wanted to study philosophy, but his father objected because of the few prospects of earning a living as a scholar. Marx began his university studies in Bonn, studying law, though he was more interested in philosophy. Marx's father insisted that Karl transfer to a university in Berlin that had higher academic standards. It was while Karl was in Berlin that he became familiar with Hegel's philosophy and adopted the atheistic beliefs of the Young Hegelians, who believed the philosophy of religion was the basis of the corrupt German state.

Friedrich Engels was the son of a German textile manufacturer. Young Engels was also interested in the philosophical beliefs of Hegel. He read Hegel's works, attended lectures while he was stationed in Berlin during his Prussian military service, and became associated with the Young Hegelians. Engels's father was upset with his son's radical beliefs and sent him to work in England in a textile plant, hoping his son's beliefs would become more mainstream. But Engels found the conditions for the working classes horrible and wrote a book about the deplorable conditions.

In 1844, Engels and Marx met in Paris, a city in which revolutionaries from many countries lived. Marx and Engels formed a lasting friendship. Engels was a communist, and Marx became a communist as well. Marx was expelled from Paris for his revolutionary beliefs, and he and Engels moved to Brussels and then on to London.

As Marx developed his philosophy about government, he deviated from the position he had taken as a Young Hegelian and expressed the belief that capital, not religion, was the basis of a government's power. He and Engels wrote the *Communist Manifesto,* and Marx later published *Capital,* in which he critically analyzed the capitalist system.

Magical Realism

ALTHOUGH AN EXACT DEFINITION of the term is elusive, many consider *magical realism* to be a fusion of the real with the fantastic, thus creating a world that is both familiar—almost routine—and at the same time dreamlike or extraordinary. Magical realism often uses two perspectives in a novel or story that at first seem totally at odds with each other: One perspective is based on a normal, rational view of reality, while the other accepts the supernatural or fantastic as commonplace reality. Magical realism is normally not fantasy; the environment in which it takes place.

It was in 1925 that German art critic Franz Roh first coined the term *magic realism* to describe an artistic style. Later, it was used to describe the painting style of American artists such as Ivan Albright and Paul Cadmus. The term is also credited to Cuban writer Alejo Carpentier, who used it in 1949 to describe Latin American fiction. It was the so-called "Latin American Boom" that made the term popular, in particular the work of such writers as Juan Rulfo and Jorge Luis Borges.

One of the best-known writers of magical realism is Colombian novelist Gabriel García Márquez (born in 1927), who won the Nobel Prize for Literature in 1982. In a Márquez story entitled "A Very Old Man with Enormous Wings," an old man with giant wings lands in a family's courtyard. The community gathers to see the old man, who cannot fly away because his wings have been injured. The woman who lives in the house where the man has landed charges admission to see him and gets rich from the money she makes. Eventually, the winged man is upstaged by another "freak" who shows up in the community—a girl who has been turned into a tarantula. Ignored, the man's wings finally heal, and he flies away. The people in the story do not question the man with giant wings; they accept him and eventually exploit him. Ultimately, the reader learns more about the supporting characters than about the man with wings. The story demonstrates several characteristics of magical realism, including unquestioning acceptance of the supernatural, a nonexplanation of the supernatural by the author, and an ironic, almost humorous tone.

Other contemporary authors who have used magical realism include Toni Morrison, Gunter Grass, and Salman Rushdie.

D. W. Griffith (1875–1948)

DAVID WARK GRIFFITH was the first to fully understand that film is an artistic medium with unique techniques and aesthetics. For this reason, Lillian Gish, an actress he discovered, dubbed him the Father of Film. The techniques that Griffith invented and innovated formed the basis of the classic narrative style (also known as the classical style), which is still the standard style of Western filmmaking today.

Born in Oldham County, Kentucky, Griffith began his career in a theatrical company, serving as an actor and playwright. In 1907, he was hired by the Edison Studio in New York to act in a film called *Rescued from an Eagle's Nest.* He quickly realized the "flickers" were a medium dependent on stories, and he began writing scenarios for rival studio American Mutoscope and Biograph. In 1908, he directed his first film, a one-reeler titled *The Adventures of Dollie.* Over the next five years, Griffith made almost 500 one- and two-reelers for Biograph—it was during this tenure that he perfected the language of filmmaking.

Among the most significant of his discoveries were: the fundamentals of editing, including the division of scenes into long, medium, and close-up shots; slowing down or speeding up the action through pacing; and parallel editing—cutting back and forth between two scenes to suggest simultaneous action. In addition to editing, Griffith experimented with camera angles, expressive lighting, and camera movement as well as symbolism and narrative flashbacks. Finally, he and his actors, including the legendary Lillian Gish, helped develop a subtle style of acting suitable to film.

Griffith attained his greatest popularity and prestige between 1915 and 1920. He left Biograph in 1913 to begin the feature-length *Birth of a Nation,* which would be the culmination of all that he had learned about filmmaking. As such, it is a masterwork of the cinema. However, the subject matter—the Civil War and Reconstruction—is told from a 19th-century Southern perspective in which African Americans are rendered as the most racist of stereotypes and the Ku Klux Klan is painted as heroic. Instantly popular as well as controversial, *Birth* made Griffith both famous and infamous. The rest of the decade is marked by the director's best work, including the four-hour *Intolerance, Hearts of the World, Broken Blossoms,* and *Way Down East.*

Griffith turned to romantic melodramas in the 1920s, but they often did not fare well with critics or Jazz-Age audiences who were no longer interested in Victorian morality. Though he made two talkies in the early sound era, he had lost his cache as the Father of Film. He died in 1948.

Opera and Concert Music in America

IN THE EARLY DECADES of the 19th century, American audiences had the choice of a wide variety of musical entertainment. Some of these performances were based on the repertories of European stage music. Operas in the Italian *bel canto* style were the most popular with American audiences, thanks to their musical accessibility and wide distribution in the European market. When Italian operas were brought to the American stage, they were translated into English and frequently mixed with other styles of music. It was not uncommon for an audience to demand—and obtain—a rendition of a popular Anglo Irish or American political ballad in the midst of an operatic production. Opera companies toured widely throughout the East Coast, South, and Midwest, presenting hundreds of full-opera performances. In some cases, these operas would even share a concert bill with more humble types of musical entertainment.

In mid-1850s America, opera and other music from European composers was folded into a culturally diverse menu of musical consumption. This began to change toward the end of the century as such music began to be idealized as part of a self-contained "high art" tradition. The issue came to a head at the turn of the 20th century, as members of the Anglo American upper class of the Eastern seaboard grew wary of a perceived "cultural disruption" caused by the influx of immigrants from Eastern and Southern Europe and the growth in the urban African American population.

This upper-class sentiment of cultural exclusivity resulted in the creation of several cultural institutions, such as museums, public parks, and a cannon of "great" musical works. Just as important, when going to see a performance of a great opera or work, a new measure of proper decorum was required for the concert halls and opera houses of large urban centers. These developments helped to cement the so-called "high culture" status of certain European-derived musical traditions (generally known today as "classical music") and their association with elite cultural and social status. While that distinction has somewhat eroded in the last quarter century, the split between "high art" and "popular culture" still exists. This difference is more pronounced in the United States than in the European countries where "high art" originated.

Gustav Mahler

GUSTAV MAHLER'S (1860–1911) SYMPHONIES and songs are now considered among the most beautiful and expressive works of the turn-of-the-20th-century Austro-German tradition, and his lush orchestral writing has been a favorite of contemporary orchestras and their audiences since the revival of his music in the 1970s. In his own lifetime, however, Mahler's success was more tentative. Not only did his eclectic approach to mixing genre conventions and "high/low art" elements draw fire from establishment critics, his ethnic status as a Jew in late-imperial Vienna was a hindrance both to his career and, in the waves of institutional anti-Semitism that followed World War I, to the permanence and legacy of his works for the next generation of composers.

Mahler's own career and aesthetic approach reflect notable conflicts and contradictions. As a young man, he identified strongly with the Wagnerian philosophical camp of "progressive" musical composition and built his career as an operatic conductor specializing in Richard Wagner's works. However, despite his conducting and directing focus on opera, Mahler never completed an operatic composition. He incorporated program music (intended to evoke representational images or moods in the listener) and other nontraditionalist elements, such as songs and choral sections, into his symphonies. But he also systematically employed the "classic" structures advocated by champions of "absolute music" (music to be appreciated on its own merits, not evocative of images or emotions).

Mahler's professional career relied on being appointed to some of the most culturally prestigious—and thus conservative—institutions in central Europe. These required a number of personal and philosophical sacrifices for him, including his conversion to Roman Catholicism in order to become director of the Vienna State Opera in 1897. However, he always held a reputation as a champion of modern music, did his best to program new works by progressive composers, and even encouraged some of the young Viennese radicals (such as Arnold Schoenberg), whose experiments would soon create a drastic split between Mahler's own late romantic aesthetics and new notions of musicality.

POSTSCRIPT

■ Late in life, Mahler married Alma Schindler, who was also a musician and composer. However, Mahler forbade Alma from composing after their marriage, maintaining that it was important for there to be only one creative force in the household. This understandably led to tensions in their relationship.

What Is Light?

To describe light, most people would talk about visible light, which consists of wavelengths of red, orange, yellow, green, blue, indigo, and violet light. These form the familiar visible color spectrum. However, visible light is just one part of the many wavelengths of radiation on the electromagnetic spectrum. Really, scientists use the term *light* to describe the entire electromagnetic spectrum, which gets its name because it consists of both electric and magnetic fields. Included in the spectrum are radio waves, microwaves, infrared light, visible light, ultraviolet light, X-rays, and gamma rays.

Determining the physics of light has been a complex process. In the 19th century, light was thought to be an electromagnetic wave, but by the 20th century, it was suggested that electromagnetic energy was emitted and absorbed in the form of a tiny bundle called a *quantum.* The energy of each bundle depended on the frequency of the light's wavelength, or where it fit on the electromagnetic spectrum. Scientists found that these quanta behaved like particles, which raised an important question: How could an electromagnetic wave act like a particle? It was reasoned that light particles could behave like waves and vice versa. This dual nature of light is still being studied in the field of quantum physics.

As scientists learn more about how light behaves, they have been able to create new technologies that utilize it. Fiber-optic cables are designed to reflect light along their length. They have revolutionized the telephone, television, and computer industries by allowing the transmission of images and information over long distances at higher rates than materials such as metal. Lasers are another important technology that rely on concentrated beams of light at a specific wavelength. The word *laser* is actually an acronym for "Light Amplification by Stimulated Emission of Radiation." Lasers have proven widely useful in a variety of ways, from performing delicate surgical procedures to scanning bar codes in supermarkets. Light is also a key component in a variety of other technologies, including X-rays, Magnetic Resonance Imaging (MRI), and optical and scanning electron microscopes.

In many ways, the modern study of light is akin to science fiction. Albert Einstein once proposed that nothing could be done to change the speed of light, but scientists are now discovering that he may have been wrong. Work is now being done on faster-than-light communications and travel, which would move matter or information faster than the speed of light. In 2005, IBM claimed to have created a microchip that could slow down light, which eventually might be useful for commercial purposes.

Lewis Hine

Lᴇᴡɪѕ Wɪᴄᴋᴇѕ Hɪɴᴇ (1874–1940) understood that photographs had the power to inspire social change. Hine was born in Oshkosh, Wisconsin, and worked in a factory before studying sociology at the University of Chicago. He bought his first camera when he was teaching natural science and geography at New York City's progressive Ethical Culture School. From 1904 to 1906, Hine photographed immigrants at Ellis Island, and in 1907 he was hired by the Pittsburgh Survey to document the gritty realities of that industrial city.

Hine also became the staff photographer for the National Child Labor Committee in 1908. For nearly a decade, he created moving images of children working in sweatshops, mills, mines, and fields for that organization. Taking such pictures often required subterfuge, as many were not sympathetic to his cause. Hine had an actor's sensibility and impersonated everyone from fire inspectors to erstwhile teachers reduced to selling insurance. Sometimes he persuaded the owners and managers that he was primarily interested in photographing the machinery. Then, he might slyly ask a child to move next to a piece of equipment to provide a sense of scale for his picture. Hine could accurately estimate a child's size by measuring them against the buttons on his vest. Sometimes, if he could not get into a facility, he would photograph children in the early morning as they went to work.

While he believed absolutely in the truthfulness of the camera, it is also true that Hine strived to compose images that would elicit sympathy and inspire action. New technology made it possible to publish Hine's pictures in newspapers, and there they attracted wide attention. Hine also traveled from city to city giving public lectures that were illustrated with lantern slides of his photographs. His motivating belief was that "The object of employing children is not to train them, but to get high profits from their work." Thanks in part to Hine's efforts, a number of states passed laws restricting child labor.

The construction of New York's Empire State Building in the 1930s became Hine's last great subject. His photographs of the workers are viewed as a celebration of labor and human dignity.

The Kennedy Assassinations

IN THE FALL OF 1963, President John F. Kennedy began laying the groundwork for his upcoming reelection campaign. Well aware of the historically thin popular vote margin that had won him the White House three years earlier, he was anxious to shore up support in the Deep South. Despite having a bona fide Texan as his running mate, Kennedy's Northeastern liberalism, though moderate, was viewed with suspicion and loathing throughout some regions of the country.

A split between ideological wings of Kennedy's own party necessitated a trip to Vice President Lyndon Johnson's home state to mend some fences. Accompanied by his popular wife, Jacqueline, the president was overwhelmed by the outpouring of affection and warmth they received. Huge crowds turned out in San Antonio, Fort Worth, and on November 22, 1963, Dallas.

It was in a parklike setting called Dealey Plaza that President Kennedy was assassinated in a hail of gunfire. He was 46. The brief shining moment known as Camelot had passed, but John F. Kennedy's ascension into myth had just begun.

The torch was symbolically passed to the late president's brother and closest confidante, Robert Kennedy. Bobby, as he was known, resigned from the Attorney General's post he held and in 1964, ran successfully for the U.S. Senate from New York. Seemingly overnight, he became a beacon of hope during turbulent times.

Opposing the Johnson administration on the increasingly unpopular Vietnam War gave Bobby a purpose. In early 1968, following LBJ's stunning withdrawal from the race, Kennedy announced his candidacy for president. To a country rocked by the April assassination of Martin Luther King, Jr., Bobby offered comfort and empathy, projecting an authenticity that resonated among the poor and minorities in particular, despite his wealthy background.

His June 5 victory in the California primary seemed to make the prospect of a second Kennedy administration inevitable. But in an all-too-familiar turn, Bobby Kennedy was tragically gunned down at his Ambassador Hotel headquarters, just moments after delivering his victory speech.

POSTSCRIPT

■ Lee Harvey Oswald was arrested and charged with the assassination of John F. Kennedy but was himself killed before his day in court.

The Short Story in English

THE SHORT STORY is a distinctive literary genre like the poem, play, or novel. Authors must be concise, for they have only a few pages to create a world and a mood, tell the story, and reach a conclusion.

Many short stories, particularly those written nowadays, do not necessarily follow this logical pattern. They may begin and end abruptly in the middle of the action. Sometimes the narrative is deliberately disjointed. Authors often experiment in short stories before employing their innovations in the longer, more challenging novel form. James Joyce called the short story an "epiphany" and emphasized the importance of "revelation" rather than development over time, as in a novel.

The short story originated in tales that were told around the fire by our prehistoric ancestors. Ancient Greek narratives such as the *Iliad* and the *Odyssey* are composed of short rhymed sections that compare roughly to the short story. Chaucer's *Canterbury Tales* and Boccaccio's *Decameron* are short stories set within a larger narrative framework. Short fiction in English, as we know it today, was developed in the 19th century by Edgar Allan Poe, who was a master of the macabre and suspense. Other 19th-century short story authors include Washington Irving and Nathaniel Hawthorne.

Since Poe's day, most novelists have produced short stories, often beginning their careers in the form. Among these are Henry James, who depicted high society, among other things; Joseph Conrad, who wrote of the sea; Sherwood Anderson, whose subject was small-town life; and Theodore Dreiser, who focused on the city.

Many short story writers set their tales in a specific geographic area or depict a group in society such that their works become a composite portrait of the subject. James Joyce's *Dubliners* (1914), for example, is made up of 15 stories, none more than a few pages, set in his native Ireland. Ernest Hemingway's first book of short fiction, *In Our Time* (1925), focuses on manly pursuits like fishing and camping. Flannery O'Connor's *A Good Man Is Hard to Find and Other Stories* (1955) and *Everything that Rises Must Converge* (1965) are set in the Deep South and are imbued with biblical symbolism.

As the short story developed in English, European authors were producing short story masterpieces in their own languages as well. No account of the short story is complete without a mention of Russian authors Anton Chekov and Nikolai Gogol and French writer Prosper Mérimée, all of whom flourished in their field in their native tongues.

Thomas Alva Edison (1847–1931)

A PROPONENT OF EXPERIMENTS and trial and error, Thomas Edison was one of the most prolific inventors in the modern world. Edison was born in Ohio, but his family moved to Port Huron, Michigan, when he was about seven years old. Teachers thought Edison was dull; his mother began home-schooling him, attributing his problems to superior intellect and deafness caused by ear infections and contracting scarlet fever at a young age.

Thomas began working for the railroad to earn extra money. When he was about 12, he saved a child from being run over by a train—the event changed the direction of Edison's life. The child's father was grateful for Edison's rescue efforts and offered to teach him about the telegraph. In learning how to use the instrument, Edison developed a method to send multiple transmissions simultaneously.

Edison then moved from the Midwest to the East Coast. During the time Edison lived in Boston he developed an electric vote-recording machine. He applied for and received a patent, but was unable to market the device—many politicians believed that the machine's ability to tabulate votes quickly would disrupt the political philosophy that favored the manual counting of ballots. From that time on, it is said that Edison concentrated only on inventions that people would purchase.

From Boston, Edison moved to New York, and then to Menlo Park, New Jersey, where he established a laboratory for testing and development. The following year, in 1877, he invented the first phonograph. He also developed a dictaphone, a mimeograph machine, and the incandescent lightbulb. Edison's inventions led to the production of the first silent motion pictures. He became known as the "Wizard of Menlo Park" and was thought of as the "father of the electrical age."

Edison patented more than 1,000 inventions during his lifetime. He held patents in the United States, Germany, France, and the United Kingdom. He continued to be active in business until a few months before his death. Edison and Henry Ford developed a friendship during the time they spent wintering in Fort Myers, Florida, and after Edison's death, Ford moved Edison's Menlo Park Laboratory to Greenfield Village Museum in Dearborn, Michigan, where it can be visited today.

John Stuart Mill

AS A VERY YOUNG CHILD, British writer and philosopher John Stuart
Mill (1806–1873) was educated according to the theories of his
father, philosopher James Mill. Utilitarians, like the elder Mill, believed
that when choosing a course of action, the overall usefulness of the
consequence was the most important consideration. As Mill described
in his famous work, *Autobiography* (1873), his father trained him from
a young age so he could eventually carry on the cause of utilitarianism.
He began to learn Greek at the age of three and had read most of Plato's
dialogues by the time he was seven. His education continued rapidly, and
at age eight, he was already studying Latin and mathematics. By the time
he was 12, he studied logic; political economy by age 13; and history, law,
and philosophy at 14. For the young Mill, no holidays were allowed, "lest
the habit of work should be broken and a taste for idleness acquired."
The only recreation was a daily walk with his father, who used the time
to quiz his son on his studies. His formal education ended at 17, when he
began working for the East India Company.

By the age of 20, Mill was a chief contributor to the *Westminster Review*
and became recognized as a leading utilitarian. In 1826, he suffered a
nervous breakdown, brought on by the rigors of his early training. Following this, he indulged himself in the writings of Romantic poets and
socialist thinkers, which he viewed as being as distanced as possible from
his father's intellectual ideals. He also met and fell in love with a married
woman named Harriet Taylor. They corresponded, traveled, and occasionally lived together over the next 20 years, until her husband's death
allowed them to be married.

Influenced by Harriet and the Romantic poets, Mill modified Jeremy
Bentham's theory of utilitarianism, which stressed implementing reason
to the point of excluding emotion. He transformed Bentham's credo of
"the greatest good for the greatest number" to a more humane interpretation of utilitarianism, stating, "actions are right in proportion as they
tend to promote happiness, wrong as they tend to produce the reverse of
happiness."

In addition to his writings on utilitarianism, Mill published many other
important works, including *System of Logic* (1843), *Principles of Political
Economy* (1848), *On Liberty* (1859), and *The Subjection of Women* (1869).

Following his retirement from the East India Company in 1858, Mills
held a seat in Parliament from 1865 to 1868, where he distinguished
himself by supporting the then unpopular causes of women's suffrage,
compulsory education, birth control, and land reform in Ireland.

Futurism and "The Art of Noises"

THE FIRST DECADES of the 1900s saw a number of significant artistic movements that created a self-conscious break with what their proponents felt was a "stale" tradition. Among the more radical was the Italian Futurist movement, which was especially innovative—perhaps foreshadowing later 20th-century developments—in its approach to music or, perhaps more accurately, to the beauty of "noise."

Chief among the musical innovators in the Futurist camp was Luigi Russolo (1885–1947). His manifesto-treatise *L'arte dei rumori* (*The Art of Noises*), published in 1913, argued that the evolution of music involved the incorporation of increasingly complex machines. Russolo maintained that "futurist musicians must continually enlarge and enrich the field of sounds," substituting "for the limited variety of notes possessed by orchestral instruments today"—which Russolo found to be outdated and old-fashioned—"the infinite variety of tones of noises, reproduced with appropriate mechanisms." In the conclusion of his manifesto, Russolo suggests that this approach would bring "a taste and passion for noises" to both progressive musicians and the listening public, so that "the motors and machines of our industrial cities will one day be consciously attuned. . . . Every factory will be transformed into an intoxicating orchestra of noises." Russolo and the Futurists were especially interested in the sounds of industry and machines, which they believed to be the true sounds of the future.

While the technology for sound reproduction was limited in the 1910s and '20s, Russolo created "instruments" that he called *intonarumori* ("noise-sound-makers"), with which he created performances of "noise-music" in a number of European cities. Regrettably, Russolo did not leave precise details about the construction of the instruments, which were all destroyed during World War II. However, there are some modern recordings that use reconstructions of Russolo's intonarumori. (An interesting 2004 compilation of a number of Futurist word- and sound-works is available on the *Salon Recordings* label.)

The musical side of the Futurist movement was relatively short-lived. (Most Futurists were visual artists or poets; Russolo himself identified as a painter rather than a musician.) However, Russolo's approach to "noise-sound" foreshadowed an increasing interest in electronic and electro-acoustic music, a tradition that really came into its own after World War II with the introduction of more widespread and inexpensive technological resources such as tape recording and musical synthesizers.

Sara Josephine Baker

Hell's Kitchen, a gritty neighborhood in Manhattan, New York City, is not where most people would choose to work. However, Sara Josephine Baker (1873–1945) took it as an opportunity—it was there that she focused on decreasing the city's infant mortality rate.

Baker was 16 when her father died of typhoid fever. She decided not to accept a scholarship to Vassar, her mother's alma mater. Instead, she chose to enroll in a medical school for women, the New York Infirmary Medical College. After graduation, Dr. Baker interned in Boston where she realized poverty and ill health were connected. She focused her medical career on improving the health problems linked with destitution.

When Dr. Baker first became an employee with the New York Department of Health, she worked as a medical inspector in the public schools, determining whether sick children should be sent home. As the result of her efforts, a citywide school-nursing program was established.

For an extended period, Dr. Baker concentrated her efforts in Hell's Kitchen. In that section of New York City, more than 1,000 infants were dying weekly from disease. Milk was not pasteurized; it was sold in open, often rusty, containers and mixed with water or chalk. Dysentery and typhoid were common causes of death; smallpox was another major health concern. Baker focused on preventative measures in her attempt to reduce the mortality rate. She and members of the nursing profession began training mothers on how to properly care for their infants: Good diets, cleanliness, and safety were all part of the program. Older siblings were also taught how to care for the infants, helping to provide mothers with the opportunity to join the workforce and assist in supporting their families financially. When Baker realized midwives were delivering babies without having to account for their qualifications, she encouraged the city of New York to begin midwife licensing.

Dr. Baker became well known throughout the world as a result of her efforts. She was the first female assistant Surgeon General of the United States. She also became the first woman to serve as the professional representative to the League of Nations. She wrote books as well as numerous medical articles and served as president of the American Medical Women's Association.

The Art of Arp and Moore

GEOMETRY HAS ALWAYS been central to art, but perhaps never more so than in the early years of the 20th century. In abstract styles such as Neo-Plasticism and Constructivism, geometric shapes—often constructed with architectural tools to achieve maximum precision—not only made up the art, they also took on symbolic significance, standing for the vitality of modern life, the efficiency of mass production, and the "brave new world" of science and technology.

In response to such work, there emerged another strain of modern art that was inspired by the forms and processes of the natural world and embodied a whole other set of concepts. The term used to describe this art is *biomorphism,* which comes from the Greek words *bios,* meaning "life," and *morphe,* meaning "form."

Biomorphism first appeared in the work of the French painter and sculptor Jean (Hans) Arp (1886–1966). Around 1917, he made a series of brightly colored wood reliefs he called "Earthly Forms," based on drawings of the roots, branches, and stones he observed on the shores of Ascona, Switzerland. In simplifying the forms of the drawings, Arp arrived at works that were abstract yet evoked their natural sources of inspiration. He went even further in his "Concretions," a series of sculptures he made in the 1930s that suggested natural processes such as growth and metamorphosis.

Arp's biomorphic works reflect their creator's faith in the power of nature to cure social dislocation and other ills of modern life. They influenced other artists of the time, including British sculptor Henry Moore (1898–1986).

Moore was greatly inspired by the natural world. The "principle of the opposition of bumps and hollows" seen throughout his *Henry Moore*

work derived from Moore's study of the flint pebbles he collected on the Norfolk, England, coastline. These and other organic objects also helped Moore develop an understanding of the natural materials (wood and stone) in which he worked. Even at its most abstract, Moore's sculpture always makes reference to the human figure.

The work of artists like Arp and Moore made biomorphism an important influence in European and American art of the 1930s and 1940s.

Quebec Separatism

O**N** S**EPTEMBER** 13, 1759, French and British troops faced each other at bayonet-point outside Quebec City in modern-day eastern Canada. Thirty minutes later, England's domination of North America had been assured, and the dream of "New France" was dead.

The British victory at the Battle of the Plains of Abraham took about 30 minutes and involved fewer than 10,000 troops on both sides. It is familiar to many by virtue of Benjamin West's famous painting depicting the death of the British commander, General James Wolfe, at the moment of victory. The French commander, Louis-Joseph de Montcalm, was also killed.

The battle, just one of many in the global Seven Years War, was the pivotal event in the North American theater. Once Quebec fell, France's 155-year presence on the North American continent was doomed. Four years later, the Treaty of Paris gave possession of New France—most of what is now eastern Canada—to Great Britain.

But a triumph of arms does not necessarily translate into a victory over hearts and minds. A war of another sort continues to this day in a Canada torn between two cultures, majority Anglo and minority French. This battlefield is political, social, and cultural. At the heart of the conflict is French-Canadian resentment from a people who have pride in their language and culture, a desire for more autonomy, and fears of political and cultural dominance by the English-speaking majority.

Quebec's position as a virtual nation within a nation has long been acknowledged. In 1867, when John A. MacDonald successfully engineered a Canadian confederation, the continuing Anglo/Franco dissension was tacitly recognized with the division of the former province of Canada into the provinces of Ontario (English) and Quebec (French).

In more recent times, the specter of Quebec separatism has gained momentum with multiple referendums, constitutional conventions, the formation of separatist political parties, and even terrorism intended to advance independence.

In the 1970s, Canadian Prime Minister Pierre Trudeau introduced official bilingualism. Quebec, however, refused to sign the new Canadian Constitution negotiated by Trudeau in 1982. In 1987, Prime Minister Brian Mulroney negotiated a package of constitutional amendments to satisfy Quebec's demand for recognition as a "distinct society" within Canada. These efforts dragged on to a national referendum in 1992, when the proposal was defeated.

Margaret Atwood

ARGUABLY CANADA's most famous living author, Margaret Atwood (1939–present) is a writer who refuses to be pigeonholed into a single genre.

Atwood's father was an entomologist and zoology professor who brought his family into the remote regions of Ontario and Quebec as he studied tree-eating insects. As a result, Atwood was infused at an early age with a love of the Canadian wilderness, and this feeling runs through her writing. Because of her lifestyle, Atwood did not attend school full-time until she was 11 years old. She began writing at age 16. In 1961, her privately printed book of poetry entitled *Double Persephone* won the E. J. Pratt Medal.

In 1966, her poetry collection *The Circle Game* won the Governor General's Award. In 1969, she published her first novel, a satire about a woman at a marketing firm called *The Edible Woman*. The woman in the story cannot eat but feels as if she is being eaten. Atwood continued to bounce back and forth between fiction and poetry, sometimes publishing a book in both genres every year. She reinterpreted how Canadians view their literary heritage in 1972's *Survival: A Thematic Guide to Canadian Literature* and sparked new interest in the field of Canadian literature. She continued to move into different areas of writing in the following years, penning short stories, a novel, and even some television scripts.

In 1980, Atwood became vice-chairperson of the Writer's Union of Canada. This was the perfect forum for her to champion books that explored Canadian nationalism. In 1985, Atwood published her signature work, a novel entitled *The Handmaid's Tale*. Grim, sardonic, terrifying, and humorous all at the same time, the book depicts a futuristic society in which women have no rights except to marry, keep house, and reproduce. The book made Atwood and her work international sensations. It was made into a film in 1990.

Atwood brings the same passion to her environmental beliefs that she brings to her writing. She has suggested that gas-powered leaf blowers and lawn mowers be banned. She uses a hybrid automobile and lives in a house with no air conditioning.

Atwood continues to produce short stories, novels, literary criticism, and poetry. There is even a scholarly group, the Margaret Atwood Society, dedicated to her work. Her signature is creating strong yet mysterious female characters in stories rich with discussions of sex, politics, and other issues. In 2006, Atwood published a collection of essays entitled *The Tent* and in 2007 a collection of poetry called *The Door*.

Oscar Wilde (1854-1900)

REFERENCING HIMSELF, poet, dramatist, and novelist Oscar Wilde said that he put his genius into his life and only his talent into his work. Certainly, he created a character for himself as dramatic as any that he placed on the page. A leader of the Aesthetic Movement, which advocated "art for art's sake," Wilde deliberately attracted attention with his long hair, eccentric clothes, and habit of holding flowers in his hands when he lectured. He was regularly lampooned in the popular press and even parodied in the character of the poet Bunthorne in Gilbert and Sullivan's 1881 operetta, *Patience.* Bunthorne was said to be a "very cultivated kind of youth" given to "an attachment à la Plato for a bashful young potato or a not-too-French French bean."

Wilde was one of the most colorful figures in the literary world in the 1880s. His witticisms were widely quoted: "Work is the curse of the drinking classes," "Nothing succeeds like excess," "Divorces are made in heaven." Entering the United States for a lecture tour in 1882, he told an astonished customs agent "I have nothing to declare except my genius." His plays were so successful that in 1895 he had two hits running in London at the same time: *An Ideal Husband* and *The Importance of Being Earnest.*

Wilde's plays were his only popular success, but he published works in a variety of genres—from fairy tales to literary criticism. His two most important works, *The Picture of Dorian Gray* and *Salome,* were received with moral outrage by Victorian critics.

In 1895, Wilde's public career ended with a crash. In response to a threatening letter charging him with homosexual practices, Wilde began an inexplicable libel suit against the Marquis of Queensbury—the father of Wilde's lover, Lord Alfred Douglas. Wilde was defeated using evidence that included his own passionate letters to Douglas; a love poem by Douglas to Wilde, ending with the famous line "the Love that dare not speak its name"; and a list of male prostitutes with whom Wilde had been involved. The libel suit was followed by criminal charges against Wilde for sodomy, using the same evidence. Wilde was sentenced to two years in prison with hard labor. Although he had several chances to flee the country after his sentence was passed, he chose not to run. While in prison, he wrote *The Ballad of Reading Gaol,* a long poem drawing on his experiences.

On his release from prison, broken physically and financially, Wilde moved to Paris, where he lived under the name of Sebastian Monmouth until his death in 1900.

Islamic Sects

Sunnis and Shias

THE TWO LARGEST DIVISIONS in Islam are the Sunni and Shia (or Shiite). Following the death of the Prophet Mohammed in A.D. 632, the question arose over who should succeed him as caliph, or leader of the Muslim people. One group believed that Mohammed had chosen a close friend, Abu Bakr, as the new leader, while another believed that the Prophet wanted power to stay within his own family. In the following conflicts, the majority who were in support of Bakr would become known as Sunnis; the minority in favor of familial succession were called Shias. Today, about 90 percent of the world's estimated 1.1 billion Muslims are Sunnis.

Kharijites

Historically, this name refers to a group that withdrew support from Ali when he was caliph after he called in arbitrators to settle a conflict with the governor of Damascus. They believed that such human intervention went against Allah. Kharijites claimed the authority to judge and kill "false" Muslims, even caliphs. Today, the Ibadiyah subsect in North Africa, Oman, and Tanzania consider themselves the Kharijites's descendants, though they reject the name and moderate some of the teachings.

Ismailis

The Ismaili sect began with a split from the Shia group in the eighth century A.D. Most Ismailis today follow the Aga Khan, the imam of their sect, who runs a worldwide network of charities and development projects. Syria's ruling Alawi sect is an Ismaili offshoot.

Nizaris

The Nizari Ismailis, known as *Assassins* in Europe, broke from the main Ismaili group in a dispute over succession to the caliphate. Founded in 1090, the group controlled several fortresses throughout Syria and Persia (present-day Iran) in the 11th and 12th centuries. They became well known for their use of targeted murder to eliminate enemies. Beginning in 1256, their main strongholds were crushed by invading Mongols and forces from Egypt. Today, only a few scattered Nizari groups remain.

Wahhabis

Muhammad ibn Abd al-Wah'hab (1703–1792) was an Arabian tribal leader who promoted a conservative interpretation of Islam. His followers consider the more liberal practices of other Muslim groups to be heretical. Wahhabism is Saudi Arabia's official state religion.

George Gershwin's *Rhapsody in Blue*

ALTHOUGH HE WAS SUCCESSFUL as a songwriter for Broadway, radio, and film, George Gershwin (1898–1937) long struggled with the goal of creating music that would qualify as "high art." At the time, the goal of defining an independently American "classical" tradition was a highly contentious issue among American musicians and critics. Those who critiqued Gershwin's music considered his success in the popular market an indication of the inherently "superficial" nature of his compositional

approach. Still, Gershwin created a number of works—popular in their own day, and still more widely performed than most of the compositions considered more "legitimate" by his high-minded critics—that sought to integrate the European-derived concert music tradition with the jazz and Broadway musicals that were the composer's bread-and-butter.

The opportunity for one such experiment came with a commission for a special concert organized by Paul Whiteman, one of the lead-ing bandleaders and arrangers of the big-band era. This concert, which Whiteman called *An Experiment in Modern Music,* took place on February 12, 1924, in New York's Aeolian Hall. It was an event designed specifically to exemplify the potentially "classical" aspects of jazz.

Gershwin's contribution to the concert was his *Rhapsody in Blue* (1924), which resembles a piano concerto (a standard "high-art genre") in its contrasts between a featured piano and a larger ensemble but makes use of musical devices (in instrumentation, harmony, and rhythm) that are characteristic of the swing-jazz sound associated with Gershwin's songwriting. With Whiteman's band performing the orchestral portion, Gershwin himself played the piano for *Rhapsody*'s premiere.

The opening of the work is especially striking and has become one of the signature sound-clips of Gershwin's music (in fact, one of the classic "sound bites" of orchestral jazz): The clarinet plays a trill low in its range and then suddenly slides far up into the musical stratosphere, blending the sound of the classical clarinet with the sensuality of jazz style.

While critical reaction to *Rhapsody in Blue* was mixed, the popular response was overwhelmingly positive. To this day, there's debate about whether this work can really be considered jazz. But no matter how it's categorized, *Rhapsody in Blue* continues to be a popular and beloved piece of American music.

Albert Einstein

ALBERT EINSTEIN (1879–1955) WON the Nobel Prize in Physics only once, in 1921, though physicists agree he could have easily won it for each of the four papers he published in 1905. These papers covered such eclectic topics as Brownian motion, special relativity, matter and energy (the origin of $E = mc^2$), and the photoelectric effect—for which he did win the coveted prize.

But Einstein, as many people know, had humble beginnings. He wasn't an especially gifted student—though, despite the common misconceptions, he wasn't dull or mentally challenged. In fact, he skipped the last years of high school and applied for ETH Zurich at age 16.

Einstein met his future wife, Mileva, at ETH. She was the only woman studying mathematics there. He spent two years searching for a teaching position but ended up working at the patent office in Bern, Germany.

Einstein was promoted at the patent office and received a Ph.D. at age 26. He moved around as a professor at various universities, including Berne, Zurich, Prague, and Berlin. During his early years as an academic, he developed the general theory of relativity, which unifies special relativity, Newton's law of gravity, and the space-time continuum. It's a form of gravitational theory that uses equations that relate space and time. In particular, as opposed to classical mechanics in which forces of gravity describe various phenomena such as free-fall and orbital motion, Einstein's theory of relativity ascribes such events to inertial motion within a curved space-time geometry. Evidence since then, such as the deflection of light, slowing down of time, gravitational waves, and even black holes, have supported Einstein's theory.

For much of the rest of his career, Einstein sought to build on his theory of general relativity and to try to unify it with all the fundamental laws of physics—in particular, gravitation and electromagnetism. His dream was to unify all the laws of physics in some grand theory of the universe. He failed on this account, but he was responsible for pioneering the field of quantum mechanics, providing a theory of the dual nature of matter, which would later give rise to string theory and other advances that have furthered his vision of a "grand theory of the universe."

During the rise of Nazism, Einstein moved to the United States and began working at Princeton University's Institute for Advanced Study. He became a U.S. citizen in 1940 and, concerned about Hitler's eye on science, helped convince the U.S. government of the need to develop the atomic bomb. He died in 1955 from the rupture of an aortic aneurysm.

Pablo Picasso's *Guernica*

ON MONDAY, APRIL 26, 1937, people crowded into the Spanish Basque
town of Guernica for the weekly market. Without warning, at least
25 German bombers flew overhead, releasing 100,000 pounds of bombs
on the village. Behind them, agile fighter planes strafed the town, shooting at those who ran or tried to hide. When it all was over, most of the
town was in rubble. More than 1,600 townspeople and their children had
been killed or wounded.

In Paris, Pablo Picasso
(1881–1973) read the headline, "A thousand firebombs
dropped by Hitler's and
Mussolini's planes reduce
Guernica to ashes." He was
about to start a mural for the
Spanish Pavilion at the upcoming International Exposition in Paris. On
May 1, he made the first sketches for the powerful and poignant work
known as *Guernica.*

This enormous canvas is about 11½ feet by 25½ feet. It was so large, in
fact, that Picasso had to tilt it against the wall so it would fit under the
ceiling of his studio. When it went on exhibition, it was attacked by representatives of both the political left and right. Today, the painting is seen as
a protest against Fascist brutality in particular and, more generally, as an
allegory of modern war.

The figures belong both to Picasso's private iconography as well as to traditional art history. Picasso described the bull as "brutality and darkness."
The horse, which has been pierced by a spear, "represents the people";
below the horse, a fallen warrior clutches a broken sword. In an early
stage, the painting resembled a Spanish arena; the horse and bull seemed
to symbolize the Spanish Republican fighters and the armies of the
dictator Francisco Franco, respectively. In the final version, the conflict
is more ambiguous, although it is clear from the spear that the horse has
become the victim of human violence. The imagery, in fact, seems to suggest the distant past. Nowhere are planes or guns in evidence. The only
allusion to modern technology is the hanging light: *Bombilla* is Spanish
for electric bulb, and *bomba* means "bomb."

At first Picasso used color. He collaged scraps of wallpaper to the image
and painted a crimson tear on the cheek of the weeping woman. The final
painting, however, includes only black, white, and shades of gray, suggesting the irrefutable content of newspapers and history books.

Sitting Bull

NEARLY 120 YEARS AFTER his death, Sitting Bull (1834–1890) remains an almost mythical figure in the pages of American history. Brave, reflective, a born organizer and leader, Sitting Bull staunchly and consistently defended his people.

Born March 31, 1834, near present-day Bullhead, South Dakota, Sitting Bull was known during his boyhood as "Hunesni," which means "slow." If this was sarcasm, it was misplaced. Acclaimed for his courage in battle, Sitting Bull went on to gain great stature as a medicine man and tribal leader.

Sitting Bull was an active participant in the Plains Wars of the 1860s, when Native Americans fought the U.S. Army, which was encroaching on their land and reneging on policies and treaties. In 1876, when the U.S. government ordered the tribes out of the Black Hills and back to the reservations, Sitting Bull was key among those who refused to obey. As head of the Sioux war council, he engineered an alliance with the Cheyenne and Arapaho to resist the order by force.

When U.S. Army troops rode into the Black Hills to enforce the decree, as many as 3,000 warriors were waiting. Their morale was bolstered by Sitting Bull, who told them he'd had a vision in which many white soldiers were falling upside down from the sky into the Indian camp. This good omen was fulfilled when the tribes destroyed General George Armstrong Custer's command at Little Big Horn on June 25, 1876.

Relentlessly pursued by army troops, Sitting Bull and his followers fled into Canada, where they suffered significant hardships. Many of the fugitives died of hunger and cold or gave up and returned to the reservation. Sitting Bull and the last holdouts finally surrendered on July 19, 1881, at Fort Buford, Montana.

The Sioux leader spent the next two years in prison. Having become as famous among whites as he was among his own people, Sitting Bull did a brief tour with Buffalo Bill Cody's Wild West Show. It is said that when asked to address the audience, he would loudly curse them in his native tongue. Having no idea what he was saying, the crowd responded with enthusiastic cheers.

Sitting Bull's stature made him a target a few years later when the Ghost Dance movement emerged among the Sioux. Fearful of an uprising, Indian Agency police attempted to arrest Sitting Bull on December 15, 1890. Sitting Bull's followers resisted, shots were fired, and he and his son Crow Foot were both killed.

Chinua Achebe's *Things Fall Apart*

FOR MANY YEARS, the books written about Africa's people and their way of life portrayed the Africans as savages, with little or no culture. Then along came Chinua Achebe's novel *Things Fall Apart* in 1959, and the world began to learn more about the rich heritage of the African people.

Albert Chinualumogu Achebe was born on November 16, 1930, in a large Nigerian village where people still lived according to the ways of the Igbo (formerly Ibo) culture. At school, Achebe's interest in Nigerian heritage blended with his desire to present Nigerian culture to the world. *Things Fall Apart* was the result.

The story centers on Okonkwo, a wealthy, respected warrior of the Umuofia clan. In a settlement with a nearby village, the Umuofia win a virgin and a 15-year-old boy named Ikemefuna. Okonkwo takes in Ikemefuna, and the child develops a strong attachment to him. Ikemefuna is also a positive influence on Okonkwo's son Nwoye. But one day, a village elder tells Okonkwo it has been foreseen that Ikemefuna must die. He can have no part in the boy's death, Okonkwo is warned. But when Ikemefuna is attacked, he runs to Okonkwo for help. Okonkwo responds by killing him, despite the warning, which sets off a grim chain of events.

The village elder dies, and at his funeral Okonkwo's gun explodes, accidentally killing one of the elder's sons. For his crime, Okonkwo is banished along with his family for seven years. To Okonkwo's new village comes a tolerant missionary named Mr. Brown. Unfortunately, he gets sick and is replaced by the strict Reverend Smith. One of his more zealous followers loosens an evil spirit, which burns down Smith's church. The bureaucratic district commissioner arrests the Umuofia leaders, including Okonkwo, and throws them into prison, where they are abused. Upon their release they gather for a meeting, but five commission messengers come and tell them to break it up. This means that the Umuofia are being denied even their traditional way of talking over problems. Enraged at the loss of their independence, Okonkwo kills a messenger, expecting his fellow leaders to rise up in revolt. When the other messengers are allowed to escape, Okonkwo realizes that they don't want to fight, and he kills himself.

Written in English by Achebe, *Things Fall Apart* also includes passages in the Igbo language. Achebe did this deliberately to show the language's complexity and how it defies a simple English translation. The novel is almost required reading in Africa, and it is probably the most famous African novel ever written.

Charlemagne (742/747-814)

Wᴴᴱɴ Cʜᴀʀʟᴇᴍᴀɢɴᴇ (or Charles the Great) inherited the crown from his father in 768, Europe was in disarray. Charlemagne envisioned bringing order to it, and for 30 years, he engaged in military campaigns to accomplish his purpose.

Charlemagne was a religious person but a brutal and cruel warrior. His wars were waged to defend Christianity while at the same time increase the size of his realm. For that reason, he is known as the king who became ruler by using the sword and the cross.

As Charlemagne planned his conquests, he decided to first attack against the pagan Saxons who lived in what is modern-day northern Germany. After several years of battle, he defeated his enemy. As they surrendered, he gave them a choice between baptism and death. The several thousand who chose death were beheaded.

For several years, Charlemagne led his warriors in battle, but as he became older, he gave his sons and other individuals the responsibility of leadership, while he attempted to secure more lands in the name of Christianity through persuasion and negotiation.

Charlemagne was loyal to the Church. He formed a close association with the Church because of his strong religious beliefs and his generous contributions. The Church cooperated with Charlemagne and supported his efforts as he conquered territories in the name of Christianity.

In 795, a Roman with a humble background became Pope Leo III. The new pope turned to Charlemagne when critics and enemies accused him of being unfit to serve as pope. With Charlemagne's help, Pope Leo's enemies were tried and sent to prison. Conditions remained unstable, and Charlemagne traveled to Rome in 800 to help bring about stability and protect the pope. Charlemagne attended mass at St. Peter's Basilica on Christmas Day. During the service, the pope placed a crown upon Charlemagne's head, crowning him emperor of the Holy Roman Empire.

During his reign, Charlemagne issued a series of administrative and legislative acts called *Capitularies*. The Capitularies involved both ecclesiastical and secular matters, covered subjects of law and justice, and had the weight of law. Charlemagne had used brutality and cruelty during his conquests, but as the ruler of the Holy Roman Empire, he improved the lives of those he governed. He established a new monetary system, heralded education reforms, and helped bring about the Carolingian Renaissance, an era during which art and literature flourished.

Gothic Fiction

Horace Walpole's 1764 novel *The Castle of Otranto* began a vogue for Gothic fiction that lasted into the early 19th century and beyond. Often showing situations, persons, and events set in a luridly imagined medieval or Catholic past or in Catholic countries, Gothic novels reveled in knights, nuns, castles, monasteries, hidden dungeons, virgins, and evil seducers. Gothic plots were romantic and melodramatic, and characters were often stereotypical heroes or heroines and villains. Their stated purpose was to produce a pleasurable feeling of terror in the reader.

Although some Gothic works are studied today, including Ann Radcliffe's *The Mysteries of Udolpho* (1794) and *The Italian* (1797), William Godwin's *Caleb Williams* (1794), and Mathew Lewis's *The Monk* (1796), few modern readers find them as intriguing as their original audience did. But for about 50 or 60 years, the genre's appeal, especially to female readers, made it a best-selling category.

Most Gothic novels were seen both in their day and ours as cheap and sensationalist. In the early 19th century, "trade" Gothic novels were sold as "blue books" (chapbooks with cheap blue covers), a tradition that would continue with Victorian "penny bloods" and "penny dreadfuls." By that time, they were already targets of parody. Jane Austen's *Northanger Abbey* (written in 1798 but not published until 1817) and Thomas Love's *Peacock's Nightmare Abbey* (1818) were both parodies of Gothic novels.

However, the Gothic style also influenced major writers. Much of Edgar Allen Poe's fiction and poetry (such as *The Fall of the House of Usher,* published in 1839) is Gothic. The most famous and influential Gothic novel is Mary Shelley's *Frankenstein: or The Modern Prometheus* (1818). William Faulkner (*The Sound and the Fury,* 1929) and Flannery O'Connor (*A Good Man Is Hard to Find and Other Stories,* 1955) are sometimes called "Southern Gothic" novelists. Today's horror fiction is one continuation of the Gothic novel, as in Stephen King's fiction or the novels of Anne Rice.

POSTSCRIPT

■ Before writing *The Castle of Otranto,* Horace Walpole started a trend of Gothic buildings in the 1740s by renovating his Strawberry Hill estate in a "Gothick" or imagined medieval style, with turrets and battlements.

■ Like many terms in literary and art criticism, *Gothic* is a misnomer that originated as an insult. The Goths were a group of Germanic tribes who plundered Europe and sacked Rome during the fifth through seventh centuries. Renaissance scholars incorrectly used the term *Gothic* as a synonym for *barbaric* to insult the style of medieval cathedrals.

Chinese *Qin* Music

Records of Chinese court culture predate the various European traditions by many centuries, and sophisticated traditions of cultivated music were in place while Europeans were still working with very rudimentary resources. The most nuanced instrument from the tradition is a seven-stringed zither originally known as the *qin,* a word that has become synonymous with "musical instrument" in the Chinese tradition (so much so that the instrument is now generally referred to as a *guqin,* "old musical instrument"). The *qin* was associated with the high-class scholar culture and also with the great philosopher Confucius (551–479 B.C.) as well as several Chinese emperors. According to legend, its practice goes back 5,000 years, and mention of the instrument appears in documents that are almost 3,000 years old.

Qin music has a complex notation system, which allows for the performance of works that were composed well before the development of musical notation in the West. However, subtleties of performance (especially rhythm, which is not indicated in the notation) are still conveyed through master-student relationships. According to tradition, there are more than 1,000 distinct finger techniques that may be used in playing the *qin,* well more than any other instrument in either Chinese or Western traditions. Modern practice recognizes about 50 primary techniques.

In addition to *qin* schools dedicated to teaching technique on the instrument, there is a long tradition of "*qin* societies" dedicated to performing, listening to, and discussing various aspects of *qin* aesthetics and philosophy. Such societies often organize events known as *yajis,* which are multimedia gatherings that provide connoisseurs with opportunities to explore the four traditional scholarly arts: *qin,* chess, calligraphy, and painting.

Playing the *qin* has been described as a quiet, even solitary activity. In fact, one distinctive aspect of performance involves sliding the finger on a string even after the sound seems to have disappeared. When this happens, the performer (or a viewer close by) acknowledges the Taoist notion of "playing-without-playing" or "sound-without-sound," because there is in fact a very subtle sound of "finger-sliding-on-string" even if the string itself is not sounding. And, indeed, since both the performer and the listener know both the instrument and its music, they can hear the music within themselves even when the instrument is not sounding out.

James Watson

JAMES DEWEY WATSON was born in 1928 and raised in Chicago, Illinois. In the summer of 1943, 15-year-old Watson entered the University of Chicago on a scholarship. He earned a bachelor's degree in zoology in 1947 and received a Ph.D. at Indiana University, where he investigated viruses that attack bacteria.

Watson had started postgraduate studies at the University of Copenhagen when fate intervened. In May 1951, Watson met molecular biologist Maurice Wilkins at a symposium in Naples. Wilkins, who headed a laboratory at King's College in London, presented early results from X-ray diffraction studies of crystalline deoxyribonucleic acid (DNA). Watson decided to investigate molecular structures with X-ray diffraction at England's Cambridge University. The decision cost Watson his stipend.

After Watson arrived at Cambridge, he started analyzing the protein myoglobin. He soon met Francis Crick, another scientist assigned to work on protein structure. But it was DNA, not proteins, that really interested the two scientists. In the fall of 1951, they unveiled their three-chain model of the DNA molecule. It was met with criticism and even ridicule. Laboratory directors ordered Watson and Crick to resume their protein work. However, they secretly pursued their interest in DNA. Combining unpublished results of X-ray diffraction experiments from the Wilkins lab and their own theories about how DNA should function, Crick and Watson proposed a DNA double helix model in 1953. The achievement earned them a Nobel Prize.

By the fall of 1956, Watson had joined the faculty of the Harvard biology department. He wrote his version of the DNA discovery, which Atheneum Press published as *The Double Helix*. Watson's colleagues had convinced Harvard University Press to reject the controversial manuscript.

Watson did not limit his accomplishments to the scientific arena. As director of the Cold Spring Harbor Laboratory (CSHL), Watson transformed an institution in financial difficulty to a successful, internationally recognized research organization. In the planning stages of the Human Genome Project, Watson served as director, fending off censures and fears about human DNA sequencing. He ensured a successful launch of the project and then focused again on CSHL.

In October 2007, Watson resigned as CSHL's chancellor following vehement condemnation from the general public and the scientific community about a racist remark seemingly linking race and intelligence.

Outsider and Visionary Artists in the United States

Roger Cardinal, an art critic, invented the term *outsider art* in 1972 to designate work created outside official artistic culture, often but not always, by people who are mentally ill. Generally self-taught, outsider artists simply start at some point to make paintings, drawings, or sculptural objects, usually from materials at hand and with little regard to durability or art-world fashion.

Much outsider art is so crudely done that it holds little interest, but a few individuals with a gift for drawing and painting have made compelling objects or imagery of note. Among these is Henry Darger (1892–1973), a Chicago janitor who lived alone and produced a profusely illustrated 15,000-page epic called *The Vivian Girls* that featured children fighting monsters, as well as imaginary U.S. Civil War battles. The Mexican artist Martin Ramirez (1895–1963) spent most of his life in insane asylums, where he drew funnellike shapes, folk figures, and trains.

Many outsider artists are completely anonymous. Some outsiders produce benign images that spring from their personal lives—wives, children, animals, and the like.

Once disdained by dealers and the public, outsider art became popular in the final decades of the 20th century and is big business today with dealers, Internet sites, and magazines that cater to collectors, art fairs, and auctions. The term *outsider art* has expanded to embrace some folk art, especially in its more obsessive manifestations, and visual materials such as sensational sideshow banners that are bursting with vitality but have no artistic pretensions. Some dealers represent fine artists whose work is said to flout tradition and call them outsider artists.

Outsider art is an elastic term that includes "visionary art"—the borderlines are by no means clear. Visionary artists claim to have found special spiritual or mystical truths that they express in art. Some visionary artists, such as Hieronymous Bosch and William Blake, have been accepted into the canon of art history and are studied and revered by art historians.

Other visionary artists are untrained individuals who have made a huge variety of works that embody their personal (usually religious) visions. These latter visionaries may work for years on their projects and leave a large, challenging visual legacy. One such artist is French postal worker Ferdinand Cheval (1836–1924). Over the course of 33 years, Cheval constructed a huge sculpture/building called the *Ideal Palace* with stones he picked up along his postal route.

The Battle of Britain

IN JUNE 1940, Winston Churchill told the British people, "The Battle of France is over, I expect that the Battle of Britain is about to begin. Upon this battle depends the survival of Christian civilization. Upon it depends our own British life, and the long continuity of our institutions and our Empire."

By this time, Germany successfully occupied a great portion of Western Europe, and its leaders believed it could beat out Great Britain. Two months after France's defeat, Germans initiated Operation Sea Lion—the code name for Adolf Hitler's plan to invade Britain—by landing more than 10,000 soldiers along England's southeast coast. The Germans amassed troops, tanks, and vessels in Dutch, Belgian, and French ports but decided to delay the invasion until its Luftwaffe had successfully destroyed Britain's Royal Air Force (RAF).

Knowing that they generally had better pilots and planes than those in the RAF, the Germans launched attacks on English airfields, factories, radar stations, and ports along the southeast coast. But the Brits fought back, and as British fighters like the Spitfires and Hurricanes were destroyed, more were delivered. Pilots who had fled from Nazi-occupied countries made themselves available to the British in the fight against Germany.

Initially, German commanders assumed they could destroy the RAF within four weeks. But as the British retaliated, the Nazis realized their goal had been miscalculated and further delayed the coastal invasion. In early September, the Germans decided to shift their plan of attack, and planes began bombing London's dock and the East End. The areas sustained terrible damage as German raids continued on a daily basis. Many attacks were carried out in the darkness of night. On September 15, the British, exhausted but determined, turned the largest concentration of Luftwaffe planes back, thus preventing the German invasion of their homeland.

The raids on London were conducted less frequently and with less intensity for the remainder of the battle. While London was being attacked, the British were able to build more planes and repair damaged air bases. The RAF was not destroyed, the Germans failed to gain air superiority, and Britain remained free from Nazi control. Although the actual battle continued throughout October, September 15 is regarded as Battle of Britain Day.

James Joyce's *Ulysses*

WRITTEN BY JAMES JOYCE (1882–1941), the monumental novel *Ulysses* was first serialized beginning in 1918 and later published in Paris in 1922. In both the United States and the United Kingdom, it was banned until the 1930s.

One of the most learned men of the 20th century, Joyce constructed *Ulysses* with great care, linking each of its 18 episodes to Homer's *Odyssey.* The Telemachus figure in the novel is Stephen Dedalus, a young writer introduced in Joyce's earlier novel *Portrait of the Artist as a Young Man* (1916). The Ulysses figure is Leopold Bloom, a part-Jewish advertising canvasser. Written in stream-of-consciousness style, the novel is highly allusive and full of wordplay.

Dedalus and Bloom wander the streets of Dublin on June 16, 1904; this is their "odyssey." Although they visit many of the same places, they don't actually meet until episode 14, entitled "The Oxen of the Sun." This episode, which is particularly complex, takes place in a maternity hospital and has been said, in its wordplay, to suggest the history of the English language, with the final paragraphs emblematic of the baby who has just been born.

The novel has been widely studied, and all its episodes are rich in literary and linguistic treasures. Especially well-known are "Scylla and Charybdis" (episode 9), set at the National Library, where Stephen expounds his theories about Shakespeare; "Nausicaa" (episode 13), where Bloom masturbates while watching a young woman on the beach; "Circe" (episode 15), in which Bloom and Stephen visit a brothel; and "Penelope" (episode 18), in which Bloom's wife, Molly, speaks her famous soliloquy, consisting of eight extremely long sentences containing only three punctuation marks.

The "Nausicaa" episode was especially responsible for the ban on the novel. In 1933, however, a landmark ruling handed down by U.S. District Judge John Woolsey declared that the novel was not pornographic and therefore could not be considered obscene.

The novel's text as well as its content have been controversial; Joyce did not leave a unified manuscript, and editors and scholars have argued about the accuracy of various editions. The 1984 edition by Hans Walter Gabler, which supposedly corrected a number of inaccuracies, is largely ignored today. Reprints of the 1922 and the 1960 editions are widely available, however.

Aaron Copland (1900–1990)

A ARON COPLAND'S DISTINCTIVE musical style has become widely associated with the sound of the American frontier and, by extension, with "American-ness." His music (and music designed to match his "soundscapes") has been widely used for commercials that attempt to evoke wholesome American values. (Think of the widely successful "Beef—it's what's for dinner" series of commercials, which are set to an excerpt from Copland's ballet *Rodeo*.)

It was certainly Copland's goal to help create an accessible and distinctly American "art sound" in the 1930s. This was a significant change of approach from his early years as a follower of European (particularly French) modernist trends. His commitment to the New Deal ideals of "art for the people" led to significant successes, to the point that he was widely acknowledged as the leader of a "school" of composers who effectively created a model for American symphonic music in the decade before World War II.

Yet Copland's clear sympathies for socialist and left-progressive causes during the New Deal years created major problems for him in the 1950s. Paradoxically, at the same time that his compositions such as *Lincoln Portrait* and *Fanfare for the Common Man* were used widely to convey "Great American Music" in post-World War II U.S. government cultural publicity efforts worldwide, he was also intimidated by the "red scare" that surrounded the McCarthy hearings. Copland was under investigation for two decades but was never charged. He essentially went into semi-retirement as a composer until his death more than a quarter-century later.

Even as he curtailed his compositional activity, however, Copland was a crucial mentor for a younger generation of orchestral composers. Most prominent among his protégés was Leonard Bernstein (1918–1990), who played an important role in the revitalization of 20th-century orchestral music in the 1960s and '70s and was an effective champion for Copland's music in the last decades of his mentor's life. Unfortunately, this came about largely because he downplayed Copland's deep progressive philosophical commitments in the interwar years.

Copland received a Pulitzer Prize in composition, as well as three Academy Award nominations. He died in 1990 from respiratory failure and Alzheimer's disease.

"Process Music" and Minimalism

JOHN CAGE's (1912–1992) experiments with chance music, additive musical structure, and indeterminacy were enthusiastically received by the musical avant-garde of the 1950s. A number of musicians developed Cage's concepts of open-ended notation and sound organization, emphasizing the idea of music as a *process* (active, verb) rather than an *object* (static, noun). While many such experiments took on a purposefully audience-shocking bent, some musicians worked instead toward incorporating process-based music into an aesthetic of beauty, or at least of consonance (aiming for a soothing rather than disturbing sound quality). This approach has often been characterized as "minimalism," although many of its proponents reject this term.

Historians tend to point to *In C* (1964) by Terry Riley (1935–present) as the first significant example of a process/chance-based work that was purposefully grounded in consonance. *In C* (which Riley and his ensemble perform around the world on a regular basis to this day) consists of 53 short musical units that Riley instructs any number of musicians to play any number of times, to the steady accompaniment of the note "C" played repeatedly in the middle range of the piano. The units are designed so that their overlap creates a pleasing musical effect; previous chance/process music often opened the possibility for harsh dissonances in the "random" coming-together of musical ideas.

Steve Reich (1936–present) also draws on process-based composition, but he focuses more on additive musical gestures, in which short musical ideas are repeated many times but are gradually extended and overlapped (so that the "process" of their extension-overlapping-change becomes the focus of the listener's attention). Reich has written works for several prominent ensembles and has been influential in moving process-based "minimalism" into the concert mainstream (also drawing the attention of experimental/progressive musicians in the rock world, such as the band Sonic Youth).

The most prominent of the minimalists is Philip Glass (1937–present), who has written for a variety of genres, including symphonies, operas, and film scores. He has been especially interested in combining his work with various types of visual media. Glass is probably the most successful "classical" composer of the late 20th century and has collaborated with superstar rockers like David Bowie as well as with established orchestras.

Through minimalism and its aftermath, the daring indeterminacy/chance experiments of Cage and his associates in the mid-1900s have been absorbed into the musical mainstream.

Indian Music: The Classical Traditions and "Cassette Culture"

THERE ARE LONG-STANDING elaborate high-art ("classical") musical traditions associated with Hindustani and Carnatic cultures, in Northern and Central-Southern India, respectively. Both derive from practices established more than 2,000 years ago. The exponent of the Hindustani tradition most renowned in North America is probably sitar player Ravi Shankar, who famously worked with the Beatles and with a number of "classical" musicians (most notably Yehudi Mehunin) and has been honored by institutions worldwide.

The Carnatic practice relies more on playing recognizable compositions as they were written (and acknowledges a series of renowned composers stretching back to the 16th century). But both the Hindustani and Carnatic traditions expect the performer to elaborate based on specific melodic and rhythmic patterns (called *raga* and *tala*), which form the basis for an entire concert. While the *raga* were historically associated (especially in Hindustani music) with specific seasons, times of day, and other functional considerations, interaction between musicians from the two traditions has led to the choice being left increasingly to the musician's inspiration and ability.

While both Carnatic and Hindustani traditions used to rely on subtle distinctions among the many regional schools of performance, an interesting phenomenon was created by the rise of recording companies (which were largely British-owned) in India in the 1930s. They established a near-monopoly in mass-distributed Indian music. This phenomenon was further reinforced by the parallel rise in Indian sound films (in which music has played a crucial role) and the establishment of "star" film singers, whose songs dominated the Indian musical scene through the 1970s. In packaging popular film music for consumption through 45 rpm discs, recording companies established a much-abbreviated three-minute version of the traditional *ghazal* love-song. In doing so, they "flattened out" the improvisational element and introduced instruments and melodies/rhythms that were strongly influenced by the European tradition.

As ethnomusicologist Peter Manuel has observed, this status quo was deeply shaken by the introduction of the audiocassette in the 1980s. That medium was (and still is) easily reproduced (often in pirated form) and widely redistributed with no need for large capital investment. "Cassette culture" thus opened a market for Indian musical activity and creativity into a wide spectrum of independent directions.

Rita Levi-Montalcini

BORN INTO A TRADITIONAL Jewish family in Turin, Italy, in 1909, Rita Levi-Montalcini's father expected her to forgo a profession and devote her life to being a wife and mother. Although she always thought she wanted to be a writer, her life took a turn in a different direction. When Levi-Montalcini was about 20, a relative died of cancer, and she realized she could not adjust to the life her father wished for her. She obtained his permission to enroll at the university and began preparing for her eventual career. After she graduated from medical school, Dr. Levi-Montalcini enrolled in a specialized program to study neurology and psychiatry.

In 1936, laws passed by the Mussolini regime prevented non-Aryan Italian citizens from academic and professional careers. Dr. Levi-Montalcini spent a period of time in Brussels as a guest of a neurological institute and then returned to Turin to be with her family as the Germans were invading Belgium. Rather than emigrate to the United States, the family stayed in Italy. Dr. Levi-Montalcini set up a small genetics research laboratory in her bedroom to conduct experiments and study the growth of nerve fibers in chicken embryos. Even though her family had to seek protection away from Turin during the war, she continued her experiments and research.

Shortly before the war ended, the Allies employed her as a medical doctor to care for war refugees being brought into Florence from the north. Afterward, she returned to the University of Turin and to academic life.

After World War II, Dr. Levi-Montalcini was invited to Washington University in St. Louis, Missouri, for a semester. She was to continue her work under the supervision of Dr. Viktor Hamburger, who had conducted experiments on chicken embryos with her in the past. She stayed for 30 years—teaching at the university and continuing to research and conduct experiments in which she isolated the nerve growth factor by observing cancerous tissues that caused nerve cells to grow rapidly.

In 1962, Dr. Levi-Montalcini established a research facility in Rome and split her time between St. Louis and Italy. She retired from university teaching in 1979 but continued to serve as director of the Institute of Cell Biology in Rome. She and another colleague received a Nobel Prize for their discovery of nerve growth factors. She also received America's highest scientific honor, the National Medal of Science. As of 2008, Dr. Levi-Montalcini was the oldest living Nobel laureate.

Chuck Close

CHUCK CLOSE (1940–PRESENT) TRANSFORMED the face of modern portraiture. His giant black-and-white portraits have often been likened to mug shots—a connection that the artist readily acknowledges. He appreciates the way a mug shot efficiently captures its subject "straight on." For Close, who has dedicated his career to portraiture, the mug shot was a means to escape conventional portraiture with its focus on celebrity and replace it with a form of portraiture dedicated to "regular folks." His portraits are always based on a photograph of the sitter.

Self-Portrait, 1977

In 1968, Close completed his first portrait, *Big Self-Portrait* (1967–68). The painting captures every nuance, line, and wrinkle of Close's face in massive scale and in a highly realistic style that closely resembles a photograph. At the same time, *Big Self-Portrait* seems to tell us little about the inner life of the sitter. The subject's cool remoteness, one of the most striking aspects of the work, is an effect seen throughout Close's portraits. He would instruct his sitters to maintain as neutral an expression as possible when he took their picture, and would do the same when he was the one being photographed.

With its hyper-realism and massive scale, *Big Self-Portrait* announced the elements of what became Close's signature portrait style. The same is true of its subject matter: Close's subject is often himself. Over the course of his career, Close has created what amounts to a historical record of his visage over time—from his loss of hair at a relatively young age to the laugh lines and crows' feet that occur as a result of the aging process.

Close's other subjects are his family and friends, primarily artists. One of his favorites is the composer Philip Glass. Close has created numerous portraits of Glass based on a 1969 photograph he took of the young composer.

In the mid-1980s, Close began to depart from his ultra-realistic style in a series of paintings that break down the subject into a series of colorful painted dots, in a manner reminiscent of Seurat's Pointillism.

In 1988, the artist suffered a blood clot that initially left him paralyzed from the neck down. Though he remains in a wheelchair, he began to paint again by means of a customized brace. He has since created haunting portraits that blur the face of their subject, continuing to reinvent the genre to which he has dedicated his career.

Toussaint L'Ouverture and Haitian Independence

THE ISLAND OF HISPANIOLA in the Caribbean is shared by Haiti to the west and the Dominican Republic to the east. The Taíno Arawak people lived on the island when Christopher Columbus landed there in December 1492. Disease and enslavement quickly depleted the natives' ranks, which led the Spanish to turn to Africa for slaves.

French colonists populated the western third of Hispaniola after it was all but deserted by the Spanish in the middle of the 17th century. Once it was officially acquired by France from Spain, Saint-Domingue (Haiti) thrived on its exports of sugar and coffee, becoming the richest economy in the Western Hemisphere. Several black revolts were crushed by the French colonists until August 22, 1791, when civil war broke out between the slaves and their masters at about the same time the colonists rebelled against French rule.

Toussaint L'Ouverture was a former slave who was self-educated, literate, and well-read. He took up the cause of the rebellion, organizing and leading black troops. He quickly rose to the head of his own slave army.

By 1793, a number of factions were fighting each other for control of Saint-Domingue, including Spain and Britain. L'Ouverture initially fought alongside the Spanish against the French but switched his allegiance in February 1794 when the French National Assembly abolished slavery in Saint-Domingue. Five months later, France and Spain signed a peace agreement that forced Spain to give up all its remaining holdings on Hispaniola.

As the only black commander to have sided with France, L'Ouverture rose in power in the new government. To stabilize his hold on the country, he agreed to an alliance with U.S. President John Adams that would prevent France from using Hispaniola as a staging area for any assault on the United States. Angered by the actions of L'Ouverture, Napoleon Bonaparte dispatched an army to once again secure the island.

L'Ouverture agreed to a truce in May 1802. Although assured by the French that he would not be punished, L'Ouverture was seized a month later and taken to France, where he died in prison less than a year later.

Distracted by war in Europe, Napoleon gave up the fight for Hispaniola. Jean-Jacques Dessalines, a former slave, defeated the remaining French army and was named the leader of what is now Haiti when it declared independence from France on January 1, 1804.

Herman Melville's *Moby-Dick*

Herman Melville, born in 1819 in New York City, went to sea on a whaling ship in 1840 after failed careers as a reporter and a teacher. His classic American novel, *Moby-Dick,* was published in 1851 as *Moby-Dick; or, The Whale.* The most ambitious of Melville's works up to that point (he wrote six other novels, as well as short stories, and poetry), the book owes much of its grim undercurrent to writer Nathaniel Hawthorne (*The Scarlet Letter,* 1850), Melville's friend, to whom he dedicated *Moby-Dick.* But the book was a commercial failure, and Melville died in 1891 a forgotten man. However, the novel was rediscovered in the 1920s and is now hailed as a masterpiece.

Moby-Dick begins with one of the most famous opening lines in American literature: "Call me Ishmael." This identifies the narrator of the story, a man who has come to New Bedford, Massachusetts, to join the crew of a whaling ship. After meeting a South Seas harpooner named Queequeg, Ishmael signs on to the whaling ship *Pequod,* which is under the command of the mysterious one-legged Captain Ahab. The *Pequod,* named after a Native American tribe that didn't survive the European encounter with America, is a strange ship painted black and covered with whale teeth and bones. After setting sail on Christmas Day, Ahab announces to the crew his intention of hunting the whale that took his leg—the legendary great white whale Moby-Dick. The *Pequod* kills some whales on its voyage, and occasionally an event happens—such as a drowning, or the ship's cabin boy going insane—that foreshadows the end of the voyage. As the voyage progresses, Ahab becomes more and more fanatical about his desire to kill Moby-Dick, pressing other captains for information about the whale even as they try to warn him off his quest. Eventually sighting the creature, Ahab's attempts to kill Moby-Dick fail and get members of his crew killed. Finally, Moby-Dick sinks the *Pequod,* and Ahab gets tangled in one of his harpoon lines, is pulled out of his harpoon boat, and drowns. Only Ishmael is left alive to tell the tale.

Numerous themes and symbols have been found in *Moby-Dick,* including the idea that the whale in its great and unpredictable power is God. (For instance, many of the main characters have biblical names.) Other themes include the idea and effects of prophecy among humans, and the limits of humans' ability to understand the world in which they live.

POSTSCRIPT

■ Melville earned just $556.37 from the initial sales of *Moby-Dick.*

Grace Hopper (1906–1992)

Aᴌᴛʜᴏᴜɢʜ ᴛʜᴇ ᴛᴇʀᴍ *computer bug* did not originate with Grace Hopper, she certainly made the term popular after a moth was found in a computer, impeding the computer's functioning.

As a member of a research team working on a computer project at Harvard University during the war, Hopper devoted her time to working with the development of the Mark I computer, used by the navy to calculate ballistics and gunnery information. The computer—big and bulky by today's standards—was the first of two Mark computers with which she was involved.

After World War II, Hopper joined Eckert-Mauchly Computer Corporation and worked on the development of UNIVAC I, the first commercial computer. Hopper stayed with the corporation when it was taken over by Remington Rand; in 1952, she invented the first computer "compiler"—software that made other computer software easier to write. Before the invention of the compiler, computer programmers utilized repetitive commands by using a numbering code in software programming. After Hopper's invention, programmers could use language commands for programming instructions.

Hopper's talents also resulted in the development of a common language used in computer communications. The language, called Common Business-Oriented Language (COBOL), is widely used throughout the world and has permitted companies to compile computerized information. Hopper's computer work was completed during an era when software technology was not patented. As a result, none of her inventions have patents.

During the 1970s, the navy used standards developed by Hopper to test computer systems and their components, such as programming languages. The National Bureau of Standards assumed the administration of these standards in the 1980s.

Hopper was awarded a National Medal of Technology during a White House Ceremony. The Data Processing Management Association also named her Man of the Year. She retired from the navy several times only to reenter service when needed. Hopper had already been promoted to the rank of captain when, by special presidential appointment in 1986, she was awarded the rank of commodore (which later became the rank of rear admiral). The Department of Defense awarded her the Defense Distinguished Service Medal—the highest noncombat award possible. Hopper worked as a consultant until her death.

The Bhagavad Gita

THE BHAGAVAD GITA (The Lord's Song) is one of the most famous and popular of Hinduism's sacred texts, and it's one of the most beautiful works of Sanskrit literature.

Written sometime between the fifth and second centuries B.C., the Gita is actually a section of the Mahabharata, the great Hindu epic that tells the story of rivalry and warfare between the Kauravas and their cousins, the Pandavas.

The Gita begins on the eve of a battle between the two dynasties over a kingdom promised by the Kauravas to the Pandavas. Their armies are massed on the battlefield at Kuru. Prince Arjuna, a son of King Pandu and a great hero who has wrestled with the god Shiva himself, sees family, friends, and teachers gathered on the other side of the battlefield. He envisions the end of the battle, when his cousins will lie dead, and he experiences a moral crisis, wondering if he is justified in killing them. Arjuna temporarily calls off the battle while he discusses the issue with Krishna, an incarnation of the God Vishnu who appears in the story as Arjuna's charioteer. The Bhagavad Gita becomes a dialogue between Krishna and Arjuna.

Throughout the 700-verse poem, Krishna leads Arjuna in a wide-ranging philosophical conversation that considers man's relationship to god, the wheel of *karma* and rebirth, and the importance of following one's own *dharma,* or moral duty. They also discuss questions of war and peace and consider the nature of action and devotion, as well as the nature of God. In one of the most famous verses, Krishna urges Arjuna to perform his *svadharma,* the duties appropriate to his class and stage of life: "Better one's own dharma, though done imperfectly, than another's well-performed," Krishna teaches.

The Gita suggests that actions done in fulfillment of one's svadharma and without personal ambition are acts of religious devotion that lead to salvation. Krishna explains that for Arjuna, a member of the warrior caste, sin would lie not in killing but in refusing to perform his duty as a warrior. The Gita ends with Krishna convincing Arjuna to proceed with the battle.

POSTSCRIPT

■ Krishna is also the major character in another important Indian poem, the Gita Govinda, written by Jayadeva in the 12th century.

Igor Stravinsky and *The Rite of Spring*

*L*E SACRE DU PRINTEMPS, a musical composition by Igor Stravinsky is surrounded by contradiction. It is one of the most widely heard classical works of the 20th century—but in its most popular context, as one of the sections of Disney's film *Fantasia,* heard in a reconfigured and arguably mangled version. The piece was originally designed as a component of a specific multimedia-dance event; it was eventually redefined as a work of abstract music, with its composer attempting to renounce both its connection to a specific story line and the multiplicity of creative voices that went into its creation. First greeted as shocking and unmusical, the composition is now an essential pillar of the canon of music history. The title is generally translated as *The Rite of Spring,* though Stravinsky himself preferred *The Coronation of Spring.*

Le sacre, intended to depict prehistoric fertility rites, was a collaboration among Stravinsky and three other equally important cocreators: Serge Diaghilev, director of the popular Ballets Russes dance troupe in early 20th-century Paris, who commissioned the work; dancer Vaclav Nijinsky, who created the choreography; and folklorist Nicolai Roerich, with whom Stravinsky consulted extensively in planning the "prehistoric" character of the music and who also provided the set designs for the production.

The first performance of *Le sacre* in 1913 famously caused a riot by its Parisian audience, which was astounded at the ballet's contrast with the more conventional first part of the evening's program. The musical aspects of the event were very provocative, to be sure: The use of instruments in unprecedented and purposefully "savage" ways, the highly irregular percussive rhythms, and the obsessive repetition of harmonically and melodically dissonant snippets were all intended to shock the ears of the audience. The costumes and choreography, however, were equally jarring to an early 20th-century ballet-goer's sensibility.

As it turns out, the costumes were almost completely lost, and the choreography vanished entirely after the work went out of the troupe's repertory following only seven performances. Many 20th-century ensembles have created alternative choreographies for *Le sacre,* but the work quickly became divorced from dance altogether as Stravinsky repurposed it for orchestral performance. In fact, he eventually claimed that the *Rite's* deepest meanings were most evident when it was experienced without the "distraction" of dance and scenery. From this perspective, Stravinsky would have approved of a long-prevalent scholarly perspective that held up the *Rite* as entirely "abstract" in its musical independence from earlier sources.

INDEX

INDEX

INDEX

E

Earthquakes, 78
Eastman, George, 211
Edison, Thomas Alva, 343
Eiffel Tower, 67
Einstein, Albert, 178, 305, 339, 353
Einstein on the Beach (Glass), 275
Eisenstein, Sergei, 329
Elgin Marbles, 25, 253
Eliot, George, 223
Eliot, T. S., 62, 307
Elizabeth I (Queen of England), 119, 183
Ellington, Duke, 70
Emerson, Lake & Palmer, 205
Engels, Friedrich, 334
English novels, 118
Enlightenment, 189
Environment. *See* Carson, Rachel; Science and nature.
Eroica Symphony (Beethoven), 37
Ethanol, 234
Evans, Mary Ann, 223
Existentialism, 147
Eyck, Jan van, 95

F

Fanfare for the Common Man (Copland), 261
Fanfares for the Uncommon Woman (Tower), 261
Faulkner, William, 307, 358
Fauvism, 326
Federalist Papers, 201
Feminism, 309, 323
Fibonacci, 162
Film, filmmaking. *See* Theater and film.
Fisk Jubilee Singers, 247
Fitzgerald, Ella, 142
Fitzgerald, F. Scott, 272
Florence Cathedral, 116
Florida Everglades, 80
Ford, Henry, 56
Foster, Stephen, 331
Frankenstein (Shelley), 358
Free radicals, 66
French Revolution, 303, 309
French salon culture, 239
Freud, Sigmund, 165, 301
Friedan, Betty, 323
Frost, Robert, 167
Functional magnetic resonance imaging (fMRI), 262

G

Galapagos Islands, 80
Galilei, Galileo, 24

Game theory, 101
Gamut, 58
Gandhi, 308
Garcia Márquez, Gabriel, 335
Gardner, Alexander, 88
Gates of Hell (Rodin), 319
Gates of Paradise (Ghiberti), 130
Gauguin, Paul, 298, 326
Gautama Buddha, 21
Gehry, Frank, 221
Geisel, Ted, 232
Gene therapy, 241
Genetic engineering, 290
Genetics, 45
Genghis Kahn, 168
Gericault, Théodore, 123
German Empire unification, 250
Gershwin, George, 352
Ghiberti, Lorenzo, 130
Ghirlandaio, Domenico, 235
Giovanni Arnolfini and His Wife (van Eyck), 95
Glass, Philip, 275, 365, 368
Global warming, 143, 157, 164
Glorious Revolution, 110
Goethe, Johann Wolfgang von, 251
Gogh, Vincent van, 298, 326
Golden ratio, 269
Gorbachev, Mikhail, 175
Gothic fiction, 358
Gottschalk, Louis Moreau, 128
Gould, Stephen Jay, 140
Goya, Francisco, 74
Graham, Martha, 252
Great Gatsby, The (Fitzgerald), 272
Griffith, D. W., 288
Guernica (Picasso), 354
Guggenheim Museum, 221
Gutenberg, Johannes, 145

H

Haitian independence, 369
Hamlet (Shakespeare), 125
Hammett, Dashiell, 204
Handel, G. F., 100
Haraguchi, Akira, 178
Hardy, Thomas, 328
Hawking, Stephen, 227
Haydn, Franz Josef, 114
Hemingway, Ernest, 132, 265, 342
Herodotus, 131
Hildegard of Bingen, 51
Hillary, Sir Edmund, 266
Hinduism, 372
Hine, Lewis, 340

INDEX

INDEX

CONTRIBUTORS

Tina Adler is a freelance health and science writer based in Washington, D.C.

Patricia Barnes-Svarney is a geologist, an award-winning science writer, and the author of more than 30 books.

Sandy Becker does research in developmental biology and embryonic stem cells. As a science writer, she writes for the general public about practically anything.

Victor Cassidy is a professional writer on art and ecology. He is the author of *Henry Chandler Cowles: Pioneer Ecologist* (2007), *Sculpture Invasion* (2007), and numerous articles in national and international art publications.

Susan Doll holds a Ph.D. in radio, television, and film studies from Northwestern University. She is the author of numerous books on popular culture, notably *Elvis: A Tribute to His Life; The Films of Elvis Presley; Marilyn: Her Life and Legend; Elvis: Rock 'n' Roll Legend; Best of Elvis; Understanding Elvis; Elvis: Forever in the Groove; Elvis: American Idol;* and *Florida on Film.*

Jane Friedman is a Chicago-based independent scholar, editor, and exhibition consultant with an expertise in Russian and Soviet art. She has had articles published in the *Zimmerli Journal* and *Studies in the Decorative Arts* and has written or contributed to various exhibition brochures and catalogs.

Martin F. Graham is coauthor of seven books on the Civil War, including *The Mine Run Campaign, The James E. Taylor Sketchbook, Civil War Chronicle,* and *The Blue and the Gray.* He has also been a contributor to such magazines as *Civil War Times, Blue and Gray,* and *World War II.*

Jerry Guo is an economics student at Yale. He has written for the *New York Times, Nature, Science,* and *The Scientist.* His first book, *Science Whiz,* was published in 2007.

Peter Gwynne is a freelance science writer based in Cape Cod, Massachusetts. He is a former science editor of *Newsweek* and has founded science and technology magazines in Asia, Europe, and North America.

James H. Hallas is a graduate of Syracuse University's Newhouse School of Communications. A military historian, he has penned a pair of World War II histories, focusing on U.S. Marine Corps campaigns: *The Devil's Anvil: The Assault on Peleliu* and *Killing Ground on Okinawa: The Battle for Sugar Loaf Hill.* He also wrote *Doughboy War: The American Expeditionary Force in World War I.*

Jessica Harwood is a freelance writer and a professor of biology at Spartanburg Methodist College.

Kathryn Holcomb is a student of 19th- and 20th-century American history. Her writing credits include a number of articles on little-known events, notably Chicago's Eastland disaster. A collector of historic memorabilia, she lives outside of Grand Rapids, Michigan.

Phillip Jones, Ph.D., is a freelance writer who has worked in the fields of science and law. His articles have appeared in *History Magazine, Nature Biotechnology, Forensic Magazine, The World Almanac and Book of Facts,* and other publications. He also wrote a booklet on historical trivia, two science books, and teaches an online forensic science survey course for writers.

William Martin is a freelance writer whose diverse portfolio of work includes creative, media, and business writing. He holds a B.A. in history and political science from the University of Toronto and lives in Toronto with his wife Marianna and three daughters, Samantha, Paige, and Erica.

Nancy McCaslin is a freelance writer based in South Bend, Indiana. She has an M.A. in American history and has taught high school history and government. A seasoned, intrepid international traveler, she has never visited a country she did not like.

CONTRIBUTORS

David A. Murray writes freelance from St. Louis, where he has taught English, writing, humanities, and film for 17 years. He earned his Ph.D. in English literature from Washington University in St. Louis.

Julie J. Rehmeyer is a mathematics and science writer and the mathematics columnist for *Science News* magazine.

Russell Roberts is an award-winning full-time freelance writer. He has published more than three dozen books for both children and adults, including the best sellers *Down the Jersey Shore* and *10 Days to a Sharper Memory.* Among his children's books are examinations of the lives of Jefferson, Hamilton, Robert Goddard, Galileo, and Nostradamus.

Richard A. Sauers, Ph.D., is the author of more than two dozen books, including *America's Battlegrounds: Walk in the Footsteps of America's Bravest* and *Gettysburg: The Meade-Sickles Controversy.* He is director of the Packwood House Museum in Lewisburg, Pennsylvania.

David Stark, Ph.D., holds a doctorate in art history from Ohio State University and is currently a director in the department of museum education at the Art Institute of Chicago.

Pamela D. Toler holds a Ph.D. in history from the University of Chicago. She is particularly interested in the times and places where cultures touch and change each other.

Cassandra Willyard graduated with an M.A. in science writing from Johns Hopkins University in 2007. Since then she has written about everything from HIV to Halley's Comet. She now works as a freelance science writer in Washington, D.C.